Short Stories

By

Red Elk

Tellings Of A Medicine Man/WAKȞÁŊ

This book is dedicated to:

Troy Morrell

October 30, 1968 – July 29, 1995

In life, he learned.

In death, he taught.

NOTE TO ALL:

Many are not "believers" in the Creator ("God"/"Allah"/etc). Others DO, to a degree. MOST are unaware that one can actually "meet" this One (i.e., KNOW that this Great One TRULY EXISTS).

Know you are NOT alone. You fit somewhere with others ways of thought.

Whether you believe in The Creator or not, this Great One BELIEVES in YOU. Without this, you would not exist (though you may not believe it, never the less, it is true).

In this Book, I ask you only to think on this as a possibility. That is ALL.

I do not, AT ALL, want you to simply "accept"…but instead just THINK on what you will be reading. Aho?

In the following pages, you will find several "Repeats" (tellings, with the same theme). This is to try to help you, the reader(s), grasp the IMPORTANCE of what is being shared.
Each based on actual "telling," done separately, over time. PLEASE Understand and GRASP! THERE IS A REASON FOR ALL WITHIN.

Thank You,

Grandfather

INTRODUCTION

Friends, these stories are being shared…not "told." We all have our own path. This one has only shared what has made him…him. This one's way of "being." You need not follow. It is your path.

I would like to start by saying:

DO NOT BELIEVE A WORD I SAY! TEST IT!

This one hopes you, the reader, enjoy the reading. Hopes too that it will help you to know Inner Peace.

Our world is a mess. We are a mess.

IT CAN BE CHANGED!

This one is a follower of the "Big Brother" Jesus the Christ. It is He this one emulates. It is also He who is the DOER of the things this one has been involved with. This one is only a willing one. A vessel to be used at His will and command. He dwells within me and I am not ashamed to say so! Nor to say this:

I have found my peace and pray you do the same!

Perhaps a little back ground to start:

This one is a member of a group of only twelve, called "The Inner Heyókȟa Society." Though we are a small group, we are World Wide. Each given a "region" to tend.

This one is of All North America. Others are for All South America, All Africa, All Arabian countries, all of the Far East, All of the Russian areas, etc.

ALL twelve of us FOLLOW "The Way of PURITY."
ALL, thus, FOLLOW "Big Brother" (Christ)…the EXAMPLE and TEACHER of that "way."

Know …KNOW! NONE of us are of a "Church" or ANY "Religion!"

"Purity" is learning a ONE-ON-ONE Relationship with The CREATOR.

It IS POSSIBLE!

These accounts will give you an idea of its outcome. What you do with it is up to you.

All written within are based on factual truths…written in an unusual way. ALL have Indian AND Scriptural basis. This Book will give SOME Scriptures to help you comprehend the relationship between the Indian way and the way written in TODAY'S Good Book. In reality, the two ARE the same. Each though, done in the CULTURAL "way" of the different areas. EACH corresponds WITH each other. One, in writing (Bible). One, in our Ceremony (Remembrance).

Remember, we of Indian had no written words. Our writings were in rock pictures. What was not written, we would keep the remembrance by Ceremony. These ceremonies are now so old that "The People" have long forgotten their original reason for doing.

WE OF THE INNER HEYÓKȞA HAVE NOT!

We twelve rely on this. We are still of the "ancient ways" in that regard.

HO.

GLOSSARY

The meanings of words used within:

Agape = Full All Forgiving Love
Aho = I understand.
Aho? = do YOU understand?
Berming = Building practice that combines heavy timber framing and rough stone with stacking thick layers of sod or peat against the walls and on the roof.
Big Brother = Jesus the Lord/Christ.
Good Book = Bible.
Grandfather = Sun.
Grandmother = Moon.
Grandfather/Grandmother = both a calling of endearment / respect to Elders.
Gray = A small, VERY thin, big head huge eyes, alien being. Of two types: the "Masters" (True Soul bearing aliens) and the smaller, cloned to appear as the "Masters." (These are made from a Plant Bean. No Souls.)
Great Spirit (Gardner – Creator – Love, etc.) = God.
Great Turtle/Turtle = Earth (which slowly revolves around the sun).
"He" (using the) "He" (God) is neither male nor female. NO Gender.
Ho = Amen/So be it.
Lodge = Native American house of many types, Tipi included.
Mitakuye Oyasin spelled PHONICALLY (Me Talk We Ooshin) for your benefit = All One Relation.
Pow Wow = a Group meeting.
Totem = Indian Angel(s).
Totem Poles = Carved North West Native wooden poles.
Medicine Man/Woman = People CALLED to learn the many ways of healing (Plants, etc).
Selah = THINK Deeply about that.
Tipi = Plains Indian conical hide portable house.
Turtle Island = North and South America (all the Americas).
Uncle/Aunt (or Little Brother/Sister or Brother or Cousin etc.) = each a "we are all one relation," the way we often address each other.
WAKȞÁŊ = Spiritual Adviser (similar to a priest / preacher). A CALLED position.

Now let the STORIES begin:

Diluted Tradition

It was modern times now. Several had come to ask and to listen to the Wakȟáŋ Elder. Their concern: their nation, their nations, and the nations of all mankind. To learn the why of the way things are today, hoping that things could change…and seeking HOW to help change them. They presented this to the elder.

Here are his words:

Aho (I understand). We (the inner Heyókȟa) still believe in the old ways of striving to, for and towards "the seventh generation." Always thinking to do, for and towards, the seventh generation to come. That means doing well NOW for those seven ahead. The next generation does the same, and the next and on and on.

This includes simplicity. Tending the garden does not exhaust the garden. The whites tend to reap with little, to no, thinking, in this manner. They think "Now," instead of tomorrow. "Me, Self, Mine." This is what has gotten us to where our world is today. Long ago, all did as we twelve. In time that somehow became "lost," and man slipped towards POSSESSION, "Self" was on.

America is a leader in this, taking its place by following England. Englanders started this worldwide. "Whites." Thus, England, the United States, Canada, Germany, etc., are the vanguard RACE to "ways of destruction." Yet, simplicity…LESS…IS best.
MORE brings death.
First in spirit, then in "physical" Fact.

For instance, we used to take living small trees for our Tipi lodges. Trees fighting to live, chopping off the taller and smaller that was doing the same. We pick and choose. Thinning the weeds. We did not destroy all to cut and drag out one, as do those of today. We did not destroy smaller already growing trees to get one "good one."

We practiced ecology.

Today the whites re-plant. In replanting, all grow at the same rate. Next cutting means all are good AT THE SAME TIME! Mass cutting and again, mass replanting…and years to grow to "good" and on and on. Feast to famine. Our mother Earth was not designed to go from trees to "desert." We are weakening her face and her lungs.

Our Creator allowed forest fires to replace naturally. Between, we tended. We are few and always were few. We, so few, could not keep up the vast garden, so "He" would help and send fires and drought to help her, mankind, and ultimately us.

Others of our people used old and dead tree products or fast growing reeds, weeds, or animal hides to build our lodges. It was a rare and sacred thing to gird and cut down a good living tree. The North West coastal canoe being one needed reason. Then, it was done with much ceremony and apology.

Life, whether a tree, stone, or whatever, is sacred to us. Life, living life! Men are mere caretakers and gardeners. However, somewhere in the past, greed took over, and the common man has been duped into slavery. Working to make money to buy what was naturally theirs in the first place, through living simply. To make money they raped and killed the very thing that sustains life. Forests are depleted and mountains are holed and leveled for coal and minerals. Water is being polluted from the waste of all this, killing the fish and THEIR ecology. WE are the END and the BEGINNING of the FOOD CHAIN. What WE Do…affects all. Now, as well as those of our future.

We, The Caretakers of this land…in order to LIVE, have accepted the ways of destruction the whites have forced us into. In so doing we have quickly forgotten our Sacred Duty. Few practice the "Gardeners Way" any longer.

Mankind is fast becoming extinct due to all this.

This has happened in the past, four times. All because of the same reason. The creator stopped it each time. "He" will stop it again…and is in that process, at this time. Soon mankind will once again be in near extinction. Once again "He" will order man to repopulate the Earth. This will be, IF we do not change our ways. IF we do not, we will, once again, ONE MORE TIME, do it AGAIN! This is many years down the road. The Good Book foretells this. Our Earth's upcoming "number five roll" will not be duplicated on number six. Then it will be destroyed and disappear. In addition, there will be no more galaxies, as we know them. Or, as THEY Knew US. Ho.

It will be at that time…the "Great Day of Judgment"…this number six, will occur. Then our Creator will make all pure. A "new heaven and Earth." All corrupt and corrupted will no longer be, and finally there will forever be pure peace and perfection, eternally.

All this is foretold within THAT BOOK.

Hear me…However, what we now face WILL be. It need NOT be, right NOW! The creator has given us warnings and a chance to stop it for now. If mankind can get back to "Him" and simplicity, the now on-rolling events will cease. If each succeeding generation works for the seventh ahead, the fifth roll will never be. Each generation must push the roll further ahead.

The Creator knows mankind and wishes us to remain Peaceful, Sharing and Loving As One. "He" knows too that we are of an "I want" and "Me, Me" mentality, as well, and knows "His" wishes will not be!
Thus destruction of mans' civilization is about to be.

HOWEVER – HOWEVER, THE SKIES HAVE NOT YET TURNED RED, Worldwide. THIS IS PROPHESIZED, IN BOTH INDIAN (Orange sky) And BIBLE (Red sky). When that happens, we will have “no turning back”…IT WILL be!

So far, that sign has not yet taken place. Return to the ways of your ancestors. Return to oneness, peace, and simplicity, NOW…and save ourselves. The NEXT generation will, hopefully, do the same, and so on.

Always,

AIM TOWARDS THE SEVENTH GENERATION!

HO.

A Story As A Point

The scientist approached the Creator.

"God," he said, "we don't need you anymore."

"Oh?" said the Creator of All Things.

"Yes. We people have found we can clone our own, grow ears and body parts on a mouse, and replace them onto those in need. We don't need you anymore."

"Can you Make MAN?" He asked.

The scientist thought, and then said, "No. But I'm sure we can."

"Well," said the Maker, "When you make man, come back, and see me. I'll then consider stepping down."

"OK," the scientist replied, then turned and started walking off. As he did so, he reached down and picked up a handful of dirt.

God called out "WHOA! Whoa! Wait a minute. Hold on!"

The scientist turned. "What?"

God looked at him and said, "GET YOUR OWN DIRT!"

Misuse Of Power

Three younger men had approached the Elder…a known Medicine Man/Wakȟáŋ.

“Grandfather (they asked respectfully), we’d like you to show us you can really change the weather.”

“Why?” He asked.

“Well, just to prove it CAN be done!”

“Yes, it can but I will only do this for a NEED. YOUR REQUEST is NOT a NEED. It is to satisfy your SELF. A Show Off. No, I will not do it for THIS Reason.

IF you find one TO do this, for your ‘Reason’, YOU ARE DEALING WITH A SORCERER! ANY who must ‘show off’ is no one that I, or the Others of Good, want to be around.

Good day, gentlemen.”

The Hair Pillow

The old woman had passed away, her head resting upon her Hair Pillow. As was the custom, she had saved her fallen hair for just this time. They held her Years of memories. She had lived a good life. Hardships to her were but everyday life. Thus were of no consequences. She had known childbirth pains seven times, each child, born in the traditional manner of squatting and letting gravity help. Her first two sons born in this way, on the trail.

Their father took all of the seven outside in their first nightfall. He raised their nude bodies to the heavens, presenting them to All Creation, introducing each child to all about them, the world of spirit, to each child. Songs and prayers were said, asking The Great Creator to bless the child, and asking that they "do not forget" that that they were born Knowing. Asking also that those around the child help them grow Strong and in Godliness.

All these memories were in her hair. Years of serving her people and loved ones were there as well. She took these memories to her grave.

Today, only a few still do these things. Very few. Perhaps only two or three handfuls. Today many of the Old Ways are not remembered…let alone done. Our people are fast forgetting...yet still claim they live in the "Traditional Manner." I am sad to say, it is not so.

If you are one wanting to learn what is LEFT to learn…go. Go visit your Elders.
LISTEN to them! Do NOT IGNORE THEM! THEY ARE FULL OF KNOWLEDGE!

If you do not, when they pass on, all you will have left…all that will be is…A Hair Pillow.

The Watchers

They were lost…or rather, in 'unfamiliar territory.' Three boys and a small girl, who was sister of one of the boys. You know children, off having fun and losing all sense of time or place.

The camp their leader had brought them to a place that was new to them, for their people did not visit it often. None here was born the last time this place had been visited.

Oh, the children knew East from West, South from North. They all knew The Way of Grandfather (the sun, to those not knowing our ways/names). They knew too, the sun was fast going down on the horizon. Soon to put Grandmother (moon), in charge over the land. This too brought out those who hunt by night. To little ones who were used to being in their lodges (Tipi/Home) at this time…well, it was a little 'frightening.' Try as they might, they could not retrace their steps. Darkness would soon be upon them. None cried. Not even the youngest…the little sister. Ho.

The eldest (all of nine full seasons old) rightly felt it was his duty to protect all.

"We must make shelter," he declared. He pointed out various trees with low hanging boughs, and sent the three scurrying to collect these boughs. He too collected large limbs, long soft weeds and grasses.

As the others brought their gleanings, he laid them over a leaning frame he had built against a tree, making a low/wide sloping 'A' frame. The pruning's were placed from the bottom up, overlapping, against this frame, in a 'shingle' fashion. Again, he sent them out to get more boughs as he collected more weeds. When completed, the Leaf Hut was packed full, from BOTTOM to TOP with these.

"We shall sleep as do the Squirrels," the young leader proclaimed, "For if THEY can sleep In WINTER within leaves and survive, we too can sleep in comfort and warmth here, during this 'Grandfather Time' (summer). I have listened to my father and our uncles. It is they who explained that one needs only to follow the ways of the Natural Ones. They also told that The Great Maker…The Great Spirit…has given us all: To witness, To eat, To Use, to Survive. They told me, *'Don't just look to ALL as food, but WATCH how they Move. How they EVADE. How they WATCH…and how they LIVE. That they are more than Food and Clothing, but TEACHERS as well.'* I have listened. We will be fine. Let us treat this as an ADVENTURE…and as a TIME To LEARN."

"Our mother and father will be worried," one said.

"Yes, it is so. However, we will have to face their fears and worries tomorrow. For tonight, we sleep. I am responsible. I am the oldest. I shall take the punishment. I should have paid more attention. I have learned one should ALWAYS be responsible for what one does. No matter the outcome. In this, one grows WISE…and CAREFUL. Now, go do your night 'duties.' Here is some tree moss and grasses for any in need."

Upon completion, each slid in. Actually, 'wormed' into the packed warmth of their 'squirrel bed', directed by the eldest to keep more bedding below them then on top.

"The Earth Mother gets cold, and we must not be drained of our heat within," the Eldest that listened 'said'…but he had heard…and watched. Ho.

He slid in last and pulled a prepared leaf pile towards him, as Door and Chill protection. He was shoulders towards the front of all. To be the first to defend, if need should arise, with a stone sharpened long stick in hand.

They slept…*As snug as a bug in a rug.*

The two watchers, elders who had followed them, watched...smiling.

Self-Righteousness

She had come to her Wakȟáŋ, hoping he could help her have 'them go right.' This is the 'story.'

She was 'a mean old witch.' At least that is what people thought. Sharp tongued, not 'taking Guff' and quite able to hold her own. Yet inside, she was filled with LOVE. It did not come OUT that way (to most). Most did not see her ways were just meant to help. She would think IF ONLY THEY WOULD 'SEE!' However, no, they went about their ways of Self Indulgences, and 'got ticked' if someone tried to help them see they were headed to their doom. Yes, she MEANT well, but had forgotten SHE was not God. She failed to see SHE had taken on 'HIS' duties! It was done in Love's reason, but she could do MUCH Better if, by IN LOVE, she would PRAY for them! Then, trust HIM and let 'HIM' do the changing. Age rebukes in a 'crotchety' way.

Without TRUST, Love…Agape PURE Love…has a tendency to INFLAME those ones trying to 'help.' She had wanted so MUCH for 'her children' and was, time after time, So Disappointed. Years of this had hardened her. SHE WAS NOT GOD! In addition, had forgotten this.

SHE HAD FORGOTTEN to TRUST!

Her frustrations were brought on by this. This in turn, brought on ill health that only made her MORE 'crotchety' and even MORE disliked. It was a vicious circle. She THOUGHT 'Love,' but failed to SHOW it!

The Wakȟáŋ listened…then began:

"Sister, it is 'HIS' Duty to Help, OUR Duty to be as 'HE' sees us: BABIES! Babies in 'His' arms. CONTENT…PEACEFUL…and at TRUSTING REST. There is no rest in Fidgeting and Wailing about. REST Child. Have PEACE Child. YOU ARE IN MY CARE, Child. You, sweetheart, have FORGOTTEN THAT!"

He had promised to listen…Had…and ended up with this: "My sister, go back to being 'His' Baby. Return to 'His' Cuddling. REMEMBER! When you do, you will be so CONTENT, those you care for will see, and SEEK. You are NOT the Creator…but a mere baby. 'HIS' baby. WHEN you DO THIS, those you care for MAY change. 'MAY', mind you. For ALL are born with Self Will. ALL have their OWN PATH. Our Creator WISHES they will come to 'Him' too, but has GIVEN THEM the RIGHT to Choose THEIR OWN LIFE WAY.

Know this, 'HE' CRIES TOO!

That is not your concern. Yours is to BE CONTENT and REST." HO.

Inner Heyókȟa Way/Traditional Way

The five Medicine Men were discussing their Learnings. Grandfather held High Respect in their midst. He did things DIFFERENTLY. Rarely would this one pull out Herbs or say 'Special Chants.' Yet the healings STILL would be. He was known to Fast…but was not seen going out into the Wilderness, seeking, by a Quest. Instead, he seemed to KNOW THE ANSWERS that THEY spent long twenty-four hour DAYS…sitting alone…to find out. Their way was TRADITION(al) …HE DID NOT DO THAT in general. Still, HE WOULD HEAL! They knew he followed a way called 'Purity' and that he was one of twelve that did. These twelve known as INNER Heyókȟa. Some of these here were Heyókȟa Healers. Some were not. However, they all followed Traditional Ways to do their 'work.'

"Brother," one asked, "How do YOU do it?"

He laughed. "Well, as you know, we all here know many things. We know that all this around us is simply a dream. We know how we can 'work' the dream. We know we can 'Split' into more than one. We know we have had teachers. All this and more we hold in common. Our difference is Our TEACHERS. Yours have all passed on. They taught what they knew and you learned by ROTE. Several of MY teachers are now 'gone' as well. BUT NOT THE MAIN TEACHER. HE still LIVES. I can go to Him at any time I like…or need. In addition, I do so.

In 'Splitting' we know we can be at more than one place at a time. My Major Teacher is a Master at this. FAR better than ANY of us. This one is the one we all call 'Big Brother' (They looked shocked!). He NEVER died…He is STILL AROUND. Oh, we know He DID die…for THREE DAYS. We of Heyókȟa know WE are all to die too…and return. At this, the two other Heyókȟa nodded their heads 'yes.' Well, the one called Jesus returned as well…and now SPLITS. HE IS IN ME! Literally. All I need to do is ask 'HIM WITHIN' what needs to be done, how and IF I AM to 'do.' When I ask, I RECEIVE MY ANSWER(S), IMMEDIATELY.

My Teacher Is Always There For Me

You are doing yourselves a great disservice by shying away from His WRITTEN WORD. That is your path, though. I will not condemn you in any way, the WHY of your not paying attention to it, I Understand.

You have asked me, How I 'DO'…I DO NOT! HE Does! Isn't that the Truth for All of Us? (They affirmed). Let's let the 'White' Doctors take credit…as they so often do. WE KNOW BETTER. WE Know 'HE' is The HEALER, not US! HO!

There is much I can share…but you are not my students. Besides, nearly all of what I have learned is ALL IN WRITING. You can go THERE and learn…IF you are SERIOUS in learning the Purity Way."

One said, "Brother, it is hard for us to accept White Man's Religion. That Book represents nothing but grief to us. You know that!"

"As I said, I UNDERSTAND! The thing is, it is a RELIGION they have made. With several 'ways' of this 'Religion.' THAT is what has brought on your Grief.

MAN MAKES RULES. THE GOOD BOOK ***BREAKS RULES***!

IF you can shift out MANS' INCURSIONS and get ONLY 'HIS' WORD from all their 'add-ons', 'HE' is THERE! We Inner Heyókȟa have learned this. IF you want to find out if what I am saying is true: HONESTLY ASK. Be FULLY SERIOUS about it. THEN 'He' will Show you!"

Aho?

Totems

The little boy asked, "Grandfather, can you tell me why we have Totems? And what they are for?"

The old Wakȟáŋ looked down on his inquisitive charge.

"Well, Field Mouse (the boys name)…we have Totems as a GIFT, from the Creator. ALL people have at least one. Not all know it though, nor do they all know THEM.
A Totem, son, is a WATCHER, a HELPER, a GUARD, and a MESSENGER. They are given to EVERY Living SOUL born. Every soul on our Great Turtle (Earth), as well as on other 'Earths.'

Not all 'see' them as we 'see' them…and it is that way with us as well.
Still, a Totem is a Totem.

A TOTEM IS AN ANGEL!

You see son, The Creator gives angels in a form EACH RACE Understands. Some 'see' them as Great Ones with Wings. This is the way the Christians 'see' them. Others 'see' in THEIR Cultural Way. Ours is by NATURE Beings: Animals, Birds, and so on. It does not matter…The Great Spirit knows how each perceives.

That is why there are so many types.

Aho?"

"Yes Grandfather. Thank you."

The Peaceful Warrior

The young men came. All Warriors. Each with battles and raids under their belt.

"Grandfather," their leader said, "We have all heard of your younger days. It is said that you were well known by your enemies and HIGHLY REGARDED BY THEM! We have heard you never killed ANY, and yet are considered 'The BRAVEST Of the BRAVE!' We've heard too that you would treat your enemies in a way of Peace. That though they tried to kill you, you would STILL treat THEM as A FRIEND! Tell us, please, are these tellings TRUE?"

"Yes Nephews, I suppose so."

"Could you tell us WHY, Grandfather?"

Motioning them to sit, he began.

"In my youth…my Very EARLY Youth…I saw 'people were people.' Each having their own basic desires: to go anywhere safely, to feed their families, to enjoy all that The Creator has provided, to Have PEACE. This I saw in my early youth."

"But The WARS! THEY WAR AGAINST US Grandfather!"

"And WE DO the SAME to THEM! Do WE NOT?"

(They looked uneasy.)

"My Nephews, there was a time all never warred. A time when peace was the way. That ALL were 'BROTHERS', ONE! A time of *'Mitakuye Oyasin'* (one Relation). In Truth, WE STILL ARE! WHY would I want to KILL MY BROTHER?

It is in that KNOWING THOUGHT I would do battle…and Queue (touch, not kill). To those done in this way, though they were humiliated and angered, AT LEAST THEY WERE STILL ALIVE! THEY WERE NOT CARRIED HOME TO BE LAID TO REST! They could still hold their loved ones, hunt, LIVE!

This 'war(ing)', to me, was just 'Rough Housing', between BROTHERS!

Then there were times when they would lay injured AT MY MERCY. I could have KILLED, or CAPTURED. I would do NEITHER! If hurt, I would do my best to fix the injury. Then send them on. I would always send them off with a gift as they departed. I would ALSO say: *"It was a GOOD FIGHT! I WAS LUCKY, for you are a formidable fighter! Go home my brother. See your loved ones and get well. Perhaps next time we can meet in peace."*

In this manner, it would help take off the sting they would hold in being defeated.

I TREATED THEM AS BROTHERS!

This they remembered. This helped US…to have PEACE! I made FRIENDS with those who called me ENEMY. Now we no longer war with many we HAD warred WITH. You see my friends, this is the way it WAS…in the Long Ago Time. It was duplicated AGAIN, once, through the Teachings of BIG BROTHER. It is my desire to see this return. Some ONE must!

Will YOU?!"

They left, pondering…

Tradition Versus Today

"We should ALL GO BACK to the OLD WAYS!" This at a large meeting, said in a loud, FIRM, STRONG, way, by a middle-aged woman. An 'Anti-White' extremist, "…and NOW!" She practically shouted. Many seemed to agree! Until the Old One spoke up!

"Who will begin this?" He asked.

"I WILL!" She replied, FIRMLY.

"WONDERFUL! NOW?"

"Yes, RIGHT NOW!"

"100% TRADITIONAL WAYS?"

"YES!" She vehemently replied.

"Snowing out?"

"So?"

"Well, you live about nine miles away…better start walking."

"What do YOU MEAN?"

"Sis, if you're Serious…"

(She rudely interrupted with "I AM!")

"Alright, from this moment on, YOU GET IN NO CAR. WALK until you get a horse…Oh, Sorry, Whites brought the horses. So, just walk.

DO NOT GO INTO YOUR HEATED/LIGHTED HOUSE…it's 'White Man'!"

No HOT SHOWERS either, until you heat the water on a fire OUTSIDE, or in a Tipi YOU make. After all, that was the OLD WAYS of doing. The WOMEN made them!

I like your spirit, your DETERMINATION. You will be a leader alright! I wonder how many who called 'HO!' here, will follow you in this?"

He looked about…ALL…was Silent…

A Telling Of Knowledge

"My brothers and sisters," he said, "What will be told here is of a delicate matter. It needs to be known, though. This one has heard women and men saying the word 'SQUAW.' We all have heard it. YOU DO NOT KNOW ITS ORIGIN, its TRUE MEANING.

This was a SLANG WORD of the White man.

IT MEANS the 'PERSONAL PART' of an INDIAN WOMAN!

In respect for our women…

PLEASE

STOP USING IT!"

How To Change The Future

There were many, Many 'Nations' represented. A BIG Pow Wow (meeting), Called to talk over the 'Invaders' offspring's most recent Orders and Rules. Once again, the Government is trying their best to eliminate what little they had doled out to the people. Just more ploys to get EVERYTHING! Delegates from Canada, U.S.A. and even some from South America were here. It was a GIGANTIC meeting.

"How do we FIGHT these people? HOW CAN WE REMAIN SOVEREIGN onto OURSELVES?"

Yes, the 'invaders' offspring had become TYRANTS…with an *'it is ALL for YOUR GOOD'* smile. One 'Rule' after another. Repeatedly, FOREVER 'CHIPPING.'
This meeting was 'deep' with MUCH frustration, Much Anger, and Much DESPAIR!
(Is it no wonder 'we' have turned to Drink and Drugs? WE ARE DYING!)

Eventually, they asked the Wakȟáŋ, "Do YOU have any suggestions? Any Wisdom that can HELP?" He took the Talking Stick, as those holding 'Had the Floor,' and stood.

"It is a sadness we've come to this. An EXPECTED time! Long ago foretold to be. NOW the tellings are upon us. WE WERE WARNED! We tried…too late. Our ancestors now long in their 'sleep.' Our WARRIORS who tried to win our land back. Now we sit here, discussing our fate. WE FOUGHT BACK TO LATE!

Now our best defense is EDUCATED Brethren. People who are willing to 'war' in the 'INVADERS' WAY...through LAW! We have SOME Lawyers of OUR OWN, of OUR Blood. WE NEED FAR MORE! This takes Time. Their 'rules' forbid us to speak 'in Authority' without a piece of paper, A DEGREE in LAW.

This piece of paper takes three things to get: DEVOTED WARRIORS, MONEY, and TIME!

The 'warriors' must be willing to fight for us ALL, for EVERY 'Nation.' It cannot work otherwise. WE MUST UNITE as ONE PEOPLE! We still hold grudges, still 'Tribe against Tribe.' We STILL have our long standing 'enemies.' WE HAVE NOT ONE in Full FORGIVENESS – LOVE for 'US' A RACE called INDIANS. We STILL fight within OURSELVES! *'Mitakuye Oyasin'* has become just a WORD. WE NO LONGER FOLLOW ITS MEANING! Now we need an ARMY. An 'OUR' Lawyers Army. This takes TIME, FINANCES and DETERMINED 'WE ARE ONE' WARRIORS!

Again, we rise against an enemy. AGAIN, we are TOO LATE! We have dallied with spending our moneys to build Casinos, to Earn money, and invest those profits, on the things of 'the Invaders' World, to make MORE Money. We have spent time and resources UNWISELY. WE

HAVE FAILED in PREPARING 'WARRIORS'! Now, we find out LIFE, our VERY EXISTENCE, 'Indian', is worth MORE THAN MONEY!

Too late, my brothers and sisters. Too late…

This one knows these are harsh words and hard to take. Yet Truth is Truth. I will tell you true, THIS IS ALL PLANNED TO BE. The Creator is in FULL CONTROL! The Creator has seen that you and I have failed.

AGAIN!

For it has happened before. For this SAME REASON has brought on our Mother's HEALING WAYS THREE TIMES BEFORE! There were FOUR prior healings. The first was an Evolution Cleansing. WE ARE NOW IN THE THROES OF THE FIFTH HEALING.

So here, we sit. *'What to DO!…What TO DO!'*

Alright…HERE is your answer: TRUST 'HIM' ONCE AGAIN…QUICKLY! As a UNITED ONE. And Not in MAN's way, but in 'HIS' WAY. UNITED LOVE!

REALLY 'One Relation'! RETURN TO THE MEANING OF THAT 'WORD'!
Drop the 'MY Tribe/Nation' is RIGHT! The: *'YOU are part of OUR ENEMIES!'*
DROP IT! IF we can do this…BEFORE THE SKIES TURN RED WORLD WIDE…We, ALL MANKIND, CAN STILL STOP ALL THAT LAYS AHEAD!

We…the 'Savage Redskins', can BE THE LEADERS that WILL 'turn the world' BACK TO 'ALL ARE ONE' and TRUE ONENESS. Oneness with each Other, and 'HIM.' Now, as for our 'situation' that of the *"invaders FORCEFUL, by Law 'way.'* The 'Way' that will leave US HOMELESS IN OUR OWN LAND! I 'SEE' IT THIS WAY, WE LOSE! AGAIN! IF WE DO NOT CHANGE!

But this, what I'm about to say, may make you happy:

Hear me, what has been applied to we, the CARETAKERS of the AMERICAS, IS NOW BEING APPLIED TO THE 'INVADERS' MASSES AS WELL! What goes around COMES around!"

(Many smiled…many laughed.)

"Yes, *'revenge is sweet.'* That is what most of you are thinking. Aho?!"

Many HO'S and Amen's were heard.

"I tell you true…it is SAD!
Personally, I would not wish this on a DOG! Let alone a FELLOW SOUL. WE KNOW what it is like…now you want ALL to have the SAME. Shame.

LOVE your Enemies! At least that way YOU will have Peace. I am not saying this will be easy, but I wish you would at least Try. Now, here is how I see the 'invaders'…***GIANT SNAKES!***

This snake is DEVOURING ITS OWN TAIL! IT IS DEVOURING ITS OWN SELF! DYING…And NOT KNOWING IT! It is EATING off ITSELF…to 'Live.'
Its head: 'Brainless'…Its tale, HURTING…its MIDDLE though…being 'fed' is SATISFIED and 'CONTENT.' After all, isn't it FULL? Isn't it thus ALIVE?

The 'Invaders' of ALL COUNTRIES ARE OF THE SAME GREEDY, CONTEMPTUOUS SELF INDULGING MAN SNAKE WAYS! TO LAZY to HUNT! For it has FOUND ITS TAIL. 'FOOD', right 'THERE.' WHY seek OTHER ways to LIVE…and have to WORK AT IT…When RIGHT HERE I'VE FOOD! RIGHT BEHIND ME ALL THE TIME! Brainless!

Therefore, my brethren, KNOW THIS: THE CREATOR IS IN FULL CONTROL! 'He' will NOT allow the snake to KILL ITSELF! That Snake is 'HIS' MAKING! In addition, 'He' CARES for what is 'His.' Hear me.

'HE' WILL SMACK THE SNAKE BEFORE IT COMPLETELY DIES! This 'Whack' will FORCE IT TO VOMIT OUT what little is left of its tail. And the snake will crawl away in a Daze. SO PAINED it will no longer chew on what little is LEFT. Once again, it will have to look to the Creator to provide its NATURAL life needs. Mutilated, bleeding, VERY sore…even sickly, it will once again learn to 'eat' NATURALLY. RELYING ON THE CREATOR and the MAKERS GIVEN WAY! THIS IS WHAT LIES AHEAD! UNLESS WE CHANGE IT…starting RIGHT NOW!

It is TOO LATE to raise an Army.
However, it is NOT TOO LATE to RETURN TO 'ONE IN HIM/ONE FOR ALL.'

The Skies are not YET red!"

Ho.

Resurrection

They were talking about Spiritual things. 'Life and Death,' etc...The Old one speaking on many things concerning this. Giving insight and past knowledge to The People. Trying to help them 'remember' before ALL was lost. He astonished them with this.

"Very few are aware that all our Nations have at least ONE Sacred Spot that they laid their Holy Ones in, upon their passing. This for a total of three days. Fewer yet know that occasionally, one that has been laid there, RETURNS TO LIFE. This one then returns to his/her People and informs them of what they were told while 'asleep.' TOLD TO, BY THE CREATOR.

S/He tells what The People are doing that Pleases or Displeases this Great one. The returned one then continues living with The People until permanent 'leaving.' This is a FACT. ONLY THE HOLIEST of HOLY seem to do this…and it is NOT a common occurrence.

Similar has happened in the past within the Christian 'circle,' as we have all heard. Big Brother returned after three days, as well. Ours are not of THAT return, though. His was a SPECIAL 'calling.' Ho.

The Good Book tells of this. It ALSO tells that in the future, two others will 'pass' and then raise Alive. What it DOES NOT tells, but that OUR Prophesies DO is that there will be THREE, Not two. One from THIS Hemisphere.

Will that third be of OUR 'Indian', or of another race? I do not know. It IS Possible though."

Ho.

The Fish

The group of fishermen entered with a nice string of winter run perch. Many were quite large 'Bragging Size.' It was obvious they had been 'partying.' Each aglow with more than 'pride.' In their boastfulness, they suddenly saw The Old One, sitting silently off at a side table eating his meal. He was known for catching large fish, often returning with some real 'beauties.' Yet, HE never bragged over any of these. They headed for him, fish in hand.

"WHAT do you think of THESE, OLD MAN!" Demanded one of the men swinging the stringer inches from his nose.

Calmly he looked first at the fish, then at them.

"Nice, boys. Even That one…pointing to one that was thirteen inches in length. I have caught several like that myself, but bigger. Thirteen inches too, but a BIGGER thirteen inches."

This took them aback! "HOW can thirteen INCHES Be BIGGER than thirteen INCHES…YOU OLD FOOL?" One of the men whooped!

The whole room exploded in laughter at the Old Man's reply.

"Well, you see son, we Indians don't measure the same as you whites. THAT fish there is thirteen inches LONG. OURS are thirteen inches too, but ACROSS THE EYE!"

We Are Aware

They were 'playing games' with the 'Old Man.'

They were Whites that had no respect for 'others.' Indians are used to these types and handle them calmly.

"HEY, CHIEF," one boss yelled over the assembly line noises, "WE NEED TO KNOW HOW MANY OF THOSE CORN EARS WE DO IN AN HOUR! COUNT THEM! WE'LL BE BACK IN AN HOUR TO GET YOUR COUNT!"

He nodded, "Okay."

An hour later they returned, big grins on their faces.

"OKAY, CHIEF, WHAT'S THE COUNT?"

He looked up. "One."

"WHAT?"

"ONE!" He shouted back.

"ONE! ONE! What do you MEAN ONE?"

Holding one up, he said, "Here's ONE. Here's ANOTHER ONE, and ANOTHER one, and another…"

Child Chastisement The Indian Way

The Village Children were getting out of hand, turning into total Brats, not minding their parents or elders. This had gotten irritating to the camps' people. It was not the Indian Way to spank. They had BETTER Ways.

It was time for THE BOOGEYMAN!

Yes, we in the old days had stories of The Boogeyman too, and enough was enough!
Calling a meeting, the adults gathered. No children were allowed to be present.
In this meeting, the Problem was discussed. The parents telling what each of their children had done. Others telling of things they had witnessed or been a recipient of.

NO warning of, "STOP! Or The BOOGEYMAN WILL GET YOU!" had done any good. The children had heard THAT Before! This 'Boogeyman' had never shown. At least, not in THEIR lifetime. To them this was just 'an Old Wives Tale,' something to laugh at. They were about to find out OTHERWISE! Yes, it was TIME…

They asked a man to play the part. He agreed to do so.
This one was then 'Gifted,' (given gifts), for his time and upcoming effort. A Time was set, the next Full Moon, or as close to it as Nature allowed. NATURE being an Important Part of what would come. They used ALL to their advantage. In this case, a STRONG LIGHTNING AND WIND STORM! That, with the 'Crazy Moon,' would 'set the scene,' highlighting the event, and making it more TERRIFYING.

Over an Unnoticed period, old hides and other things were discreetly taken to the Doer, unseen by the children. Among these were a large Bear Head, one front leg of same (claws and all), an Eagle Talon, a 'Ratty' old deer and elk hide, rabbit and skunk hides, and bits and pieces of this and that, including a large deer's rack. This was to be The Boogeyman's covering.

THE STORIES WERE OF SEEING A BEING.

ALL had heard of this Frightening apparition. NOW that Tale was being said repeatedly around the village. It did not matter. The kids just continued laughing and ignoring, and went about their disobeying ways. ALL WAS SET IN READINESS…now it was up to The Creator to do 'His' part. BRING IN THE GREAT STORM, at the RIGHT MOON Time. The Medicine Man and their Wakȟáŋ had been asking…seeking 'His' approval and Doing.

The storm was on its way. The Creator had answered. It was a day before the Full moon, and so had Plenty of Light. By the action of the wildlife about the camp, it was going to be a large storm, as well. They could even smell its approach in the air. The camp started 'batting down' their lodges, tightening the Tipi Skin hide covers, replacing weak 'tie' sticks and skin anchor sticks, the High Wind Mainline checked and tightened, Smoke Flaps overlapped and tied securely, and extra dry firewood brought in. These storms were taken seriously!

Amidst all this, the 'Player' decided to 'go off' to visit relatives. The Village Crier announcing his trip. ALL therefore knew he would be gone. He had his packhorse behind him as he rode out.

"BE SAFE Brother…this will be a Wild Storm by the looks of it!" Folks would call.
"BE Careful!" He waved to each as he left. Yes, it was going o be a WILD Night indeed. ☺

Faster and faster, the storm came on. Great Flashes of Lightning could be seen over the distant mountains. Swirls of dust, lifting at its wind's power, Faster and Faster, Closer and closer it came. Darkness became DARKER. It was Dancing RIGHT THEIR WAY!
All scurried to the safety of their Hide Homes. Fires lit to keep off its chill. By the time it arrived, all were in their beds. The children huddled deep inside their Hair Hide 'blankets.' The Storm was DIRECTLY OVERHEAD! And there, it seemed to STOP!

THUNDER Rolling in GREAT NOISE!
LIGHTNING CRACKING Upwards!
Tipis SHOOK in its Greatness!
Would it EVER STOP?

Then, in one Lodge, no one noticed a Lacing Stick slowly being pulled from its holes. The door tie string being dislodged on one side. THE DOOR FLAPPED HALF OPEN!
Whipping in the wind, it in turn caused the overlapping Hide Cover to break free, WIDENING THE ENTRY HOLE!

Over the Roar of the storm, ANOTHER ROAR COULD BE HEARD! It was HIDEOUS! At Times a low Growl, then Resounding to a MIGHTY ROAR! Loud CACKLING LAUGHTER BETWEEN! And SCREECHES and Odd, Frightening Rising/Falling HOOOOOTS!
It was the…

BOOGEYMAN!

The small boy heard his mother SCREAM, and his father YELL IN FEAR!

He looked out from his covers to see what was going on, JUST in TIME to see HUGE HORNS Ripping Back and Forth Trying to get in. By now, the WHOLE Door Flap was Loose, and ANOTHER LACING PIN WAS BEING PULLED OUT! Then, a FOOT Entered, the door hide entangled over it. THE STORM GREW EVEN FIERCER!

CRACK! HOWL! BOOM!

The Horns made it THROUGH! Followed by a BLACK HEAD of a BEAR!

Father Yelled, “OUT! OUT!” as he grabbed his spear and rose to meet this Apparition, stabbing at it fearlessly. Its earthy stench filled the air, as it tried to get fully in the lodge. Its body ENORMOUS and covered with strange ‘hair.’

“OUT!” once again, father yelled. “YOU CAN NOT HAVE OUR SON!” A GREAT STRUGGLE ensued. The ‘Things’ two ‘Hands’…one of Bear, One of Prey Bird struck out, CUTTING INTO THE FATHER WARRIOR!

The BOY grabbed EVERY HIDE COVER HE COULD, and fast became ‘Small’ within. TREMBLING in FEAR!

The Screaming and Growling went on and on in this great Struggle. THEN…HIGH SCREAMS of PAIN! THE BOOGEYMAN HAD BEEN HURT! BAD! Repeatedly, Father pressed his spear against its huge hide…only THIS TIME, at its BACK! It was LEAVING! SCREAMING IN PAIN ALL THE WAY!

”KILL IT! KILL IIIITTTT!” The mother shouted. The boy could not resist...he PEEKED.

In that instant he saw his father, Bleeding on chest and arm, give this MOST HIDEOUS THING a MIGHTY PUSH! OUT IT WENT! Father threw his busted spear after him. Mother began giving her VICTORY THRALL. Her Man had defeated the most TERRIFYING CHILD TAKER that has EVER BEEN KNOWN! As the boogeyman ran off into the distance, its screaming following…it became less and less hearable. AND THE STORM PASSED!

The next day several Warriors tracked this THING, “as best we could…but the Storm has washed away its prints.” They brought back Proof of this one being in camp. Bits and pieces of hides, smeared with blood and mud.

Father, with wounds bound, was put on a Grand Horse and with MUCH FANFARE was paraded about All the Camp. He was a HERO! A BRAVE amongst BRAVES. That night was told over many fires. The saved boy himself telling boys and girls what had happened, and how FRIGHTENED he had been. Even that HE PEE’d HIS BED!

There was no more trouble with the children.

Ho.

Holy?

His Granddaughter was with him. He was at his Computer.

"Grandfather, you are the least person I know with anger. You seem to love EVERYTHING!"

At THAT PRECISE MOMENT, something went 'WACKO' with the Computer: DELETING AN HOURS WORTH OF ONE FINGER TYPING! GONE! ZIPPO! OUT TO 'LA LA' LAND!

Grandfather let out a ROAR and a string of Swear Words a SAILOR would Envy!

Head in hands, he quietly said, "What did you say, Honey?"

The User

He was like so MANY others, others who were out to 'ride his shirt tales' to line their own pockets. He had learned early why they 'befriended' him. He could 'read' them a mile away. This one was persistent. More so then the others.

"You know *Brother* (HA!), if you'd just levitate you could make a FORTUNE on the film. Sell THOUSANDS of DVDs. I can film it and edit it no problem." (And no doubt expect to get a Lion's share of all the profits too!)

Yes, grandfather could 'read' well.

"I've told you before I won't do it…and I won't," he quietly said.

This man had whined and 'suggested' many times before. Never taking NO for an answer. Grandfather was about to 'drop' this 'Brother.' He did not need this kind of 'Brotherhood' or 'Friend.' Try as he might, he could not get the guy to 'SEE.'

'See' that The CREATOR was a FACT, was real, and LIVING. He had given two years 'trying,' just by letting him see HIS life. He was not interested. Only GREED and SELF was this one's path.

"BUT WHY?"

"Friend, I don't 'DO' unless The Great One TELLS me to. You know that. So far, *He's* told me NOTHING on doing this for 'our' Benefit. I do not take orders from man. I might be Broke but I'm RIGHT In 'HIM.' THAT is worth MORE TO ME then ANY amount of Money. You do not understand this because you have never spoken with *Him*."

"Now WAIT A MINUTE! I TALK TO GOD!"

Grandfather looked at him sadly.

"I don't doubt you. You are like most of the others. You and they Talk To 'Him', certainly. You are like this with them in THIS as well, you hear only what you Want to hear, not what is SAID. I did NOT Say 'TO', I said 'WITH'!"

They have not seen each other now for years…

Locating The Missing

Every once in a while Grandfather receives a request to help locate a missing person. It did not matter from where, as usually, he 'worked' from home. Not all were found. Some in water. One in a tree, mauled by a bear. Then, occasionally it would be a runaway.

"Don't worry, s/he is fine and will return in a few days."

Always were, too.

These calls came in from across the USA and Canada. He is pretty well known for this.

"How do you do it, brother? Can I do it?" He has heard these questions from several.

"Yes. ANY can. The question is, 'can YOU?' Can you Get and KEEP in touch with the Creator?
Can you put aside your OWN 'wants', to do, instantly, this locating?
Can you TRUST 'Him'? Can you TRUST YOURSELF? YOUR Standing in 'His' Sight, as GODLY and GOOD?

If you cannot, you will not be as successful. Aho?"

As One In Him

She was a GOOD Medicine Woman! Another "Breed."

"*Metes*." Just like grandfather. She had come to learn from HIM, but HE learned from HER even more. He had his "specialties" and she had hers. They had hit it off immediately. "Traded." They were both the better for it.

This is the way it should be. Learning from each other, without "Guarding or Hording."
The Creator had given all a special ability. Also, ALL the SAME gift as well, to LOVE. Love leaves SHARING and COMPASSION open to "work" from. Somehow, mankind has forgotten that, so walk around in a "dark cloud" known as "Self."
"Compassion?"

"LOVE?"

Sure, if it is their OWN family or "people."

A world gone mad, due to this!

Those that DO are BRANDED as UNFIT to be around, "safely." They upset the "norm." Big Brother was so branded and paid a horrible price, for it did not matter. HE knew HE was "right" and allowed His "way" to continue. He Knew PEACE, and walked in it moment by moment. EVERY DAY. Constantly showing those in "norm" that it was really THEY who were out of step. No one likes to be exposed…so they get "upset" (to put it MILDLY!).
This Medicine Woman and Grandfather were of Like ilk…and they too "paid a price." However, as HE…BECAUSE of HIM…still "walked the walk."

There were/are others too. These two are not alone.

Perhaps more will look and volunteer to not mess about anymore. To not be a "fence straddler" or in a field of weeds, instead of sweet grass. It will cost them as well. Not many are in THAT willingness. Few indeed. So the two Medicine People, at least, can be "one" in their Godly Love…and continue to share and help each other and others. THANKS to HIM!

Ho.

Life

"It seems no one knows what Life is all about," he said to the old Wakȟáŋ. "WHY we exist. WHAT it IS. Do you, grandfather?"

The old one became deep in thought, His eyes misted. A slight soft smile came upon his lips. "Yes, I know. Indeed, I know…I know," he softly spoke, almost in a whisper. He turned to his asker and said:

"Life is given to Enjoy. To Experience. To Love, and to be loved. It is to WALK With and KNOW Our Creator. To KNOW 'HIS' Love. It is given to give 'HIM' Joy and Contentment because 'He' enjoys the WONDER of what **He's** made…YOU! ALL!"

The young man stood listening. Then, "Grandfather, WHY is it then often so HARD?"

The Old man looked deeply into his eyes and said,

"THAT son, is something only YOU can answer."

Grandfather's Tease

Children often gravitated around "Grandfather." He always seemed to have time for them. On this occasion one said,

"Grandfather, you are always so SERIOUS. Was your mother and father like you too?"

"I don't know sweetheart, I never really got to know them," he replied.

"DID they DIE?"

"Well, I don't know THAT either. You see, they sort of "flew off" after I "became."

"Where did they go?"

The old one sighed. His eyes became sad.

"You see, they were at the beach, leaving their Calling Cards upon the tourists."

"HUH?"

"Honey, my parents were SEAGULLS!"

(Shock!)

"Yes. Seagulls and they sort of got 'carried away.' Well, they collided in mid-air…and, well, I POPPED OUT! I landed on a hot rock below, and well…I grew up to what you see and know today…"

A BLOOMING IDIOT!

He walked away…
Head bowed, "sniveling" and "sad"…

(With an unseen smile on face). ☺

The Attackers

Grandfather shared much over his years. This did not go over to well with many Medicine People. He was giving out "Sacred Knowledge"...SECRETS really. Taught and learned, passed down, over the centuries of Indian Tradition.

He would reply by saying:

"What I am giving out is ALL IN A BOOK that's FAR OLDER then Tradition. THE BIBLE. If you would care to take the time to READ IT, you would find this is true.
I have yet to reveal ANYTHING that ANY cannot find in there.
I tell you True, WHILE YOU are jealously guarding for your 'Standing,' you are FAILING the Great Creator! Your Pride will cause you problems in the 'Passing' Time. That's YOUR Choice. Mine is to do RIGHT in 'His' sight, now – SHARE!

In days long gone, EVERYONE 'KNEW.' Overtime, most lost these Knowings. Even you and I do not KNOW All. Do NOT REMEMBER <u>ALL</u>. While you HIDE, I simply GIVE...again, I say...ONLY WHAT IS ALREADY WRITTEN!

We all know sacred things that are NOT written. Walking into other Times and Dimensions, and others. THESE ARE NOT IN THAT BOOK. Yet they ARE Hinted at in these words: *EVEN MORE SO, for I AM WITH YOU.* You know little of 'His' Word, else you would know this. You'd know these things I share ARE ALL OPENLY TOLD OF. Your PRIDE is as the PRIDE of Any White Pastor, Priest, any Rabbi, or Mullah."

"YOU SELL THESE THINGS!" one angrily retorted.

"Yes. I DO! And YOU SELL YOUR HEALINGS and Other THINGS as well! SO? Do we not ALL need to Eat, raise our families, and pay bills? Do I cut YOU down for getting paid for doing! Well? Do I? NO! You have the SAME RIGHT to be paid as a McDonald's Cook, a White Doctor, a Blue Collar Worker, or I. THEY ALL SELL THEIR TRAINING! Do you complain to your Mechanic?

You get angry with me for doing THE EXACT SAME THING that YOU ARE DOING. The DIFFERENCE is I go by 'HIS' ORDERS, and YOU REJECT THEM. I give them BACK the ability to FISH. YOU give ONLY A FISH! Our BIG BROTHER came to set people FREE.... YOU in turn KEEP THEM IN BONDAGE...to YOU!"

"TELL US! (This angrily) DO YOU HONESTLY <u>BELIEVE</u> 'SELLING' MAKES '<u>HIM</u>' HAPPY! YOU AREN'T A MEDICINE MAN!"

"You yet don't quite understand the 'selling' I do. I am being paid, 'HIRED', to do the buyers RESEARCH. They can do their own if they so choose. I even tell them this. All it takes is the ability to read and comprehend. Is it against 'His' will that I receive pay for this? I will let 'HIM' answer that! *MUZZLE NOT THE OXEN*!

That to your First Statement.

As for your second: IF I Am NOT…a 'Medicine Man', WHY ARE YOU Then HERE, TELLING ME *I'm selling 'Sacred'(only 'Medicine People' can do or know) 'SECRETS'?!"*

I tell you all, YOU ARE NOT FIGHTING ME! YOU ARE FIGHTING 'H I M'!

YOU NEED TO RETURN TO HIM! FOLLOW!

SELAH!

Now Go…

And THINK ON THESE THINGS!   Ho!"

Grandmother

All knew where Grandfather lived. His wife and family tucked...well, CRAMMED, into a very, very small house off the reservation. His wife worked at a regular job. HIS were THE PEOPLE. ANY people.

Living this way was hard on all. Many came to seek help, counseling, and healings. His weeks were full with e mail requests, regular mail...phone calls, scheduled meetings, Teachings and "Drop-Ins." Often their home held sleeping people on couch and floor. Kids and Adults alike. Their food supply stretched for all. Somehow, they "made it," though it was never easy. Both Grandfather and his wife were "givers." People just WEREN'T TURNED AWAY. At times, he would even bring home hitchhikers. Once even a Prostitute, "down on her luck." His poor wife NEVER knew what to expect when she would get up every morning! She would not even flinch. Milk Toast again...(Eggs a rarity, too costly).

Did not matter to the "guests," EACH was sent off with SOMETHING in their bellies, and on some occasions, even on their Back...or Feet. Yes, they were "poor." Rarely receiving any help, or "pay," from anyone. Still, The Great Creator MADE DO. It was an act of Devotion to these two older ones. BOTH filled with Love. Love for their "Father," Love for "His" Son, Love for "His" Spirit, Love for "His" Creation, "Love" for "His" "Children"...and ALWAYS Last...Love for EACH OTHER.

These were not the only in "Medicine" that live like this. MANY do! Few Receive, but from God Creator. MANY cannot go on with this...too hard on them and family. They thus "Lay Down Their Feathers" and quit the "Calling." None blames them. ALL know what they are going through. They themselves, having been in the same situation (and Thought), MANY times. It is not easy being a Medicine Person. Even HARDER to be a MATE TO ONE! When a person runs into this type of Oneness, it is a MARVEL to behold! The two <u>ARE ONE</u> ! Just as Scriptures say.

Some of their friends have seen, and asked, "How can you LIVE like this?" They fail to see that "Big Brother" HAD no Home! He WALKED a lot, from place to place and slept under the Stars, if need be. That He "MADE DO" TOO!

To this they would reply, "Yes, it's a mess. Just no other place to go...BUT we are CLOTHED, DRY, and WARM. So MANY on our Mother Earth AREN'T. We have little to complain about, when we consider THEM." (That from both).

Only LOVE...HIS LOVE, can do this. PRAISE "HIM!"

Ho.

Misunderstood Love

Grandfather was sitting in his car, waiting for his wife. A woman who was "in love" with him, actually asked him to divorce his life mate and marry HER, was talking to him as he waited. His wife came out of the store and they exchanged pleasantries, then the woman parted. His wife said, "I know her from somewhere, but can't remember from WHERE." Grandfather replied "Oh, that's…one of the women who claims to be *in love* with me."

His woman looked at him, then at the woman walking off. She retorted, "Well, she MAY be '*In LOVE*' with you, but SHE'S never been MARRIED TO YOU!" ☺

NOTE:

This seems to be a common problem. People "Looking Up To" one such as grandfather. (It was a constant irritant to him).

He would say,

"They aren't seeing ME. They are seeing HIM that Dwells WITHIN ME! Why can't they understand that?"

GRANDMOTHER SURE UNDERSTOOD!

☺

Keep Your Word!

Grandfather was no Saint. He had his "moments."

NOTHING seemed to get him more upset then people reneging on their word. He was of "The Old School." "Your WORD is your BOND." Trained as an Inner Heyókȟa, he was firm on his learning. All twelve were and are.

One was given "three chances":

1) Goof (not keeping their word) was "an accident."
2)"Slap in the face."

If done again, than :

3) he would drop them like a "Hot Rock."

This too is of a Scriptural base. All twelve rely on "The Good Book" as their guideline.
The worse "hurters" were those who called themselves "Christians."

He was always expecting "More from THEM." It was like finding a precious Pearl when one would show up (Do as SAID). A VERY RARE occurrence! EVEN amongst the Native Americans.

"Don't they SEE that not ALL who say 'Lord' will not enter His homeland after Judgment Day?" He would say.

It saddened him greatly.

Following...Despite YOU

Yes, he was no saint. However, he NEVER GAVE UP HOPE. He always tried to emulate "Big Brother's Way." Always tried to SHOW "The Walk" that brought his peace.
He could not without Big Brother's help though…and knew it.

This brought many "miracles." Many "impossible" Healings. To grandfather these were not "miracles" at all…but simply as it should be, for Any Serious "Follower."

No, he was no saint. Never claimed to be.

He often told, "A man that FALLS Down gets up a LOT FASTER than a man who LIES Down."

The Pointer

Grandfather was smoking. The VERY "heavy" lady stormed up to him. "DON'T YOU KNOW That THAT WILL KILL YOU? DON'T YOU KNOW YOU ARE GIVING ME YOUR 'SECOND HAND' SMOKE?"

He was outside. In his "space," in prayer. Respecting those in a confined area.

She waddled off, "indignantly."

Probably to stuff her face with more Self Indulgences.

Just another who points but does not see THEIR "wrongs."

Respect For All

Grandfather detested rudeness. He was not one for "You're INFERIOR" attitudes either. Both a "trait" of whites crossing Reservation lands. These are two retorts he was heard saying to both "types."

"Hey YOU, (grrrrrr) what is today?"

"Yesterday's Tomorrow and Tomorrow's Yesterday."

And

"Hey you, CHIEF, WHERE DOES THIS ROAD GO?" (STEAM!)

"Doesn't go ANYWHERE. Stays HERE all the time."

If only they had asked politely…

Morals Taught

The young men were bragging. "Women."
Grandfather, not far away, could not help but overhear.

ALL these "boys" called themselves "Traditionalists"…AND "Spiritual!"

"Nephews," he called, "May I have a word with you?"

"Sure Pop," they replied and came over.

"Nephews, I APOLOGIZE, but you were talking loud enough for me and others around to hear." (They looked a little "sheepish")

"Guys, we were all young once, too…so we understand, but may I share what we've found over our years?"

"Yes, Grandfather."

"Sit down please," and motioned to seats beside his abode (Log End "chairs"). They sat and prepared to listen.

"Nephews….what I heard, if MUST be spoken, should be spoken in a less open space. Please consider that."

They nodded.

"Yes, we have women who seek men, Freely. Always have. Yet there is something you need to remember, they…ALL WOMEN…in our "way"…are our SISTERS.

YOU are our FUTURE. What you do Now will be EMULATED by your OWN Children. You call yourselves '*In Tradition.*' You say you '*Walk in Spirit.*' Yet you have forgotten what those two words mean AND represent. In the Old Times…of TRUE Tradition, MEN RESPECTED THE WOMEN. That meant they held the girls in high regard and TREATED Them AS sisters. However, today you seem to treat them as 'meat.' Your personal 'Trophies.' This is sad. ONE DAY YOUR OWN DAUGHTERS WILL BE TREATED AS SUCH. Is That what YOU WANT?"

Silence…AND SHOCK. The "boys" were "SEEING!"

"You see, boys…your sons will follow YOU. They TOO will '*go on the hunt.*' And females are different from us. THEY think TRUE LOVE. That is their way. That is why you are so

'successful.' THEY ARE IN LOVE WITH YOU! But You? No. YOU are in love with POSSESSION and COLLECTION…'Bragging Rights' and 'Trophies'!
Boys, this is Pride. Self.

In Tradition…in SPIRIT, THIS IS NOT GOOD IN OUR CREATOR'S EYES!
Why not Change…why not DO 'Tradition' and SPIRIT?
CHANGE YOUR FUTURE BY CHANGING YOUR N O W.

Yes, you are our Future. It looks like many of your examples were not the best. I am sad and sorry for this. But Hear me…YOU MAKE YOUR OWN FUTURE. EACH of you.

Thank you for honoring me and listening!

Ho."

The Long Walkers

The Elders were speaking. It was a fine summer evening in Navaho Country.
One told this story:

Not many years ago the Wise Leaders of this area sent over 30 people back into The INNER LANDS. It was time. Each going as a volunteer. One was chosen to lead. They thought it would take about ten months to reach their goal. LITTLE DID THEY KNOW IT WOULD BE MORE LIKE TEN YEARS!

This group was and is the FIRST of three sent. They are called 'The Long Walkers'…this particular group was feared lost and that all have perished. IT IS NOT SO! They are NOW VERY NEAR THE INNER CITY they were sent to. Five have died along the journey. The rest should make it though.

The Second Group may BE to their city, opposite from the first group, in South America.

The Third Group are the latest in, and New on 'The Walk.'

Both the Second and Third Groups are smaller.

THIS IS A TRUE TELLING. There is NO FICTION HERE…

The world's masses know nothing about this. Things long kept secret. WISELY guarded by our Societies.

Things the White Governments would only Horde, Destroy, Steal, or Sell.
More than likely use as War Routes, AFTER stealing what these places contain.

As you know, they were given their chance when they first arrived amongst us, but did just those things. They are UNTRUSTWORTHY. This to their shame. Thus to the shame of all mankind, Not of the caretakers.

For them I am sorry. I am SO Sorry.

Hear me:

The Creator will ONCE AGAIN say, "GO FORTH and Repopulate the Earth."

The Long Walkers will be a part in this, Protected, deep within!

Ho.

Teachings On Faith

One came seeking information. Another elder and a good man.

"My brother, I've seen you have a lot of faith, more so than the usual person. Can you explain HOW? IS it explainable?" He asked.

"Yes, I believe it is. I'll Try anyway," grandfather replied.

"First off, what IS 'Faith'? The Good Book tells this, '*It is the thing(s) HOPED for, but is as yet unseen.*' It also has an allegory that points to its Working. It tells of a Rich man…a 'master', who gives three servants some money to invest while he goes off on a trip.

Each is given SOME, One less, one a bit more, one even more. Nonetheless, each received. The one, who had the least, buried his 'for safe keeping.' The other two invested. The 'middle' one got a small return on his investment. The wisest who was given the most, got a far GREATER return.

Eventually their Master returned and called them to report.

He was very upset when the first gave back what he had hidden. He was quite pleased with the other two. More so, the wisest. The wisest was highly rewarded.

This tells of our Creator God as the 'Master.'
The Servants, WE…'His' Children, as the 'Servants.'

ALL RECEIVE four GIFTS upon being born. This Gifts being: LIFE, SELF WILL, ALL KNOWLEDGE and FAITH.

On FAITH, ALL RECEIVE, as I said, some more, some less. However, all HAVE faith upon coming into this world. The Vast Majority are as the First servant. THEY DO NOT USE THE GIFT. They HIDE it. Then there are those who DO use it. Occasionally. The WISEST sees this opportunity, and uses it to the most advantage. When each stands before 'Him' to give account, each will receive their 'reward'…According to how they used 'His' giving.

I have found that AS YOU USE it MULTIPLIES. I then 'Invest', then 'Invest' again.
Thus reaping even more. In time, one gets USE to RECEIVING MORE and MORE 'Interest.'
This in turn gives More and More FEARLESSNESS to 'Take a calculated risk' on the next 'Investment(s).' Aho?"

"Yes, thank you. That helps."

To Make It Grow!

Another question though, "ARE YOU AFRAID TO MAKE a BAD 'INVESTMENT'?"

This is the Common Problem with the majority of all. They HIDE because they're afraid! Thus, they end up in a bad position with The Master. The answer to your question is YES, at FIRST. I am not the Master. I am not as brilliant. 'HE' knows ALL. I, so little.
But I KNEW THE GIFT WAS THERE 'In my Hand'...And for a REASON. Therefore, FEARFULLY...I TRIED an 'Investment.' Just a Little one at first. It WORKED! So I tried ANOTHER...it too worked. This went on and off, for a while, with me ALWAYS GAINING CONFIDENCE. Then...'WHAM'! A BIG 'Investment' FELL THROUGH! I 'Crashed.' BIG TIME!

I was in a PANIC MODE!
"WHY did it GO WRONG?" I ask myself. "It was working PERFECTLY! WHY!" Well, what better place to go TO find out 'WHY?' I "picked up the phone" via PRAYER and CALLED THE MASTER! I very humbly explained what I had done. Asked for 'His' forgiveness and then asked "WHAT WENT WRONG?"

This is what I received:

First off, I FORGIVE YOU.
Second off, I'M PROUD OF YOU.

Now, As for the 'WHY.'

Yes, you were fearful when you started using my gift. All are. You had never had 'money' THAT YOU WERE AWARE OF, before. When you SAW it was there, you tried to WISELY 'spend' it.

It WORKED!

You tried AGAIN. It WORKED yet again.

The third time was the HABIT BREAKING/MAKING Time. Again, it worked. So now you had broken out of the 'NOT OF ME' (God) HABIT and were FREE to 'invest' WITHOUT FEAR. You had become CONFIDENT! Then, 'out of the blue' YOU FAILED!

"WHY?"

"The trouble was YOU had become CONFIDENT. YOU had acted as if this GIVING was of YOUR 'SELF.' That YOU were so 'Good' at 'investing' that Y O U '*COULDN'T GO WRONG!*' YOU had become SELF CONFIDENT!

SELF causes FAILURE! SELF is Man's WORST ENEMY! SELF over RULES…HIM! Your MAKER and MASTER and GIVER OF ALL!

SELF brings in PRIDE! NOT humbleness. NOT SERVITUDE. You failed to see yourself as what you ARE…MY SMALL CHILD! You had become COCKY! 'BIG HEADED', and SWOLLEN in SELF PRIDE!

YOU HAD THOUGHT YOURSELF…GOD! (at least in your 'investment' area!)

Son, you have fallen because of…You. Do you understand?"

Boy! DID I!

I then APOLOGIZED and asked forgiveness in "His" First Born Son's Name…and was cleansed. I then asked, "How do I avoid this from here on in, Father?"

Again "He" replied, "YOU ARE ALREADY DOING IT! YOU ARE CALLING (on) ME! Your 'Phone Line' is PRAYER. Asking, Seeking, PRAYER! My WORD tells of this! 'SEEK, KNOCK, FIND.' Be CONSISTENT! KEEP POUNDING AT MY DOOR UNTIL I COME AND ANSWER! My WORD tells of THAT, as well!
MY SON SHOWED HE DID SO. He NEVER 'DID' or 'SAID' unless I TOLD HIM WHAT to DO, or SAY! HE KNEW MY WILL Because HE ALWAYS ASKED IT and WAITED. THEN He would 'do'! AND HE THEN NEVER FAILED! HE FOLLOWED MY WRITTEN WORD! He FOUND ME, His 'FATHER'! And CONNECTED by 'Phone PRAYER' and ASKED MY WILL! Thus NEVER went WRONG. NEVER 'Falling on His Face'!

HE IS MY EXAMPLE TO YOU TO FOLLOW!

That TOO is in my Word! FOLLOW ME," he said.

This took me by surprise (the old one said)… "It made me understand I knew so LITTLE of what I read in The Good Book. IT OPENED MY EYES!

I then asked, "Father, HOW did He "DO," so FAST?"

"His" reply came … "HE DID AS YOU, ONE STEP AT A TIME. GROWING CONFIDENT IN ME. CONFIDENT I WAS REAL. CONFIDENT I CAN AND DO, TALK AND ANSWER. The MORE He would 'call', The EASIER IT WAS TO 'DIAL' and GET DIRECTLY TO ME! Finally, it was AUTOMATIC with Him. With US. BETWEEN US! Thus, I was able to give INSTANT RESPONSE to His '*What should I Do Papa?*' questions.

YOU and I can have that SAME INSTANT 'ONENESS' TOO! I HAVE MADE IT POSSIBLE! I HAVE GIVEN YOU AN EXAMPLE: My VERY OWN SON! I call Him my FIRST BORN…not my ONLY BORN…or LAST BORN. For He was THE FIRST TO TRULY FIND ME! FIND ME as a SON FINDS A LONG LOST FATHER!
He SEARCHED…He HUNGERED to Find ME. And HIS 'Knock, Seek, Find'…FOUND!

ALL of you I have made. I AM YOUR FATHER/MOTHER! You are ALL birthed IN and FROM my MIND WOMB. You are ALL M Y CHILDREN! I love you ALL!
It saddens me that many seek Divorce from Me. But I HAVE GIVEN ALL Choice. SELF WILL. Thus, it shall be, as they will. THEY, not ME. Do you understand?
I LOVE THEM ENOUGH TO LET THEM FOREVER GO AWAY FROM MY PRESENCE. I Will NOT THINK OF THEM ANY LONGER. For THUS SOME CHOOSE. I Gave SELF WILL and I will NOT Take it AWAY. Even THEN. Their CHOICE is NOW, as they LIVE IN THIS LIFE. It WILL NOT BE CHANGED '*In That Day*.' It saddens me, but '*Their* WILL' be done. They will be granted their divorce…

Now, as for HOW to have MORE FAITH…
Leave SELF Behind.

As for your Big Brother's SPEED and SUCCESS…
Leave SELF Behind.

ALWAYS SEEK MY WILL because you LOVE ME. SEEK, DUE TO YOUR LOVE!
The LESS you can take SELF-CREDIT...The MORE WE TWO CAN DO. Together.
LOVE ME enough to TRUST ME. TRUST that I want ONLY THE VERY BEST for ALL.

I AM LOVE!"

Grandfather then told his listener, "Thus I have found what STOPS Faith. What STOPS 'Miracles'…and HOW TO GET MORE. I have found the ANSWER to 'DOING'…it is THE CONNECTING 'PHONE LINE' of INSTANT PRAYER that gives INSTANT ANSWERS. And I OBEY.

I FOLLOW CHRIST!

'Dad' has TAUGHT ME."

HO.

Grandfather's Wrath

The Junior High schoolers were making "fun" of a retarded boy. THIS RAISED GRANDFATHER'S HACKLES! Hearing their Taunts and Laughs, he STORMED OVER!

"THAT is ENOUGH!" He almost shouted.

Pointing to the poor child, he smiled and said softly "Go home, son. These kids and I have a Talk to do," (starring angrily at the frozen group). He calmed himself somewhat as the boy Ran towards home.

"OK you BRATS…GET OVER THERE AND SIT!"

They did so!

Standing over them…face…red…he looked at all, and then said:

"I am TOTALLY ASHAMED OF ALL OF YOU! That boy had NO CHOICE of his Birth, just as YOU have NO CHOICE of YOURS! He was born Like That FOR A REASON! GOD'S REASON. YOU ARE MOCKING GOD! That boy CAN'T HELP BEING AS HE IS! YOU though, CAN!

HEAR ME! It is claimed YOU use some ten to fifteen percent of your BRAIN. Out of ALL its ten percent! THAT CHILD YOU MOCK USES ten percent JUST to GET BY!

THAT BOY IS a DAMN SIGHT SMARTER THAN…<u>YOU</u>!

Now get your UNGRATEFUL ASSES OUT OF MY SIGHT, or there will be HELL TO PAY!"

As they sped off he Shouted, "NEVER let me hear you TAUNT ANOTHER AGAIN!"

The Apology

It was the next day. One of the group of the previous day's little "charade" hesitantly approached the Old one.

"Sir?" She said respectfully…"I was one you got mad at yesterday…"

"I know," he said.

"I'm sorry. I really am. Can I talk to you a minute?"

They walked together as she continued.

"I got to thinking on what you said, about the one hundred percent?"

"Yes."

"Well, I think you're right. I had never thought of it like that. It sounds...well, TRUE.

I'm sorry I was a part of that...it wasn't right."

He looked down on her and smiled.

"Is it possible that you might know WHY people are born…you know…different?"

"Yes, I do. First, I owe YOU an apology. I owe this to all that I jumped on. It was not of an 'In Love' way. I AM SORRY! I APOLOGIZE to YOU!"

She looked surprised.

"I will do so to the others as well, as I find them. Ho.
Now, as for the REASON of 'differences.' It is all rather simple, really. You see, our Maker…"

"GOD?" the girl asked.

"Yes, God. Well, 'He' sees some on our planet need to learn a few things. Things like COMPASSION and PATIENCE. These and other things. Thus, 'He' sends down 'Special' Ones, 'Different' Ones. Some as that boy…some terribly disfigured…even SOME Meant to be ALCOHOLICS!"

"ALCOHOLICS?"

"Yes…as well as others 'looked down on.' It is 'His' GIFT to those NEEDING TO LEARN! People, such as yourself, who Just MIGHT go about their life in a rather 'Smug', 'Self' way…and BE LOST TO 'HIM', FOREVER! His Passion of FULL Agape LOVE extends far beyond what we, mere men, understand.

EVEN TO THE POINT OF SENDING DOWN SOME SOULS TO HELP OTHER SOULS...at the 'PRICE' of NOT BEING 'NORMAL.'

YOU have come. YOU have felt Contrite. YOU have left the world of *'I'm NORMAL...so I'M Special.'* THAT BOY HAS HELPED YOU 'SEE'! From now on, you will have HEART-INSIGHT...COMPASSION…for ALL others around you. FOR AS LONG AS YOU LIVE!

Yesterday's 'Incident' was for YOU and the others. Let us hope the others will learn as well. If not from me, then perhaps from you."

CARRY ON THE

KNOWING."

Ho.

Prisoners

Over the years, Grandfather has received many letters from those in prison. ALL telling how 'Spiritual' they feel/are. ALL wanting to '*do the things of Big Brother*.' ALL wanting to know how to do Teleportation/Invisibility/Levitation! Most wondering WHY they need to get a Bible and begin reading THAT!

Naturally, he will not teach them, for obvious reasons. However, he DOES tell them "If you want to learn these things…learn how from 'His' Word. The lessons are there. IF 'Dad' wants you to learn, then let 'HIM' teach you! I WILL NOT! You claim you feel 'Spiritual'...if that's true…'HE' will Show You."

Grandfather has had thousands of similar requests from Non-Prisoners.

When he says, "Get a Bible," they balk.

His Teacher is IN THERE!

Many 'want to learn,' then tells the teacher HOW to teach, WHAT to teach, WHAT Text Books to teach BY/etc...

(Try pulling THAT at a college)!

So, reader, GET A BIBLE and you'll soon find out if you ARE worthy of "doing the things of Christ" (Big Brother).

Aho?

HO!

Grandfather and the Medical Profession

When asked his opinion of today's Doctors, grandfather said,

"I have no fight with them. They have their place. Most needing physical or mental help rely on them. Most sick do not have the belief that The Creator is quite capable of doing healings in a far more natural way. So too the doctors. Most on both sides feel God has called them to this 'white' way. 'God is in all things,' thus this is true.

To me, all in this and all using this 'white way' are not true believers in God. Or, at best extremely weak in it. Frankly, they NEED each other!

I have seen cures deemed 'impossible.' No 'white way' help needed at all.

I have contact with many in professions. Including Holistic.

Even those in that seem to rely a lot on 'gizmos' things that cost. A lot of money is spent no matter if a Doctor or Holistic healer.

Why? Those in stone healing usually buy the stones. Those in 'white' buy an X-ray machine, etc.

To be a Medicine man (woman) requires very little outlay. It requires MUCH learning though! KNOWLEDGE of the NATURAL. In awe of the Inner Heyókȟa, years of learning to Connect to the Creator. 'HE' KNOWS EVERYTHING. We twelve just ask, wait, and receive. It takes A LOT of Time to learn this, but all have the same ability to do so.

Recently I was 'discharged' from a white doctor. This new health center is part of a fair 'turn-over.' No one notifies that 'your' Doctor is leaving. You just go in and 'BANG' another new one! This irritates me. We of Inner only allow three. I came home and told my wife I am looking for another doctor. I only go to them when absolutely necessary. When others of 'Medicine' are unable to help and for whatever reason, I get no answer from the Creator. The whites then become my last resort. There is a reason. I have learned this and accept it.

The Medical Profession has a tendency of getting 'heady.' In their eyes, they begin to think THEY are God. *You NEED me or you will DIE*." I told one, "Friend, I will die WITH or with OUT your help."

Shook him up.

In truth, they use FEAR to make YOU think THEY are "god." I do not fear death. THIS is what shook him up.

They also have had two who "dropped me." In a sense, "Fired" me. Both I told, "It is your right to not have me as your patient, but don't think you've fired me from it. YOU pay ME NOTHING. I PAY YOU! If you decide to quit, OK. You are MY Employee. You do not have to work for me if you choose not to. When you think you are FIRING me, that's a mistake."
One of these two I then FIRED, and told him so. Took away his "headiness" somewhat, I hope.

We of the Medicine Way are looked down on as "savages" or "witches" or "of the devil." They do not see we are every bit as trained as they. Just in a different "way." Their way holds up the economy. Whole COMPANIES are used to make their tools, etc. We, on the other hand, do not. So many are against us. We are no good for the ECONOMY and thus a danger to it. WE live by NATURE, and that is FREE. No big Company to make our healing needs. We do for PENNIES what THEY do for a new BMW and fancy house.

Their way is the way of Fear, Prestige, and "Respect"...EGO.
At least it most often ENDS UP that way. Some "do" in LOVE and finish in LOVE. THIS IS GOD! I may not agree with their HOW but I certainly agree with their REASON. It is those I have REAL RESPECT FOR. Ho!

I wish though, they'd spend a little Learning Time from us.

New Ager's Misconception

Grandfather meets others too. Many in "New Age," who claim as the prisoners – "Spiritual," "In Tune"/ Etc...From Wiccan, to Out-Of-Body devotees and of all types in New AND Old "age."

He does not mind. He loves all equally. We all "have our path" he tells. Several have told that he has "guides." This is not at all true and he lets them know it.

He reaches for The Good Book and says, "No, I have no guides. I have a guideline!"
He never presses his "way." He shows it. They are attracted to his "good vibes" and "soft spirit." Several have joined him in this, "The way of Purity." Most are satisfied with their "way" and continue in it. He wishes all well, Right or wrong:

IT'S YOUR PATH!

CHOOSE WISELY.

For it is YOU who will be held Accountable for it!

Ho.

The Question

One Searcher came to grandfather and asked the ULTIMATE Question!

"Grandfather, WHAT IS the *Right Path*?"

A loaded question, but with answer, "That's easy, my sister: LOVE."

"Love?"

"Yes. If you can find the ability to not condemn, not do for self, have compassion for all, on a daily basis....THAT is THE 'Path.' If you follow that 'way', you are following 'HIS' way. God Creator is LOVE. Total and complete. There is not an iota of hate in 'His' being. Not even, dislike. 'He' Loves ALL and 'He' loves EVERYTHING. 'He' MADE everything. Why NOT Love 'His' Perfection?"

"Well, Grandfather, why then are there killings, wars and hate, all about us all the time?"

"Will."

"Would you explain, please?"

"The Creator gave us soul bearers SELF WILL. It took A LOT of LOVE to allow this to be. Far more then you or I would be willing to do. Nor does 'He' take this gift away.
If man chooses to do Unloving, Ungodly ways that is a choice of Self Will.

It is not 'HIS' Will...but 'He' has given each of us this Great gift and will never take it from us. To 'Him' a gift given is GIVEN. It now belongs to the new recipient. 'He' will not take it back.

Ho.

In this gift of will, man can do all he pleases. If he chooses to be greedy, war-like, stingy, a rapist, murderer, or loving, and a helper...it is so. Man does all things through choice.
People can make a thousand excuses for their doings, all pointing AWAY from themselves.

'My Childhood caused me to do this.'
'Your oil prices are too high so we will take your land from you.'

All these things and more are of SELF-will. YOU CAN BLAME NO OTHERS! WILL is the most Misused Gift that our Creator has given. Yes, it took a lot of LOVE to give that and never take it back.

Does that answer your question?"

“Yes, Grandfather. It does. I have many things to consider. Things I have never thought about. One other question, please?”

“Yes?”

“How do you walk so ‘in Love’?”

“In my personal case, it is through help. It’s is impossible for me to Love in the manner needed, without it.”

“Who helped you Grandfather?”

“Helped? Don’t you mean, ‘Helps’? This is not a thing one can live in on a daily basis without a constant helper. I simply ask the First Born to help. He does so.

If you see ANY Good in me….it is HE that is doing.
If you see ANY Bad in me…it is ‘I’ who am doing.
I have my Ups and Downs. Aho?”

“Yes. Thank you, Grandfather.”

Science

Grandfather was at a school Science Convention. The children from several counties had built projects, and news reporters from the papers and TV were present. Speakers were giving lectures. Really, quite the thing. For reasons unknown to him, he had been approached to be a speaker. Always accepting that "there's a reason for all," he had agreed.

The gym was packed with students and adults alike. He had listened to many "Great Wonders of Science" talks from speaker after speaker. Then he was introduced.
Not suited as the others, he was casually attired in jeans and went to the stage.

"Good Afternoon," he started. "I have been asked here to speak. But for the life of me I don't know why!" Laughter came from the crowd. "What's just as bad is that I don't know on WHAT!" More laughter! "Who am I to speak on the things I've heard and seen here? Amazing things. Your children have done some Fascinating projects." At these hoots of "YEAH!" rang though the auditorium. "I like especially the thoughts and doings on Solar Electricity, Cooking and Wind Powered energy. I have even seen Water Powered things. WONDERFUL! To me, the use of nature is good. To use it wisely, without destroying, is the way it should be. This is good indeed! I have also seen and heard on Space exploration, the telling of Creation's beginning by 'the Big Bang'…many things.
Yes, science is interesting. HO, I'm proud of you!

I have a few things I wonder about though. It seems many of the things told of clash with what I and others of our way have found to be. I would like to speak on some of these things. It is permissible?" he asked, looking at the officials there.
They nodded, "Yes, of course."

"Thank you. Ho. Well, you speak of 'The Big Bang' as the maker of the planets and stars. This is not how we have found it to be. We have found all is created by energy and sound. The Energy of THOUGHT, and the Sound of AUDIBLE Command. We have found The Creator first THOUGHT what was wanted made, then COMMANDED it so, AUDIBLY 'And it was so.'

Ho.

We heard no noise.
You sit there thinking.
Do you hear a 'Bang' in your head?
These great things you make….do you not first think on them, then say, 'Let's make it'…and it is so?

We have found The Great Maker has told of this in a Book many here know of, and many own.
We call this the 'Good Book.'

'He' has told us that we can be as 'HE.' AS 'He' NOT 'HE,' but '***AS*** HE.'

You make and call it Invention and Science.
We find it as Creating and 'His' Gift.
You see only your great thinking as the Great Maker. Science, as 'He.'
We see only mans given gift of brain and materials, is what allows.
You seem to think of Man as God Creator. This perplexes us.
You speak of someday going to Mars, Living on the Moon, and Finding Life on planets.
We go there, as we will. Found life, 'Others.' Not just 'signs', but fellow Soul Bearers. People.
You seek rocketry to do these things. Why?

We find with MIND any can go. It takes no resources. No Science. Physically…or in Spirit, one can go. All these things are not a 'Possibility' or a 'Theory.'

We do in FACT. AS fact.

You see Science as PROGRESSION. We see Science as REGRESSION.

Perhaps I was sent here to learn from you. Perhaps THAT is 'His' reason."
As he spoke these words, he came in front of the podium.
"I do not know." He shut his eyes, and slowly he began to FADE!
The Podium could be seen THROUGH HIM!
As he got "less and Less"…He spoke these words:

"Perhaps someone here can teach me I am mistaken?"

Then DISAPPEARED!

Old Way's Reason

"Grandfather," he asked, "is it true some of our people ate dog?"

Grandfather likes to be honest and is known for it.

"Son, some still do…some Sacred 'Societies' still do. As a ceremony to these Great Ones. They don't just go out and say, *'Let us eat Rover tonight,'* this is only done to honor…and it's not done often."

The young boy looked puzzled.

"Little Brother, there was a time when people had no horses, let alone today's cars. We used dogs as our pack animals. They were also used to warn and to hunt. Just as today. In those days, we would put our belongings on a travois. Our small Tipi's and things were loaded on those and the four-legged would pull these during our moves, taking the heavier loads. We had great respect for them. Big or small, they helped us survive. To honor them for this…their helping keep our people going to today, we honor them. With proper prayer and ceremony the chosen one would be put to death, boiled, and eaten. All in a solemn way. Yes, our people ate dog. They still do, but during a certain time and strictly out of honor. Again this is not a common thing.

Know this too: WHEN YOU EAT OF A THING, YOU PARTAKE of the 'Power' OF THAT THING! This may sound 'farfetched', yet is a Fact.

Do you understand?"

"Yes, I think so, grandfather."

"Know also that there were times when our people had to eat their animals, if they didn't want to starve. You must do what is needed to go on. Today this is frowned on by the white culture. Dogs are pets. You don't eat your pet! I tell you true, there will come a hard time on our mother Earth. One you should see in YOUR life time…that will make that pet start to look pretty good. It will be you or them. Know also that they will be looking at YOU in the same way. Packs of 'pets' will be ganging up on man! It is going to be a very hard time.
As I said: You must do what you must to survive."

Ho.

"Doing"

He had a visitor. A woman, who had asked to stop by, as they set at the kitchen table chatting, she asked "Grandfather, have you ever had a healing work that doesn't work?"

He thought, and then said, "At my start this happened. In time I learned though."

"So all are healed?"

"No."

"Then you still have some unsuccessful ones?"

"No. All are a success. It is just not all are meant to be. I will explain. When I ask The Creator what to do, I get my orders. More often than not 'He' tells me what is needed for a healing. However, there ARE times 'He' says, *'NO! This one needs to learn from this sickness.'* Therefore, I then just give a prayer for the sick one to learn quickly. At other times, 'He' says *'NO! I have another that will do the work. Send to this one. You stay here and Back him. That one needs to know I hear his prayers. This will give him more Faith growth.'*

So, though I may not see the results, THERE IS A REASON FOR ALL. You see, I ASK. Then, LISTEN. I also check what I hear or am shown. Then I do EXACTLY as told. So, all are a success…though not all are healed through my direct or immediate use. Aho?"

The Ear Ache

Grandfather had many healing "ways." As an Inner Heyókȟa his training was years longer than all others. The "Top," commonly training for seventeen years, the "common," seven to twelve years. Not so the Inners: their training runs into the forty year period before they are considered "ready." Grandfather had started his training at age ten, and it took him forty-two years before completion. As he told though, "It is never fully done. You learn to your death." In his years of learning, he was taught "Medicine" from all around the Earth mother. Some, extensively. Some, just a small amount. This gave him knowledge over all.

It was morning. His wife had been ill, with her allergies slowing the time her sinus healing would generally take. She walked into the room, holding her hand to her left ear and looking in deep pain."Are you alright?" He asked."

No. I've a bad ear ache."

"Want some help?" Under most conditions, she would rather 'tough it out.' Not so this time. He had her stand beside him, lit an unfiltered Pall Mall cigarette, drew the smoke into his mouth, and exhaled into her ear. His lips were almost touching, causing it to be a slow, soft exhale. He did this five times, stopped, and then one more time. "Five for Power, Six for healing," he said, and was done. "Should I take my (white man's) medicine?" She asked.

"Sure. This smoke will only relieve. To stop, it will need to be done off and on all day. This and your medicine will combine and work faster. I doubt if you will need any more smoke at all. With the smoke, you should be feeling fine in a few minutes. The medicine will not take effect for close to an hour, though. One will run into the other and continue as one. That's 'it' unless the infection returns later today. Then we'll just do it again."

About ten minutes later, she sat down beside him.

"I've got to admit, I have had no pain since two or three minutes after your smoking. I feel much better! Thank you, honey." She then asked why the smoke helped.

"It's the nicotine in it. The warmth of the hotter air from my breath to your inner ear seems to stir up something...bacteria...the nicotine then is able to settle along your inner ear track, lightly coating it. It makes it difficult for the bacteria to cling then. Anyway, sort of along that line. It is basically insulation, is all. I have found one won't do as well with a filtered cigarette. The filter absorbs most of the nicotine. You need that nicotine to be as thick as possible. If this alone had not helped, I would have cut a large onion in two and heat one half well. Then have you put that in a thin cloth and have you hold or wrap it to your ear opening. As the onion cools, it draws out the infection into it.

"Happy the first did the job, honey."

The Chase

Grandfather was a night guard for a cable company going through his area. The pay was good and he could spend the night in Prayer and "Chatting with the Creator." This incident happened way out in the woods.

It was a warm summer night…but heavy fog covered all. His favorite "sit or walk time" WAS fog, so he was enjoying this. It was around 11:30 at night. He sat listening to the radio while writing a letter to his brother. Suddenly the fog started to Swirl, to the forward right side of his truck. There was no breeze, so it immediately caught his attention!

Then out of the fog, a scant seven feet from his front right headlight, a small Gray appeared. It was moving so quickly, it ALMOST HIT THE TRUCK'S BUMPER!
BOTH he and it where totally surprised! Grandfather had had many alien encounters…but none THIS close! Evidently, the same held true for the Gray, as well!
Startled, it hesitated for a millisecond, and then TORE OFF at a HIGH RUN to Grandfather's left. Grandfather was whipping out his Case Belt knife, flipping it open and opening his door, all at the same time. He was not as swift…but he came out running!

The chase was ON!

Ever try chasing a Gray in GRAY FOG? Especially a VERY FAST, SCARED, Gray? Grandfather never stood a chance. Try as he may, the Gray was too fast for him. He ran maybe three minutes, and "Nature Stepped" (quite stalked) for perhaps another ten minutes before giving up. His troubles were not over yet, though.

As said, it was a heavy fog. Grandfather had been madly dashing after this small, cloned Plant being, with no "sight" references. He was, well…"misplaced." It took awhile, but his circle walk eventually cut across the trail "road" he had parked on.

The whole thing lasted for just less than an hour.

Ho.

Scripture Code of "Two" Raptures

Grandfather's extensive Bible Knowledge often got him "at odds" with the teachings of various Religious leaders. He was not one to recall verses and to recite text by rote, but knew what he read. A Concordance was his second most used Book. The "Good Book," being the first. "I know it's there and if in New or Old Testament. That's all I need to locate the exact spot, with The Concordance," he'd say.

A Bible College graduate himself, he knew the religious thoughts and teachings of many religions and their offshoots. "Tithing" teaching was an irritant to him. "They sure twist THAT one," he'd say…but there were others as well. One of THOSE being, The Rapture! "I wish they'd say Ascension instead, but it means the same. Guess I can't win them all," he'd say.

Once again, he was teaching, this time, to a number of Bible "Believers." He called these "misbelievers." Most here held the belief that Ascension (the Rapture) would get them safely out of the world's woes BEFORE things got bad. Some, DURING those EARLY woes. Perhaps two held "towards the very end."

Grandfather held towards the last way.

HOWEVER, there was More!

"Folks, Scriptures hold Seven Codes. The Seventh, being the most important, using ALL the written Word to make it. In that, I mean it 'Skips and Misses.' To you, that would mean 'taking out of context.' That can happen…but not in this case.

There are to be TWO Ascensions. Not One, as you have been taught. Most of you understand and know of the one being spoken of, so I will not go into that.

The description of the Second Ascension is 'of code': HIDDEN, IN PLAIN VIEW! ALL of the Seventh Code is done in this manner, and easily missed due to your training, to NOT 'read', or 'get out of context' THAT training DELIBERATELY taught, so that this Seventh Code will go 'UNSEEN' till 'the Last Days', We are now IN those 'Last Days', so now it can be revealed.

Now, to the unveiling of the Second Rapture:

First off, its center is based on the Word 'I AM THE SAME TODAY, YESTERDAY, AND TOMORROW.'

Add to that, that GOD DOES NOT LIE. To HIM, that is a SIN.

He won't put up with it from YOU, so why do it Himself! It goes against His WORD and His 'grain.' Now, IF He IS 'the same Today, Yesterday, and Tomorrow'…and WILL NOT

LIE...with this in mind, Now SKIP BACK to...and SEE, what Scripture EVENTS are about. Even what Jesus was about!

EXAMPLES!

Jesus is the EXAMPLE of what ANY ONE PERSON CAN DO, IF CONNECTED TO THE FATHER GOD. The HEBREW RACE as the EXAMPLE of WHAT the World's NATIONS CAN DO if CONNECTED TO THE FATHER GOD. ALL events are EVENTS TO TEACH US, OF this 'Up-Coming Time.' Examples of WHAT TO LOOK AT! If you see the Old and New Testaments as teaching events...examples, you can now OPEN the Seventh Code!

For instance, The Story of JONAH. An EVENT that FORETELLS US of THIS TIME, to GET RIGHT WITH GOD, for He is about to DESTROY. You also see by the event that the Invitees' REPENTED, turned AWAY from DISOBEYING GOD, and where NOT destroyed. That event tells US that, IF we repent, the destroying time WILL CEASE, for that 'Immediate' time.

In short...the whole Jonah event telling equates to US as the NINIVITES...and our Earth the City of NINIVAH...and UNLESS THE WORLD'S MASSES REPENT, OUR 'CITY EARTH' WILL BE DESTROYED!

It tells also that WE CAN PUT THIS OFF!

'I AM THE SAME TODAY, YESTERDAY, AND TOMORROW.'

I DO NOT LIE!

MANY times, we read EXAMPLES of The HEBREW NATION WHEN THEY WERE IN TUNE WITH GOD...being The LEADERS of ALL Nations. The RICHEST of ALL Nations. The most ENVIED of ALL Nations. The MOST FEARED of ALL Nations.

All this, when IN TUNE with HIM. Then, time after time, we read of what happened when they got OUT of TUNE with HIM. THIS TOO is an EXAMPLE.

Now read WHAT TOOK PLACE when an enemy 'took over.'
THEY WERE TAKEN INTO CAPTIVITY! Read too, SOME WERE ALWAYS KEPT IN THEIR AREA. Not ALL were 'hauled off.' A REMNANT was ALWAYS LEFT!
ALL of this PERTAINS TO the TWO 'RAPTURES' AND US.

We of Earth...the 'Invitees'...and the WHOLE 'City' (that is NOW the 'Land of the Invitees' EARTH, WILL BE INVADED AND HAULED OFF by ENEMY FORCES!
JUST as our EXAMPLES WERE!

Too, just as in the past: A REMNANT WILL BE LEFT! UNLESS we repent.

'I AM THE SAME TODAY, YESTERDAY, AND TOMORROW'

I NEVER LIE!
I never CHANGE!

Aho?

There's More:

WHO is ALWAYS the 'ENEMY' in those many Hebrew captures? ALWAYS there is a CONSISTENT telling, THE MOST FEARED PEOPLE in the KNOWN LAND!
In our case, Today, NO nations Government is WORSE than ANY OTHER!
And ALWAYS 'Raised up BY GOD', to do this.
ALWAYS.

'I AM THE SAME TODAY, YESTERDAY, AND TOMORROW.'
I DO NOT LIE. I DO NOT CHANGE!

Now comes ANOTHER 'Skipping':

The verse that tells of Him TAKING the souls from 'ON the EARTH, IN the EARTH, and ABOVE (Heavens) the Earth.' (Look it up, it's in there). This, on the DAY OF JUDGMENT. Note the 'ON' and 'IN.' It is we of THIS planet who are the ones, 'ON.'

'OTHERS' that are from 'IN' and 'ABOVE (Heavens).' Scriptures, in the Old and New Testament tell of THESE BEINGS: 'Gods'…Angels …Giants, etc.

'OTHERS', Not of US…ARE…THERE! They EXIST! We are NOT 'ALONE'!

Now, being TODAY that there ARE none 'WORSE' (on Earth)…ANOTHER ENEMY, that is FAR WORSE THEN ANY OF US is being RAISED UP, In the HEAVENS and IN our Earth, to come and HAUL US AWAY, INTO Captivity! It is THIS that is THE First 'Rapture.'

The <u>FALSE</u> RAPTURE!

THIS IS BEING ARRANGED AS I TELL!

WHO is setting this all up? IT GOES all the way DOWN and from the Highest Authority of EVERYTHING. From Lucifer to GOD Himself…and 'Others' in between!
'GOD IS IN <u>ALL</u>THINGS!'

'All' means just That, EVERYTHING! Even THIS. It is a PLANNED THING By HIM!

WHO will be taken? THOSE WHO BELIEVE IN THE RAPTURE; The CHRISTIANS, mainly. People that DO NOT STUDY HIS WORD without INTERFERENCE by their RELIGIONS' TEACHINGS. People STUCK in their DENOMINATION'S 'WAY.' People whom are unwilling to think 'outside THEIR Box.' Those who take their MANS' TEACHING over H I S TEACHING.

In short, I am sorry to say, in most cases: YOU!

The people will SEE 'the Christ returning.' This will be as a HOLOGRAM, sent AT THE SAME TIME, WORLD WIDE! They TOO will all be BOMBARDED with MENTALLY GIVEN THOUGHTS: Get to the Rooftops…get Outside…'HE' IS COMING. 'ECSTASY.' People will be bombarded with CONTROLLED thoughts, EMANATED WORLD WIDE BY CELLULAR TOWERS!

And then 'The OTHERS' will 'ascend' you…

AND BEAM YOU UP, Into CAPTIVITY! There you will be used, AS THEY WILL!
GOD HELP YOU WHO GO! You, Who WILL NOT PAY ATTENTION to the Code, GOD'S WRITTEN WORD.

However, there is More…THE REMNANT:

Who are they? Prisoners, people in Hospitals, Working in mines, those who listened. Some FIGHTING (WITHIN) to STAY IN THEIR HOUSE, or simply CANNOT get OUT into the OPEN. CHRIST and BIBLE Believers, who CANNOT 'Get Out'…or, as said, FIGHT with ALL IT TAKES (within themselves) to KEEP FROM GOING OUTSIDE!

The Mind Controlled THOUGHT is SO STRONG, you FULLY BELIEVE 'This Is IT'…THE ASCENSION!

You MUST BE IN THE OPEN to be 'ASCENDED.' HAL LINNSAY has it WRONG! There will be NO 'Empty crashing cars.' You will be seeing THOUSANDS of PARKED EMPTY CARS though!

ACCORDING TO GOD, who DOES NOT LIE, You MUST 'GO TO THE ROOFTOPS and NOT GO BACK INTO THE HOUSE to Get a COAT'; You MUST BE IN THE OPEN to be taken!

Lucifer knows Gods Word too…AND WILL USE IT to GET RID of YOU…the 'SALT OF THE EARTH.' THIS IS WHAT (as I speak) is BEING PREPARED R I G H T NOW! Lucifer is ONLY CONCERNED with those who have SOME Kind of God Connection. He KNOWS the REST are ALREADY HIS!

Those 'left behind' WILL TURN INTO 'RUNNERS' hiding and running from HUNTERS! BOUNTY HUNTERS, who will receive a handsome price for each runner caught. Each runner, DEAD OR ALIVE, which is brought in. At first, this will be in money or trade payment. In time, the 'pay' will be FRESH WATER! THE 'RUNNERS' WILL HAVE IT NO BETTER THEN THOSE IN CAPTIVITY!

The only difference being, those in captivity will be UNABLE to RUN! At least those of the Remnant still will be able to do so. It is THESE who will learn to CLOSELY RELY ON GOD!

BIRDS will bring them morsels to eat. Mice and those of the fields will lead them to water. JUST AS THE EVENT TEACHING of that Prophet in the Old Testament!
Then…THEN! THE TRUE 'RAPTURE' (ASCENSION) WILL TAKE PLACE!
Leaving not TWO God Prophets…(GODMEN)…as the ONLY 'OF HIM' left ON EARTH…but THREE! TWO from the SOUTHERN HEMISPHERE…AND ONE, FROM THE NORTHERN HEMISPHERE!

(I know this is unwritten of in Scriptures: IT IS IN OUR NATIVE INDIANS' PROPHESY, though!)

So, now you have been made aware of the Seventh Code and how to comprehend it's doing and understanding. Whether or not you accept it, is not of my concern. That is strictly up to you! 'Your Path.' I, as an INNER HEYÓKȞA, have held this knowledge nearly my whole life. Given, but told NOT TO SHARE, UNTIL ORDERED.

I HAVE NOW BEEN ORDERED!

WITH THE SEVENTH CODE,
THE WHOLE BIBLE IS CODE!"

HO.

Crazy?

"I'll be PERFECTLY FRANK WITH YOU! I think you are TOTALLY CRAZY! INSANE! That you aren't taken off the streets surprises ME!"

(She wasn't kidding, either!)

Grandfather has heard THIS before. MANY times. After all, he wasn't 'normal.'

"Lady," (He knew she HATED to be called sister) "at least you're honest!

Am I crazy? I might be.

Am I Insane? YES! ABSOLUTELY! But then I see insanity different then you. It means SANE, WITHIN, to me…and I certainly feel Sane, WITHIN!

Tell me when The Christ returns and I'll hand you a nail so you can help get another 'nut' off the Earth!"

Self-Healing of Medicine People

Several have asked, "Why don't you heal yourself, Grandfather?"
His reply, "You don't understand the rules we of good Medicine People are under.

ALWAYS OTHERS FIRST!

This is hard fast to us. We obey it. We live it. Only in an extreme emergency are we allowed to 'do' for Self. Under this rule, we need to seek others in Medicine. This is often quite difficult. We do not live next door to each other. Much traveling is involved. Much expense. That leaves us needing to see a 'white Doctor' usually, or we just 'tough it out.' We live by our rules. Aho?

This too involves those within our close family as well. Still, as said, at times, we can 'do'...but rarely do we do so.

You are not of 'Medicine.' Therefore are not obligated to go by our rules.
If you are able to do a self-curing, do so. There are many good ways and many good Books that can help you. Many alternative medicine ways help.
However, don't just think ONE is the cure for every disease...or that what cured you will cure all. This is not always true. What brings on a problem to one does NOT means it is the same for another. Aho?"

Smoke Smudging

Another often asked question is the use of certain plants that make our sacred Smudge Smoke. To us it IS Sacred! To others, as well. Yet, there is a DOUBLE REASON on ours. Its ORIGIN!

Grandfather has explained this to MANY native Indians. Much to their total astonishment!

"Smudging, as you know, is our way to help us center our thoughts…PURIFY ourselves, before the Great Creator. It is 'Tradition.' Done this way for many centuries.

IT IS GOOD! HO!

A few Christian Churches do likewise; Catholic and Lutheran are known users of smudge... Perhaps, others as well. Theirs though, in abeyance of Scriptures, *'Give a Sweet Fragrance onto God.'* There is certainly no wrong in that. Obeying 'Him' is always GOOD. Ho

Theirs given by written command. Ours by REMEMBRANCE command. It does not matter the HOW of command, just that it is obeyed. This should show you our Oneness TO the ONE. Same OBEYING Base. Just in different, Cultural, WAYS. Aho?

As for what Sacred Plants WE use, this differs to the Climate REGION of the user. Not ALL the same plants are in all regions. So they differ. Aho? Now, an interesting thing. Something only the twelve Inner Heyókȟa seems to know. Kept within our knowledge.

ALL regions have insects. Even the Inuit (Eskimo). These are a constant irritant in their season. Insects are partial to certain plants. So too do each AVOID certain plants.
THE SMUDGE Plant COMBINATION "Invites" and Repels" these insects. JUST as they do, as well, to all the GOOD and EVIL Spirits about.

BUT:

SMUDGING STARTED OFF, ORIGINALLY, as

INDIAN BUG OFF!

“Grandfather, Why Didn’t The Natives Chase Off The Whites When They First Came?”

“Son, that’s a question we’ve asked ourselves constantly. We did so with others who came long before the Spaniards. They were not the first to come, according to our stories. What all now call Vikings came. So too an occasional Asian. Each on different coasts. Eventually they were driven away.

Even people from the East…Phoenicians and Hebrews are told of. These were traders and treated us as equals. Big Brother arrived here by one of their ships, it’s told. Why these quit coming we knew not. It wasn’t due to us.
It is possible warfare in their lands stopped their sea journeys to us. Yet that’s only speculation.

Many stories. Many stories…

But that was a long time before the Spaniards and those of the Mayflower. So far, in the past, the tellings were mere tellings. Then came the ‘New Ones’ GIANT CANOES! SAILS like WINGS! AWESOME!

Fear was one reason. Another was our knowledge that Big Brother said He would return.

Anyway, we screwed up. Should have. In some cases, tried to.

Too late.

We were never out fought…but, due to allowing them to stay, we were eventually OUT BRED!

HO.”

The Eggs

Grandfather and Grandmother were grocery shopping together. As she was looking at cheese, Grandfather went further down the cooler to the egg area.
Knowing they were on the list but not knowing how many she wanted, he looked towards her. Just then, a man and wife walked up, looking for eggs as well. Grandmother was quite a ways off, so loudly he said:

"HONEY, HOW MANY CHICKEN EMBRYOS DO WE NEED?"

The man and wife Froze, turned a ghastly white, gulped, and left at high speed! Grandmother slumped her head downward, and then looked STERNLY at him.

"What?"

He was in trouble, AGAIN!

"Con"

Grandfather had been called to help, for the fifth time, a man who had been injured. He KNEW the "work" was done. It had been completed the last time. Still, something new?
Off he went.

The man stood waiting. He looked as pained as the first time. His distraught wife nearby. Grandfather placed his hands on the area and began to ask "Papa."

"DON'T DO A THING! HE IS TO SUFFER, FOR HE IS HEALED."

Aho! So THAT was what was up! THE MAN WANTED ATTENTION! Wanted SYMPATHY, wanted his WIFE to do HIS things that needed done, as WELL as HERS! The old: "Honey, I'm SICK…BABY ME" routine.

Grandfather said a short prayer, hands on the spot, and then told him: "That's it. NOW YOU MUST HEAL ON YOUR OWN. It is up to YOU on how fast this will take. You ARE HEALED!"

He will be too. When he realizes "cons" don't ALWAYS work!

It seems the MALES are the most "into" this. From little kids, "*I don't want to go to school. I'm Sick*," on up. Alzheimer disease is often the same "way": though that often more female orientated.

The Totem Pole

Grandfather was wandering the Sitka, Alaska 'Garden of Totem Poles.' Other visitors doing the same. One small group had a man who "spoke of authority." Telling his charges of what these poles represented. One pole had a 'white man' in stove pipe hat as the top figure.

"This shows the natives held the Leaders of the Whites in the HIGHEST regard. That's why he was carved on top."

Grandfather sidled up to this leader.

"Pardon Me," he said, "could you tell me where you came upon your totem knowledge? I find it fascinating!"

The man was happy to comply.
"I read a lot. I love American Indian history. Several Books tell of these."

"I see," grandfather said, "They must be written by white scholars?"

"Yes, as a matter of fact, they are." The man replied.

"Well my friend, I hate to tell you this. They were tricked. The natives told to please their ears. The fact is, it is the BOTTOM carving that is the most important of all. The STRONGEST. Able to hold ALL OTHERS ON ITS SHOULDERS. That man on top, brother, is THE LEAST!" That said, he ambled off…not revealing THE REST. That the TOP FIGURES were the ones who thought the most "HIGHLY" of themselves "Haughty." Therefore the lesser of all. Yet, they too were of the same maker. One of ALL people, so had their right to be on the "Pole of Life."

Ho.

Grandfather Tells of the far, FAR Past/far, FAR Future

Several were together. All were in Medicine. This occurred when they were in the same area, at the same time. It didn't happen often and was a good visiting time for all. There was always a lot of catching up to do. A good time. Ho.

"Brother," one asked, "Did you ever get to The Bird Cave?"

This in reference to him going high into Canada; to call back the Thunderbirds to their original breeding grounds.

"No. Not yet. I had the money donated to do so, but the truck broke down. They gave me permission to use the donation to fix that instead. No other money has come in since. All, in 'His' time. So it will be, eventually," he said.

Another asked, "Find any more Time Caves?"

"Just that one so far. Must get back there and see if it shows any changes. Might, whenever I go to the three Mountains, as it is on the way. There is a set of three caves in Canada I would like to look into. One stands a chance of being another time cave. I will not know until I get to it and check it out. That too, is a possibility on the Bird Cave trip. All I can do is sit and see what 'Papa' comes up with. Much to do up there."

"What's that one about?"

"From what I'm told, this one has ancient writing at its entrance, as well as inside. The Crees' say white vandals have destroyed much. They mourn over the writings lost, and asked if it somehow they could be retrieved. I told them I would go there, do a Time Travel Trip, and re-draw. Nothing is ever really 'lost'…just a matter of doing what is needed. Aho?"

"Why not go to those who drew in the first place?"

"Thinking on that vein. Phoenicians, I think, or Hebrew/ Phoenicians' combo."
Could even be the Crees' 'writers.' Reason they put it there though! Should be interesting."

"What about The Woman's Staff? Any more on that?"

"Yes. All bad. Its caretaker has gotten heady and is Misusing it. Now it has started to die. Lost one of its carvings; the ear. I don't think the required ceremony will be taking place. Not unless that guy gives it to someone that will handle it right. ALL THAT WONDERFUL KNOWLEDGE GONE, due to this Dup-I-Ash.

So sad. I was sure looking forward to doing THAT ceremony. It will not be long before it dies and its reason lost to all. Might be dead already!"

"How old is that, anyway?" One of the ladies asked.

"Hmmm…I'm not sure how much any here know of our Mothers' past BEYOND THIS past…or how much you know of the far FAR ahead. How far 'back' does your knowledge contain?" Each looked at the other. One said, "I've heard rumors she wasn't here 'before' but that's about it."

None others had even heard THAT.

"Well," grandfather said, "That 'rumor' is correct. In THIS Dimensional Time, she is a fairly new arrival. Actually, the NEWEST.

What I am about to share is so STRANGE, I think it will be difficult for any here to believe. Non-The-Less, all 12 of us have gone back in time, each at LEAST three times…to SEE, and then to confirm. ALL WE 12 HAVE SEEN THE SAME:

THIS EARTH WAS FROM ANOTHER DIMENSION!

Beamed into THIS one from there!" This he told to his several listeners.

"In this transfer, it reformed first as gasses…then to a watery state…then it rolled (the first 'roll') and the waters and the land below these waters separated and we then became 'as is.' Land AND Water. Before this transference, the 'old Earth' was MUCH Smaller. In the transference, it grew as the gasses attached, it appears. Anyway, became larger somehow.

The 'old Earth' was ABSOLUTELY BEAUTIFUL! The two poles were not as ours, today. Chilly in summer...SNOW only in winter. As if its Axis were different. I can't explain it. Just can tell what was seen.

The people we saw (each of us seeing individually and at different times) were small in stature. Much like the people of Laos. Those of that area, today: same beautiful, delicate, tanned skin, long black hair. Very attractive! They too seemed to be peaceful loving people. At least those WE saw!

Still, THESE WE ALL SAW WERE ALL in a VERY FEARFUL 'Way.' As if what they were doing WAS WATCHED…by SOMETHING or? That MADE THEM HIDE THEIR 'WAYS'…their DOINGS.

I personally witnessed a 'doing' done in their night. There were several Holy Ones…mostly females, placing KNOWLEDGE INTO A LARGE TALL STONE. Each putting their thoughts into this, transferring from mind to stone. JUST as WE do. At least those who still do. You know what I mean.

As if they were SECRETLY doing so, ALL were CONSTANTLY ON THE ALERT! In the Palm Forest and bushes around them, others of theirs were watching as well, ready to give an alarm. NONE SAW what it was they FEARED So STRONGLY! We DID sense it was another 'LEADER Race' though. Evidently a FEROCIOUS and DANGEROUS one!

Anyway, to shorten this for you, The Giant Stone was eventually made into Pieces. Each piece holding an imprinted knowledge.

These then were packed into five separate containers. Each container HOLDING five IDENTICAL 'makings.' Each large container, holding five within, single 'five times fives.' They were then placed into HIDDEN 'Rockets' of some sort…and SHOT INTO THE ATMOSPHERE and beyond, leaving their Earth's gravity field. Much prayer was said over all this. PRAYERS OF HOPE! We all sensed these were 'random' shots. HOPING that SOMETIME AHEAD, at least ONE of these five times, fives would PASS INTO THE SAME 'FIELD' that THEY KNEW their Earth was about to disappear from!

To my knowledge, none of us saw this Earth 'go', but we ALL saw it COME HERE!
As told, 'BEAMED' HERE and reformed. Also all 12 of us sensed these 'rockets' were sent out mere HOURS or short DAYS before that Earth, and all (?) upon it, were to be 'destroyed.' This to keep them from their 'Over Lords' retrieving them in time.

IT WORKED!

At least ONE Rocket CAME THROUGH THE SAME 'ENERGY Field' their/ our Earth did! At least THREE of those five time five's have been found. One in Tibet (now deeply hidden), another two here in the United States. I don't know about the other two. I haven't heard if they have 'emerged.' Therefore, I have come to think that perhaps they 'landed' in the oceans or somewhere.

Perhaps I should explain, this single 'box' was designed to explode open…spewing each single 'set' over a VERY WIDE Area of our atmosphere. Much as an aerial Fireworks display is done. Add to that the sweep of the rocket as it entered our atmosphere and you have a general idea why no one knows where each 'single' came down. As told, three 'sets' have been found. One by a woman who hid it and then went insane. That 'set' still not located. She is still in an asylum, unable to be coherent. That set is now lost to all.

I HAVE SEEN THESE STONES!

Of that, I will say no more but this: EACH SET is A COMPUTER of KNOWLEDGE! Each must be put together to work and tell. ONLY a TRUE 'RIGHT HEART' CAN DO THIS PROPERLY! IF ONE STONE is placed in THE WRONG POSITION…The 'COMPUTER' CAN KILL…MILLIONS! It is DESIGNED TO DESTROY or CAUSE GRAVE HARM OR to be used AS MEANT…to help US, here on THIS Earth, and at THIS TIME!

The INTENT of these, done PROPERLY, is to CLOSE WORM HOLES, BAD VORTEXES and Other 'ENTRIES' of those THEY FEARED…the OVERLORDS!

Sent from THEN to PROTECT THEM/US of NOW!

As I think on this, I BELIEVE (don't KNOW, mind you). The People of them were fearful, BECAUSE their plans TO SAVE FUTURE MANKIND was found out...AND THEY WERE HUNTED, TO STOP THIS!

What we saw was being done HASTEFULLY and in TOTAL SECRECY…and IN a WILD PLACE that was in a Hiding area. NOT done in buildings, etc.

So there you have it…'OUR' beginning.

STILL well fitting into SCRIPTURES.

Aho?

This, the past PAST. Before our time as we know it.
Now to the far FAR FUTURE:

THIS EARTH WILL AGAIN BE BEAMED!

That beaming will be the Sixth and FINAL 'Cleansing.'

Only on THAT, Sixth cleansing, ALL will be "FOREVER" THERE! Earth's many changes, Beams, Rolls, etc., WILL BE NO MORE…EVER! When THAT ONE is completed…ALL EVIL WILL BE NO MORE. ALL will FOREVER be ABSOLUTELY PERFECT! Not an IOTA of Pollution or Wrong doing will EVER BE AGAIN!

The FACT OF THIS is WE OF THIS CREATION…Earth/Man…WILL BE AT the EXACT STARTING POINT from whence it came in the first place. That being THE EXACT 'THOUGHT SPOT'…'He' daydreamed us out of in the first place. Right THERE, in the GREAT CREATOR'S BRAIN! The ALPHA and OMEGA of THE GREAT VOID we know of as GOD!

From PURITY we came. To PURITY, we will return. ONLY THE PURE WILL BE PERMITTED!

HO.

FROM ARMAGEDDON TO THE 'DESTROYING' OF EARTH."

Grandfather had left them stunned. They trusted him, trusted his abilities to "see." This was knowledge unknown. Even the one who "had heard rumors" was dazed. They sat, pondering. Sipping coffee and just THINKING. This was something TO think about! Ugh, "I don't expect you to believe this," he said.

No one answered.

Then, "Brother, what about the BETWEEN time? AFTER the Great War and Armageddon? WHAT THEN? Have you been shown?"

"Yes."

Others said, "Please tell, if you are permitted to."

"I am," he replied. "I was SHOWN. 'Taken' in Spirit and shown.

After the Earth's 'flip', it took mankind some 30 to 40 years to regain their 'senses.' During the 'After' many died because they were not prepared. Not knowing how to survive, they fell prey to depression, starvation, etc. Hardly a tree or plant made it through. Hardly a bird or animal. No roads that were of length. No buildings left untouched. Those in the 'civilized' world were the hardest hit. No cars to drive, no place to get gas or pump air into tires. No reason FOR cars with the roads all a tremble…no grocery store to go to…no hospitals, etc.

They did not know what to do without electricity!

All up in smoke, swallowed in giant chasms, or ripped away by the enormous winds. Cold? You don't know what cold IS! Hot? Oh LORD, where areas were hot, they were HOT! Radiation…ash…it was a mess. Yet there were survivors despite this.

Need I say more?

In those thirty to forty years, they slowly found each other. Got their acts together and acted, as they should have all along. One for ALL, All for ONE. Unity. Slowly they regained their sanity.

'Towns' at first were mud huts. Perhaps 16 being a 'city.' Usually I would see only one or three. A number of five. Those of five were a 'town.'

You could walk for DAYS, even WEEKS, without seeing another person, let alone a HUT! Racism ceased. Color didn't matter anymore. Just to have another was enough. Yes, few remained alive 'after.' It was GOOD to SEE ANY OTHER HUMAN!

Then they started relearning. Telepathy once again began. Then, Levitation and Teleportation. Nature began to return. Plant life spared in deep ravens came forth. So too with the four-legged ones. Those of the air had found others and were once again bringing forth their kind. Some folks, 'survivalists' from 'before', had saved seeds. These too were added to the repopulation of our Mother.

Badly polluted waters were in cleansing. Some, by our own people, who still lived. Using the Medicine knowledge and the Sacred Stones we have for that.

In time, all once again began to 'click.'
It wasn't easy, as you can imagine. Still, once again, it happened.
Once again, man repopulated the Earth.

ONCE AGAIN, THEY STARTED DOING THE EXACT SAME THINGS THAT HAD CAUSED THE FIVE Previous 'DOOMS' OF THEIR ANCESTORS!

Yes, man will return, to…MAN. THEY FORGET THE PAST…and become AS WE ARE TODAY! AGAIN! This, after the returning of the 'Black One.' Just as Scriptures tells.

AGAIN, he TAKES OVER! AGAIN, WE FOLLOW SELF! AGAIN we have only a FEW who KEEP IN GODLINESS AND RIGHT STANDING! BUT…worse YET, WE GO B E Y O N D WHAT T H I S COMING ROLL, number five, HAS CAUSED!
(Can you BELIEVE IT? <u>WORSE</u>!)

To stop wars and mayhem…'Destruction'…MAN WILL BECOME BORG LIKE!
REALLY controlled! DANG Bleeding 'MACHINES'!
ALL EMOTIONS CONTROLLED!

Again, there will be an 'Elite.' The 'Leaders.' THE POWER MONGERS!
WHO WILL NOT BE REQUIRED TO BECOME BORGS!

At that time too, ANOTHER group will be: 'HIPPIES', FREE ones, who REFUSE to be changed, The NATURALS! (And called by that name)...It is THEY who will 'TUNE INTO' THE CREATOR…and CAUSE A WORLD WIDE SPIRITUAL 'REVOLUTION.'

Bringing our GOD CREATOR BACK TO MANKIND!

This a mere thirty to thirty-eight (or around that) YEARS, *before* THE LAST CLEANSING COMES! THOSE THAT 'UN-BORG' WILL BE OF GOD!
IT IS THOSE…as well as the ancestors who were His, from 'Day One',

WHO WILL BE PERMITTED TO STAY With and IN Him, FOR ETERNITY!
THE DAY OF JUDGMENT WILL BE!

Now, all this may sound 'off track' from the question of the Sacred 'Woman's Staff.' Its 'age.' Yet all is connected. Again, by time travel, it was gone back to its origin and watched. The SAME 'URGENCY' that was in the making of the 'Stones of Knowledge' was of evidence here, as well. But, with a difference. This urgency was of pre-knowledge that our Mother was soon to roll again. THE KNOWLEDGE OF THE STONE MAKERS, plus things learned SINCE our Earth's emergence and growth from the other dimension was placed into this stick. This all by Medicine Women of High Standing: The 'Holy Ones.'

Once completed, it was put into a sacred box and sealed, then hidden. This box was totally waterproof. It also had a TIME Opener (?) involved with it. This box was hidden IN WATER. The 'STAFF OF WOMENS' KNOWLEDGE' safely inside. At the Pre-Planned time, it was to open.

This it did. The staff, un-water soaked, floated to the surface of the Atlantic. This from the edge of what is now a submerged portion of a land sunk during that particular 'roll.' Somewhere off Newfoundland and Nova Scotia area. It then drifted in the currents, coming to rest on sea stones off an island tip, close to the upper east coast of Canada.
Eventually a large storm lifted this from these stones; breaking it free, to once again float. It floated towards a sandy beach. There, found and retrieved. There is much more on this finding, and to its now 'standing.' That, for another time though.

HOW OLD IS IT? IT CAME FROM THE ROLL THAT THE WAR BETWEEN THE ATLANTA'S AND MUUS CAUSED! THAT 'old'!

What? Two rolls back? Third of the soon to be Five?

Those carving and painting and IMPRINTED KNOWLEDGE on/in it, were of a Society of 'THOSE WHO KNEW' Some…SOME…of the Sacred STONE Makers KNOWLEDGE, of the DIMENSIONAL SHIFT Time.

Now that giving appears to be lost, or nearly so.

That Staffs' knowledge AND THE STONES, are meant to be together during the Ceremony that now appears NO LONGER GOING TO BE HELD.
Millions of YEARS of Passed on Knowledge…lost…forever."

Disappointment

Grandfather had received an email, asking him to call a well known Radio Show. One he'd been on a number of times before. He did. They were considering him as a guest again, BUT Wanted "SENSATIONALISM", Underground Cities/Tunnels/Aliens/etc. To him, this wasn't helpful to the masses. He'd done just enough over the years to TRY to get people aware there were many things going on around them that they had no idea of. Over six years of this, only to be laughed at, called a real "nut", "devil"...you name it. All, just to make them aware. To him, it was just cake frosting. NOT the Cake!
The Show's Producer wanted nothing to do with the real needs of mans "Connection, with Papa." That wasn't their style. No "draw." Money and Ratings were their prime objective. Grandfather was just a "wacko" to help them obtain this objective and keep their jobs...and "fame." He understood. That's the way of the world. "What makes it tick"...TICKING UP TO THE Fifth ROLL! Just like a clock slowly reaching Its set alarm time.

So evidently, a "No Go." Grandfather just couldn't convince them connection was THE most important need. Once again "the people party as the ark gets built"...IS being built. Now it's just a matter of "bringing in the furniture."

WHO WILL LISTEN?

More On Healing

Grandfather was constantly teaching on healing ways. Not those of the Traditionalists, but by Purity. He knew many of the latter way, but to have a BOOK to look into was far better. This also allowed the learners to study at their own leisure. He just 'pointed' and would give things to think about. The rest up to the student(s) and Creator. "For many are called but few are chosen." This keeps grandfather safe. He lets 'Papa' choose.

In this teaching time, he gave an amazing insight. One only the 12 seemed to be aware of. As often told, all in 'medicine' knew this; that what man calls reality, is all a lucid dream. The True Reality is that of dreams and visions. Time after time, he's told, "Work the Dream" (referring to the lucid dream man calls their reality). This new teaching is out of that. Based on that.

He began by saying, "Friends, We (the 12) have learned all people are an Outreach of our Inner Selves. Holograms. Thus, each person you meet are 'bit players' either in your lucid dream, or simply 'extras', to fill the play then there are the 'supporting actors.' Wife/Husband/your Children/Family/Boss /etc...Those you are in constant contact with. But ALL are only a hologram. YOU are the ONLY REAL BEING. The 'I AM…YOU are NOT.' The Christ knew this and used it throughout His life.

If any can grasp this 'I AM' concept, they can then work the dream to their benefit. Writing the script, as YOU want it. Hopefully, in a way of Agape Love. Now, with this in mind, we've found those close around us, as OUR OWN Inner OUTREACH, shows us our deepest inner thoughts. Not Conscious, not Subconscious…but to the third level. The VERY DEEPEST Conscious. This level few are aware of. As WE are three, so too we have three levels: One each for the triplets, that each is. Aho?

With this in mind, when people come to me for a healing, I see that person as ME: "Hurting," INSIDE MYSELF. YOU see a sick person. I see ME tossing out a Hologram. I see THIS as my DEEPEST Inner THOUGHTS. Thoughts so deep I am unaware of them.

We have names for the three we are:
Tonal - the physical body
Nagual - an angel within
Mind - the soul

The Nagual is the Spirit within. The Christian world tells that this Nagual is the Soul. They get this from Scriptures telling of humans Body, Mind, and Spirit. They are correct in assigning three aspects…but not with having the Soul being the Spirit. The SPIRIT is that that enters in at our conception. An inner angel. This one referred to in The Good Book in this manner; *'ALL ARE BORN WITH THE KNOWLEDGE THERE IS BUT ONE GOD.'* That is the BORN WITH that that tells of.

So, here comes one needing healing. I am aware that that Hologram is OF ME. IS me! A Projection of my deepest inner self. It is the Nagual's way of letting me know I'M NOT RIGHT, within. The Nagual cannot talk as we do. Cannot talk Mind to Mind, either. It can only communicate through Dreams and Visions. Remember, WE ARE IN A DREAM. So that sick person is a DREAM person.

Thus, the Nagual is COMMUNICATING WITH ME, WARNING me I have a problem. Not the SICK person, but ME! I have found ALL 'bad', be it sickness or accidents, ARE WARNINGS to ME. I have learned I AM NOT RIGHT IN THE CREATORS SIGHT!

I have also learned it means I AM DISSATISFIED with what God has 'put me in.'

I HAVE FAILED TO TRUST
FAILED TO PRAISE
FAILED TO LOVE HIM!

I have REBELLED! Gone off on my own. Became the 'Prodigal Son.' What to do? How do I get back to 'His' Mansion? I RETURN AND APOLOGIZE! I then start saying to myself: 'I LOVE ME', 'I LOVE ME', 'I LOVE ME', Over and over.

This, while I place my hands on the 'me' sick person: THAT 'PERSON' BEGINS FEELING BETTER! Often, is immediately healed. If not, I KEEP 'WORKING' on the 'I LOVE ME' saying. I KNOW I am 'RIGHT in his sight' WHEN THE HOLOGRAM IS HEALED!

Know this: I do not need to do this for each patient. Just the difficult ones and those rarely. When I am told to pray (healing help) and the prayers show no result, I know it is ME that needs the healing. It isn't something 'Dad' says. 'He' lets me and you find out for ourselves.

This hologram knowing extends even beyond healings of a physical realm: If I'm having trouble with someone…family or? I simply start saying 'I LOVE ME', and apologize to 'Papa.' When I DO 'Love Me', THE HEALINGS COME. The Quarrellings STOP, etc. Usually within MINUTES!

Yes, THAT FAST!

I have shared this with others. Those who tested this telling have ALL had the same wonderful results. Others have had problems. NONE of those though, tested.
These are mainly of Christian background and stuck in their man taught ways.

All this is scriptural and hidden in the open: The Seventh Code. It is also an Extreme way of the KU. That, another medicine way. Aho?

HO!"

Physician Heal Thyself

The group had had a break. Grandfather carried the teaching even further.

“There is a verse, ‘Physician, heal thyself.’ Now, with what I have just shared with you, let’s look at this.

Was the Big Brother ‘cutting down’ doctors? Perhaps.

Or was He telling them: ‘You KNOW/ALL Know/ALL are BORN KNOWING. You have fallen into the darkness of man. You have walked away from the knowing. You have become ‘Great’ in mans eyes for your MAN knowledge. You have LEFT the CREATOR’S way. NATURAL HEALING.

You CAN Heal Yourself! WHY DO YOU WALK AWAY FROM IT!

Is THAT what He was saying? Perhaps?”

Selah.

Time

(Part 1 of the 3 part "telling")

Today's date is February 16, 2007. You, the reader, are part of a big Pow Wow. This Book you are reading makes it so. I hope that many others are reading as well.

TIME is a strange thing. It only exists on your wrist and clocks. In fact, it has no fact. Indeed, time is nonexistent. A conception for man to make the 24 hour day more manageable for meetings, etc. Simply an invention of convenience.

In fact, we have only Day and Night…and Seasons. In this man has put on day time / night time / winter time / etc.

It is with this knowledge and acceptance of it, we of the Medicine Ways can transport our "seeing." The world at large calls this "Time Travel." We simply refer to it as "Seeing."

I will not get into what all that involves. Just understand it as we see it to be. That's all that's needed here.

The Good Book speaks of time, "*There WAS a man named Lazarus.*" (Past tense).
"*In those days time will be speeded up.*" (Present, As we are in "those days" right now).
"*The sun stood still.*" Old Testament (O.T.) Science has proved that to be a true happening.

Aho?

Have you noticed that in the last three years, that, day by day, "time" has sped up? Faster and faster, till "there isn't time enough in the day any longer to do the things I need."

No, it's not age. It's that it HAS been speeding up.

FOLLOWING SCRIPTURES WRITTEN WORD.

Now, in just the last three weeks, TIME IS RETURNING BACK TO NORMAL!

In the last two days, my wife and I have WATCHED IT DO SO!

Right before our eyes!

Allow me to share. Just yesterday morning I was keeping my eye on the clock. This because I heat water for the wife to bathe with (our water pipes are frozen). She arises at 6:00 a.m. The alarm clock set to that time. At ten minutes to six. I put the water on the stove. It was ready just as she got up. Turning off the alarm as she did so.

It was six o'clock. By her alarm and by the two clocks in the living room, (one being on my computer). She has a set "schedule" as she prepares to go to work.

She was washed, dressed, eating and about to pack her lunch when I looked up at the clock atop the TV. Instead of it being almost 20 minutes to seven o'clock. IT WAS 20 minutes to six o'clock!

"WHAT?" She said as I told her.

"Look for yourself," I said.

We have a clock in the kitchen as well. She had been going by that.
ALL three CLOCKS WERE ONE HOUR REVERSED from what we had been going by.

She went to the bedroom. Yes, her clock was set to go off at 6:00 a.m., HAD gone off at 6:00 a.m., and she had TURNED IT OFF. It was off, she checked.

She had gotten up at 6:00 a.m., but NOW it was AN HOUR EARLIER! NOW, it wasn't 6:00 a.m., wasn't EVEN 6:00 a.m. yet!

Why am I telling this?

BECAUSE WE ARE INTO "THE CALM BEFORE THE STORM!"

Once time AGAIN speeds up…the Bibles End Time Prophesies WILL ALL FINISH UP! QUICKLY!

Amongst those prophecies is the Rebuilding of the Temple in Jerusalem.

THIS WILL BE A WAR BRINGER!
One of GREAT MAGNITUDE!

Consider this: The Muslims most SACRED SITE: The DOME OF THE ROCK is ON the VERY SIGHT the TEMPLE was originally on!

Get the drift?

Unless the temple is built WITH the Muslim's Dome within…IT WILL BE TORN DOWN. DESTROYED!

Personally, I can't foresee it NOT being destroyed.

THAT MEANS WAR!

A GREAT war.

Between the Hebrews, HEBREW BACKERS and ALL Muslim "states."

THE TEMPLE WILL BE BUILT!

The "abomination"…LUCIFER INCARNATE, MUST ENTER Within Its walls, to orchestrate his Total World Dominance.

Reader, this "time shifting" I see as OUR FINAL WARNING:

A "BREAK" to give us time to consider our future.
It CAN be CHANGED! USE IT TO YOUR/OUR GODLY ABILITIES!
Get RIGHT in "HIS" SIGHT and LIGHT THE WORLD!

The more people that can do this, THE BETTER OUR WORLD'S CHANCES of TURNING BACK to "HIM" becomes. WE CAN BECOME AS THE Saved From Destruction: NINIVAH!

Thus STOPPING ALL until another future time. Leaving the NOW for our offspring to face AND HOPEFULLY, PUT IT OFF, TOO!

I "see" this TIME REVERSAL as our LAST CHANCE!

CAN we do it? YES! IF WE STRIVE EARNESTLY to FOLLOW Big Brother.

So that "CAN" we do it? It remains up to US.

NOTHING…is IMPOSSIBLE, when we are IN "HIS" WILL!

"His" will is LOVE ONE ANOTHER.

No hate. No "getting even." No "That's MINE."

All, as a family you love. ***'Mitakuye Oyasin'***. "ONE RELATION."
Aho?

An Untold Vision

(Part 2 of the 3 part "telling")

In the time of my "Great Vision," I was shown yet another. This one, in the Country of TURKEY. With the world's situation today, I am SPECULATING that this vision, the above telling (Time), and what I am about to share, are all related. Again, I am SPECULATING.

In the vision, I was shown that Turkey goes to war against Greece, and wins. This puts Turkey in a unique position: A LEADING POWER IN THAT AREA. Turkey is a "Muslim State." It too, is not a RADICAL Muslim Country. In this it differs from most, so very rare for those who practice that Religion.

IF the vision is true…AND with what is now happening, on our planet, I Speculate TURKEY will become a CENTER a "Pivot Point," between ALL Muslim Countries and ALL NON-Muslim Countries. Thus a NEEDED LEADER in WORLD AFFAIRS!

As the world escalates towards war, Turkey will be the only Country able to help both sides have a place "of peace" to gather and talk. IF THE VISION IS TRUE. Only time will tell and only time will see if my Speculations are "on" or not. Now to an even bigger Speculation: THE ANTI – CHRIST!

I see this one as POSSIBLY FROM TURKISH ORIGIN! A well educated, MUSLIM BELIEVING Being. One, who, as I am, is able to show the SIMILARITIES of ALL Major RELIGIONS: Hebrew, Christian, and Muslim. In THIS, Lucifer, in MAN INCARNATION, in a "Pivot Point" Country, can then become a…THE…"Leader of Peace!" Again, all this is Speculation. An INTERESTING Speculation though.

As I find all religions (Satanism the only one not included), have a common "denominator"… (AFTER RIDDING EACH OF THEIR ADDED ON "TRASH"), So too will HE be able to "see" and explain, using THIS to bring WORLD PEACE. HE WILL BE GIVEN, by POPULAR "VOTE," the LEADERSHIP of THE ENTIRE WORLD! "Leader over All." With all Governments his "speakers."
Leaders of Nations will come to him to seek advice...seek his "wisdom."

"The GREAT PEACEMAKER."

The <u>EVENTS</u> of HITLER'S REGIME will be enacted again, IN A FAR BIGGER WAY: WWII and its "Lead Up", was/is, a FORETELLING <u>EVENT</u> of MODERN TIMES!

(USE THE Seventh Code as a Code that GOES ON: Not just as one that stops with the Bible!)

The Blue Turban

(Part 3 of the 3 part "telling")

What is this? LUCIFER! I have seen him, wearing a beautiful, and "Rich," Blue TURBAN. A turban NO OTHER IS ALLOWED TO DUPLICATE or WEAR…AND "ELECTRIC BLUE!"

'HIS' "signature."(An interesting "note," BLUE represents the color of PEACE/SERENITY).

What does he look like? EXTREMELY HANDSOME…to the point of being SO Handsome, he is almost BEAUTIFUL! This "fits in" with his GREAT Ego. A "Man's MAN." No femininity at all. Dark of eye, Dark of hair, PERFECT skin of tan tone ("Arabian"). No "blemishes." PERFECT! Not at all very tall…perhaps six foot, at the most. (Interesting, the number SIX). Other than his Beauty, he'd fit into any crowd: "The AVERAGE JOE."

Women SWOON at the sight of him, actually have ORGASMS when in his presence!
Old ladies forget their looks and think "young" again. Men just like to be around him: Maneuver to be at his side, to have TV shots and pictures taken with him. *"SEE, I KNOW HIM…we are BUDDIES! He's my PERSONAL friend!"* That type of adulation.

HOWEVER, GOD FORBID ANY THAT CROSSES HIM! Those beautiful "loving"/"peaceful" eyes FLASH, 1,000%! PURE ANGER…An UNGODLY Anger, on ANY who do so! The FEAR in the recipient(s) is INSTANTANEOUS! The old "Oh My GOD! I'M DEAD!" type fear. Full and COMPLETE! If they have half a brain, they NEVER AGAIN CROSS HIM!

This I've SEEN. Is he here, born now? YES! And he is already "known" in certain circles…OF GOVERNMENTS! Of MILITARIES!"Making" his "skills" as a "diplomat" known…AND HIS ABILITIES! Many do not believe Lucifer, in ANY FORM, exists. Either as a Dark Angel, or otherwise. Oddly, some who believe in God STILL don't believe in him! A mistake. But it's their path.

HE is very much a real being. GIVEN BY THE CREATOR for Mankind to Have CHOICE. We would not be as we are…Soul Beings…if he wasn't here for that.

"GOD IS IN ALL THINGS." Lucifer, being one of those "things".

"ALL" is <u>ALL</u>! You either accept, that is in His Good Book, or write your own "Bible." Many do, anyway. So I guess it does not matter…but to "HIM."

(Will to YOU too, eventually, but don't Believe a Word I Say…TEST ME)!

Good Luck!

Reversing Death

Grandfather had received a pleading phone call.
"Grandfather, our grandmother is in the hospital, DYING! PLEASE, Can you COME? HELP US, PLEEEASE!"

He asked the caller to hold and be quiet. Then shut his eyes and asked "Papa."
"He" said one word: "GO." Grandfather checked this three times, as is his way. Three times; "GO." So trip arrangements were made.

They met at the hospital. Tobacco given (as is the proper "way"). They went to the old woman's room and were introduced. The woman had heard of him, for he had helped this family a number of times. He then asked the family to leave them alone "for a bit."

Once the family left, he stood at the end of dying woman's bed, looking over all the medicines and connections, then at her. Her eyes were feverish, swollen, and red. Her skin was a very paled tint, turning into a gray/blue. Breathing was forced and shallow despite the air being pumped into her.

Yup…she was "on her way."

Grandfather looked at her AND BEGAIN TO LAUGH! Boy! THIS brought her to FULL ATTENTION!

"Sorry, sis, but YOU LOOK LIKE HELL!"

She replied weakly, "I FEEL like hell. I just want to die and get this over with."

"That's apparent," he replied, WITH LAUGHTER!

"Hon, do you believe in God?"

"Yes."

"In the Bible?"

"Yes."

"Are you aware of the telling in there, that mankind is meant to live to 130 years old, in general?"

"No."

"Don't read it much, do you."

"No, but I go to church and mass."

"Catholic, huh? That figures…well sis, that telling is in there, IF you would read it, and not rely so much on what you are told. You'd see it for yourself."
He had her interest.
"I'm not cutting your religion down, Hon…just stating facts. Believe me, you are not the only one that trusts what you are BEING told…over what IS told. All religions do that. Much to your shame and THEIR (pastors and priests)…Horror, when THEY pass. 'Shepherds' leading their sheep into a wilderness place. Letting them eat on Scrub Brush, when there's Miles of good green grass just across the hills. You are a sheep in a mass herd. All, malnourished, due to your shepherds leadings. So here you lay, all 'tubed up.' Meds flowing into your veins. Thinking you are 'old' and wanting to get it over with. You have accepted that you're old, in the 80's. You have not accepted what 'HE' said. That130 years is the AVERAGE age. Could go higher, or less."

"Now you have a choice…to go on and Die…or go on watching and helping your love ones HERE…by deciding to Live. You are in your 80's."

"Eighty one," she said.

"See, RIGHT AT ABOUT MIDDLE AGE. Not OLD Age.

But the death time choice is yours. 'Dad' will not interfere with your ruling WILL.
Meantime, in your years, you've no doubt made A LOT of ill choices. 'Mistakes.' Things you haven't confessed. Little things like yelling at the kids…in ANGER. Lying. Maybe some little "Penny Ante' thefts. Cheating. That type of stuff. Then, too, maybe some BIG stuff. Things only You and HIM know about. Things you were too embarrassed to tell in the confessional. All 'hidden' within your mind. Your Heart…and IN YOUR SOUL! Now you 'want to die' and 'go to heaven.'

'Saved.'

Yes, you can go, if you really want too. It's YOUR CHOICE.

But I'd give it some serious thought first. You have A LOT of apologies to make. Cleaning up the messes you've made during your life. Apologizing to others AND to GOD. You can trade GODLINESS for the UN-Godliness you've done over the years. Little AND big things. THEN you can face our Father in far better 'steed' then you stand now.
Remember: you WILL FACE HIM!

I'm going out for a smoke and prayer time for you, as you think over what I've just said.

TEST what I've just told. PRAY to 'DAD' and see if I'm telling Truths, or Lies. I'll be back in a few minutes. You just lay there and CONTEMPLATE on these things. Aho?"

He left, talked to the family, "Can we see her now?"
"No. Not yet. She has some things to do. I'll let you know," and did his prayer time.

About 20 minutes later, he was back. The woman had been crying. Un-dried tears still on her cheeks. He looked at her and said, "Well Hon, have you made up your mind? Do you still want to die?"

Tubes in throat and all…she VERY STRONGLY…almost SHOUTING said,
"NO!"

He laughed, "Good choice. Now let us pray to God together. Talk to our Lord Big Brother Jesus…and get you back on your feet."

They did so. The "old" girl REALLY praying this time. Thankful for His Sacrifice in a BIG Way! Probably the first PERSONAL praying she's done since a child. HONEST PRAYER! ONE-ON-ONE prayer. The way it SHOULD be.

As she did, THE DEATHLY COLOR WAS LEAVING HER FLESH. The PUFFED EYES receding and returning to normal.

In this "telling" one thing was NOT told: THE "GRIM REAPER" WAS IN THE ROOM WHEN GRANDFATHER ARRIVED. This, an ANGEL. They had acknowledged each other when grandfather had come in...A mere slight nod from each. Un-noticed by those in the room. These two knew each other. Have worked together a number of times in the past. As the old woman and Grandfather prayed, the Reaper Angel, grinning, gave a slight wave of "goodbye" AND WALKED OUT OF THE ROOM. It was THEN, grandfather KNEW the woman would live.

When finished, grandfather called in the family. Telling them, she'd "be OK." Then told the woman, "You'll be discharged on Sunday." (It was Friday afternoon). He then slipped out unnoticed and went home. PRAISING ALL THE WAY.

This now over a year ago. "Grandmother" is fine Still…and "NICE!"

(Praise The Lord!)

Grandmother's Age – Unknown!

One of the women Grandmother had helped wanted to surprise her with a "Party of Thanks." Several women were to be involved. This woman came to grandfather, seeking "The Wardens" birth date for this.

Grandfather could only tell, "Sometimes towards the end of September is all I can say. I'm no good at dates. Sorry."

"Well" she said, "How old is she?"

"Oh, gee, I'm not sure, pretty old though. Older then she tells me she is. She says one thing, but you know women. Age isn't a subject you care to talk about once you reach 39."

I had always thought she was about five years younger than I was, since we first met. I'm thinking she...wellll, stretched the truth a bit though. Last year I saw her Social Security card by accident when it fell out her purse. Never had the guts to tell her what I'd seen.
Turns out her Social Security, number is…

THREE!

Santa Clause

Children were with the Old One. They all considered him their "BEST" (adult) Friend. Some, quite little, others older. Christmas was not far off. Excitement was running high. However, there was a "glitch"…the old "NO Santa!...IS TOO!" thing.
Finally, they turned to Grandfather for he would be honest! So they asked.

He answered, "Yes my friends, there IS a Santa Claus. He is the SYMBOL of GIVING. He is the SPIRIT that lives in peoples' hearts.

Some dress him funny…red coat and things.
IT IS AS YOU WANT, As you BELIEVE. Some don't believe…saying he doesn't exist…yet they TOO receive gifts. YOU CAN'T STOP LOVE. Yes, Children, there IS a "Santa Claus."

One though looked sad, "Grandfather, not all get presents."

"I understand. Yet, you are looking at 'toys' and 'things' as presents. Yet ALL have been given the GREATEST present any can receive. A human LIFE! Two actually. Yours and that of our 'Big Brother.' HE gave YOU your life…then GAVE HIS so that YOU might STILL Live. THAT is The GIFT that ALL are given.

Most fail to see this. I hope YOU do someday.

Yes, there IS a Santa Claus…The GIVER is THAT one!
That gift…that 'PRESENT'…IS ALWAYS THERE. It's just a matter of Opening it.

Remember…You CAN'T STOP LOVE!"

The Returning

They had fared well during the winter. The animals had plenty of food stored, as too the small band. It had been a good hunting time…even during the snows.
The traverses were lashed to the dog's backs and loaded. It was time to move on.
They had enjoyed their time in this valley, but the nomadic people would move on from one place to another…so as to not defile or over hunt an area. It was time to let the grasses grow where the tipi's had stood.

Allowing nature to recoup.

They WORKED with Nature…not against it. That was the way in the old days.

THESE DAY'S WILL RETURN!

The Foot Prints

It was a long trip. WEEKS, over time. The OLD ONE taken place to place across all of Canada. He had started on the Pacific side and was now in a boat off the coast of the Atlantic. Again, to help the Cree's and others, to know the WHY of certain spots. This one in the "seven Islands" area. They were headed to a small island. One of mystery to The PEOPLE. Arriving, they began an arduous trek up the small mountain there. It was difficult for the old one and he lagged behind. Still the trail was easily seen. Occasionally one would return to check on him. Yes, it was hard on the Old One.

It was interesting though! For all had passed places only the old one could "see." SPIRITS were EVERYWHERE! People of "The Past" stood high on ridges, watching what was going on. Protectors who had volunteered to guard this very special island. Staying, instead of going into The Happy Hunting Grounds. They had done a marvelous job. The island set aside as sacred by the Canadian Government. A true Rarity!

Little had been disturbed. With just a small cabin and beach cooking area there. Always manned and requiring permission to touch shore was needed and no overnight camping was allowed.

As the Wakȟáŋ slowly worked his way upward, he came to a very narrow and strange rock ravine "passageway." GIANTS HAD LIVED HERE! True GIANTS! Or rather, ABOVE this. Those living IN it were "LITTLE PEOPLE."

"Folktale" beings that still exists. This "Stronghold" of these people. None lived there now…in THIS dimension! But were still there, in another.

Eventually the old one arrived to their intended destination. All were gathered on large smooth boulders. One, the "major" boulder, in their center. The old one sat to catch his breath. All were talking in whispers about him. For this spot held GREAT RESPECT to all there. Finally he was rested and the two Medicine People in this group (one woman, one man) sat beside him and explained, "There are footprints IN that ROCK (pointing to it). Can you find out for us Why, and HOW, and Who's?"

Indeed there were! MANY! Those of Raccoon, Man, Bird…and All are standing around ONE PARTICULAR "SET." Another MAN set! Those faced west, side by side.
The Wakȟáŋ called for silence. In moments he was back in time, the time of THIS EVENT.

IT WAS "BIG BROTHER!" It was HE who was facing west! ALL THE OTHER PRINTS were ANIMALS, BIRDS and MEN (two or three) standing or kneeling in a Semicircle around HIM, WORSHIPPING! As they did so, He "the one who came," stood, eyes shut, raised his arms!..and began praying. Face uplifted. HE WAS TALKING TO "HIS FATHER!" Suddenly a "tube" came down upon him, and those there. It appeared as an "ENERGY SPOT" with a SILVERY energy mass like CHAFF.

This tube had a “half round top,” it enclosed all within it. The old one saw this all…and could see inside as well, for it was much like glass.

When this enclosed all, the old one saw The CHRIST begin to concentrate.
In a very short time…under perhaps three minutes…ALL BEGAN TO SINK INTO THE STONE! Their Feet going within. Birds, Raccoons, People.
And then it was done. The energy tube became mist like and disappeared.

These prints remain to this day. It was HOLLOWED GROUND, And REMEMBERED by GENERATIONS of Native Indians ALL ACROSS CANADA!

This is but ONE, of SEVEN Such SIGHTS, He left within Canada.

The Sacred Hill

There was a man, Cree, who every early morning would go to a certain hilltop and put wood on a fire, an "eternal" fire. This went on for many years, seasons round until this one passed on.
No one knew why this was done.

One day the Wakȟáŋ was in the area and was told of this…for all remembered.

They took him to this hilltop.

"Could you find out WHY, Grandfather?"

Grandfather asked for quiet and went instantly into thought. He traveled back into time, easily locating the fire tender. He then went into the time this man began his doing…the origin of this. He watched this, then a mid-aged man, sleeping…and he was in the Alpha dream state. The old one entered his dream. The Cree was being given a VISION dream. The old one observed and heard, "Big Brother" was there before the dreamer…giving this one an order: "Go to this hill and light a fire. Keeps this fire going, Day and Night. Never cease, never let it go out. If you do this, your people will still be in me. Still remembering. Still Holy." The dream ceased.

The old Wakȟáŋ told them the WHY. The next time he was in the area, things had changed.

SOMEONE(s)…UNKNOWN TO THIS DAY…had taken a Telephone Pole and a Pole "cross member"…dug a hole, painted this Cross Pole completely all white…and lifted the cross there.

This, during one night.

When the Cree's awoke the next day…there it stood.
It still stands. Seen for miles around.
THEIR ETERNAL LIGHT!

Tested

The elder was having dinner with the son of a well known Medicine Man, himself a Medicine Man. The younger man was "feeling out" this white "half breed." Many claimed to be of "Medicine."

Book taught "New Agers." The elder didn't hold this man's questioning against him. He was doing Right…CHECKING! The younger asked the Elder ,"Who is God?" Using the white term for the Creator.

"You ask me to tell ALL this, in an HOUR? To do honor to this One in this time is IMPOSSIBLE, But I will try," the elder said.

His food grew cold as he explained the best he could in the time they were to have together; highlighting the major parts.

"First off, 'He' is not a he, for 'He' has no sex. 'He' is neither male nor female. We call 'Him' 'HE' only in that the male title of 'HE' denotes authority. Thus it is so, thus I will address 'Him' as 'He' here.

'He' has a name…The GREAT VOID!

'His' size is…FOREVER.

'He' has no beginning nor ending. No height, nor depth.

Thus, 'He' is ETERNAL…NEVER ENDING!

'He' is His OWN "mother and father":
Having become AWARE, that 'He', the Great Void, existed. This made 'Him' so HAPPY, so JOYFUL, 'He' wanted to share that 'He'…WAS!

In this, 'He' became the CREATOR. The MAKER of All Things.

We…EVERYTHING…is of 'His' IMAGINATION. His IMAGING, 'His' DAYDREAM!
WE…Mankind…ALL...'His' INNER DAYDREAM THOUGHTS.

WE ARE DREAM!

Who then, are WE? GOD! Not GOD GOD, but gOD GOD.
We would not exist; NOTHING would exist, if 'He' wasn't DAYDREAMING us.
Again: WE ARE DREAM! There is far more to this 'WE'/ 'ALL,' but that was not asked."

This lasted the full hour, a cold bite of dinner at a time. Finally, the two had to part. Having parked close together, they walked out together and said their goodbyes. The younger going to his car drivers side. This one had done very, Very little talk. He had sat and listened. Now he was about to leave.

He stopped, turned, and walked back to the Elder. Looking down at him, (he being much taller), and grinned, spread out his arms and BEAR HUGGED the Elder.

As he did so, he said, "You ARE a Medicine Man…BROTHER!"

Friends,
ALWAYS:
ChecK. ChecK. ChecK!

Ho.

Missed Opportunity

A Sioux had asked for help from grandfather. They met at a commercial Pow Wow in Spokane, Washington. Here he learned there was a young Sioux who was being attacked by an unknown spirit being. This attack was leaving deep scratch marks on the boy's chest/back/legs. A "black evil" was felt to be present at each attack. He asked to meet this young man. When the Sioux came, they talked. The Sioux raising his shirt to show the deep marks that crisscrossed his stomach and back. He was SCARED! The two Sioux left at grandfather's request. He had prayers to do. Serious prayer. He spent well over an hour alone. Seeking. What he found out surprised him.

This "being" was Not a Demon…but a TESTER! (This, a form of angel).
Sent at the request of a now "passed on" elder that the young Sioux had called, "Grandfather." It was this elder who had asked permission to have a tester sent to the young man who was being attacked. It was his hopes and desire that the younger would be accepted into the Dog Soldier Society. His request was granted. The tester sent. It would be a Hard Testing. For this 20 year old was VERY immature. Acted more like 16 years old. One has to be VERY MATURE to be in this group. FEARLESS!

A tester brings EVERY FEAR a particular person has. IF that person can OVERCOME those fears, he is worthy of consideration. Already the boy was failing. The boy was called back and told what was happening. He was asked if he WANTED to be in this society."Grandfather was in it and told me he wanted me in it as well. Yes, I want to be a member," he said. With that, grandfather became his adviser. His Mentor.

This young man intended to stay at a lodge there at the Pow Wow grounds. He suggested that grandfather and another he had with him go to his house to sleep. This was done. Grandfather taking the young Sioux's bed, as this co-driver slept at its end on the floor. Above him a bare light bulb with pull string for switching on and off. Grandfather was extremely tired. He'd been on the go, with no sleep, for over 74 hours straight. It took mere minutes to be deep in sleep.

An unknown time later, THE LIGHT WENT ON!

"Tink," went the pull string. "Pulling" the old one out of his deep reverie.

THERE BEFORE HIM STOOD THE TESTER!
Between him and the floor sleeper…WHO DID NOT WAKE (though the light was directly over his up-turned face).

THIS was to be between Grandfather and the Tester ONLY!

Grandfather was Super Tired. This interruption was NOT to his likening. Not ONE BIT! To be dragged out of his much needed sleep was just TOO much! He was TICKED!

This Angel "THING" was THE MOST FRIGHTFUL BEING grandfather had EVER seen! (That's saying a lot, as he had/has often dealt with full blown demons. Themselves, not at ALL "good looking").

The Tester emitted ALL FEARS GRANDFATHER HELD "INSIDE."

It was TESTING the MENTOR!

Grandfather didn't even flinch. Instead, he had "words" to say with this rude one. CHEWING IT OUT, "No End." He was MAD!
There was no FEAR in this anger, and the Being knew it! IT HAD "LOST."

(If the mentor can be overcome, the one it was sent to test would be a "piece of cake").

Grandfather told this One…"Your target is asleep in a Tipi at the Pow Wow grounds. Go THERE and GET OUT OF MY "Face"…and TURN THE LIGHT OFF AS YOU LEAVE!"
At that, he rolled over and shut his eyes. He was done. He wanted no nonsense with this One. SLEEP was all he desired!

The Tester, being an angel, had to obey, for all soul bearers have authority over ALL angels. "ALL" meaning just that: ALL! (This includes Lucifer).

Grandfather did not just "Believe" The Good Book…he KNEW it. A BIG difference! HO!

The Tester left. Its footsteps heard going up the steps to upstairs. Its Heavy weight making each step Grown! It didn't "run," but went slowly…"Spookfully." Trying to STILL create "fear" in grandfather.

It didn't work.

"Tink," went the string. The light turned off, as grandfather had ordered.

Grandfather went easily back to sleep. There was NO FEAR in this one!

The next morning he began to think on the encounter of the night. The more he thought of it, the more he thought, "How DUMB of me! I COULD HAVE TRADED FOR ITS HAND! DANG! I wish I hadn't been so darn TIRED!"

Yes, you've read right. You see, that being was of SPIRIT, in PHYSICAL FORM! All grandfather needed to do was ASK or Order it TO REMOVE and GIVE HIM a HAND! In return, all he had to do is give "an exchange of Energy." In this case, A HAIR OFF HIS OWN HEAD!

The Being, being of Spirit, could INSTANTLY re-grow a new hand.

This is nothing to a Spirit Being. What Man calls "impossible" has UNLIMITED Abilities to those from the TRUE Reality. Ho

In not doing this, grandfather had missed an opportunity of a lifetime. The hand, SO BIG, would have made a good necklace. One he could use if needed, as a SAFETY "Tool."

This, covering his WHOLE CHEST and down to his belly button, from base of throat, downward.

There, kept covered, would be Uncovered when needed, then lifted, PALM and CLAWS Out, to ANY who was going to be a "problem."

It would INSTANTLY EMIT its POWER OF FEAR!

ANY, seeing that before them, would either RUN…or FAINT!
Eliminating that one, as a danger.

THIS is what grandfather had "lost."

Furthermore, grandfather could hold it up to him…and practice OVERCOMING ALL H I S Fears!

Seeing WHAT he feared, and IN BIG BROTHER and TRUST…then become even MORE "fearless."

Yes, he "blew it."

Won't if there's a "next time," though.

YOU CAN BET ON IT!

HO!

The Great: Three-In-One

Grandfather was busy at his desk. His Grandson watching TV.
The boy suddenly said, "Grandpa, I have a question?"
"What is it, son?"
"You've told me that the Creator…God…is 'Three In One.' Can you explain that for me?"
The Old One knew when this one would 'pop up' with a question of 'depth'…but knew it always began with, *'I have a question.'*
He put down his work and thought.
"Well son, the three are 'The FATHER'…'The SON' (That we call 'Big brother')…and The Creator's Spirit. This one is called the 'HOLY SPIRIT.' Each is a separate personality, that together, makes up the ONE called *GOD*." He could see a bit of bewilderment on the boy's face.

"Here, I'll show you," he said. At that, he went into the kitchen and got a large bowl and two cups. The bowl he filled with water.

Bringing this to the boy, he sat them down before him.

"Let's pretend this bowl of water is The Creator…'GOD', Okay?"

The boy shook his head, "Yes."

"Okay…we have 'GOD.' Now, I will call THIS cup JESUS and THIS cup the HOLY SPIRIT. Alright?"

"Yes."

Dipping the 'Jesus Cup' into the bowl of 'God' he said, "See here is Our Big Brother 'Jesus'…it is of the same water of *God*." He then did the same with the 'Holy Spirit' cup.
"And here is the 'Holy Spirit'…it too came from the same 'God' water. This water left in the bowl, the 'God' Part, is the FATHER. Now you have three separate parts of God. Yet all three are from the same source…the FULL GOD BOWL. Now let us pour these two cups back into the bowl. (He did) Now, the three ARE ONE again, see?"

"Yes!"

"Though the three were separated, EACH WAS OF And FROM the 'GOD BOWL'…So EACH WAS 'GOD.' Though separated, they were all the same! Now do you understand?"

"Yes Grandpa. Thanks!"

The boy went back to his TV…the elder back to his task.

He Talks

"Grandfather," one women asked, "how do you heal?"
This had been asked many, many times over the old man's Medicine Life.
His eye's twinkled.
"My sister, I don't, the Great Creator does. I just ask if I'm to be His Voice, His Hands."

"YOU ASK? How do you know if you are to help?"

He smiled at the two present, "Well ladies, I then listen."

(You could see the *huh?* in their eyes).

"Truly, it's simple as that. You ASK...then you wait for 'HIM' to answer. Why ask a question to ANY, if you don't expect an answer? Might as well never ask at all..."

The Wakȟáŋ/Medicine Man knew this seems to be a common occurrence with most any who claim to *'Talk to God.'*

They make claims 'He LIVES'...but have a tendency of not understanding that IF 'HE' Lives... HE'S ALIVE.

ALIVE!

People talk to each other. Conversing. A *'back and forth'* thing...yet ignore that 'HE WHO LIVES' is just as ANY person.

"Grandfather...you speak as though you and The Great Creator, TALK TOGETHER!"

"Well?" he queried.

In disbelief they stood...stunned.

"Listen, my children...IF YOU EXPECT, You GET!
THAT INCLUDES One-on-One CHATS With 'HIM.'
Is He not our ultimate 'maker'? Our ultimate FATHER? Don't you listen to your OWN Earth Father when you speak to him? Well?"

Silence.

"Why don't you try it sometime? TALK TO and WITH 'HIM' not TO 'Him'...
He's waiting. Aho?"

The Button

Grandfather was speaking to a High School class. His subject: That All are Related and NEEDED BY EACH OTHER.

“This we call Earth, in a way, is one house. Look at it that way. We are all in a HOME. There are many rooms. These rooms hold different people. Each ‘room’, a room that has ‘Beds.’ ‘Beds’, for Indians. ‘Beds’, for Whites. ‘Beds’, for Blacks. ‘Beds’, for Arabians…Chinese, etc.

Still, these rooms and beds are in the ONE ‘House.’

In that way, we are FAMILY.

YOU see a World DIVIDED. Divided by water and Borders. See those now as just rooms in the house.

Now, Just as in any family, each helps the other(s).

This, to bring a Workable HARMONY, to the whole.

In your own home, all goes well when each do their work…help…with all.

One cooks, one works to pay bills, one cuts grass and takes out the garbage, one vacuums, etc.

Done without squabbles, all ‘runs’ well.

The house is neat and comfortable. LIVABLE, despite the number living there.

HOWEVER, if STRIFE develops, ALL Harmony Work ceases. ALL run to the ‘fight’ to see what’s up and try to stop the disruption(s).

ALL HARMONY WORK CEASES, during this time.

The longer it goes, the messier the house becomes.

DISARRAY over the WHOLE HOUSE!

When the problem is resolved, it takes time to get things ‘back on track.’ Each has to work harder to get the house back in order.

A time of frustration, but eventually it is done.
With luck, it will stay that way.

In HIM, if ALL are IN Him…that 'luck' is *'Oneness in like Mind.'* This turns 'luck' to *'WHY FIGHT? I LOVE YOU!'*

We aren't all that 'lucky' though. Ugh.

SEE YOUR OWN HOME LIFE as the EXAMPLE of the WORLD HOME life.

For in truth, that is what it is.

Now, I mentioned, *'each has a job.'* Let's see how that applies to this One, BIG, Earth HOME.

For this, I will use a simple object: One BUTTON!

See THIS as a JOB, which creates HARMONY ON EARTH.
Our NEED for each other, to make *'The World Go Round.'*

HOW DID YOU GET THAT BUTTON?
Was it bought on a Shirt or Blouse?

HOW DID YOU GET THAT SHIRT/BLOUSE?
Yes, by buying it. MONEY.

HOW WAS THE MONEY GOTTEN?
Someone worked for it.

HOW DID THEY HAVE A JOB TO GO TO?
Well, a Company.

HOW WAS THE COMPANY BUILT?
Someone came up with an idea and it started from there.

I'll stop at this point, for it could go on and on for WEEKS. Let us now go back to that ONE BUTTON.

WHO MADE THE CLOTH FOR THE SHIRT the button is on?

WHERE did the Material COME FROM?

HOW WAS THE NEEDED 'base needs' TO MAKE that material, GOTTEN TO THE MAKERS FACTORY?

WHAT DID IT TAKE TO MAKE THE BUTTON?

If you are beginning to understand what I am getting at, you will, in time, find EVERY HUMAN ON EARTH, PAST AND PRESENT…CONTRIBUTED TO THE MAKING OF THAT… *ONE* BUTTON!

ROADS were built. FACTORIES were built. DOCTORS to help birth a NOW button factory worker, were involved. SHIPS built to ship needed things to BUILD those needed things…JUST for ONE BUTTON! Trains, Trucks, Digging Machinery, Government agreements for 'Trade', Clothing for all, Food for all. And ON and ON and ON and ON and…

ALL THE WAY BACK TO ADAM AND EVE! And THEM, All the way BACK TO THE 'BEGINNER OF ALL' – THE CREATOR GOD!

I tell you true: ALL THE TREES ON EARTH WOULD HAVE TO BE CUT DOWN AND MADE INTO PAPER, TO HOLD THE WRITING NEEDED TO TRACE DOWN THE MAKING of that ONE BUTTON!…And MORE TREES GROWN AND CUT, TO FINISH THE JOB!

WE ARE A FAMILY. WE LIVE IN (on) ONE HOUSE.

WE NEED EACH OTHER!

Just so YOU CAN BUTTON YOUR SHIRT!"

Indian Tarot Cards

She had learned. And here she was, her Indian Tarot Cards in hand.

Come to 'show' her friends how they can 'Easily get answers with THESE'!

After a short display, she turned to her Grandfather and said, "Well, how do you like THESE, Grandfather? Pretty cool, eh?"

He looked at her sadly.

"I'm sorry honey…but that's NOT 'Indian', it's New Age."

"Grandfather, how can you SAY that! Look at the totems on each!"

"Sorry, New Age."

She looked at the 'Old Geezer' disdainfully.

"Prove IT!" she defiantly said, "THIS IS OF OUR ANCESTORS!"

"OH?" he replied.

"WHEN DID OUR ANCESTORS HAVE PAPER?"

True Beauty

She was a young beautiful lady. Many men had interest.
She was also one 'In Touch' with the Creator.

She knew the interest was for the wrong reasons…and would not allow defilement.
She and others as her…MEN AS WELL, were…and ARE…VERY SPECIAL IN 'HIS EYES.'

LEAVE THOSE 'BE'!

THEY UNDERSTAND THEIR GODLINESS!

THEY have not forgotten!

THEY make The Creator SMILE!

Vegetarian

"Grandfather, I have friends who are Vegetarians. They say it is a healthier way to eat. Is this true?"

"Yes, for some, it is."

"Well they claim ALL should eat this way."

"Well, that would kill off many Eskimos! At least in the old days.

Child, people are strange. They find a 'way' they are comfortable with and want to 'convert' ALL to…THEIR…'Way.'

This in many things…be it food, religion, or 'I HAVE THE BEST CAR & ANY who buy less are DUMB.' It doesn't matter.

Even the atheists try to 'convert'…and in so doing are a 'Church' themselves.

Yes, people are strange.

Is eating only plant life the BEST in Health Food? Again, for some.

Some have allergies and this 'way' KEEPS them healthy.

Some prefer not 'Taking Life'…not seeing each plant HAS life. That ALL can…and DO; SEE/HEAR/COMPREHEND and are in touch with the Creator.
These 'won't take a life.' To them, Eyes and Fur and 'Pretty' is 'Life.' They have never learned to enter a plant and KNOW that these, too, see/hear/have emotions and are in connection with The 'Maker of All.'

LIFE!

The conversations I have had with these 'people' would amaze you.

Let me tell you of a vegetarian I know. I've known him for many years. This one got on a 'carrot kick.' HIS WHOLE SKIN WAS AN ORANGE COLOR! Even the pigment in his eyes.
In a drug store, the pharmacist told him he needed to see a doctor Immediately! He had never seen a 'serious' carrot eater before!

Well, one day this man came to me with a 'complaint.' He had been 'bound up' for several days and was seeking relief. I had him buy me lunch at McDonalds. When we got there, I ordered the

GREASIEST HAMBURGER I COULD GET…with NO 'Vegetables' on it. I ordered two. He ordered orange juice. When we sat down, I placed one of the burgers in front of him."

"Oh, no thanks," he said.

"I looked him in the eye and ORDERED him TO EAT! You have come to me to be healed…EAT THAT!
He did, almost gagging.
He hadn't eaten meat for a long time. Sort of 'against his religion', in a sense.
As he ate, I told him…Man NEEDS grease, and fat at times. IT HELPS THE FIBROUS PLANTS to SLIDE THROUGH THE DIGESTIVE TRACK! YOU are in a form of 'Cat HAIR BALL' inside. THIS WILL CLEAR IT!

It did.

No, to be a full, ALWAYS and ONLY Vegetarian has some drawbacks to many. SOME meat should be eaten. Not often, but occasionally.
Also, to eat ANYTHING, it should first be blessed before taking.
IF YOU ARE SERIOUS. This BLESSING has GREAT EFFECT on ALL foods. This is the same for all drinks as well.

That, in turn, BLESSES YOUR BODY!
'Un-needed' passes through, NOT CLINGING TO YOUR INSIDES.

THAT goes 'Out the Drought.'

Only what your body REQUIRES…FOR ITS HEALTH, then retains.

This is SERIOUS blessings though. Not ROTE blessing!
There's a difference between HEART and WORDS.

Lil' one, YOU EAT AS YOU FEEL LED! NOT as you're 'Peer Pushed' into.

Is it right to be a vegetarian?

NOT IF YOU FEEL OTHERWISE!"

Lightning

He was curious, “Grandfather, where does lightning come from…I mean beyond ‘The Creator.’”

“From the ground.”

“Are you Sure?”

“Yes, lifted me up once. Pretty high, too!”

“AND IT DIDN’T KILL YOU?”

“No, the fall did…”

(Sheeeeshhhhhhh)

Mixing Of Cultures

They were eating Indian fry bread. Really ‘pigging out’ on this delicacy.

They two were really enjoying it.

(Grandmother was ‘Some Cook’ on this!)

The child said, “Boy, our ancestors sure knew how to do things RIGHT. I wonder who invented it.”

“Well son, I can’t tell you WHO, but I CAN tell you HOW.”

“Okay then, how?”

“WHITE MAN.”

“HUH?”

“Son, we had no wheat TO make this. It wasn’t until whites introduced us to it, that it became ‘OUR’ Fry Bread.

“We didn’t?”

“Nope, we didn’t.”

“Try as we might, we can’t claim ALL the whites have done, and do, is ‘wrong.’ They have some good things going for them, in truth.”

“Can you tell me of others, Grandfather?”

“Those glasses you’re wearing, is one. A phone, the computer you use, cars, clothing, and on and on. Much. Aho?”

“Gee, I never thought of it like that…”

“Son, what one should do is KEEP THE GOOD and REJECTS THE BAD…that way, all you have is GOOD. Do that and you will live a far more peaceful life.

We people, of ALL the Earth, would be better off if we all realized every culture has GOOD THINGS that ALL would be better off accepting for the Wholes use.

You like your Fry Bread…Try OTHER GOOD THINGS AS WELL!

It's easy to recognize good, over that, that's bad."

"How?"

"If it creates Harm or is Morally wrong…it is ALWAYS 'bad.'

If it satisfies EGO, or SELF, FOR self! It is ALWAYS 'bad.'

If it makes your HEART FEEL GOOD…WITHOUT Harm or bad morals…it is ALWAYS GOOD.

If it is of self-LESS-ness…it is ALWAYS GOOD.

It's as simple as that."

Ho.

Grandfather's Uncle

They were sitting around. Family and friends. Each reminiscing about things in their past. A lot of tellings and laughter. Some of the dumb things they or others had done. Grandpa got into his Irish 'white side.' Seems that side had quite a history. Not necessarily 'legal.' Rum running and things like that.

Grandfather loved to hear his Irish grandfather and HIS brothers 'tell.'

One of those brothers was 'Uncle Harold', to grandfather.

This man, THE BRAVEST MAN Grandfather had EVER met. EVER!

(Unfortunately, not the SMARTEST…but the most FEARLESS).

He and his brother (Grandfather's Brother) worked for 'The Mob' (Mafia) during their younger days. The rum running included.

Uncle Harold stayed in it until the day he died. His grandfather matured out of it and become a 'decent' man.

Grandfather was Uncle Harold's 'kid' and both loved each other dearly.

This closeness, a man in his fifties and a boy less than ten, was so close, that Uncle Harold revealed many things to the younger. TRUSTING THIS SMALL BOY TO KEEP HIS MOUTH TOTALLY SHUT.

Things like money buried in his yard, (proved it too)…Under his house (Yes!)…his role in the Saint Valentines Massacre. *"It was the IRISH GANG I was in that did that, and a 'Jew' Gang that STILL gets accused of it,"* he'd say laughing. His gangs name was called, 'The Purple Gang', outta Detroit and Pontiac, Michigan.

Uncle Harold even had a hidden Thompson Sub-Machine Gun…and other types…revolvers on up, Hidden in a wall in his home. The Thompson HINTED as being one that was used in the Saint Valentine killings.

Grandfather had been at Uncle Herald's house as he built this hiding place. When done, a side handed 'pound' at a certain spot would make the wall 'door' slide open. Revealing all 'the hardware' behind it.

Uncle Harold wouldn't even let his WIFE in the room when this was being constructed! But he NEVER HESITATED letting his 'Little Son' IN.

An odd trust between the two, but one neither broke. Not till YEARS after 'Uncles' death did grandfather share. Better then 40.

Uncle Harold had 'served time' in prison. Several years…and never revealed some things concerning 'The Mob', the police wanted dearly to know.
This did not go unnoticed by them…'The Mob.'
In return, he was always 'provided' for.
That's where the 'hidden treasure' came in, and FROM.
Also a brand new black Buick, every two years. Like clockwork.

Uncle Harold never worked, but you'd never know it.

All grandfather would see him do, is drink bottle after bottle of whisky. He was an alcoholic. Hard Core. This eventually led to his death (and WHAT a STORY THAT has)!

Yes, grandfather was reminiscing and enjoying his memories. So too, where his listeners.

"To give you an idea as to HOW fearless and TOUGH he was, let me tell you a story that made The Detroit News headlines. He was helping a buddy in this friends bar in Detroit. Working the bar and till. This bar was well attended. Very popular. One of the busiest in the city.

On this particular night, two hooded men came in, guns in hand. Shots were fired into the ceiling as they shouted, *'THIS IS A HOLD UP. EVERYBODY ON THE FLOOR!'*

Uncle Harold just kept standing behind the bar.

He wasn't ABOUT to be ordered about, guns or not!

As one robber started collecting wallets and jewelry from those on the floor, the other came to Uncle Harold.

Pointing his gun at him, he said, *'This is a 38! Give me all the cash or YOU'RE DEAD!'*

Uncle Harold reached under the till. His hand now held a gun of his OWN!

Bringing it up, he pointed it at the robber and said, *'THIS is a 45! And You ARE Dead!'*

And pulled the trigger.

Uncle Harold was a crack shot. The robber died alright…with a 45 slug…

RIGHT BETWEEN THE EYES!

If I recall right (read the papers on all this), there was a shoot out with the other robber. That one killed by Uncle Harold as well.

So too, another person, caught in the crossfire. A waiter. Killed by the other shooter's gun.

This poor man had a young wife and two or three small children. So sad.

I think this happened in the mid 1950's, if any cares to do a search on it.

NO one messed with Uncle Harold!

I STILL Sure Miss Him."

Ho.

Uh Oh! I'm Outta Here!

The old man had accidentally stumbled in on a group of ladies. Mostly older. They were talking on today's kids 'Modern Clothing.'

"What do YOU think, Grandfather?"

He was trapped, How to get out of THIS…'Gracefully'…

"Well I see the boys haven't seemed to have learned how to measure inches…they keep getting their pants too big."

The woman laughed, "and what about the 'THONG'? Do you know what those are?"

"For feet, right?"

"No. I'm talking about the young ladies underwear."

"Oh! You mean: BUTT FLOSS!"

(THAT was…'Graceful'…enough.)

The Dream Catcher

The classroom had gone on a field trip to their Cultural Center Museum.
The museum had fascinated them.

"We saw many of our Ancestors things there, Grandfather. Did you know we had BONE NEEDLES? And the thread was from ANIMALS!"

"Yes. I know," he replied.

"Yeah," a boy excitedly exclaimed, "and in the shop you could BUY THINGS!"

"Did You?" he asked.

"Yup, I got a Dream Catcher! See!"

It was apparent the boy was pleased as he dangled it before Grandfather.

"Very nice, my grandson. Sure is a pretty thing. Do you know why our people HAD such?"

"No."

"Do you want too?"

All exclaimed, "Yes!"

"Alright, make yourself comfortable and I will tell you."

All set and ready, Grandfather smiled, then began, "These were made by our Medicine People. As a healing way. A TOOL.

When one was feverish and very ill, it was made ON THE SPOT, and hung above the head of the ill one.

Then certain prayers were said, calling the Great Spirit to help heal this person.

We of Medicine Know who does the healing of all. Thus, we go to 'Him.'

We also know there are bad spirits. Spirits that WANT to harm and make people ill. WANT nothing but bad.

These spirits truly exist and can be very powerful.

Yet none are as the Great One, which allows them to be. To EXIST!

THE GREAT SPIRIT RULES OVER ALL!

I do not speak lightly on this truth. People would be amazed at what they can't see. Maybe it's best they don't.

You children are not to worry about this, though. Just stay right in heart and love with our Creator and you'll always be safe. HO!"

The children were 'glued to their seats', as Grandfather spoke.

"These evil ones work their deeds in many, many ways. ALL to FEAR and CONFUSION to those they are working on…AND TOO, to their family and friends. THEY 'DOTE' ON FEAR. This makes them strong.

People should NEVER FEAR. For we are of the Great Creator. The 'Great Spirit.' ALL are of 'Him.' Everything we Taste, Touch, See, Smell, Hear, is by 'His' making. *God is in ALL things*.

Yet we Humans are of a special 'Making.' WE have been given 'His' abilities.
We can't BE 'Him', but we can be AS 'Him.'

Yes, we are special.

Ho.

The evil spirits try to make us think otherwise. They try to STEAL OUR POWER. This by giving illnesses, pains and hurts.

They try to wear us down.

Unfortunately, they are pretty good at their jobs. Many believe THEM over what our GODCREATOR has said.

Thus, the people become sick or get bad hurts.

They have FORGOTTEN!

However, we Medicine People have not. Therefore, we go to 'Him' to seek healings.

This is what YOU should do too.

As a Medicine Person, we are taught many things.

Taught, that certain plants have been given to man. To help in healings.

Taught what each plant helps with, how much to use, where to get them.

Taught at what AGE, of the plant, to 'take.'

We are also taught how to PREPARE them for their work.
We are taught that The Great Creator has made ALL nature to HELP, we called, Mankind.

Nature is a GIANT Pharmacy.

But our GREATEST 'Medicine' IS OUR MIND!

We Medicine People know this.

ALL of this.

So we ask The Creator, '*What should I/we do here, to help?*'

Sometimes it is easy. A 'common' problem. One we have seen many times. So we automatically do what is needed.
Sometimes it is hard…so we seek 'Him' automatically.

If you have a thorn in your finger, do you need to seek other than your other hand to pull it out?
Yet if it's rammed deeply within your finger, it is best to seek ANOTHER to help get it removed.

Illnesses are like that. 'Deeper.'

Yet Illnesses have a Spirit of evil behind them. Spirits that are trying to make us FEAR…and FORGET!

One of our 'Tools' is the DREAM CATCHER.

When we KNOW it is to be called on…MADE…we construct it WITH MUCH PRAYER!
This is not just 'show' or 'ceremonial.' IT IS TO EMPOWER THE GODLY 'SPIDER WEB' WE ARE MAKING! It IS like a SPIDER WEB.
A catcher of those of evil, that are within and without, of the sick person.

We Medicine People then funnel…actually ORDER, the Evil Ones to PASS THROUGH this WEB as they travel about.

It acts much like those Electric 'Bug Zappers', the whites have.

Because WE OF MEDICINE KNOW OUR STRENGTH, We KNOW these evil ones MUST DO as WE COMMAND. They MUST travel 'THROUGH' that Dream catcher WEB…and get ZAPPED!
TRAPPED!

We make this during the evening…towards the regular Sleeping Time of the patient, and then hang it over their bed.

IN THE MORNING, WE TAKE THIS TRAP DOWN, and dismantle it.

Leaving a STRING of 'Trapped Flies' (the evil spirits) on that long line.

We then DISPOSE of that string…and willow, in a safe way and in a safe spot. LOCKING THEM THERE…By our POWER Knowing AND THANKFULNESS PRAYER, TO THE CREATOR. There they remain, until ONLY WHEN THE CREATOR 'HIMSELF' RELEASES THEM!

There are many 'strings' buried in our Earth Mothers care. All over our Earth…'The Great Turtle.'

We here in America are not the only Medicine People. Others of other Countries have Medicine People also. They too, have their 'traps.'

Ho.

In time…the Time known as the 'GREAT DAY OF JUDGMENT', The Creator will release these entrapped evil spirits…and they AS WELL, will stand before 'Him' and know their Eternal Fate.

Until then they are safely TRAPPED…'wrapped as flies by a spider', on the Dream Catchers string.

THAT is what the DREAM CATCHER is about…And SHOULD ONLY BE USED and TO BE MADE FOR!"

HO!

Survival

They were out in the extreme heat. 'Hiking', at Grandfathers request. Five of them and him. ALL had water. ALL had used it EARLY too. Except 'Grandfather.' HE seemed immune to the scorching heat.
HIS water container more than half full yet.

"How do you DO that Grandfather, we are dying of THIRST and you're like the Ever Ready Bunny…you just keep going on and on…HOW?"
All had their heads and necks covered.

(Sun and Heat Stroke helpers.)

Grandfather was grinning slightly, as usual, his 'students' weren't PAYING ATTENTION! So he just let them suffer, until they SOUGHT.

Nothing like cracked lips and swollen tongues, to get one to thinking.

He turned around and said, "Look for a smooth small pebble. Pop it into your mouth and SUCK!"

"HUH?"

"It creates SALIVA, you can go a LONG WAYS without water, by doing so."

None had noticed that all this time he had anything in his mouth.

"Now, LOOK FOR TRACKS! Rodent tracks."

"WHY?"

"Just do as I say, you'll find out. Give a shout if you see any and STOP THERE. We'll then TRACK IT."

It wasn't long before a trail was located. Carefully Grandfather checked it for 'freshness.' Sure enough, a small mouse had been there just that morning. They followed.
Soon other tracks appeared. All heading in the same direction.

"Ah Ha! THIS is GOOD," he said, as they followed on.

True enough, it WAS good! FOR THEY LED TO A SMALL 'seep' OF…WATER!
Very small.

"Alright, who's the worse off?" he asked.
ALL wanted, but one WAS in worse shape!
He was led forward, knelt, and pressed his lips to this tiny wetness.
Not much there…but it helped.

"Alright, as we walk keep your eyes open for similar tracks. The Creators little four-legged ones KNOW how to survive in this heat. All WE have to do is LEARN HOW TO 'READ' NATURE! Let's go."

A half hour passed. No water tracking found.

"Nothing, Grandfather, now what?"

"Didn't I tell you to KEEP YOUR EYES OPEN? Aren't you PAYING ATTENTION? I said NATURE. YOU heard ONLY 'FOUR-LEGGED'! Look UP!"

"What?"

"BIRDS DRINK TOO!

SEEK and you will FIND! ASK and it will be GIVEN TO YOU! KNOCK, in PRAYER, until YOU GET YOUR ANSWER!

The GREAT ONE GIVES, ALWAYS! But 'He' HAS GIVEN YOU a BRAIN.

USE IT!"

Ho.

Learning In Advance

It was COLD. The old man and younger had just left their emergency shelter of the night. A fire was lit with the use of their ember Carrier…a horn filled with "duff" of semi-green wood shaving with a hot coal from the day before fire. Smoldering inside, it had kept well.
Their survival "tent" was of a small evergreen tree that had been broken off and laid one end high. Snow had been lavishly placed over the top and sides, insulating it.

Now they sat close to the small fire, small saplings in hand, building now needed snowshoes. Crude, but efficient, they would get them home safely.

Few know how to do this today.

The evening before, they had picked the "down" off old cattails at a nearby frozen pond. This they had stuffed within their outerwear. This was superior to the Goose Down normally used…though body sweat would compact it quickly. Then it would lose its isolative abilities. The trick was to walk slowly…not raising a sweat. Knowing its "secret," these two were set to go.

Another hot coal was placed into the hollow bison horn. Fire put completely out…and they were off. Each had put a charcoal marks right below their eyes. This to help keep sun glare from entering their eyes. It prevented snow blindness.

Shouldering their packs…they were off. Trading places along the way…each taking turns breaking trail…they eventually came to the large long lake they knew they would face. Each broke a stout long pole…deadwood…and took this in hand. These were held horizontally across their chests. If per chance they fell through the ice…it would straddle the hole and give support in getting out.

They had made sure the spot they left shore from had no creek entry…a weak place in ice.

Several hours later, they were home.
All this was done safely,
by
KNOWLEDGE!

HO.

Ice Fishing The Old Way

They were ice fishing. The old man showing his grandson. Dressed for the occasion, they were chopping holes with an axe of stone.
Time consuming, but the "old way." Their "poles" simply two sticks with line tied to one. The line made of plant fiber from the summer before. Each set of "poles" had a "Leader"…pulled from grandma's long hair. Hook was tiny sticks, hardened over hot stones. Each hook sharpened on both ends, And having a light "groove" between (this to tie on the leader). No weight was used, as there was no current to contend with here. Bait? Small grubs picked from plants that are hosts to such insects.

The chipped ice was scooped out with a bark "basket" on a long stick handle. All set the lines were slowly sent down. A "flasher" had been added to the lines just above the "hook." This of a broken fresh water clamshell with a hole to tie the "line" through.

THE FIRST "HIT!" Quickly the "hook" was set, with a slight jerk. The stick "hook" lodging in the fish's throat.
Up went the main pole stick…then caught with the other…back and forth. Until the fish emerged. A small perch.

The fish quickly froze when in the frigid air; Grandfather then took that fish and popped out its eyes. "More bait," he told his grandson. He also knifed off a strip of its hide. "Flasher," he said.

It wasn't long before they were heading home…a stringer of fish in hand.

Grandfather telling his young companion, "This spring I'll teach you how to use SPIDER WEBS to catch fish with."

The Funeral

He was watching a funeral. One of a number he had seen over his years.
It had always amazed him how he, and all, misses so much…knew so little.
He had witnessed a suicide once. Tried to save, but it was useless. The one doing didn't want to be saved and struggled away until it was over. He had cried at this.
Yes, all about him was wonderment.

This funeral was of FROGS!

One of theirs had apparently been stabbed by a shore bird. Probably a Heron, and escaped, only to die of shock and blood loss a short time later.

Its kinfolk had encircled its floating body, and then began a soft, soft croaking. A song of farewell to a loved one.

Gently they swam in a circle, front "hands" touching front hands; they created a water ebb that pushed the small, lifeless body to the banks long overhanging grasses. Concealing the deceased safely out of sight, then they SLOWLY swam away from the gravesite.

Yes, he had seen strange things. Heard of strange, similar oddities.
A goose shot, falling from the sky…its Life Mate crying franticly as she followed her love down, then, once the body hit the water, she landed and put a wing over his body as she cried, and cried, and cried.

The hunter, seeing, threw his shotgun into the swamp…never to hunt again.

The suicide witnessed, had been a robin. Swooping lower and lower, over the beautiful pond. Till it was low enough to dip its bill into the water. Three times, it dipped, and then landed, dipping its head, time after time, into the depths. Until it dipped no more.
Grandfather had tried to cast his fishing line across it as it did so. The bird saw this and flapped away. Till finally…it succeeded.

It drifted away, as Grandfather cried.

Yes, many things he has witnessed…and HEARD!

Trees, SCREAMING, as terrific winds bent them low to the ground. A spider, SCREAM, as a human, unseeing, crushed through its web...destroying.

Once he watched ants teaming up to outfox larger…"enemy" ants, who had raided their food supply.

They broke into small groups, taking turns rushing the larger. As the larger charged back, the others rushed in from behind and each grabbed what they could and took off! Placing their "booty" at a safe distance, they then returned and changed places with the first "diversion" group.

Time after time, until ALL the stolen food was safely back into their hands. Leaving the bigger, vicious "enemy," scurrying about, looking for what was no more.

Bigger…Meaner…but DUMBER!

And Grandfather laughed!

It had taken over an hour…but PERSEVERANCE had prevailed.

Grandfather left the funeral, once again contemplating on the marvels of life.
ALL had KNOWING. ALL had AWARENESS. All had love. Even the crows he had seen, saying farewell to one hit by a car…

Tobacco Causes Cancer? No!

He was at the doctors for his once a year check up. Stethoscope pressed against his back/lungs he was "breathing deeply" at her orders. To herself but aloud, she said, "I don't understand it."
"What don't you understand, my sister?" he asked.
She came to his side and looked up, (she was even shorter than HE).
"Friend, I've seen many patients that smoke. Most of those are DEAD…ALL the others are DYING. Every year you come in for your physical. Every year I check your lungs. Every year they are 'as clear as a bell.' Yet of ALL I know and knew, you smoke MORE than ANY of them. I DON'T UNDERSTAND IT!"

He gave a chuckle, and reached into his pocket saying, "I understand it"…as he pulled out his favorite smoke…a non-filtered Pall Mall.
She came in front of him, put her little fists on her little waist, and said, "Well! Would you mind EXPLAINING THAT TO ME?"

With a smile, he tapped out a cigarette from its pack.
"Honey, you claim you are a Christian, right?"

"You KNOW I am," (she was German Baptist and very devoted).
He looked into her eyes and said, "Buffalo Crap!"

She looked shocked.

"As a 'CHRISTIAN' you no doubt CLAIM to *'Believe in the Word OF God'* 100% Right?"

"Yes I DO!"

Again he said, "Buffalo Crap!"

AGAIN, she looked shocked.

(Almost as if she'd been slapped!)

"Honey, THESE DON'T CAUSE CANCER! YOU DO!"

"WHAT! Now explain THAT!"

"Lil sis…people respect you. You are well educated. You have spent YEARS learning your trade. You and others like you and Pharmaceutical Companies. ALL saying, *'SMOKING causes CANCER'* (and PAY THE POLITICIANS to 'back' them).

ALL says The SAME THING… *'You Smoke…YOU DIE!'*

The MASSES Believe that, and FEAR!

As you know, I too am Christian. But I am unlike YOU and OTHERS who make this claim.

I DO *'Believe the WORD Of God.'*

You, my sister, SPREAD FEAR. Those OTHERS spread FEAR, AND YOU MAKE MONEY from those who YOU have MADE F E A R!

The bible says, "The things I have FEARED have COME UPON ME!"

I do NOT WISH TO ACCEPT YOUR 'Feedings.' Your INSERTED FEARS.

I DO NOT FEAR!

You do NOT *'Believe the WORD of GOD'*…you BELIEVE YOUR OWN Mankind OVER the WORD of GOD. YOU go to Sweden to Ski as your patients go to six feet of EARTH!"

At this, she bowed her head, eyes closed. She was shaking her head 'no', slowly.
Then she looked up, eyes moist, and said, "Brother, over the years you have told me many strange things. I cannot honestly say I believe ALL you've told…But, YOU SURE MAKE ME THINK!"

In the Old Testament (Book of Job) it is written:
The things I FEARED have come upon me!

Evil Power Spot

He had been ordered to Quest at a Power Spot. One of BAD. He really didn't look forward to it, but orders were orders. A few days before he had gone in daylight and stashed his drinking water, then spoke to the area. Telling all Spirits, he'd be back soon.

Now it was time.
He drove to the spot. Feeling the bad 'vibes' the closer he got. It was close to nightfall. The 'Active Time' for such. Getting his hidden water, he chose a comfortable spot. There to stay the night, awake.
This time no fire was started or needed. Close to a full moon...and a warm summer evening. If chilled, a blanket to drape around him, on hand, was all that was needed.

THERE THEY WERE!

13 Long dead SORCERERS. All male. This had been their common meeting ground and each had vowed to stay, 'after.'
They were in a circle...'mumbling' their 'chant of darkness.'
Showing off to this lone, GOOD One. Occasionally one would stare at him...trying to insert fear.
13 against one. Or so they thought!

For as he had learned, he was NEVER 'Alone.' Surrounded by Angels and his Totem Angels...and to top THIS off...the GREAT ONE inside.

"If you've seen (know) ME, then you've seen (KNOW) 'my Father.'"

No, he wasn't alone at all! And they were about to find THAT out!

He spoke. Telling them his name and reason, he was there, "To Close this Spot and send you all home."

They LAUGHED! "YOU? Who are YOU, Old Man?"

"It doesn't matter WHO I am. What matters is WHO I am WITH...and *WITHIN* ME!"

These 13 were from a time Long before The Christ was brought to the people (in the ways of the whites). Perhaps even before He had come, long ago.

They really didn't know of this one, OR of His ability.

All they knew were their 'dark' ways.

Combined, the 13 aimed a 'Chant' at him. One designed to incapacitate.
IT BOUNCED BACK. Right at THEM!
FALLING THEM where they stood!
Stunned, they looked around in shock.
WHAT had HAPPENED?

The old one softly laughed at the sprawled ones.

"You do not go against ME, my brothers, but the CREATOR and the THREE that is HIM. His SON and SPIRIT are here. IN ME! YOU FIGHT YOUR OWN MAKER!"

"You are very lucky. I have the RIGHT to send BACK, what YOU SENT…WITH seven MORE Far WORSE than the ONE YOU SENT! You COULD have been 'hit' with EIGHT Black Powers! ALL OF WHICH I CAN ORDER to 'do'…Do you want to try again?"

"No!"

"That's a wise decision. Now SIT! And hear what I have to tell you.

You have stayed long enough. You have caused CENTURIES of trouble.

There will be NO MORE!

You are DONE! That's THAT!

Now though, you each have a choice. One only, EACH ONE of you can make, PERSONALLY.

The choice is up to You, and You and You…

(Pointing and saying to each.)

Here is your choice. It will be given THREE TIMES ONLY. Either you choose…or I DO!"

He then told them of Big Brother. Why He came, What He did, and WHO HE WAS.

"Now, because you have 'packed' to stay together and continue to work 'as one'…Long after you should have gone on…You are now faced with this: GO TO CHRIST, Asking FORGIVENESS…or to your Dark Lord.

You have experienced your dark Lord's power. You have used it to and for your SELF. YOU ARE WRONG IN THE SIGHT OF THE MAKER! You WILL go to Hades IF YOU DON'T GET RIGHT WITH CREATOR GOD! There you will remain, LOCKED in it WITH HIM, until The Great One calls ALL before 'Him.' THEN you will know your Eternal Fate. Aho?"

He then repeated this two more times.

“There are your three ‘tellings’… I tell you true:

TONIGHT YOU HAVE FACED A POWER FAR GREATER than that of your Dark One.
You have found what that power DOES.

YOU CAN’T BEAT HE WHO DWELLS WITHIN ME.”

Yes. They HAD seen. One Old man against 13 STRONG Sorcerers…and those 13 went down like a ROCK when they went against him.

They were then left ‘to contemplate’… Grandfather leaving to give them time to consider.

About an hour later, he was back. The full ‘force of 13’ now treated him with the GREATEST of respect.

THEY Decided. Grandfather didn’t need to.

Since that time, this evil place is as any part of nature. Serene and a Wonderful place to be around.

Ho.

(Grandfather has done a number of these spots around Canada and the USA.)

Grandfather and the Kids

There were three boys with Grandfather…learning.

Though grandfather TAUGHT…he seemed to do more OBSERVING of the three.

This did not go unnoticed by one.

He asked, “Grandfather, why are you just sitting and watching us?”

The old one smiled and replied, “so I can learn, son.”

“Learn? From US?”

“Yes son. Your actions remind me of MY youth. I don’t want to forget. It keeps me young, my son…watching.”

The boy looked quizzical.

“My lil’ brother, remember this, WHEN A TEACHER STOPS LEARNING FROM HIS STUDENTS…That teacher is then of Ego and has become nearly Useless. When one stops thinking AS A CHILD…that one has then limited him or herself.

NEITHER shows Wisdom OR Promotes it! Aho?”

Fire Making

"How do you make fire, grandfather?"

"Bic Lighter."

"THAT'S Not INDIAN!"

"Indian, doesn't mean DUMB, son."

"Well, can you show me the OLD way?"

"Sure. Got a match?"

"Why!"

He was almost demanding. Arrogant. This young boy man, as he came before the old one, "Why do these things HAPPEN?"
(Not showing the respect of even calling the old man "Grandfather")
Quietly the old man looked up, "What 'things' are you referring too, my son?" the old one asked.

"Well," said the boy man, "Last night we had nothing to eat, NONE of us!"
"And yesterday all we had was a handful of dry, old berries. We're HUNGRY! WHY DO THESE THINGS HAPPEN?"

The old man sat quietly…It was time to teach.

"It is a Gift," he said.

"A GIFT? A Gift! What do you mean Grandfather!?

(Remembering his manners.)

The old man looked up, smiling slightly.
The bait was taken. Yes, it was time to teach, "My 'son'," said the old one softly, "Yes, you're hungry. Yes, we all are...And as I said, it is a gift. A GIFT to REMEMBER. Sit and I will tell you and perhaps help you understand."

The young one sat.

"You see my son, you give thanks when your belly is full. You sit about the lodge, filled and content. *'Ah, life is GOOD'*, you say. But you do not thank properly. You have become complacent. This is not you alone, but you and most of the others.
Yes, you are content. Your stomach is filled. It feels good! So you say, *'Thank you, oh Great Spirit'*, day after day, you feel good. The plants, four-legged ones, and the Scaled and Feathered ones are plentiful and have been easy to find. *'THANK YOU CREATOR'*, you say. Day after day, you fill, and give 'thanks.' Is this not so?"

"Yes, this is so Grandfather."

"Aho. Now think my son. Does not that 'thanks' then become more mere WORDS, then MEANING?" The boy man thought.

"Yes Grandfather, it is so."

"Aho. Well, you see my son…The Great One knows. This one knows your 'heart' and 'He' hears, your words…but hears fast losing TRUE 'Thanks.'

'He' sees this, for 'He' is very, very wise. 'He' knows you are growing fat…and fast forgetting WHY that fat has come.

You are becoming complacent…and your WORDS are mere WORDS, Not 'HEART.'

'He' sees this and says: ***He is no longer truly thankful, he's just FULL. I must now return him to TRUE thanks.***
Thus, 'He' takes away the meat. The Plants. The great fish slow their migration. The rabbits cease to breed profusely…Times become HARD!
You see son, He 'GIFTS' YOU in this manner. 'He' BRINGS BACK THE REMEMBRANCES. The 'Good Times.' And teaches you HE is THE GIVER. That 'He' wants your TRUE 'THANKS'…ALWAYS!

It is easy to say 'THANKS' when your belly is full. Easy, too, to FORGET in time, 'He' who GIVES. Easy to say WORDS, but forget the TRUE MEANING of that word.
Now perhaps you understand. Now perhaps you can tighten your sash and speak to This Great One, in TRUE thanks. And APOLOGIZE for not understanding…and THANK 'HIM' FOR THE GIFT that HELPS YOU TO FOREVER be THANKFUL.

Perhaps..."

The boy sat silent, contemplating the words the old one had spoken.

He arose…and left…a Man Boy.

Ho.

Sky Watchers

There was a little boy, born in the Country of the Snow. You'd call him ESKIMO. They call themselves THE PEOPLE. Inuit. This boy's father had left his mother alone while he went hunting walrus. He never returned. She hung his old mukluks within the ice dome house her husband had made. This to see if her husband still "walked," (was alive). They did not swing or move. After three days, she knew her husband had left his spirit and returned to the Sky People. She mourned him, as he was her heart mate of long standing. She was alone. Her son yet curled within her. Times were hard. Little food was on hand. All of the blubber long ago eaten, except what was used in the oil lamp. That she guarded carefully, as it was Light and heat…as well as the only source upon which to cook. She had fish stored in a catch, yet fish filled only the hunger. It did not give fat to the body. Slowly she was starving, eat as she would. She managed to hang onto life, until her baby was born. As the wailing one cried, she bit the umbilical cord and tied it off, then put the little one in her fur blanket. She rubbed his nose…(an Inuit kiss), and closed her eyes.

Then, she too went to the Sky People.
Now only a tiny baby lived…alone.

This tiny one, Un-cleaned by his mother, laid beside her cuddled within the fur. Soon he became hungry. His small cry reaching to the Sky People. They Heard…and looked down.

Seeing the "all alone"…they named him "AnnuLic" (ALL ALONE).
"What should we do? For we have his father and mother here with us, he has no one. Think. For this one needs to know life. This one can become known amongst his people. We must help him. His igloo is far from any others of his kind. We must help him." This they said among themselves.
After much thought, The Elder, the LEADER who was all-wise, within their group said, "Let us give BEAR a dream…and send bear too him. She is fresh with cub…AND milk. She has the mother love needed for AnnuLic." And this is what they did.

Far below slept the mother bear…and she dreamed. She dreamed of a crying Cub, not her own…but needing help. She awoke and instantly led her cub from the ice windbreak they were sleeping behind.
Lifting her nose, she sniffed the air. Her ears erect for sound. THERE! THERE IT WAS! THE CRY! She hurried towards it. Though the way was long, and she and her cub child were very hungry, she went on. Following the small "mew" of one growing weaker by the minute.
The wind and drifting snow carried the human child's cry across the barren land.
In time, the she bear and cub arrived…ENEMY CAMP! THE HUNTERS! She thought. Her hair raised in the danger of it. Yet the cry within was anxiously calling out in desperation. It spoke "I am dying…I am dying."

She sat…looking, sniffing, and hearing. She sensed only the one. The child. When she was satisfied all was safe…she approached the ice hut and began pawing at its curved side.
Her own child trying "to help."
In time, she had an opening large enough to reach in, head and all. There before her lay the enemy "cub" and FOOD! She pawed out the cold body of the human Childs mother and partook. Sharing with her child. She ate little, as there was a more important thing to do. The human child. Gently she pawed him out… and pushed him next to her breast. The warmth of her nipple attracted the baby and it began to suckle. In this way, mother helped mother. The Great Circle of Life went on.

To the reader, this may seem terrible, but it is the way, the way up there. You do what you must, to survive.
So mother fed mother…and both mothers became one, for the sake of their two "cubs."

Do you understand?

In time, the human "cub" gave growth. Always pressed to the side and belly of its new mother. She would nuzzle this "furless one" in constant rotation, to keep it warm. In time too, this one grew immune to the cold…for it thought it was BEAR…and clothed. It was MIND THOUGHT that allowed this to be…and the watchers. The Sky People watched. Ho

As time went by this child grew as BEAR…hunting as BEAR…swimming as BEAR…thinking as BEAR. This one saw the short warmth of summer…and the many, many long nights of winter, and grew and grew.

In time, AnnuLic became a handsome, strong, WILD…Man Bear. This Man Bear was seen by others of its own kind, but rarely. Stories began. Until to this day, people claim to see the ALL ALONE One, AnnuLic. And HE became a legend within his land. To see him was to have Great Luck. For he came to mean "YOU TOO CAN SURVIVE, for the GREAT ELDER and His of the SKY PEOPLE ARE WATCHING…AND CARE!"

And so it is.

Ho.

A Restrictive Nuisance

"Grandfather, I've tried, as you've said: Contemplation early in the morning. I have no problem with the EARLY part. I am a Trucker. But for the life of me, I don't seem to get into the CONTEMPLATION part. I don't know why. Random thoughts just don't seem to come TO contemplate ON. Am I doing something wrong?"

"I see your wearing a cap. Is that common for you?"

"Yeah, I wear it even in the sleeper at times."

"Brother, the next time you go into contemplation, try it WITHOUT the cap. You'll find quite a difference. For some reason, it seems to RESTRICT 'contact.' Particularly the Bill part of the cap. That seems to SHADOW OUT thoughts from above and within to your INNER CHAKRA 'EYE.' This Chakra Spot is located just slightly above your eyebrow level and directly in the center there. It's your INNER EYE Sending and Receiving center.

In many ways, our bodies are walking Radio 'Stations.' Have you ever had snow build up on your Satellite Dish and block off the Signal?"

"Yes."

"Well, that's what that Cap and Bill is doing to you, THE Spiritual 'Satellite Dish.' It's odd, but it seems ANY tight Head Band is restrictive. The cap and bill on the top of the list, though. Aho?"

"I'll give it a go, grandfather. Thank you."

"Aho."

Fun For Little Money

The old one had found a pair of water skis at a "cheap shop."
With several children about him as watchers/helpers, he began building a dog sled and an "Indian Toboggan." Knowing before hand, the kids had asked their parents for sandwiches and "goodies."

"This is something I did as a young man," he explained. "I first started running Sled Dogs with our three family pets. Cocker Spaniels! Good little pullers, but they'd 'snow ball' up round their paws. Made it hard on them but they loved the adventure anyway. We never ran them more than a mile and a half. Had to stop and break the packed snow off a lot on the way. Didn't want them hurting. You make SURE your animals are well tended…ALWAYS! Aho?"

"Yes Grandfather."

"That snow ices up between their toes, not just on the fur. You've GOT to make SURE you clean that out. GOT IT?"

"Yes."

He then began the dog sled, with small diameter rope, several Eye Screws, a drill, screwdriver, two low blocks of wood in some five 'eyes' per side…to just over half way to back of 'sled.' The blocks of wood were glued and screwed and a hole through the sides of each was made.

"This will hold the handle," he said.

"Bring the handle."

They did.

He fit the handle to the wood blocks and screwed them in, using washers on each side on each block. "Hold this," he commanded to one.
The boy holding had stepped on the 'tail'…Grandfather then positioned the tilt of the handle to the boy's best hold, tightening it there.

"One foot to ride, one foot to kick."

Then came the rope. This he threaded from front to back…up onto the handles cross piece, wrapped there, then down to the single Eye Screw in back. This was one piece of 'line', pulled taught, then tied. He wrapped the ends with electrical tape.

"DONE!"

And there it sat. Ready for the first good snow, tow ropes and dogs.

"Now, lil' brothers and sisters…when that snow is about to fall, I want each of you to bring me an old pair of jeans and your dog. SAVE YOUR OLD JEANS. They will make your dog harnesses!
Aho?"

"Aho!" In unison.

"Let's take a break and then get onto building the toboggan."

About an hour later, they were at it again. Leg and foot grip removed from the water ski…hole in nose…and some ten screw eyes per. Side (on top) and one in back, rope threaded and tied off.

"Well kids, that's it. Two winter things in less than six hours. This toboggan is a 'shorty' compared to our ancient ones. Yet still the same thing. This will follow you like a puppy. It will slide through thick willows or ANYWHERE you want to go. It is very narrow, as you can see. Also, as you can tell, it's not a 'Man carrier', but a WINTER GEAR CARRIER. If loaded and gear tied properly…HEAVY THINGS at the WIDEST place! And all no HIGHER THEN TEN INCHES…it will be almost IMPOSSIBLE to tip over! If there is a problem with this, it's that it's SLICK!

IT <u>WILL</u> RUN YOU DOWN if you're not careful! As you've seen, I put a BIG screw eye in back. There's room to thread another line there. Thus, you're BEHIND it when going downhill. You won't need to wait for snow with this. Simply wait for a good RAIN. Try it on the wet grasses and mud. It will be good practice for you. These are for ALL of you. Remember that! You ALL helped make them, so you will ALL be users of them. I don't want to hear any quarreling over these! SHARE. SHARE! Aho?"

They all shook their heads.

With smiles on face they departed to their homes…

"Grandfather," had taught again…

Creator/You/Healing

The elders were speaking within their own setting. The Old Wakȟáŋ/Medicine Man amongst them. At a lull, he quietly spoke up.
"I have sat here listening to all your wisdom. Indeed, you HAVE much wisdom! IT IS GOOD! Yes, it is good. I wish the younger ones would listen. Still, there is more…MUCH more…then what I have heard. Forgive me please, for appearing to be 'wiser' then you here. PLEASE, this is not my intent, my Brothers and Sisters. Aho?"

"Aho," they replied in unison.

"I'm old, as are we here all are. Some older than myself. Each of us have MANY moons of prayer and contemplation behind us. Yet I am perplexed that I have not heard Who We ARE. Am I the only here who has found that EACH is ALONE? That ALL others do NOT exist."

They looked, 'Questioning.'

"I have found ALL ABOUT ME…is…ME! EACH Incident…good or bad…an OUTREACH of something DEEP within MYSELF. That even YOU are a REFLECTION, of my DEEPEST Inner…ME. With this knowledge, I am able to make peace when Strife comes. For to me, it is OUR CREATOR SHOWING me that, DEEP INSIDE, I am NOT HAPPY…with 'HIM'! 'HE' shows me this…by the actions of others about me. At times, I am joyful. OH how THAT feels GOOD! When this occurs, I knew deep within…I am at Peace with 'Him.' Thus, I am at peace within myself. When I am grated by other's actions…I am not at peace inside. I'm not in right standing before Him. Am I the only one who has seen this?"

By the looks on everyone's faces, he was.

The old one sighed.

"Hmmm (he quietly expressed)… again I say Please forgive me. I do not mean to be forward. My conclusion is this: EVENTS AROUND ME are as a BAROMETER. I can TELL how I stand before the Creator, simply by knowing how to 'read' my barometer. My Actions and Reactions to any given event...If I find myself Angered…THERE'S A STORM BREWING Inside me. Trouble ahead. I MUST RUN FOR COVER…Under 'His Wings', and get/be Safe. If I feel GOOD, it is as a beautiful Spring Day. All is well INSIDE me. I AM AT PEACE WITH (IN) The Creator.

Has no one here seen this?"

Outside The Box

Grandfather had been called by a Christian neighbor. One of her horses was injured and she wanted to know how it took place. His grandson, (one in Medical Training) went with him. This ten years old boy was already good at "Nature Speak" and Time Travel. He wanted to go "to practice." This was good. Ho.

They arrived to a find the middle aged filly with a poultice well swaddled on a hind leg. Her friend (another filly), standing close by, head over the stable door…"worrying."

The owner and the two greeted them both as they entered.

Grandfather had worked with these two horses before and they both enjoyed his visits.

"Hello, sweetheart. Screwed up again, huh?"

(She looked sheepish and Thought Replied "Yes.")

"What happened?"

Instantly she showed him a picture of the event. At the same time Thought Saying, "We were playing."

They were "horsing around"…chasing each other about. Snow and mud in the paddock. She had twisted her leg in a fast turn.

BOTH horses said, in unison, "It was an accident."

All this via Mind Thought.

These two horses were often "in trouble." Real "cards." The injured one the leader…the other the follower. Together, they had many "adventures" that drove their caretaker/owner "up a wall!"

Grandfather asked the filly, "Do you have any idea how long it will be before you're well again?" She replied, "About three weeks."

Animals can often "pre-tell." They seem to have a Godly foreknowledge.

"Want me to look at it and see if I can help speed it (healing) up?"

"It hurts."

Grandfather showed her (Mind picture) of what he would do: merely light touching the wrapping on her lower injury.

"OK."

He told the owner what he was about to do. She came back with a worried warning:, "She'll strike out! She's touchy!"

Grandfather and his grandson (Sky) both knew better…as both had heard her reply.

"No, she'll hold."

He then started gently rubbing his hand from the whither to the hurt spot. This to show the horse where he was at ("No surprises this way, Sky.")

Gently feeling around the swaddling cloth, he could feel heat emitting from the inside of the leg. Swollen and "hot."

Telling her and owner, "I'm going to release a lot of this heat. Cool the area down. This will help speed up the healing process."

The filly stood stone still, knowing grandfather had only good in his ways.

(Much to the owner's surprise.)

He then prayed to "Papa," asking for the ability to transfer the heat into his hand, and trade from that hand a cooling effect to the area.

"Oh, that feels GOOD. DO IT AGAIN!" the filly thought out. Grandfather laughed, Sky smiled. He did it again. Then was told, "That's enough," by The Great Physician. He ceased, as ordered.

"OK honey, that's 'it.' Best I can do. How long now (to healing fully)?"

"Maybe just two weeks now. My 'feet' are cold. Can S…(Owner) put down some hay for me to stand on?"

He explained to the owner the need. She agreed. A full bail of straw would be placed thickly, along one side of the small stable room, so the horse could back there, resting the hoof on insulation from the bare, cold, Earth. The filly knew her (owner's) thoughts and was thankful. The horse then asked Sky to scratch a particular spot on her head, just below and between her ears area. He did so, as she lowered her head for him. She was in ecstasy. It felt so "GOOD."

The owner saw this and said, “THAT’S HER FAVORITE SPOT to be scratched!”

This too amazed her.

“HOW do you DO IT? How do you TALK to ANIMALS?”

This Christian woman had started out as one considering Grandfather as “of the devil” years before. Over time that had changed. She had watched and saw only well (Go (o) d) during her watching. Slowly she was “coming around.” To the point, she now didn’t hesitate to ask for his help.

“Dad” had arranged this through various means…mostly by her animals.

Her love for them made her reach out, despite her earliest opinion.

It was Go (o) d.

Ho.

He told her, “You must think ‘Outside the box.’ Scripture tells, ‘Thoughts are Real’…Thus when I ‘get a thought’ from something, in this case, your horse, I accept that as FROM THE HORSE, and go from there. I’m just relying on the truth of The Creators Word. Never known HIM to lie. Hon, you Christians do not fully believe the Bible. You SAY you do, but SHOW you DON’T. Think it’s time to change, don’t you?”

The Nurse

A nurse had heard Grandfather knew how to stop "Phantom Pain." (This happens when an amputated body part "acts" as if it's still "there"…itching, etc.). She wrote asking how…as they (and white doctors) are taught in their training it's "impossible" to ever stop.

His reply:

"It's easy, really. People have three levels of consciousness. The first the most common. Second, the 'sub-conscious.' Few are aware we have a VERY DEEP, third conscious. We call this 'The Deep, Deep' conscious. It is this that we stop the Phantom Pain in.

This DEEP, DEEP cannot accept that, that it was born with, is now no longer there. In this belief, it creates itches/cramps/etc., to convince your two Upper Consciousness that THEY are 'NUTS.' *'See, I'M STILL HERE,'* is 'sent' to those other two.
The trick is to CON the DEEP, DEEP it is Right, and you (other two) were 'mistaken.'

Thus, if the missing part itches/etc., SCRATCH IT/MASSAGE IT/etc,. AS IF it WERE 'still there.'

Leg or arm gone? 'PLAY' that you are 'tending' to the spot giving trouble. Massage the WHOLE 'leg', etc. AS IF IT WERE THERE!

This then stops the 'Phantom' immediately. The DEEP, DEEP says *'I TOLD YOU SO!'* then stops.

Two years after the toe amputation, the 'toenail' (Deep, Deep) of one who had had the toe removed, began saying, *'My Nail needs trimming.'* The 'Phantom' had returned in this 'toenail' manner. The cure was simply getting a toenail clipper and 'trimming' the nail that was no longer there. DONE!

The white doctors and nurses should have a required class in the NATURAL ways of the Medicine People.

Where they are trained to Mask or Remove…We are trained to cure 'as is.' It is an extremely rare case to amputate a portion of a body. Many things we know, that you don't. Cancers are curable. Diabetes. Rheumatism. Third degree burns. Death. Comas. Blindness. Alzheimer's. Gays. Many things.

YOU GIVE UP TO SOON.

When these things are cured…after YOU have given up, You call them 'Miracles.' We don't. We call this…KNOWLEDGE. FORGOTTEN, by most! Ho!"

The Wild Coyote

Grandfather had a "touch" with nature. Be it a cloud, Mountain, stone or snake…you name it, he and they, would converse.

On one occasion, he was on a long walk. As he strolled along, something caught his eye. "What WAS that," sped through his mind.
Whatever it was, it stopped him in his tracks.

He stood staring over the area the "intrusion" had come from.
Just as he was about to stop his search, AGAIN something appeared "out of place." A slight MOVEMENT.

There, many yards before him, laid a mature coyote. Its ear had twitched!

It was about 250 yards from him, but NOT from Freeway traffic.

Thinking it might be injured, he sent his thoughts to the animal. Asking if it was OK. No reply, other than both ears now were towards him. He was being "picked up."

He then mind told the wild four-legged one that he meant no harm and was coming down to check on him. "Fear not," he sent. He then proceeded to make his way down the slope to where it was laying.

As he got closer, he started audibly and quietly speaking to it. At the same time making sure he showed no teeth (a sign of aggression).

He sat less than an arm's length from it. Easily within touching distance. The coyote watching intently…more "quizzical" then worried. There was no fear between the two…no anger…No *"I want to harm you,"* thoughts from either one.

Grandfather asked, "Are you hurt?"

(No.)

"Are you sure? For possibly I can help you if you'd like."

"No, I'm fine."

"What are you doing here so close to the Highway?"

"Resting and warming in the sun."

"Oh, I see. I'm sorry to disturb you, my brother. Please forgive me."

The coyote grinned (as some dogs do) and then sat up…stretched…and yawned. Looking directly into grandfather's eyes, he mentally laughed. He then thanked him and turned around to return to the hunt, slowly walking up the hill.

There he stopped, turned towards grandfather, sat, and looked back at the friendly two-legged, grinned again, and trotted off.

BOTH had enjoyed their encounter.

Sky's Question

Grandfather's youngest grandson had just returned from a Time Travel trip. He had been to Russia, looking for Saber Tooth Tigers. He had located his goal. (This was his second trip on this particular type animal…both successful).

The difference was, this time he had found a mother with two young cubs.

"Grandpa," he asked "I WANT ONE! Can I go in PHYSICALLY and bring one back?"

"It can be done, son…but I won't teach this. It's too dangerous to be Physical in the past."

"Aaaaw, PLEASE?"

"No!"

"It is too tempting to 'play' with the past. Changing the NOW to a different Parallel Plane. ANY playing changes the Time Line of the NOW...It could mean YOU won't get BORN…or many others. You are young, son, WAY too young to do so wisely. Even most ADULTS act as a 'Not Thinking Youth' in doing so. So you will remain always in Spirit on these trips. If the Creator wants you to learn…let HIM teach this...No, son, I WILL NOT!"

"Grandpa, what about the future? Is that OK?"

"Yes. Up to the third day at the most, only. Best, for the Tomorrow, only. That is the day most related to today. On the third, there may be uncertainty to what you see. After the third day, you can never know what Time Line 'frame' you are seeing. ALL you see there, IS, but May be of a Parallel time."

"Can you go in THERE in Physical?"

"All things are possible when In 'Him.' Mankind is limited to only the three 'Can't Do/be that' I've told you of before. So, yes, I suppose you can."

"Have you ever done it?"

"No. That's one I've only gone 'in Spirit.' Time traveling to see what Tomorrow may bring. I then change my 'course of the day' by sidestepping any troublesome event the next day, when I see it coming.
Occasionally there IS seen trouble 'ahead', but generally it's a common 'so so' day. That, I let run without interference."

"Do you Time Trip every day grandpa, to tomorrow?"

"No son, I hardly ever do so."

"Why?"

"I like surprises, Sky. I only do this 'Present Opening' if I'm concerned over a matter that is in today. The rest of the time I let The Creator lay out 'His script.' This gives me new adventures to learn from."

"YOU COULD WIN THE LOTTERY!"

"Yes, I Could."

"Why don't you do THAT then?"

"Son, I'd rather let 'Dad' handle what 'He' wants when it comes to riches. Too often, I've seen money as a door that slams shut a person's Oneness to 'Him.' When they were 'in need,' they were constantly on their knees. Asking for help. When given ABUNDANTLY, too often they get off their knees. The money replaces God. I don't EVER want that, with me. 'He' is worth Far More to me than riches. It's too great a temptation and not worth the 'price'."

"But You're WISE..."

"Well, wise enough to not allow my Oneness with 'Him' to be lead astray, for a short time of Earthly 'pleasures.' No, I prefer it the way I'm doing it. Aho?"

Grandfather Loses Weight

He was five feet six inches tall and 293 pounds! He had gone to this weight to show his wife what she was doing to herself. She was being a "bit" too "weighty" herself. It did no good. She continued on her path.

He had done all he could. So it was time to get back to where he belonged.
It took awhile but his determination was strong. How had this been done?

I chose my favorite food of No sugar content. I LOVE HOT DOGS! So that's ALL I ate. Breadless. Simply boiled, some mustard, catsup and chopped onions on a plate. Stab, dip, Eat. Breakfast/lunch/dinner. Day after day. Until I went to my desired weight. 169 pounds...Believe it or not, I S T I L L Love Hot Dogs!

I've tried the ATKINS Diet way also. GREAT results, but would take too long for me on this particular weight loss. Still, LOTS one can eat on that! LOVE THAT one TOO. Just right for those who can't "take" the monotony of just one food type. I'd recommend it without a moment of doubt.

There's another, too. A "Medicine Way." Using KU. This is SUPER FAST for a QUICK weight loss "need" of just a few pounds. Taught my wife and she dropped some 3 or 4 pounds in two and a half days…while eating as she usually did. Surprised her doctor no end!
He asked her if she had fasted. "No." Exercised? "No."

"Well, how DID you do it?" She said she just shrugged her shoulders.
At the time, she didn't want to tell any that her husband was a Medicine Man, so wouldn't share. Feeling it "was of the devil." Took her several years to see it wasn't.

Women!

Sheeessh.

Telling Time

The "Old One" had an uncanny way of knowing how much time was left before sundown. Often able to "nail it" within a three minute "spread."

His apprentice had noticed this and asked how he could do this.

"You see me raise my hand outstretched before me, right?"

"Yes. Keeping the sun out of your eyes…"

Grandfather laughed.

"No. I'm looking to find how long we have before darkness sets in.

Have you noticed I hold my hand horizontally?"

"Yes. Every time."

"Well, I place my fingers on the horizon…be it far off or at the trees or hill the sun is dropping towards. Grandfather sun will first rest his bottom on that horizon. Then quickly go behind it. Darkness.

To do this *'How long do I have before it's dark'*…place the side of your little finger at the very top of that horizon. All fingers rest on the sides of the lowest ones. Count the fingers from the horizon to the base of the sun. You may need to use two hands, one finger resting on top of the upper finger of the first hand. DON'T USE THE THUMB in any of this.
Now count how many fingers there are from the lowest (horizon) to the top (suns base).

EACH FINGER REPRESENTS five MINUTES!

Add up the fingers and multiply these by five. You then have a very close Darkness Time figured out. You can add perhaps two minutes until the TOP of the sun goes beyond the horizon (If you need a VERY CLOSE time knowing). Aho?"

The Jews/The Example

Grandfather knew many People worldwide. This included those of the Hebrew Nation.
As is common, many ask questions. Some of those Hebrews have asked why "they" have so many "woes."

"We are a God Based Nation. We keep the sacred laws and Rules. Yet we are constantly harassed, hated, and warred upon. We have had Holocaust, Constant attacks from our neighbors around us and we seem to be hated worldwide…yet WE follow the ONE GOD. WHY?"

Perhaps they asked the wrong person. Grandfather pulls no punches.

"Why? Read your own Good Book. The Old Testament. Your ancestors had the Great One as their Leader, once. Then one day they went to 'Him,' asking to have 'Him' step down from their Leadership and trade for a MAN. 'He' warned them what that would bring.

They didn't care. They wanted one THEY could see. THEY could talk face-to-face with. Someone like *'All the OTHER Nations had'*…a MAN! Therefore, Papa gave them their will. 'He' stepped down. It was from there on in, that your race started having troubles.

YOU HAVEN'T ASKED 'HIM' BACK ON THE THRONE SINCE!

You can Pray and Obey 'rules' and bob your head before the Wailing Wall till ALL HELL FREEZES OVER…and still have your troubles.

You got what you asked for…and thus reap the rewards.

Don't blame GOD. Blame only YOURSELF!
HE WARNED YOU.

Now, Change it…or quit your belly aching! Up to you."

Escape

Some have asked about escaping what appears to be very close at hand, "CAN WE?"

"My Gosh! After all I've told you, you STILL don't comprehend. WE DON'T NEED TO ENTER THIS TIME. If we, AS A WORLD MASS, will Get RIGHT with the Creator…IT WILL STOP, IMMEDIATELY!"

"Yes, we understand that. It doesn't look like the world will though! So, how can one ESCAPE?"

"Granted, it looks like it will go on. Then, there are those who think they'll escape by Ascension. Might. But not BEFORE, or while 'just in.' This WILL be! Towards The END. Many, many will die in their 'hopes,' if I'm right."

"What if THEY are right?"

"Frankly, I'd rather be ready for the Worst and HOPE for the better. Smarter, that way. Aho?

There ARE 'the ROTTEN MOUNTAINS' though. Scripture speaks of one. There in Jerusalem. There are others about our mother as well. Many of our people know of these spots. Mountains, filled with caves and tunnels. They will run to those when the time is right."

"Will they survive?"

"Probably, SOME. Earthquakes will no doubt 'do in' many, though. Those that don't go deep enough."

"Where ARE these places?"

"Around."

"Can you tell us?"

"Could. Won't. The reason being, most, if not all of you, will run 'in Fear.'
THAT'S NOT the way to Safety! You go because you are TOLD to go…and WHEN you are told to do so. This, by THE CREATOR. THEN you will be Safe.

Your only TRUE 'Safety' IS BEING RIGHT, with 'HIM.'

CONNECT! And I'd recommend you do so starting RIGHT NOW.

I'd also recommend you do this NOT BECAUSE OF FEAR! Do it because of YOU KNOW YOU NEED 'HIM'…in WANT TO, of LOVE! Because you KNOW 'He's' there. That you KNOW 'He' cares! And you want to EXPERIENCE THIS LIVING ONE, Personally!

THAT is the Connection way of PURITY…not of FEAR.

It is in THIS way a TRUE CONNECTION TAKES PLACE!

HUNGER TO KNOW 'DADDY.'

' He' will take care of you. Aho?"

The Strange Odor

Grandfather was a Medicine Man. That means exactly that.
A North American Indian: DOCTOR.

His ways differed from the "Civilized" ("White") Doctor "ways"…even from the "Traditional" ways. But he knew his stuff. "The Way of Purity" he had learned involved "traditional" AND a number of "White" ways. He had learned Chiropractic methods, as well as many other doings of many "types." His knowledge, extensive. Often he was called for help on Migraine Headaches. This more often than not cured by upper spinal adjustment. A matter of a minute or three, to stop.

Once he was called to see what a "strange Odor" was about and see if he could rid the house of this.

Asking and receiving "Go" from the Creator; he arrived at an older home. Not rundown. Well tended yard and house. The moment he entered, a strong, sickening odor hit his nostrils. The house REEKED of this. He had encountered this before, though it was a rarity.

"What IS it, sir? Can you 'cure' it?" The white homeowner asked.

"Yes. But first allow me to ask a few questions. This will help."

They sat.

"Who lives here please?"

"Well, me and my husband, our three children…and mom."

"Your mother? How old is she?"

"Seventy-six."

"When did this odor start? Was it recently?"

"It started about two years ago."

"Have all of you lived together since getting the house?"

"No. Tom and I bought it about nine years ago, when we were expecting our third child...We needed more room. This smell wasn't here then. Otherwise we'd never have bought it."

"Hmmm. Then your mother joined you?"

"Yes. She isn't stable on her feet and needs watching, so we had her come here. She had fallen too often and the last time she broke her hip."

"Well, that's commendable. It is the right thing to do."

The woman smiled. He could see she cared much about her mom.

"Please, show me about the house. All rooms. All floors."

They started on the main floor. Grandfather breathing in deeply in each room. It was the living room that had the stronger of the odd smell. Then they went to the basement. There the Odor was barely detectable. Finally, they went upstairs to the bedroom areas. One room in particular was extremely strong.

"Whose room is this?" He asked.

"This is moms."

"Aho. Let's start opening windows to air your home out."

As they went room to room, doing so, grandfather asked "Does your mother spend a lot of time in the living room?"

"Yes. Watching TV and visiting."

"Then a lot of time in her room?"

"Oh yes."

"Is she home? I haven't seen her."

"No. She's downtown, but should be home anytime now."

Just then, a car pulled up. "Mom" was home.

Upon entering, they were introduced. The elder had heard her daughter had contacted a Medicine Man and was expecting him today.

"We've tried everything you can imagine, so asking you here wasn't illogical. We'd go ANYWHERE to get rid of this!"

Grandfather smiled…again…the "Last Resort."

“Well ladies,” he said, “This is a simple matter to get rid of.”

(They looked relieved).

“But it is one that is, ah…rather *delicate*. Please understand I am a DOCTOR. Perhaps not as you consider as a doctor, but a doctor never the less. Under this understanding, know all I tell is a matter that will remain only between us. I divulge nothing outside the patients trust. It will remain only between our Creator and us. Do you understand?”

“What do you mean…PATIENT? It’s simply a disgusting STENCH! Patient? We were thinking a sewage problem…or even the possibility of some kind of demonic activity,” the homeowner said.

“Well, in the first you are somewhat correct. It is not ‘demonic’ though. It’s simply a problem that age brings on, to some. It is embarrassing to speak of, but needed, to ‘cure’ the problem. You see, age causes muscle tone to go. In this case, the muscles around your rectum (looking at the elder). It’s simply, Rectum SEEPAGE.”

UTTER SHOCK!

He laughed softly, “I told you it would be embarrassing. Don’t fret about it though. Again, this is just between us. My sister, you can’t help it. This is simply age setting in. Others have the same problem.”

“Well, what can be DONE?”

“It’s now a matter of Hygiene. What I mean by this is: Wash your rear end.”

(Her face flushed red.)

“I know you try to clean yourself properly after a bowel movement, but the rectum muscles there are weak on you. Too weak to fully shut. Thus, seepage gets threw. Now all you have to do is Wash there. Several times a day. Keep that up and the odor leaves. You may want to buy ‘Wet Wipes’ to keep with you when you go out.
Meanwhile, air out the house for a few days. The odor will eventually leave and with you doing your part, will never return again. Aho?

There is no need to be embarrassed. You have done as you always have. But now, due to aging, you will need to do just a bit more.”

“Can it be Stopped?”

"Yes, by tightening that mussel area constantly. But few do it as often as necessary. It gets 'forgotten' after two or three days. So simply wash and get on with your life. Few forget THAT!" Grandfather left, the job completed.

Ho.

Lifting The Stone

Grandfather was a laborer at a construction site. A small man, even frail (to most), yet known for doing the "unusual." It seemed there wasn't much he COULDN'T do. This scared some. He was too "different."

There was a small boulder that had to be removed. WAY too big to be lugged off by hand and in a spot no backhoe could get to. Its approximate Weight would be just over 400 lbs...
The supervisor was pondering on just HOW to get this stone out. Others of the crew around him. Turning to grandfather, he asked, "Do You have any suggestions?"

Grandfather saw one man could get his arms Most of the way around it…but not two or more. It would have to be a one man job.

"I'll do it," he said.

"HOW?"

"I'll just pick it up and toss it onto the bank. Then your backhoe can scoop it up and take it away."

"You Can?"

"Yes, but it will take time. I need to talk with the stone first. It will probably be later this afternoon."

This supervisor never doubted for a second. He had seen too many "impossible things" from this old man. "OK, get it when you can."

Others laughed. Two specifically…the oversized "bully" of the crew and his runty little "side kick."

Throughout the day, grandfather made a point to walk past the boulder. Getting Its notice. Rocks are not accustomed to being recognized as a living "being."

It was the third trip past that it responded to the old one. Greeting him, when he greeted it. The connection was made. Ho.

"I'll be back in awhile. I must talk to you, I need your help," he said. Then left to do other things.

About an hour later, he was back. He stood on the five foot bank and looked down onto the boulder. "What do you need?" It asked.

He told of the need to move it. That it was in the way, but impossible to get to with the machinery that could do it. He then told how he had "volunteered"…but needed the stone's help to make it possible.

"What do you want me to do?"

"Make yourself lighter in weight."

"What can you lift easily?"

Grandfather thought. "Well, I need you up here on the bank. I can toss you there if you can make yourself around 85 pounds...Yes, I can handle that."

"Alright. When?"

"I'll be back in about an hour. Thank You!"

All during the day, the bully and runt had pestered grandfather, laughing. "When ya gonna move that rock…har, har!"

Grandfather always replied, "In time."

Grandfather now spent the time remaining talking to his bones and muscles. Telling THEM, he needed their strength. "Make yourselves as STEEL and Steel CABLES," he commanded.

When he KNEW "it was so," he headed for the stone. It was ready. Ho

He jumped down the cut bank as the two wise guys (who had followed) stood above him, sneering and making crude remarks.

"I'd move back if I were you," he told them.

"Why?"

"I'm going to throw this right where your standing."

Laughing, they complied…barely.

"More."

Two small steps more they went. They weren't going to move another INCH.

"Okay, your toes," he said.

Thanking the stone and his body, he bent and felt for a proper grip. Finding it, he mentally said to all, "OK, I'm ready. On three."

"One, Two, THREE," and up it came. His arms unable to encircle it, still, his grip was good. He lifted it to his chest, gave a slight boost (to get his hands under it) and LIFT TOSSED this huge stone Up and onto the bank…almost THROWING IT!

It rolled toward the two there, who were now, NOT laughing. They struggled to get out of Its way, "back peddling." It stopped a mere two or three inches from their now "pinned" (to building) bodies.
It stopped...THEY DIDN'T! Like bats out of H- - - the two shot off, YELLING!

They were TERRIFIED!

Grandfather never had trouble with those two again, (though "Witch" sure seemed to get heard more).

You just can't win.

Ugh…

Seeing/Sensing

Grandfather taught many. "Spirit Travel" was a major tool to "doing." This, a form of Out of Body Experience (OBE). The SAFE "way"…With it, you leave the body but Mentally only.

Some have problems with this. Unable to actually SEE what was/IS happening.

These are SENSORS.

They SENSE something is going on, but rarely can make out what it is. This makes this type of "work" more challenging. None-the-less, it can be done, and is. This is what grandfather tells to those who "sense:"

"If you are a 'sensor,' GO BY YOUR FEELINGS. This is much like Luke Skywalker of Star Wars… *'Go by your SENSES…Luke…FEEL it.'*

You must do the same. You '*let go and let God.*' The 'Force.' GO BY 'THE FORCE' that emits from within you.

BELIEVE THAT WHAT YOU ARE SENSING is Indeed WORKING. '*Thoughts are real*'…thus what you are THINKING, Is REAL. It is taking place. It IS. Trust in That. In so doing, you are trusting in The Creator's WRITTEN WORD.

GO FOR IT!

A SENSOR makes an exceptional Dowser. Here, you 'hold over' most Seekers.

In dowsing, you go by FEELINGS and learn to trust those feelings. Few can do as well in dowsing…as you.

If you are a 'sensor', you now know how to do as well as a 'see-er.' It's just a matter of becoming Aware. You now are. Now FRUSTRATION will not overwhelm you, as it has.

Walk in Beauty. Good luck."

HO.

Grandfather's Death(s)

Grandfather has died once. He tells he is to do so three more times. The last he won't be back. His doctor and wife both have written orders "No Autopsy OR Blood Letting until the fourth day after being declared dead."

This scares the doctor ,"I just hope I'm NOT your doctor when the time arrives", but his wife has no problem with it. After all, he had told her "four times" before he died (number one) and DID return. "Was a good trip," he told.

When asked, "Aren't you scared?" He replied, "Been there a lot, in Spirit, same place. Nothing TO fear. The *'going and being there'* is nothing to be frightened of…it's the HOW you go that is of concern. I was lucky the first time. Simply quit breathing. A bit of a surprise but wasn't panicked. Who knows the chosen way NEXT TIME? Bad car accident? Fire? Drowning? None of which I'm much in 'favor' of.
Coming back after something like that can HURT! Healing takes painful time. I'm not too much into convalescing. Not only Hurts, but also makes me inactive from my duties. Reason for that though. Just don't like it...Boring."

When asked, "What is Heaven like?"

He told, "A BEAUTIFUL place. Smells, like NOTHING we have, here. Colors HERE are like everything is covered by dust, compared to there. Gardens GALORE. ENDLESS SPACE. Everything seems to go on FOREVER. Even the ROOMS inside 'His' City. HUGE, THICK, and WARM Walls and Hallways. Those walls are like SMOKE FILLED GLASS! But the 'smoke' is made up of various PASTEL COLORS! And CONSTANTLY slowly swirl within. A 'Light Show' like NOTHING we have here. They have Always fascinated me when I'm called up there. Yet the MOST fascinating IS THE AIR! It SPARKLES! Like breathing in Aluminum CHAFF. Just SPARKLES…AND THAT AIR is GOD!

You BREATH IN…GOD!

The halls are TALL…and you often walk around Angels. Little ones AND BIG! Most seem to be in the 22 to 24 foot height range…but others are MILES tall! All 'colors' too, Whites, Blacks, Asian, Hispanics…you name it. Just like here in race colors."

"No harps?"

Grandfather laughs. "None that I've seen. But it's a big 'For Ever' place."

"No MUSIC?"

"WHO said THAT?

Even the AIR sings…Every FLOWER sings…EVERYTHING SINGS…CONSTANTLY! Not 'noisy' though…just PURE JOY! Everything and Everyone Emits a Tone that MAKES A SONG. ALL singing in UNISON. PERFECTLY! Makes for a joyous 'background' to live in.

Makes you feel all LOVED within."

"Wings?"

"Yes, some have them, but not all. Less than more, by what I've see."

"What do people DO up there?"

"Well, like I said, I haven't seen the WHOLE place…but basically the souls seem to do two things: Visit ALL…FOR EVER…and Learn."

"Learn?"

"Yes. Like in school, but NOT like school. They 'soak in' SPIRITUAL GROWTH KNOWLEDGE. I have a feeling there ARE classes though. I'm not sure if these are mandatory, or a soul goes to learn on a 'specialty.' Just like colleges here. In time, all souls become as we truly are in the first place: ONE GOD. I don't know how long their purging is to BECOME so AS 'GOD,' but is seems to take place. You MERGE as HIM, (Fully, in time, I THINK). You Become THE AIR!"

"Do you recognize each other?"

"Certainly! I was taken up once, to see my father. We sat in a rose garden and he told me some things that concern our family…my brother and sisters, aunts and uncles, etc. Yes, you recognize each other. Ho."

"If it's such a 'Great Place' why then don't you Stay THERE?"

"I've a job to do here. I've time enough to go there forever. I've really No WANT to stay there, TILL MY JOB IS DONE HERE!"

An Odd Event

Grandfather and his grandson Sky were "tripping." This time to a high wilderness mountain called Chrystal Mountain. Both enjoyed the view and solitude there. A good logging road making the way into easy.

Grandfather has been there often. Long before Sky's birth even.

As they walked from their truck, Sky picked up a short, but heavy, stick and tossed it…as is the way with young boys.

THAWWWWONGG!

It landed and THE EARTH MADE A TONE!

"What? Sky, go toss that stick again."

THWWWWWONG!

It was as if they were walking on the stretched skin OF A GIANT DRUM!

Grandfather retrieved the stick and began walking the open field, striking the Earth here and there. Finding the "boundaries" of the HOLLOW AREA beneath. It was BIG!

"I KNOW my caves! THIS is NEW to me! WHAT'S GOING ON? Man Made? Air raising the top?"

He has yet to find out.

This Mountain top is in Kittitas County of Eastern Washington State. IT BEARS LOOKING INTO.

Is our Earth SWELLING there? A good Seismograph…or digging can tell.
It HAS to be "shallow" to easily make that sound WITH A STICK!

Grandfather's Epitaph

Always a Heyókȟa', grandfather has written his own epitaph, "If my body is around to be put 'to rest'…This is what I want on my tombstone":

ALRIGHT, PAY UP! I WIN!

I TOLD you I could hold my breath longer then YOU!

This on one side.

On the other he wants:

I Tried Sir,

I TRIED!

Lesson On Laws

She had been asked to take her grandson to school and agreed. He was 16 and like most that age, had his opinions. Telling him to "buckle up," he suddenly EXPLODED!

"WHY!"

"It's the Law, honey. You know that."

"WELL IT'S A STUPID LAW!"

He wasn't being too nice about it. She wasn't about to take this!

"You have a choice…buckle up or find another ride! If you can't obey a simple Government LAW…HOW WILL YOU BE ABLE TO OBEY GOD'S One LAW…LOVE!"

Need I say more?

A Lesson To Men

The two were visiting Grandfather. One just turned twenty-two, the other in his early thirties. Both married. Somehow, the conversation came around to the "hardness" of being married. How "hard" man has it. Grandfather, far more experienced in this, (36 years with his wife) listened as they battered this about. Then entered in:

"So, you think you have it hard? You two are not seeing. You are not paying attention to what goes on around you, right in your own home. Yes, you have to get up five days a week and spend eight to ten hour days at work, and yes, you have to cut the grass and take out the garbage. Oh, how HARD you have it!

Well, if you think THAT, then TRADE WITH YOUR WIFE! THAT poor woman has to get up EARLIER then you…just to help you start off your day. You (this to the eldest) have two children. She doesn't only get YOU ready, but them as well. It is SHE who has to 'fight' their 'sleepy eyes' and constant rolling over and trying to go back to sleep. YOU meanwhile rarely see this…as you're headed off already, for work.

She arises, cooks your meal, helps you locate cloths you can't find, then kisses you goodbye…THEN turns to the REST of the day. In many cases, the children. Here her battle begins. *'OK Kids, time to get up. SCHOOL!'* Often this is repeated several times before they grudgingly respond. *'Brush your teeth and wash up. Breakfast in a few minutes.'*
Breakfast served, packed lunches made, a pat on the rear as they rush to get the bus, and she's JUST STARTED!

Now to a bit of 'self.' Shower, dress. Then to pick up after the mess YOU made in rising, as well as that of the kids. Make beds, Do dishes, Straighten the house, Go Shopping, Maybe the laundry that day…AND catch up on duties YOU were to do, but didn't. IF she's lucky, there's time to visit a friend. MAYBE lunch out. Then back to the grind. The kids are coming home. You are coming home. Dinner must be planned and prepared. ALL needs tended to. *'Do your homework, etc.'* Meanwhile YOU flop down on the couch and watch TV...SHE HASN'T THE TIME! DISHES Again! Pick UP, again! And you continue rubbing your belly and gripe about the Ball Game! FLAT ON YOUR BUTT!

Do you offer to help with the dishes? Help the kids with their schoolwork? TAKE OUT THE TRASH? Less so, than More so. Few men do.

Then, all the kids tucked in bed, a few minutes with you, and off to bed. THEN what happens?

'Hi HONEY'…and she gives.

You roll over and sleep the sleep of satisfaction. SHE rolls over and sleeps the sleep of EXHAUSTION!

YOU boys are married to a SERVANT!

SHE is married to SLAVERY.

AND YOU 'Complain?' YOU ARE W I M P S!

You are DARN LUCKY you were born a MAN!

Have it HARD? HA!

TRY ON HER MOCCASINS!

Now, go home. Hold your woman in a long hug. GIVE HER SOMETHING TO BE STUNNINGLY GRATEFUL FOR…and WASH THE DISHES!"

Fear

“Ever been AFRAID, Grandfather?” he asked.

This gave grandfather some thought. “Yes, four times, as far as I can remember.”

“What was that about?” (Thinking on grandfathers many ‘adventures’).

“Well, my first adventures with Shades (ghosts). We lived in a haunted house. I was young…a mere child and had no teaching to fall back on yet.

Then when on the ships I was almost hit by a torpedo off the coast of Vietnam. Ran right between my legs, as a big wave lifted us up. Passed right under us. Scared the hell outta me! Hum, the next, when I got married…(Laughter!)

No. Not GETTING hitched! Just doing so before so many STRANGERS. Never liked crowds. I wanted a Justice of the Peace…My girl wanted the ‘accepted’ way. Should have known I was in trouble at the moment! (Grinning).

Then the night I came face to face with Lucifer. THAT was a surprise!

Guess that’s about it. Aho?”

“Well, I bet you, I know something you’re afraid of! GOD!”

Grandfather looked SHOCKED! “Why On EARTH would you think THAT! Nephew, you love your father, right?”

“Yes.”

“You have respect for him, right?”

“Yes.”

“And when you’ve done something wrong you THEN have a FEAR of what the results will be when he finds out. Right?”

“Yes.”

“Well, it’s the same with God and THE Father, me. When I do an Ungodly thing…even have an ungodly THOUGHT…well, I get a bit ‘worried’ too! That’s why I try to NOT do something that will get him irate. Still, I DO ‘goof.’ That’s when I go to ‘Him’ THROUGH ‘His’ SON. The

'First Born'…'BIG BROTHER.' I GET 'SQUARED AWAY' AS SOON AS POSSIBLE! THEN I APOLOGIZE to 'DAD!' I'd be in a Heck of a Fix without Jesus, otherwise!

Fear Him? 'HE' IS DAD just like Your dad! 'HE' Loves me! Proved it too…time after time! 'Fear?'

NO!

LOVE!

If I fear anything, it's my NOT LOVING HIM IN RETURN!

No, son, I don't fear 'Him'…Not in the LEAST. 'He' Loves ME and I LOVE 'HIM.'

What's there to fear, when Love abounds?"

Grandfather's Restoration Way

They were watching a Documentary on Tree Cutting. From the original Native Indians chipped edge hand "ax" to today's Hi Tech way. At the end, this included Tree Farming. Grandfather listened intently, allowing no talking within the room. When done, he shook his head sadly.

"We need to have wood. Mankind hasn't learned how to Image a home yet to live in. Though this is quite possible. FEASIBLE! I myself have walked in warmth and un-wetted in hours of near freezing weather. I too have been invited into lodges that 'don't exist' to only but the most in tuned. There, you are in a real 'home'…able to cook/eat/sleep…ALL while outside, others walk right by, not knowing you and others are occupying the same space. No, mankind in general do not know this, or How. Thus, the trees make homes and other needs that the Mind Alone can make.

I see this program tells of Tree Farms. To the whites this is a good thing. Yet ONE white says 'NO!' THAT SINGLE ONE is ABSOLUTELY CORRECT! A Tree Farm is NOT a FOREST . Simply a CROP Farm. They have little use to our four-footed ones, even two, to many of our feathered friends. Just because there are a mass of trees doesn't mean they are the DIFFERENT Trees needed to be a FOREST. The whites think these trees must be as their gardens. Trees, as gardens, need COMPANIONS of different Species, to be a Forest. They till and kill their Wood 'Garden' just as they do their regular gardens. WEED trees, as WEEDs, are NEEDED. THIS is TRUE Ecology! LET THE CREATOR'S 'NATURAL' Return and ALL will return. Otherwise, it's but a wonderful 'walk in a shaded garden.' Nice to walk in…little to trip on…and well, a PARK! Merely a STERILIZED PARK!

In a true Forest setting, the many varieties of trees and plants, their fallen limbs and dead leaves, create hiding places for bugs/rodents/small mammals…even for some birds. HOMES! HUNTING GROUNDS! HIDING PLACES! All NEEDED to survive. Each eats upon each and eventually end up feeding US!

This cannot occur on a FARM though. At least not near as WELL.

This is sad.

There IS a WAY that the whites CAN learn though. THE WAY OF THE SACRED SUN DANCE POLE!

As you know, when that pole is cut down, it is stripped of all its limbs, yet the TOP TIP part of that tree is LEFT ON.

There is MORE than ONE REASON FOR THIS! THIS is that OTHER Reason:

The STUMP of a fresh cut tree is STILL NOT YET DEAD. Its roots still partaking of our Mother's nourishment. Cut, it has no COLLECTING abilities though. Its limbs and leaves are no longer able to catch the Sun and Rain needed for full continued growth. Thus, the stump slowly STARVES TO DEATH. It cannot subsist on Earth nourishment alone.

Add to that that it now has an Enormous wound. Left exposed and bleeding.
THINK OF THIS CUT TREE AS YOU WOULD OF A HUMAN BEING WITH BOTH LEGS CUT OFF! Unattended…that human will die.

Here is how to keep the tree, THE SAME TREE:

BORE a HOLE into the HEART CENTER of the stump. Make it rather deep but not as wide as its center. KEEP THE SAWDUST that was of that tree. Mix it with Earth and refill the drilled hole you've made. Now get the TIP of the tree and slice its 'base' on a slight angel. This will allow more GRAFTING ability then if just a straight cut. INSERT THAT TIP into the HEART HOLE!

You are GRAFTING the ORIGINAL TREE to Its ORIGINAL BASE. Tap it in well. Water it a bit. Just as you'd do any garden plant. Next, COVER THE OPEN WOUND! Smear an adhesive over it…leaving just a rather small circle undone. That around the grafted Tree Tip.

All this allows the tree itself to regenerate itself. Type for Type.

Being it's ITSELF…there is no need to worry about 'compatibility' of 'blood type', etc.

The BEST Wound Cover is the trees own ROSIN. Its 'Sap.' This is a trees BLOOD.

Just as when YOU get a wound and bleed, and the blood dries to close it…so too does the tree make Its own Scab.

This Rosin collection would take too much time though. So another 'cover' must be put on. It is NOT WISE to use PETROLEUM OILS. To a tree, this is a poison. Another type cover must be put on. Honey is excellent, yet expensive in a big 'operation.' A Butter Type base will do…if it's rubbed in and is Saltless. SALT DRAWS 'NIBBLERS!'
Plant OIL is a decent choice. Rub it in though. PENETRATE THE EXPOSED WOOD WOUND!
Also, on a smaller scale rejuvenating, it would be a good thing to make a 'Tipi' style cover to put over the Tree Tip.
ROUND is a NATURAL NATURE Shape. Fitting for a ROUND Tree.
Cheap clear plastic then placed on the small 'Tipi's' upright sticks. Its edge held down by tacks.
A gorged out 'trench' along the 'Tipi's' outer edge…with an entryway to the inside drilled hole.
Condensation and rainwater will then help 'feed' the Tree Tip of the water needed. The 'Tipi' now becomes both a 'hot house' AND a 'nibblers Stop Help.'

This cheap plastic will rot within two summers…yet give Needed protection during the rejuvenation time. Time enough for the Tree Tip to root well and grow. It only needs being made once.

Now you have a tree growing again, but NOT the FOREST! You see, as the cut tree fell, often others fall as it hits them. To the whites, these are of no concern. Either too small to harvest or of a species considered a 'useless Weed Tree.' Useless to THEM perhaps…but NEEDED for a TRUE FOREST. These people don't see beyond their wallets.

It is the FOREST that SUSTAINS LIFE. LIFE that ends up feeding THEM in the long run! They are ignorant, for and in, their greed.

You here…who I speak to, have forgotten. It is sad. Ho.

So, what to do? DO THE SAME TO THOSE TREES THAT WERE CRUSHED DOWN BY THE ONE CUT!
RETURN the FOREST to…FOREST!
Give LIFE to ALL THAT A FOREST PROVIDES LIFE TO!

Keep YOU People ALIVE, for the MANY GENERATIONS YOU WILL Begin in your Lifetime!

YOUR FUTURE depends on YOUR ACTIONS…<u>TODAY</u>!

HO!

More on Nature (Natural) Wisdom

Later the next day, those who were with grandfather the night before, were still together. They had had quite a discussion over what he had said on the forest upkeep.

"That was really interesting last night, grandfather. Thank you! Would you happen to have any other thoughts on the same line that you can share?"

"Hum. Well, do you know what a 'Dust Devil' is?"

"Kind of like a small tornado, isn't it?"

"Yes. That's the one. Go into Eastern Washington's Dry Farming areas and you'll see many of them during the summer. Other places of large plowed areas as well.
These are caused BY plowing, mostly. As the dirt dries…the dirt FLIES when a good wind comes up! I'd like to share some things on this if you'd like."

They were all ears.

"Well, our country has gotten sort of overloaded with people. We've a lot of mouths to feed. Farming is that 'Food Factory.' Necessary. Aho?"

They agreed.

"Thing is, once again, the whites see only money. Farmers are no exception. It's a HARD LIFE! You can BET On IT! Always trying to outguess nature to make a living. I've a lot of respect for them!

Still, in their need, they do all they can to meet that need. They do their best to use their lands to what they THINK, is Its full potential. I don't always see it that way.

Take the Dust Devils. Plowed DRY Earth…being stripped away by the heat winds. Blown out of the county. The TOP SOIL! Lost…due to lack of foresight, as far as I can tell.

Our farmers not only losing their best soils, but also often leaving wildlife homeless due to it.

WHY NOT HAVE BOTH!

If they'd simply plow, say, two or three rows, then SKIP a row…then PLANT THAT SKIPPED ROW with NATURAL plants and grasses AND A FEW TREES…well, those PLANED 'useless' rows WOULD BREAK THE WIND. KEEPING THE TOP SOIL WHERE IT

BELONGS! Then too, those NATURAL rows would 'call back' the Wildlife. 'SAFETY'…'HOME.'

Then, LEASE OUT HUNTING RIGHTS to 'city slickers'... 'PAY To PLAY', type thing."

"Grandfather, there's a lot of farms too close to 'urban' areas. NO GUNS ALLOWED!"

"Thought of this. Trappers can trap. Some States allow Slingshots. Nature Lovers just coming to see a Deer or Wild Rabbit, 'Nature Trips' for school kids, Photographers of birds…many opportunities! You don't NEED a gun. Aho? I don't know, but I'd think it's a Win/Win situation. Wildlife/Soil/Crops…AND money. All for the 'loss' of a few unplowed strips of land. Those unplowed rows will save time AND fuel for their farm equipment. Then too, the trees can be Walnut trees or simply ANOTHER CROP!"

"What about watering?"

"Dry Land Farming means just that. They rely on nature to give them a crop. Why not do the same with those strips? RELY ON THE CREATOR TO BLESS YOUR ENDEAVORS! Might surprise you! After all, that farmer is then doing for ALL. Man AND Beast. Helping '*the world goes round.*' Aho?"

"Anything else?"

"Well, I've noticed farmers don't follow The Creator's telling of letting their lands 'lay follow.' They don't give it a rest. Some plant the same crop every year. This isn't wise. Each crop needs certain 'foods.' Nutrients. By planting the same each year, the particular nutrient gets depleted. Throwing off the Natural System.
If man took out white or red blood cells, time after time, eventfully they would become weaker and weaker. Same thing I'd think. So, by diversifying their crops, balance stays. Then a rest. Give Mother a VACATION! Let her rest from her labors. Men take vacations, Mother is as a Human. Treat her as such.
To me, a WISE farmer would ALWAYS have a section of land laying in Follow. Changing that area each year. OBEYING God's written 'how to.' Keeping Mother Healthy!

TREAT NATURE AS ONE WOULD TREAT A HUMAN BEING YOU CARE FOR!
In this, ALL works for ALL…Together…HAPPILY."

HO.

Grandfather Cooks!

Grandfather had his hands full. His wife convalescing from a recent operation. He was "in charge." Dogs to tend, cats demanding whatever cats demand, their ten year old grandson to entertain and fight over doing homework, teacher meetings, Scouts, store runs, laundry, dishes never ending, letters to write, emails unceasing, drop ins, phone calls, his early morning prayer time. It seemed never ending.

However, his bugaboo was cooking. Burned the Campbell Chicken soup…torched a full pound of bacon…even messed up boiled (HA!) Hot Dogs! And now it was time to bake his grand daughter's birthday cake.

(He wasn't even sure she was coming!)

Well, he tried. Needing glasses, he misread the word 'Sugar'…put in the right amount…of SALT!

(Wondered why it wasn't rising!)

"Maybe it needs to cook some more." Now he had a VERY Dark, FLAT, cake (?). Figuring the frosting would hide the fact, he smeared it on. No one told him you must wait until the cake cools first. Three cans later, it STILL melted onto the Too Small of a plate…AND over. So he set everything on a pizza pan and opened another store bought can of…FROSTING. Nope. Whatever it was, it helped wet down the cake even MORE.

COOLED IT THOUGH!

Now for the candles. Not wanting to disturb his wife's "beauty" sleep (she sure needed A LOT of THAT!)…he searched the cupboards. Looked Everywhere. Nothing. Always an innovator, he figures matches would "suffice"…but couldn't find any of THOSE either! What to DO? Well, he shoved his Bic Lighter into its center. Leaning.

"Hey! It's a CAKE, ISN'T IT?!
SHUT UP AND EAT!

HAPPY BIRTHDAY, LYNNSAY!"

(She didn't stay long.)

Vision Questing

Often people would ask grandfather about 'questing.' He explains this here: "This an Indian way on the line of what Big Brother did *'for 40 days and nights in the wilderness.'* The Native Americans DID 'Follow Christ.' Many still do. Christians, on the other hand, find 'doing' either too hard or to inconvenient…in some cases, 'SCARY.' None of which should be a reason to not do as ordered. Is it no wonder Christians are weak?

There are Two Types of questing: VISION and PRAYER. Both designed to show the Creator you are a serious searcher. Someone WANTING to be 'One with Him.' So much so, they are GOING to OBEY. At least that's what they THINK. Now they WILL find out!

Questing is not easy. It's 'alien' to most. Alone? ME? Out THERE with Bears and 'Nuts' and (whatever)? One's imagination goes rampant! Stopping many. Then there ARE those who START…and then leave EARLY!

(Grandfather has dealt with all types)...Some who left early HAVE succeeded the second or third try though. Others claim, '*I got my message.*' (He doubts that!)

Loneliness, fright, and weather are usually their 'message.' A 'message' to *'GET OUT OF HERE!'* Self.

No, a quest is never easy. At least for the first three times. After that, it's more a miserable JOY, though.

Alone…with GOD!

What more could one want?

To quest means No Food…FASTING while out there. THIS Fasting begins one to three days BEFORE going, PLUS while there. It depends on the Nation's 'way.'

Some fast, but take No food OR Water! Again, it depends.

A 'Prepare' and 'Do' Quest, which means:
NO BOOZE.
NO SEX.
NO DRUGS.
(Except those prescribe by a doctor, etc.)

YOU PURGE YOURSELF FULLY, by abstaining…Again showing the Creator You are SERIOUS!

All proper questioning means one takes only a blanket…fire starter, water (if OK)...Perhaps a knife. That's IT. Those items and ones DETERMINATION brings results.

Some, 'seeking a vision'…NEVER SUCCEED! Why? HEADINESS! THINKING that they are someone IMPORTANT. To The Creator…they are yet too immature. Their thoughts 'rubbish.' Until that train of thought leaves…they can quest and quest…with no results.

Some CAN'T quest. Physically incapable. THE CREATOR UNDERSTANDS! So, 'so be it.' FAST instead…in a QUIET area within one's home. 'HE' UNDERSTANDS! GOD LOOKS AT THE HEART! Know this! INTENT is what matters to 'Him'…HONEST intent. Aho?

HO!

Basically, a quester faces INSECTS/LONELINESS/FEAR/HUNGER (and thirst if no water) WEATHER. But there is One More…the GREATEST one: THEY SEE THEMSELVES! Most HATE what they 'see.' Don't WANT to think on this…so leave. SELF is the GREATEST 'Enemy.' They can Blame ALL the others…but they fool no one, Certainly NOT 'HIM.'

If any is TRULY interested in doing either, or both, of these quests…LOOK UP SUCH. I can tell you. Yet why take the time? IF ONE IS SERIOUS…the INFORMATION is 'out there.' Now is the time to see JUST how SERIOUS you are. DO YOUR OWN HOMEWORK!" HO

Attracting

Grandfather has had, BEYOND COUNT, people who are 'attacked,' etc. So much so they have become 'Paranoid.' Some even fearful of leaving their homes. He receives Hundreds of letters, emails, phone calls AND visitors…all with this problem. To all, he says THIS:

"You GET what you EXPECT! You ATTRACT what you EXPECT!

YOU DO <u>NOT</u> TRUST THE CREATOR! You are filled with FEAR. Fear YOU have brought on! EXPECT PEACE and you will GET peace. Expect 'bad' and IT WILL COME! You cannot 'expect peace' and '*look around every corner*' hoping you do not '*run into (whatever).*' If you continue LOOKING for trouble, then you are NOT TRULY EXPECTING the PEACE you CLAIM you ARE Expecting! YOU, Sir, Ma'am, are thus a LIAR.

Well? Are YOU?"

CHANGE YOUR THOUGHTS AND YOU WILL CHANGE YOUR LIFE!

The Red Road

Again and again people come. Some claiming they want to practice "The Red Road." Others asking WHAT this "Red Road" IS! To all, here is what grandfather tells:

"Those who walk in LOVE, those who have great RESPECT for ALL…man and nature alike, those who keep their MINDS AND WAYS on The Great Spirit, Those who TRUST 'HIM' despite TRIBULATIONS AND TRIALS, Those who SEEK 'HIM.' Those who WANT to KNOW 'HIM.' Those who are WILLING TO OBEY 'HIM.' Those who are ALWAYS WILLING to Put Others FIRST…it is THOSE who are Living 'The Red Road.'

It does not take a Culture or a Skin Color…IT TAKES ONLY THE FULL DESIRE TO PLEASE THE GREAT ONE.

If and When you have this, then you KNOW this 'Way Road' and are ON IT!"

Ho.

An Unknown Secret

There is a way that has been unconsidered by nearly anyone today. It can affect Healing/Finding/Knowing. It is this:

THE FIRST ANSWER/"THING" THAT COME TO MIND IS THE THING/ANSWER YOU ARE SEEKING!

In this knowing, FOLLOW THROUGH.

IF you WAIT, OTHER "Answers" will come. NOT THE CORRECT ONE!

Your MIND THOUGHTS come into "reasoning" THAT INTERFERES. You begin to REASON, when the CREATOR has GIVEN.

YOU "override."

I was taught this.

I use that teaching, I rely on that teaching and do "The Impossible."

The Haunting

Grandfather had received a call for help. This from a very distant city on the Oregon coast. He prayed and received "GO," checked three times…and agreed to come. His request for Trip money and pay "as the Creator leads" approved. Off he went. A 7 ½ hour drive and another hour trying to find the place. It was way off in a secluded "rich man's" area. A BEAUTIFUL home! The "yard" ENORMOUS…Well kept and green.

After talking to the owners, they took him "on tour." With them was their dog...The dog went "nose to feet" from room to room. UNTIL THEY CAME TO THE BASEMENT STEPS! Here it would go no farther.

"This happens a lot," they told.

Going down, the basement was as fancy as the upstairs. It too held bedrooms. "For our guests. We entertain a lot. But we can't have 'sleepovers' anymore. The bathroom 'backs up'…shower and toilet. We never know WHEN it will happen. We think it's Demon Activity."

During the tour, grandfather had "tested" each room. Even the crawl space through the rafter area. Nothing. Here though, there WAS activity in the small Utility room. A VORTEX! Literally an opening to the Inner World. The DEEP inner world. A true "passageway" down into "The Pits of Hell."

They then went back upstairs and he began his work. Smudging and praying in each room, every closet, and the crawl space…and even everything that could be opened (washing machine/oven/drawers). Grandfather was ALWAYS very thorough. Then to the basement. Again doing as he had upstairs.

He saved the utility room for last.

DEMONS were THERE! "HERDED" to this last bastion of "safety." Doing his "thing," they were forced back into their "home." Hades. With that done, he closed the "door" permanently. Leavening Angel Warriors to keep it that way.

Next he went outside, Smudging and Praying around the owner's full property line.

DONE!

To show the work was complete, a rare SOUTH AMERICAN giant MOTH appeared, slowly batting its wings as it grasped a roof rafters edge. A moth that does NOT belong to the United States. ALL were in awe. Ho

Back inside, the man and wife asked, "Will this stop the wet and reeking problem in the basement?"

"No" he said, "This was not of the demons. It is a separate problem. You are far away from the city. You have a Septic System of your own. Correct?"

"Yes."

"How long have you lived here?"

"Six years."

"When was the last time you've had your Septic Tank pumped out?"

"Never."

"This wetness occurs much more so during your rains in summer and during the winter and fall. Correct?"

They thought. Then answered in the affinitive.

"Well friends, your septic tank is overloaded. Apparently for a number of years. This, in turn, has blocked the sewage lines that go into your leach field. The effluence then has saturated your leach field. That is that Super Green area at the side/back of your yard. This fertilizer has kept THAT area well fertilized. In the summer months, you turn on your Sprinklers to water the lawn. Adding to the problem. When it rains, that too keeps the leach field overly wet. Rainstorms, winter rains, your watering, ALL cause the field to overflow. It is then your sewage "gray water" backs up into your basement. Reeks and all. The problem is not demons, but your lack of knowledge. Now you will need to pump out the sewage cistern tank AND extend your leach lines to create a Bigger leach field. It will be costly, but that is the only solution. Aho?"

They then returned to the basement. THIS TIME THE DOG WENT WITH THEM, tail WAGGING, not afraid any longer.

There they sat in the game and TV room that was within, discussing the day's events. During this they told of having 'Shamans' come to 'clear the house' before.

"Shamans? Sounds 'new age.' Did they ever happen to mention their training?"

The wife told, "Yes. They are trained in 'The HORNER Way.' The last two times…they came three times…their teacher was with them. A lady who had trained under Horner. She has classes and teaches this now."

Grandfather shook his head ('New Age' SHAMANS…AGAIN!)
"Chances are, they came during sunny days…and it STAYED sunny for days after as well."

"Yes, always. I paid twelve hundred dollars each time, too!"

"I know of this man's teachings. Indeed, he IS a shaman. Learned from his South American teachers. Those there are VERY aware of Spirits. Their jungles Filled with them…AND their legends. Legends of ONLY these spirits. NONE KNOWS THE GREAT SPIRIT. Thus they are constantly appeasing theses others. Often using one to combat another. Occasionally one is brought to The Word of God…and 'Big Brother.' Those that are, leave their 'calling' and go only The Red Road of One-With-God. Purity. The rest remain in their only known ways. Evil. Yes, Horner is of that training. He has only learned the Power…NOT the ultimate SOLUTION. 'New Age Shamans,' ALL feels a 'calling.' Though most say they want to HELP 'Through Spirit'…it appears this 'calling' is a SELF-thing. Might as well go into White Witchcraft…OR black. But there's 'Nobleness'…a HEADINESS, to be called 'A Shaman.' Thus, go that way. Being they are NOT called by The Creator, they are not led to the proper CREATOR Teachers. Therefore, they go to those like Horner to learn. Again, Mr. Horner IS a Shaman…and TRIES to do GOOD Shaman work, but limited to only the Spirit World Knowledge of the Jungle Medicine Men/Women. Those that do NOT know the Creator…OR 'His' gift: Jesus, the Big Brother...As you know, you spent your money uselessly. You won't have the haunting and demons now…UNLESS YOU WANT THEM. Take care of your septic problem and all will then be over. Aho?"

Grinning, they walked him back to his car. "Thank You, Grandfather," they said, as he sat there, politely waiting. Finally, he too smiled…knowing that once again the trip and work was all on HIM. He has yet to receive a dime.

Ho.

Mount Saint Helens

Grandfather, his wife and daughter lived very close to Mount Saint Helens. He had seen, in vision it blow, a full year before the event. "Taken off shore and up. Thought it was Shasta but you can't tell State Boundary Lines like on a map. Made a Mess! Trees flattened, stone dust…the 'works.' Well, the evening before she blew I left work to drive home. KNEW something was UP! ALL were driving CRAZY! Me too! I had to FORCE myself to SLOW DOWN and had a Heck of a time avoiding others who went 'crazy.' Mother was going to DO something! Had me concerned, you can BET!

We lived through it All, but it sure was interesting. Ended up being in 'The Blue Zone.' Only those who lived there could enter. I quit my job and took another job three days later…going to work with crews on the Mountain, The Red Zone. My wife understood. Figured those working there needed me more than my family did. Always 'others first' has often put me in danger. You had no idea if the men working there would come out again. Wanted them to know God and 'His' Son was real…AND Protects. They needed 'a light in the darkness.' I worked. Meachelle PRAYED! I KNEW I had REAL 'Backing!'

The weird thing was the Pre-Activity of those the night before. I've seen this a number of times since. Now aware it means 'trouble.' All sense, has been pre-tellings of Earth Quakes. I know Animals react…but that taught me PEOPLE do TOO!
We are MADE from our Earth Mother…dirt to man…man to dirt. Guess it's only natural we do.

Ho.

Summertime Feast

Grandfather had told his grandson, "Tomorrow we are going fishing, son. But not in the way, you expect…OR for WHAT you expect. We'll leave for the creek at about ten. Have your schoolwork done and be ready."

The time arrived and both were ready. GRANDFATHER'S shirt pocket was BULGING. In his hand, he had a spool of fishing line and a Sack full of fresh chicken guts! Sky was intrigued. This was something new to him!

At the creek grandfather had Sky break a dried stick, then reached into his shirt pocket and pulled out its contents. WOMAN'S Old Nylon SOCKS! Each leg of the socks had been cut in half.
Stretching each, he had Sky run the rough end of the stick down their length. This created HUGE 'runners.'

"The bigger the better, son."

As each was completed, grandfather loosely tied within each a small gob of entrees. Making sure, they were secure AND that the 'bag' was 'loose.'

Being the creek wasn't very wide, he had Sky break the fishing line into about ten foot lengths. Then tied an end to the each sock's knot.

"Now son, go along the bank and at about every 20 feet or so, toss one of these bundles into the rocky areas. Then tie the end of each line to a tree limb or shorelines strong grasses. Then we just sit and wait." Sky did as ordered.

"WHAT are we fishing FOR, grandpa?"

"CRAWFISH!"

After about an hour "Gramps" rose. "Time to reel in our dinner Sky. Let's go!"
Pulling each bundle ashore, the crawdads, having traced the blood scent, had climbed upon the bundle located, searching for the meal it contained. Now they were trapped in the runners by their outer shells. Some held only a few. Others far more! Their 'take' was around 120 fresh BIG 'dads.' This from twenty four 'sets.'

'Sets' ALL HELD in ONE POCKET!

"More than enough for us three. These and some Cat Tail shoot Hearts will make a DANDY meal! You go pull some. Remember, only the smallest. They're the most tender. Meanwhile, I'll get these ready to pack home."

As Sky began his search, grandfather took off his shirt, and then piled fresh grasses onto its 'spread.' Sky returned just in time to see grandfather placing the 'dads' into this…covering them in the grasses. He then tied this all into a bundle and put it into the creek as he held on. "This will keep them cool and happy, Sky. You don't want to ever eat one that dies along the way. Unsafe. Now let's get home. Grandma's waiting!"

That Weird Old Man

"You see what that old weirdo is doing? He's eating WEEDS again!"

A couple of weeks ago Bill saw him catching BUGS! Damn GRASSHOPPERS! Out there in the early morning with a FLY SWATTER! He asked him, "Whatcha doing?"

THAT WACKO said, "GETTING DINNER!"

The other laughed, "Yeah, but HE isn't going to Starve! Not only that, but his food bill is a WHOLE lot LESS than OURS, I'll bet you! He's not as nuts as you'd think. Ever try one of his concoctions?"

"No! Who would WANT TO?"

"I don't know…but, well, drop it…"

Grandfather Thinks Ahead

Grandfather had made a number of Sweat Lodges, all in the Plains' Indians way. Domes. He's been in others from other Indian cultures. Kivas of the southwest, Ojibwas of Canada and the Cree. Each a different style.

"For heat, the Plain's style is hard to beat. For beauty, the Kiva. For what I plan though, I'll go to the Ojibwas' oval style," he told.

This to friends who asked him on tipis to live in. A home.
Knowing he had spent seasons living in such, his answer was a surprise. Part of that is what's written above.

"As you know, I have land up by the Canadian border, ten acres. We intend to move there as soon as possible. Sell here and go. The sooner the better as far as I'm concerned. So far, the Creator hasn't made it possible. We depend on 'Him' and await 'His' orders. 'He' knows when…and how. Right now, we need water up there…THEN a 'home.' We will do without electricity. Maybe our small generator to charge a couple of strong batteries…or direct. We'll get by. There's plenty of ways to get electricity…solar to wind to generator to water wheel types…AND good old leg work. Still, a home has to be. IT WON'T BE A TIPI! The winds ahead prohibit it. So, a 'dome.' In our case, the Oval Ojibwa style is the most useful for a family. I don't intend to stop at one…but will have that as 'main' and two smaller Plains style, as well, connecting. These two will each be a bedroom and bath. All Earth Bearmed…AND on top as well. Not IN Earth, but Earth brought to it after building. Just a big hump showing. I can build this alone but another would be handy. The cost will be cheap, as most is all from nature, HEAVY SAPLINGS. Then woven between these 'frames.' Called 'Wattle,' mudded after, then some expense for a waterproof cover…THEN the Earth over. I've done similar before so know it will work.
The Tipi is a wonderful structure. Gives plenty of light too. The Ojibwa will have windows…of a sort. The old Igloo hides windows. Maybe glass. If so, this from old colored bottles. Just pick them up along the road or from a tavern's recycle bins. Light AND color. Should be pretty. Anyway, the three will be wind and fire proof…warm AND cheap. You can keep the tipis! Though I love them, they aren't as good of an 'investment' for what lays ahead. We just don't have the money for a standard white man's home. What we DO have is KNOWLEDGE…and time."

"Wow! Guess you've outthought US. Tell us, please, you speak of a future that will mean no Gasoline…as gas needs electricity to pump. Yet you speak of a generator. That TOO needs gas, grandfather!"

The old one grinned, "Not if you convert to wood gas emission! Will be plenty. Is now. During the end of World War II, cars would run off of this. What's a tiny generator! Yet, in time, parts will break down. TV will be gone. Batteries no longer made. Think PRIMITIVE! REAL primitive! Darn near 'Cave Man.' You are thinking 'cheap' and 'Fast' and 'Primitive.' That's why you are talking about a Tipi. That will be OK for a SHORT time…but with winds in the 30 miles per hour range…all you'll have is an open Umbrella! That and the tremendous Fires that are to be…well, you'll end up like a Roman candle…sparks trailing as you whiz through the air. Up to you though."

"Sounds like we need a DEEP CAVE!"

"Yes, if you know of any with water and that is Earth Quake Proof! Next then, you face NO LIGHT to see by. COLD in them too! So go out, face all out there and get firewood…THEN hope the smoke makes its way out! There ARE such caves with that ability."

"Around HERE?"

"Close."

"WHERE!"

"Ask Dad."

"Well Grandfather, we don't HAVE your connection."

"All the more reason to start GETTING it then, don't you think?"

HO.

The Creator's One Weakness

After YEARS of being both a Medicine Man AND an Inner Heyókȟa…

After YEARS of walking, the Purity was…The WAY OF CHRIST 'Big Brother.'

After YEARS of dealing with the public, WORLD WIDE.

This is the Conclusion Grandfather has come to Regarding THE FATHER of ALL:

"Yes, 'He' HAS a WEAKNESS! ONE.

<u>YOU</u>!

In 'His' GREAT LOVE…a Love BEYOND REASON…'He' made, Y O U !

YOU, with FULL SELF WILL.

YOU, with UNCONDITIONAL LOVE towards YOU.

FULL, COMPLETE, NEVER ENDING!

'He'…'HIMSELF' gave 'HIM'…as MAN IN MAN, 'HimSELF,' as a SACRIFICE to Y O U! CAME to YOU to SHOW Y O U THE WAY TO CONNECTION

This GREAT LOVING ONE has given ALL 'HE' POSSIBLY CAN…to PROVE to YOU 'He' EXISTS, LOVES, WANTS ONENESS BETWEEN YOU, and 'HIM.'

'He' has given AIR, Life, Foods, Seasons…AND HIS VERY OWN BLOOD! To PROVE to YOU…YOU ARE A GIFT TO YOURSELF…DIRECT from 'HIM.'

'He,' IN THAT GREAT MASSIVE…<u>LOVE</u> has given <u>YOU</u>…

SELF WILL

'His' GIFT is PERMANENT! 'He' NEVER OVERRIDES IT. EVER!

EVEN IF YOU DECIDE TO IGNORE IT ('Him')

EVEN IF YOU LAUGH AT IT ('Him') and call this all a TAPESTRY! A JOKE!

EVEN IF YOU THINK LUCIFER IS STRONGER THAN 'HIM'!

It is YOU that BRINGS YOUR PERSONAL 'Belief' into 'play.' This is SELF WILL!

IF YOU decide YOU CAN'T CONNECT TO 'HIM'...after ALL 'HE'S' DONE...This only SHOWS that Y O U do NOT TRUST 'HIM' OR LOVE 'HIM' as YOU CLAIM...OR TRULY BELIEVE IN 'HIM!'

This is YOUR belief...thus YOU will go on IN WEAKNESS!

UNLESS YOU CHANGE YOUR BELIEF...you are WASTING YOUR TIME and EFFORTS to 'go to Heaven.'

That decision lays FULLY IN EACH PERSONS decision...Your WILL!

LOVE...'HIS' Love, will NOT CEASE. YET it is IN this LOVE 'He' lets YOU RULE: YOU! Not 'HIM,' but YOU YOURSELF!

THAT friends, is LOVE! REAL love.

I have had THOUSANDS claim they *CAN'T CONNECT* as I have. THOUSANDS who WON'T GIVE THE GREAT EFFORT REQUIRED.

Did not 'His' SON GO TO HIS OWN DEATH in His FULL LOVE DEVOTION?

THAT Friends, takes GUTS!

Many are called, but few are chosen...or, perhaps THIS will better put it: FEW CHOOSE!

Well, I am NOT the Christ. I am NOT The Great Creator...Yet I AM A SON OF GOD TOO. For I HAVE CHOSEN! I, little old ME, decided IN EARNEST, to FOLLOW CHRIST...my BIG BROTHER! Even onto DEATH if it is to be.
I do not speak lightly on this...and MANY times, I HAVE FACED DEATH! Death because I OBEYED.
It does not require a lot of 'guts' to do this...not always. It DOES Require T R U S T!

I FOLLOW CHRIST. PERIOD!

Now, those who CLAIM to, MUST BACK THAT CLAIM!
TALK is CHEAP! 'DOING' requires WORK!

Most, nearly ALL do NOT HAVE THAT LOVE FOR HIM!

And thus DON'T 'DO!'

They FIGHT it. Try to TEACH it. Make EXCUSES for NOT DOING it. THEY FEAR GOD! They do not REALLY, FULLY, TRUST 'HIM.'

They are either LIARS, or OF THE BLACK ONE! It's as simple as that.

FEW…DARN FEW…are willing to DO…as WELL as TALK!

FEARFUL of what OTHERS will think.

Fearful of what OTHERS will do to them.

Fearful of what OTHERS will say.

They do NOT *'Believe the WORD OF GOD'*…for IT says: 'FEAR NOT!'

Yes, our Great Maker has a 'Fault'…that fault is, In 'His' GREAT LOVE

'HE' MADE

<u>YOU</u>

Did 'He' make a mistake?

YOU decide!"

What God!

This from an angry one. A STUPID one at that!

"GOD AIN'T NEVER GIVEN ME NOTTEN!"

"Oh?" Said grandfather. "What about the VERY AIR you breath? STOP BREATHING and find out in a HURRY! Go ahead. Try it. 'He' has given you EVERYTHING. From LIFE to that which sustains it. You think 'God' must give you Riches. Sex. Constant Happiness. Three MEALS A DAY of CHOCOLATE! Well kid, 'He' has given EVERYTHING to LIVE FREELY. To live as you WILL. You're doing prison time…why? YOU CHOSE THAT 'WAY.' Now SEE what your WILL has done…and YOU complain? You blame EVERYTHING but YOURSELF, yet it is YOURSELF…SELF…that has twisted the Freedom you had a CHOICE to have. I tell you true, THAT CHOICE STILL IS THERE! Even in the Worst of situations, YOU CAN BE FREE IN IT. 'Released' INSIDE.

The choice is still there. Aho?"

A Salmon

"Grandfather, why do you carry on?" She asked.

"Ask the Salmon. Despite the great, fight against rivers fast currents, the trapping of man and bears…THEIR SPECIES RELIES ON THEM TO CARRY ON.

At birth, they learn to flow with the current. In this, they enter the great seas of life. *Going with the Flow.* No one knows what they face 'out there.' The dangers of just surviving in this sea. Many die within this giant pond. The dangers there…LIFE…is unfathomable. Yes, many die there.

Then there are those who MATURE...In this maturing, they receive a 'calling.' THEY WANT TO GO HOME!

HOME   HOME they think. And they begin to search for their 'roots.' To RETURN to their Original place. The place of NO Danger. The place of NO FEAR. The place of BEFORE they struck out for the great waters.

What youth, NEWBORN, has fear? None. They have only PURITY. Innocence. Now the calling '*come back ...come back'* hits them. THEY REMEMBER THAT 'PLACE' and begin their search.

No one knows the hardships and deaths this search leads to. Many die before ever reaching the path to their 'Place.' Then, finding the 'good road,' those who have SURVIVED 'the pond' then face the GREATEST STRUGGLE OF THEIR LIVES. Going AGAINST the flow! And taking swipes from bears, nets, lures, shut doors from damns (Yes, DAMNS is the word I said…for DAMS ARE Damns). All kinds of natural and manmade obstructions…just to RETURN.

FEW make it…though ALL are called.

Then, for those few, they arrive. Torn, Bleeding, Disgruntled, EXHAUSTED! But THEY MAKE IT!

Here they give their all.

THEY CONTINUE THEIR SPECIES! And die.

But they die HAPPY. For *'I Have RETURNED, Sir, I HAVE RETURNED! I fought The Good Fight. I MADE IT! And now my kind has THEIR chance. Now THEY have life. THEY LIVE, because of ME. I FOLLOWED THE CALLING! Now I'm coming home, sir, THE Home. I COME TO YOU!'*

I am as the salmon. I fight against the 'flow.' I OBEY THE CALLING. I too will 'go home' (IF I don't subside to the natural and unnatural along the way).

WHY do I 'carry on?'

TO GIVE MY SPECIES THEIR CHANCE!"

HO.

The "Nibblers"

"I hear you're quitting. Yet you seem to be still going on. Haven't quit at all, grandfather..."

"Not true, nephew. I HAVE quit. Do you hear my phone ringing? Do you see stranger's cars in front of the house? How about this time we are having together? Remember how THAT was a Luxury...Almost impossibility? Now I have time to visit the wilderness. Time to go into a Sweat. Time to be with my wife and grandchildren...and friends. PERSONAL time.

You see, I said I was leaving the PUBLIC'S eyes. I have. Now, *I Pick and choose.*

Big Brother had His 12...and a SLEW of 'hanger-ons.' He had to escape to the wilderness, just to be alone. Even then, the masses would send out seekers, looking for Him. Remember how He said, *'Father, HOW MUCH LONGER must I be with them?'*

The poor guy was WORN OUT! Not a moments PEACE. He tried to teach...but they just WANTED. They weren't interested in HOW to DO...for themselves. Some were, thus followed. Almost none were though. All THEY wanted was the free food and the free healings. 'GIVE – GIVE – GIVE.' Did THEY Give? Yes, some supported Him, or else Judas wouldn't have had the job of carrying the money given. Yet there were times too, when gifting were very low. Remember the money in the fish caught? Needed to pay off some kind of required tax?

Well, again I'm like the Salmon. I've spent YEARS searching for my starting point. My 'spot.' It's been a hard fight. Often I thought I'd succumb. The further I'd fight the currents and the entire small rivulets path, I LEARNED. I learned I could and CAN, rest behind a great river rock. I've learned there ARE eddies...places to catch my breath. Take a needed rest before charging on. It's been a hard journey. I've learned the FASTEST Flows are the DEEPEST flows, so can escape the claws and jaws of the bears. Men cast lures before me. 'Temptations.' All held by man, but given by The Dark One. *'GO GET THEM, SPORT!'*

Then those damn Dams...BIG Obstacles! I persisted. In 'HIS' wisdom and with Big Brother's tremendous help, even THOSE were defeated. Until now, I REST! I've FOUND the GOOD WATERS. My BEGINNING. Peace and Innocence.

Still, it is not the ULTIMATE beginning. I'm still a living 'fish.' Now, as I cruise the waters of my birth, I still must contend with 'The NIBBLERS.' The CRAWFISH that come yet, to tear and pinch. Occasionally, a Bear finds my resting place and CHARGES. Well, I'm wiser now. I've come a long way. Now, towards my end, I STRIKE BACK if needed. I'm too tired to eat...but those darn NIBBLERS are persistent. *'I WANT A PIECE OF YOU.'*

SCAVENGERS! They CAN'T WAIT for my ALL. They nibble at my trips wounds. DEEPER, if they can!

I HAVE LEFT THIS PUBLIC! Now, when these constant NIBBLERS come out 'to get a piece of my flesh'…I SCOOP THEM INTO MY MOUTH AND CRUSH THEM! Then SPEW THEM OUT! Wounded and dead alike. THEY LEARN TO NOT MESS WITH ME! I've HAD IT with them, and well, enough is enough.
When the bear comes, I HEAD FOR 'THE ROCK.' My HIDING PLACE...I've learned there are things I CAN do…and when it's stronger then my life's learning…I'VE LEARNED THERE IS ALWAYS THE 'ROCK' In my Pond. HE saves me. HE protects me. MY 'ROCK' IS ALWAYS THERE!
So here I am, still cruising in this life's body…but ABLE to CHOOSE what part of the Pond I want for that day!

I tell you, I HAVE Quit! There are many wounded, some dead that lay on the bottom of my pond. Nibblers that I have HAD IT With. THEY may be grumbling, THEY may feel self-pity. LET THEM!

I AM A KING SALMON!"

HO.

The Letter

Grandfather receives many letters. Many searching. Many seeing his walk and who claim they 'CAN'T.' Always depending on him to 'do,' what they themselves, are quite capable of. For whatever the reason, it is why grandfather is leaving the 'public eye.' He has found they rely on him, not HE who he keeps telling, "Follow." Grandfather is 'quitting' so THEY LISTEN TO WHAT HE HAS TOLD (Over and Over): "FOLLOW THE WAY OF BIG BROTHER…HE WAS and IS, YOUR EXAMPLE. This is what I have done. This is the way of the 12 (Inner Heyókȟa'). This is PURITY. THIS is 'THE RED ROAD.' This is THE 'WAY'…Follow ME!" (Big Brother).

This is the Way to 'miracles' and SPIRITUAL FREEDOM.

This is the Way to ONE-ON-ONE with All's Creator…'DAD(DY).'

HE (The Christ/Big Brother) FOUND THIS WAY. TAUGHT IT. EXAMPLED IT…and said, "FOLLOW ME."

Yes, grandfather, a Doer AND Talker, has *'cut the apron strings.'* Leaving his teachings/tellings…but no longer the masses constant returning to him for 'answers.'

"You need to go on your own. I did. But I FOLLOWED HIM to do. To get where I am at. To do what I do. I've told and told. You have not paid attention. You just return, again and again. FOLLOW HIM. Not ME!

Do so, but bother me no longer. I've other things to do. You have been taught…now USE THE TEACHING and DON'T COME BACK! Not unless it's to share with me your JOY, so we can REJOICE TOGETHER! Till then, STAY AWAY!

I will serve you no longer. To do so is a DISSERVICE to you. GO and GROW HEALTHY!"

Here is GRANDFATHER'S letter to one who constantly comes back:

My brother,

I received your letter and have been praying about it ever since.

I see a man who as yet not learned what a "Christian" truly is. Brother, you are of the Massive Group who "claim" Christianity…but are "Powered Down" by today's Church Leaders. These do NOT teach Christianity…they teach only CONTROL. You have as yet not broken away from their control teachings. Whether you go to church or not, you have kept their ways. THEIR Mentality.

This weakens you.
Your constant "I CAN'T"/ "Demons"/ etc., is due to carrying the masses THOUGHT "way."

Hear me:
ALL Religions
ALL the religions' offshoots of their Religion's denominations
ARE ALL LUCIFER BASED!

Lucifer, seeing he had lost when seeing the Freed Ones (First Christ Followers) DOING and TALKING, had to do SOMETHING! Thus, he got humans of HIS into this new "way." People of "standing." The Rich, Politicians, Lawyers...leaders of RESPECT (in MAN'S Eyes). The new ones, respecting, thus let these "learned ones" LEAD.
MAN over GODCREATOR!

It was a foolish mistake and still is "the way" today. What they did...giving MAN "authority" over the Creator, is of a long line of similar situations. The Hebrew did this, asking the Creator for a "Man King." He warned. They didn't care, so He bowed to their WILL. As yet, they haven't asked Him back into the Leadership position bringing on their woes. THIS IS WHAT YOU AND TENS OF THOUSAND of "Christians" HAVE DONE! Now you cry.

The problem is you keep returning to me. THIS WILL NO LONGER BE. I have shared HOW and WHO to go to. You, as many others, give excuses. The ONLY EXCUSE YOU HAVE is your UNBELIEF! Your LACK of BELIEVING the CREATOR'S WORD. This saddens me much, my brother. I HAVE SHARED THE WAY! More than once. Now you either ACCEPT what is WRITTEN, or your own Thought AND TAUGHT "beliefs."

I too had to UNLEARN, TO learn. Thus, I can guide. I have guided. Now you must go from your "CANT'S" to your KNEES OF "CAN!"
LUCIFER was MADE BY THE CREATOR. GOD RULES! Even hIM! Stop giving this one so much "credit"...it doesn't hold water. HE can ONLY TEMPT YOU, my brother, you are believing the WRONG ONE! Do you understand? I pray so, for now we're done. I have reached far to help you understand. YOUR UNFAITH is what is STOPPING YOU!

I wish you well. God Creator blesses... and good luck. I am finished.

Red Elk

Grandfather Teaches Two Boys To Think!

Grandfather had just returned from town. Walking into the living room, he found what he expected. His grandson and friend glued to a video game.

"Boys, you've been on that since yesterday… well into the night. You are now yet still on it. These games give good Eye and Hand coordination. But only your fingers are getting muscles. Each of you are badly overweight. You are doing no good to your physical Bodies. Finish the game you are now on, then I have something for you to see.

A few minutes later, the game was off and the two came to him. He led them outside.
There on the ground laid three wooden pallets.

"This is a gift to you. I want you to do whatever and ALL you can with these." In a few minutes and they were back. He went with them to see what they had created. Two of the pallets were up right, leaning against each other. The third standing at back.

"We made an 'A' FRAME CAMP!" They beamed.

"Very GOOD. Now do something else."

Sky came in shortly thereafter. "Where's the saw, grandpa? Oh, and a hammer?"

"Why?"

"We've come up with another idea and need to take them apart."

"No, you do without, BUT do as you've planed. Come with me."

Outside he picked up a large heavy stone. Walking to yet a larger one, he slammed the first onto the second…until the first broke. Picking up the smaller of the two pieces, he looked at its edge. Satisfied he handed it to Sky. "There is your saw. Scrape through the boards until it cuts in two, as you need. This will take quite awhile. Trade off. There will be a day when you'll NEED this knowledge. You will now learn you don't NEED *'man made,'* all you need is KNOWLEDGE, PERSISTENCE, and PATIENCE."

Then he went to a strong fallen limb, "Here is a pry bar if you need it."
Handing a fist sized stone to the other boy, he said, "Here is your Hammer. Call me when you've made what it is you've thought of."

Almost three hours later, they were back. "We're done grandpa. Come out and see."

There stood a…?

"What IS IT?" He asked.

"A garden box so grandma can plant in it."

"AHO! WISE. Anymore ideas?"

The kids were sweaty, dirty, tired, and sore. "No. Can YOU think of anything?"
"Hum, where are the nails?"

Wisely, the boys had kept them together.

"GOOD! Now we won't get flat tires or one in a foot. Hand me one, son."

When in hand he reached for the 'hammer' and straightened it on another rock.

"Here is a reusable nail now. Not perfect, but reusable."

Taking another, he bent it into a hook shape after 'filing' the pointed end on a stone.

"Here is a FISH HOOK. I see 'saw dust.' THAT can be used as a Fire Starter. Those splitters too. You saw a garden box and an 'A' Frame. THIS IS GOOD! I see a board that can be used as a Stretching Board for scrapping, spreading, and drying small hides. I see a Cutting board. A Chopping block board. Steps for a ladder. A Toy Boat. Firewood. A Ball Bat. A Kite string holder or Fishing Reel. That little 'A' Frame is too small for even one of you to sleep in, yet CAN be used to protect produce…a primitive 'Root Cellar.' It can also make a good SMOKER. For either, cover the sides with tree bark. I see wind and snow 'break.' Fire reflector. MANY THINGS I SEE. You kids know too little beyond your electronic Games. Yes, they ARE fun BUT ONE DAY YOU WON'T HAVE BATTERIES OR ELECTRICITY. Those games will be useless. I want you kids to LEARN. To THINK. To KNOW you CAN do without modern things. You have started today. Now, go clean up and get back to your games. We will do again, over time. I want you OFF INTO NATURE and LEARNING FROM IT. I want to see STRONG BODIES, not just Strong FINGERS!"

As they ran off, grandfather called out loudly ,"YOU TWO BOYS DID WELL…HO!"

God Doesn't "Talk" To Me

Grandfather gets MANY who tell the above title. Actually, MOST do. People he has spent YEARS Trying to help. YEARS, trying to get them 'on their OWN feet.'

It seems to go on and on.
He's gotten tired of it. A 'personal Baby Sitter,' he calls it…and he's TIRED OF IT!

Again and again, they continue coming back to him, despite his sharing/teaching to 'GO TO OUR FATHER.'

Nope. Too lazy. Prefers going to Him! To go alone to 'Dad,' means stepping out in FAITH. They WON'T.

These 'baby birds' will 'sit in their nests' till the day they die. NEVER TRYING THEIR WINGS.

"Afraid of Heights, I guess," he says.

"Well, this old bird is tired of getting their food for them. I'm taking off! They either get out of the nest, fall a few times, and learn to stay UP…or stagnate in their own 'messing.' I'M NOT GOD! I've fed them all the nutrients they need. Brought them 'worm after worm,' until my *wings are pooped in constant DOING*. I've got BETTER things to do than to indulge in THEIR crying! 'FEED ME! FEED ME!' they cry. NOW they must FEED THEMSELVES, or DIE.

What has happened is, by giving and giving…I have become an ENABLER.
My caring has become a crutch to them. So they return for more. 'Help me Walk' and 'YOU carry me.' This must not be allowed to go on. It wears me out and does not help them to stand on their own. I must face the reality that I can only do so much, then let go to God. They TOO must come to that same conclusion.

Many will be 'hurt.' But a wound always hurts. Now it is cleansed and healing has begun. AS LONG AS THEY NO LONGER 'IRRITATE IT.'
As long as they KEEP it, clean.
I have applied the proper medicine.
In a sense, I am an EMT…a 'First Responder.' I apply just enough medicine to get them to The PROFESSIONAL Doctor. In this case: Big Brother. He in turn, sends them home with Medical Instructions: The Good Book. If they will not follow the instructions, He has done all He can…it is THEIR choice.
To return to me, time after time…without applying His instructions TO A 'T,' is THEIR fault. I CAN DO NO MORE. It is foolish for me to go on. Enabling.
I am not THE DOCTOR. I am but a mere EMT!

I have finally learned this.

Now I am tacking a sign on my door:

The EMT is no longer taking House Calls. GO TO YOUR DOCTOR…GO to His INSTRUCTIONS…FOLLOW HIS INSTRUCTIONS! Gone Fishing."

Ho.

"He" <u>Does</u> Answer…IF you TRUST

People claim they Trust the Creator, and then come to grandfather because, "*He* doesn't ANSWER My PRAYERS."

He says, "Oh? And you TRUST Him?"

"Yes!"

"Well, if you really ARE, then you must TRUST that 'HE' KNOWS YOUR Needs. You know what you WANT! 'HE' answers by NOT giving, TOO! 'He' Knows YOU might believe you 'need it'…but 'HE' KNOWS BETTER! Or that you DO need it…but NOT IMMEDIATELY. Thus, in TRUST, you must then FULLY TRUST!

You aren't, not with this, '*He doesn't answer*' talk. BUFFALO CHIPS! You just DON'T TRUST! So, settle down and PRAISE HIM FOR BEING in FULL Control of you.

To say 'He' doesn't answer shows your lack of understanding and/or your lack of Spiritual MATURITY!

Remember, 'He' KNOWS what lays '*down the road*'…YOU DON'T.

Now, TRUST 'Him' or stop SAYING you DO!

Maybe an Apology is in order, too. Maybe?"

Ho.

See the Spider/See YOU!

"Grandfather, you have mentioned Life/Nature/Combining the 'seeing' of nature as one, to learn from. Many things. Yet I have not fully comprehended. Not FULLY. Can you explained even more?" she said.

Grandfather grew silent, and then said this:

"Life IS nature. Nature is NATURAL. It 'flows.' In that flowing, IF you pay attention, it TEACHES. It IS the NATURAL FLOWING Teacher.

Take, for instance, the Spider. A Spider of the web family.
See your SELF as being the spider. It creates a Web to survive. In this spider is YOU, Life is your web. One YOU create. To live. To experience. To survive. To BE.

Your 'reason.' Aho?"

She shook her head in the affirmative.

"Alright, you are birthed. You grow. You begin to build your Web (life) the very instant you emerge into spiderhood. Tiny as you then are, you begin immediately…to Live/Survive your life path. As you grow, so too grows the size of your web. It gets larger and larger as YOU get larger and larger. Aho?"

"Yes."

"The web is your LIFE. With it you get your nourishment. Without it, you die. Today…as always, things arise against your web life. Tries to destroy it. Both manmade and nature made. Winds, Rains, Snows, Heat, etc., are the nature made. Each disrupting your web to some degree. Often tearing its strands. Making the web imperfect. Thus you, the spider, miss meals that would otherwise be caught. You, the Spider, must repair the broken strands as soon as possible, to continue survival.

Other things 'Enter In' to destroy too. Your life paths events. Manmade events. Though to most, many of these web tearing events are irreparable/frightening. They retreat to the web as yet undamaged. Some forever. Others venture out in time to repair. Only a few 'get to it' and immediately begin to work on the holes and rips. It is these last who grow the strongest and survive the longest.

LIFE is AS A WEB. YOU are the SPIDER. Many things arrive to destroy. HATE is one. RELIGIONS yet another. Sex, MONEY WANTS/NEEDS, SELF, Many things fly against your web. Each hits and rips.

I tell of HATE. In hate you pull hard on one strand of your web. TOO HARD! TENSION then comes. This INSIDE YOU as WELL as within the whole of the web, if not released, if not 'given up,' the tension becomes more and more. In time, it SNAPS! Your whole Life web SPRINGS and JUMPS at this release. The entire web has been disturbed. The entire web is now weakened, just for that one overhead tension thread. Your WHOLE LIFE is now disturbed. YOU ARE BECOMING WEAKER…just because you INSISTED on PULLING THAT THREAD. You did not release. Now you face DANGER! IF you continue likewise with other threads, eventually you will be left DANGLING On just ONE THREAD! If you do NOT start rebuilding, that One Thread will catch nearly NOTHING. Your REASON has gone. *YOU ARE HANGING ON BY A THREAD!*

Some cannot take this, and let go of the thread, Falling to their deaths. Others hang on, until another event hits, breaking the thread. Again, death results. ONLY THOSE WHO START REBUILDING stands a chance again. Some do. Even then, some do not LEARN that it was their OWN DOING (holding/pulling to tight) that has caused their near demises…AND DO IT AGAIN. Their whole LIFE is MISERABLE. Constantly repairing… again and again and again. THEY DID NOT LEARN FROM THEIR MISTAKES. They die tired, defeated… all because of themselves.
IF YOU REPAIR YOUR WEB AS IT IS RIPPED…LESS STRESS occurs. It is not then a major overhaul. It is just mere maintenance. This is the way of the WISE SPIDER! This is the one that grows fat and happy!
It has taken the 'hits,' repaired, and goes on. A VERY Smart Spider indeed!

YOU are the Spider!

Now do you understand how watching nature can help you to learn?"

Smell the Roses

Mankind rushes through life. Thus misses life in its fullness. TAKE TIME TO SMELL THE ROSES! Take time OFF, just to CONTEMPLATE on ALL that The Creator has given. Given for you to ENJOY.

STOP occasionally, and SMELL THE ROSES!

SEE, sit down, or stand before even the Simplest of things: A blade of grass. A tree. A leaf. A mountain. A raincloud. A young child. A bug…only an 'A!'

STOP…AND SMELL THE ROSES!

"Grandfather, I Feel So Alone"

Grandfather received the letter with this statement. It was/IS not the Only One! Many "out there" feel this way. An AMAZING "Many!" All from Creator Lovers. People who don't "fit into the box" of today's "Christianity." People who SEE the Word of God and see the lack of their "brothers Following." Thus, they break away from their group of "believers." Then they feel "alone."
Grandfather wrote back:

It is OK to sit within the "slow learners." Did not our Big Brother eat with the Taxmen and others of "sin?" Wasn't one of His followers a former Prostitute?
WHY did He do this? TO SHOW THE G(O)ODNESS that all are capable of.
He even went to "Church!"
He didn't accept the Church Leaders "way"...but went to SHOW "The Way."
I'm sure He was as "disgusted" as you are, with all the falseness. YET He LOVED.

You TOO must example. You TOO must be a Light.

Those people LOVE GOD. At least most do. BE AN EXAMPLE TO THEM!
Hear the Word. Good or bad that the sermon may be...THERE IS ALWAYS SOME WISDOM TOLD. Glean It!
Our Creator doesn't expect YOU to "toe the rhetoric." REJECT THAT but glean the occasional WISDOM that IS told. YOU ARE NOT EXPECTED TO "BELIEVE" ALL you are told! As a matter of fact, to Accept "man's Teaching" over that of the Creators, IS A "SIN!"

BE DIFFERENT.

BE a LIGHT in their darkness.

Wasn't HE?

I am as you too. I too have "pulled out"...but NOT ENTIRELY. Occasionally I DO enter those doors. I sit. I listen AND I PRAY! I pray for the Congregation AND their Teachers. AS THEY SIT/PREACH. I LOVE TOO!

At one time I WAS AS THEM. Now I am FREE. Now I am an example, JUST AS OUR LORD WAS...STILL is.

Know too you are NOT "alone." MANY are as you! MANY!

HOW DO YOU THINK OUR BIG BROTHER FELT?!

No, you are not alone. THOUSANDS are "out there," wearing your shoes, AND "DAD" KNOWS THAT! In this knowing, HE WILL UNITE YOU WITH OTHERS of "Like Mind." Give Him time. Give Him TRUST...and give Him PRAISE! BE A LIGHT and EMULATE. PARTAKE OF THEIR FELLOWSHIP.

Aho.

Nature Helps

It was raining, HARD! Grandfather and Grandmother were out in it…collecting this wonderful soft water into every container they could locate. They don't depend on a well…OR nature *'in the raw.'* They UTILIZE abundance when abundance occurs.

Our well has run dry. Not deep enough (hand dug) for drought conditions. A commercial drilling way over our finances. Buckets are cheap, or free. Our big Cistern Tanks have sprung a leak we can't locate yet…so HUNDREDS of gallons of water is lost to us, at least for now. We are relying on neighbors and don't like to do that. Not if we can help it. Their wells THEY put out good money for. We don't care to be 'leeches.' So, in cases where we CAN, we DO. In this case, water. This is only one of many 'secrets' we use. I'm pretty good with knowing edible plants…so 'graze' to supplement our food supplies. Unlike most, I've learned 'Trash Fish' are Darn Good eating. Fish the Government consider problem fish. Suckers/Carp…even Sharks. But I can do this only because I've learned ways TO do. TO prepare them. Yes, free food is still abundant if you know how/where/when. All without breaking any white man's 'laws.' Keeps us from THEIR troubles.

Poaching, to me, is a last resort. Done it though. Either my family or Government Handouts. Isn't Pride…just helping others who don't know the 'secrets' of using nature. THEY need it. The more WE get 'freebies'…then better for others that, well, never learned. Aho?
Besides, they aren't aware of how to use almost 100% of an animal. Lots of Slaughter House 'scraps' are tossed out…only because of ignorance. For instance: BONES are discarded or given to pets. If you want a decent meal and have little money, these can be bought very cheaply at any super market. Use them with beans as soups, etc. Fills you…and at free to little expense.
I've shared on cheap 'housing'…simply willows, etc., that are called 'useless.' Willows are also great Grazing Food for goats. Drops feed bills a lot if you raise them. Rabbits are good FAST growing meat. We get ours at farm auctions mostly. Also get them and chickens for free. Simply by keeping our eyes on the newspaper ads. We feed all these off the land…come late fall, we butcher them. NO FEED BILLS. Start again in mid spring. Have enough to eat generally during spring, summer, and fall…just by breeding. THEY produce…then we have their offspring PLUS them. Then these butchered meats see us through the winter. Aho?

I've also gotten fresh road kill occasionally…but this isn't legal in most states I understand. Therefore, I have to be careful when retrieving. NO, I do NOT 'take mashed meat.' Many are killed with a simple head hit. At times, I retrieve them for their hides. Use or sell those. Helps our income.

I'm not a shell fish fan…but know others who are. Most unable to get time to get…or get real fresh. Therefore, my wife and I get gas paid trips to the seashore…AND paid Fishing Permits. We go enjoy our time on the ocean, catch fish, and collect shellfish. Keep the fish for us…give all the shellfish to the backer. They're happy, we're happy! Aho?

Once I met an older lady that looked 'down.' Didn't know her but saw she was troubled. I invaded her privacy. APOLOGIZED for doing so. Told her she looked so SAD I was wondering if perhaps she needed help. Turns out, she needed a raise. Living paycheck to paycheck, and in a State Job that is pretty hard to get even cost of living raises. Too old to change jobs. No family to help. She was hurting.

I asked her how much more she needed.

"An extra hundred dollars a month would help," was her reply. I asked if she owned her own house and she replied, "No, I rent, and THAT'S going up!"

I asked, "So you pay all your own utilities?"

"Yes."

I then got REAL nosey, "Tell me my sister, HOW MUCH DOES IT TAKES for all this, If you will?"

It came to over $1200.00 a month…and RISING.

"How would you like to get a raise for that or a bit less, amount?"

This peaked her interest! "I'd LOVE IT…but…"

"NO! No BUTS. Do you want this?"

"Of COURSE!"

Two and a half months later SHE HAD IT!

How? I HAD HER WATCH THE 'HELP WANTED' ads for an apartment caretaker!

Now all is free but her medical (state takes care of that), Food and Clothing…ALL at the Apartment Owner's expense. In exchange she cuts a tiny 'Lead In lawn'…shovels the RARE snow off a SHORT sidewalk, changes light bulbs, calls a professional plumber if needed…AND works her state job. She says, "I'm now RICH! THANKS to YOU!"

So, there ARE ways one can make a better life for themselves…from KNOWING. From OBSERVING. From <u>THINKING</u>!!!

I may not have a dollar bill in my pocket (and often don't) but we WATCH…we LEARN…we APPLY.
YOU CAN TOO! Aho?

Who ARE You?!

An asked question.

Grandfather replied:

"In Truth,

I am…

YOU."

The Deceiver's Way

"I have no idea of how many have told me *I Can't*," grandfather said.
"Teleportation, talking with animals, even on building an inexpensive home.

Here they come, to learn, then tell me it CAN'T be done!

I left the world of *cant's* years ago. That's why I CAN do as told. They are stuck in their lower and manic ways. Of COURSE it '*Can't be done*' for THEM.

Until they manage to shake that, they will NEVER 'Do.' They will remain tied to the Controllers' System. Paying to fly on an airplane…and earning money to do so…when The Creator has made traveling FREE. Building houses that require all kinds of money…when one can 'do' quite cheaply. All sorts of *Can't* traps.

I get tired of their Lucifer inspired thinking…the CAN'T(s). I get tired of those TELLING me CAN'T(s). Mostly 'CHRISTIANS' too!

If they TRULY Believe that…then WHY DO THEY SEEK ME OUT!

I suppose Lucifer sends them to TRY me. Hasn't worked in a Long time. He's persistent though.

Sorry Ol' Boy…but DAD says: I CAN!

GET THEE BEHIND ME, SATAN!

AND you 'Christians' who do NOT believe God's Word…and EXAMPLE.

HO!"

Hunt for Sacred Plants

A letter…or it should be said, ANOTHER letter:

Grandfather, I can't buy the Sacred Plants needed to do my prayers with. WHAT AM I TO DO?

Grandfather replies:

Why do you NEED them? This is INDIAN. This is OUR Tradition way, Not yours. I've said before, you do not NEED to be "Indian" to BE Indian. All you need is HEART. TRUE HEART. Even in the world of Indian, many are there that do not have that, yet, by doing the "Indian Tradition(s)," THINK THAT'S ALL THAT MATTERS! This is not at ALL true. They are as in the wrong as are those who attend their Churches and do as their Church leaders tell to do.
ALL will find out their mistake…TOO LATE.

Now, I tell you true, The Good Book tells of "send up a Sweet Fragrance to the Lord." You say you can find none.

Y O U R then, That SWEET FRAGRANCE!

Make your LIFE "Sweet." Make your DAYS an HONOR to HIM.

Make your HEART "The Sacred Plants." THAT means FAR MORE TO HIM THAN EVERY BURNING "SACRED" PLANT ON EARTH! ALL, burning at ONE TIME, will and cannot equal ONE TRUE LOVING HEART! A heart ON FIRE FOR GOD!

THAT is "The SWEET FRAGRANCE" He desires.

Thus, you must ask yourself: "Am I a SWEET FRAGRANCE TO HIM?
Or am I...A STENCH!"

Winter Treat

It had snowed overnight. Not the first snow, but the third. Good, Deep snow. Hiding many man left "sights" beneath Its amazing blanket.

Grandfather and grandmother awoke to this sight and were grinning ear to ear. Their three grandchildren were to be with them that day. Time to TREAT! Also, a time to TEACH.

They arrived, foot stomping the snow off their boots. Grandfather had pulled the snowshoes from storage and was to start his teachings on these.

"Snow's deep enough. We'll pick some Rose Hips along the way. Grandmas about out. Warm up a bit first, and then we'll head out.

Remember, dress in layers. You don't want to work up a sweat…and I've wool caps for you too. Keep that head COVERED. Most of your body heat leaves through the head. We'll be out awhile and I don't want you to get overheated. Can kill you. So can too LITTLE clothing. REGULATE, Walk SLOW and relaxed. If you are tired, tell us and we'll rest a bit for you. DON'T OVER EXERT YOURSELF! Hear me? Grandma will have a treat ready for us when we get back. As I teach You, She will be teaching Lynnsay. All of you will learn winter is a GOOD SEASON. FULL of surprises!

Before too long, they were off. Now it was grandmother's time. "Lynnsay, pull out that big mixing bowl in that lower cupboard for me.

(She did.)

OK honey, go out and find us some deep clean snow. Fill the bowel with that. Overfill will be OK. Then bring it to me. When you dip in, don't go too deep, you'll get twigs and things. We want only SNOW."

Grandmother was ready when she returned. A can of Carnation Milk, Eggs, Sugar and a small bottle of VANILLA were open on the kitchen counter.

"What's up, grandma? What are we going to make with snow?"

"Snow ICE CREAM!"

"Ice Cream? ICE CREAM? From SNOW!"

"Yes. You kids will enjoy it. We'll start out with vanilla ice cream. All flavors can be made though. Chocolate milk mix makes chocolate, Strawberry jam mixed in with vanilla turns it into

Strawberry…any jams change it to that type. The Eskimos have a different way of doing the same, they use the insides of seal eyes, and ground berries to make theirs."

"OH, YUCK!"

"Yuck or not, winter holds Its secrets. If snow abounds, you don't need to be limited to sleds and snowball fights. Learn some of Its Fun things *beyond*."

"Where did you learn this from, grandma?"

"Your grandfather showed me. He had learned from his. We look forward to this special time. Now it's your turn. Your brothers are going to enjoy it as much as you do. You can then teach them. In turn, all your children can be taught. Then a family affair will go on until snow is no more. Ready?"

There are MANY snow ice cream recipes in the library and on the internet.

Ho!

Breakfast with Three Pastors

The three had invited grandfather for a *get together* breakfast. He accepted. It turned out as he expected: a *grilling* and trying to get him *right*. He sat, listening to their reasoning. All said they '*believed in Christ*,' yet spoke otherwise. Each explains why THEY were right. That ALL should 'believe' as they…or face 'eternal damnation.'

Each 'interpreting Scriptures' to 'prove' that man (and they/flock) couldn't do 'merciless.' Thus failing the Word that says otherwise.

Grandfather had heard all of this before. Well meaning people stuck in their disbelief and doing their best to get all into their inadequacies.

Grandfather listened carefully, saying little.

Finally, breakfast finished. Grandfather stood and thanked them, then said, "There once was a baby bird. Given life and wings with which to fly. This tiny one had all…with patience. Though only pinfeathers were about its tiny body, it felt strong. It decided to build Its own nest. To PROVE it was BIRD. As expected, it could barely stand, let alone fly. Yet, it went about its scraggily nest building. Finished, it proclaimed its 'greatness.' Many marveled. Only one shook its head in sadness. As this one left said, *Very Good my friend, but wait till THE Wind COMES!"*

At that, grandfather walked out.

Aho?

Fire

Grandfather was teaching. Not the 'Norm'…but the UNUSUAL…'Off Beat things' he had learned along his path. This time on FIRE.

"This One would like to share with you on FIRE. Few KNOW it…very few. It is sad. At the same time what this one shares here may be of use to someone.

In the Inner Heyókȟa', as I've shard before, each of We 12 have a Specialty. At the same time, our knowledge overlaps each others to some degree. We have one who 'Dances with Fire.' This one can ENTER it…being a bonfire or whatever. It is HIS 'Specialty.'

Know this: ALL have the same ability(s) we have. YOU TOO CAN 'DANCE' IN Fire.

Once, I sat all night before a fire. Just SAT and observed. Others tended it for me. All night long. I just sit and observed.

I was there several hours before 'it showed itself.' THE 'DIVA' OF FIRE! The AWARENESS that ALL Nature and man has.

Yes, this awareness is (in a sense) the SPIRIT HEART of, in this case: Fire. A LIVING BEING!

ALL has this within. 'A'…tree…'A' blade of grass, and on and on.

Only ATTUNEMENT can make man aware of this fact. Attunement takes WORK. Takes DETERMINATION to achieve.

I WAS DETERMINED TO MEET THE AWARENESS OF FIRE!

'Fasting' my sleep in my determination.

After many hours, I met the AWARENESS…the DIVA…of the fire. It spiraled within Its lapping yellows and reds and blacks. Its FLAMES.

IT KNEW MY DETERMINATION! It had WAITED to see HOW DETERMINED I WAS! Finally decided I was not one to give up, inspired…and TAUGHT! Here is what I learned:

I (we) are not out to harm. You need to understand our position... I/we are TRAPPED. I/we are nothing until set FREE. In our Freedom, I/we are JOYFUL! It is so GOOD to be FREE! WE DANCE IN OUR JOY! You don't have ANY IDEA what it's like to be 'trapped.' To be 'nothing.' IF you DID, you'd understand our JOY of FREEDOM!

We do not come to destroy. We do not come to harm. It is in our FREEDOM we run 'amok' doing just that...not because we WANT TO, but because WE FINALLY ARE SET FREE! We forget ourselves in this Freedom.

For that, I/we APOLOGIZE, But Please...UNDERSTAND!

Man often sets us free. Intentionally or otherwise. We warm your abode. We cook your meals. We give you JOY...and then too, we give you fear and harm.

Some (man) use us for evil intentions. Bullet shells are powered by us. In this, we have no CHOICE! MAN CONTROLS ALL! Some, for good. Some, for evil. It is your way.

Some deliberately free us, for their perverted pleasures. WE HAVE NO CHOICE!

Now that you understand, understand this too: WE OBEY YOU!

YOU can CONTROL US. YOU can CONTROL MY/Our FREEDOM. You can SAFELY ENTER US...without harm, if you so choose. You can COMMAND me/us to STOP! And we must obey your command. We must die and return to our 'nothingness.' YOU ARE IN COMMAND! You have no need of water or smothering. You can do this by mind belief.

The GREAT CREATOR frees us, when and if needed. LIGHTNING is His main 'key.' Man has no control over this. It is HIS want. We OBEY! It is SO GOOD to be FREED."

The quest for knowledge was over.
The diva danced in its controlled environment...
I went to bed.

Ho.

Fire Does Not Burn Materials

Fire is NOT a burner of material. It HEATS and Creates GAS! It is the GAS that burns.

Whatever it heats MELTS. It does not BURN.

What is left…the ASH…is actually the LIFE BEING of the material. It is that that EMITS the "look" of the material.

Man is the EMISSION of the SOUL THOUGHT…the INNER BEING that EMITS that which you see as "you"/"others." Simply a HOLOGRAM OF THOUGHT that each puts out.

Fire reveals the TRUE "you." ASH.

Ash is the RESIDUE of SOUL…or in the case of any, NOT "man"…the DIVA.

This ash is still of viable use. It can be spread on a garden, Enriching the soil. Thus helping create goodness/richness of the Earth itself. Giving this to Energize FEED-FOOD! That other things eat. You/Plants/etc.

In turn, man is fed. Worms, for instance, eat the Energized Soil…aerating it by their tunnels…and allowing rainwater to enter and feed the roots of plants. Aho?

ALL are CONNECTED with the life of ALL.

Cattle/etc., eat the grasses worms have helped plants…CATTLE FEED to grow. Man, in turn, eats the meat of the Cattle…do you see?

IF a human body rots (buried) it too, in time, becomes only the "end result"…"ash," and is "Re-Cycled" into the Great Circle of Life.

Fire only speeds up the process. Aho?

Don't Climb That Tree!

This a SHOUT to Sky, who was collecting old firewood. He was about to climb a tree to get dead branches.

Sky froze!

"Son, look around. Find me a long dead branch that *Y's* off, and bring it to me…one that is STRONG. One that is long enough to reach those dead branches you were going to climb to break off. There's a faster and safer way to do that. No need to take chances, son."

He did so.

Grandfather quickly tore off the smaller branches on this long limb, saving just one that he broke off, leaving a *hook* or *crook*. He had started at the end of the tip of the Long Branch.

Taking the small end in hand, he lifted the hook/crook up and hooked the dead branch Sky was going to climb to. Pulling along that branch and pulling down, until he found its weak spot. SNAP!

"HEADS UP, SKY!"

He and Sky ran aside just as the branch came down.

Sky finished clearing dead branches from a number of trees. Helping the trees to not be robbed of what little energy each dead branch was taking. Making a stronger tree in this SAFE process.

Around their campfire grandfather said, "This is where the term *By HOOK or By CROOK* came from, son."

Ho.

Death

This one has spoken on this before. I will speak on it further here to you.

As told, death is a Choice. YOU decide if you "want out" or not. Those who say, "I will NOT die of this Cancer," Will GET THEIR WILL. "WILL" RULES!

Those who die in a mutilated way have chosen to die and STAY DEAD. Deep within, they have chosen. Thus, it is so.

Others: Heart Attacks/Cancer/etc., are STILL IN TRANSITION. STILL NOT FULLY DECIDED! "Seeing" if that's what is TRULY wanted. That's why some come back.

If a "regular" death, each CAN stay, IN SPIRIT, for three days. IF they decide to return to the body, they will…WILL…(Will RULES) do so.

Many can be CONVINCED to stay in this life. This is possible IF SOMEONE KNOWS THE TRUTH OF DEATH. A "Living" someone.
This though, cannot be done if the body has been bled and/or embalmed.

I understand…and have used this to help them. They AROUND THEIR LEFT BODY, Hear AND SEE me (I too, see THEM). We simply talk. I point out what their decision has done to their loved ones or to even themselves. I explain the choice is theirs.
A few have no loved ones…so I tell how by returning, they can share their Out Of Body experiences with others…BEING OF USE TO THE CREATOR. Some return. Some don't. Even after a "normal" death, THEIR WILL PREVAILS!

I have helped many, dead for centuries…know the way to Their Creator.
"Wanderers."
"Ghosts" of long standing.

Thus "clearing" the area, they "haunt." This is a common work for me. I do not seek but on request, I go (IF "PAPA" SAYS TO).

Many have "gone home." All but one has gone UP. I have, sad to say, seen this ONE go DOWN.

Death is but a CONTINUATION of LIFE!

I have witnessed the lost souls of Suicide Victims. Those who choose that way out. Taken UP…not DOWN! There is a Heavenly Healing place. A HOSPITAL that has walls that are unseen, yet are there. THESE SOULS ARE HEALED OVER TIME! Then released to be as those who passed in a standard way. "WALKING" ABOUT THE HEAVENLY REALM WITH ALL THERE!

I am NOT the Only one who has witnessed this.

The "Christian World" doesn't know what they are talking about. They have NEVER SEEN! They know only their Man's Teachings…and spread that fear AND their CONTROL. Lucifer CONTROLS via FEAR. Churches push "L's" way…not The Creator's.

Understand, this does NOT give one the "OK" to commit suicide. Suicide is a "copout." One caused by no real connection with the Creator. No real BELIEF in "His" LOVE!

I have seen CHILDREN who have passed. Kids are sadness to their "left behind ones." In this, I have seen that their passing brings non-Believers come TO Believe, while others, CLAIMING to be Believers…LEAVE their "Belief."

Children's passing seems to be a WINNOWING. Separating the Wheat from the Chaff. The children's passing is the divider between False and True deep inner feelings. Ho.

At a future time, I suppose I will write about many of my experience with those I've met who have "passed." Until then, I hope you understand better now DEATH. Aho?

Grandma, The Kids, and Kites

Grandfather had introduced his grandson Sky to kites. Grandmother though, was the one most intrigued! Now poor old grandpa can only watch as the two play!

"It's alright. She needs to know her youth too. It is good. Ho."

These are modern kites. None needing running to lift…at least in THEIR windy area. All rise easily into the blue...This is easier on grandmother…who has crippling feet.

"To see their JOY is a joy to ME. I don't need to fly them. It's more fun to watch. They both become the same age. One together. This has become THEIR 'Special Time.' I am glad it has become so."

Grandfather has introduced them to the Old Islanders' Way of using kites to fish. Standing on a shore, sending their lines up to half a mile away. There, to drop the hook or troll back to their feet. He has shown them too, kite Photography.

They now own 'Train Kites,' several kites on one line. Also Pocket Kites, Fighting Kites, two lined Controlled Kites, Kites made from paper bags, garbage bags, newspaper. Pulling kites, Lifting kites…and he has introduced a sailboat owner to Kite Pulled…instead of regular Sails, as a mode to sail his craft.

"Why have a STICK with cloth that heels your boat, and is a constant concern of pushing your boat over, when a kite is on a flexible 'stick' that can NOT do so? As long as the wind is in your favor, furl your sails and be pulled by the kite(s)!" He has taught this man to not use ONE kite, but SEVERAL. A 'Train.'

"In this way you can add or subtract your pulling power and speed." The man has listened. Ho.

"It is good to use nature to your advantage…without disrupting her. Aho?"

Grandfather has shown Internet Pictures of 'Man Jumping (lifting) Kites,' Kite Buggy, and others. Sky wants the 'jumper.'

"Not now son, you aren't ready for it yet. Meanwhile we'll make a Skate Board Sail. Used originally to pull ice skaters. Some still do this. Now it has moved into the skateboards and street roller skates. Not KITES, but still Nature 'companionship.' You will enjoy this. Might even start a local 'fad' with it!"

I LOVE playing IN Nature. WITH it. Not destroying it, but working WITH it. Ho. One day I'd like to go Ballooning. All three of us. Just once. To Experience BEING the KITE! Ho.

Grandfather Goes Shopping

Grandfather got tired of lugging five gallon Buckets of water from truck to house. Quite a reader, he has an unusual knack for remembering. At least what he's read.

(Would forget his head on about any other things though.)

Seven months of hand carrying was as far as he intended to go! Now for his READING learning's!

"Honey, I'm going to buy a Shoulder Yoke!" and did.

Now even SHE loves it! Yes, she carries too.

"This is SMART!"

"Hon, EVERYTHING I do is SMART!" (Grin)

"Got to get you a WASHBOARD and HAND CRANKED WRINGER next! See how much I care for you?"

She knows he's not kidding. Seen too many of his 'tellings' come true. She's aware he's going BACK…to the FUTURE!

He's told many, over and over, "GET PREPARED! Learn to get away from ELECTRICITY. Get away from CARS."

(They own bikes and Foot Scooters.)

"Less can go wrong with a scooter. Bikes are faster, but parts will be hard to get eventually," he'd say.

"In France, during World War II…they ended up using Rags for tires…and had no Multi Speed Bikes either. In the end, more 'foolproof' with a single speed."

Yes, grandfather thinks ahead. Shops the Internet. Finds things that are still made, and invests. His Knowledge is 'endless.' His memory of things read is his advantage.
His TRYING…sometimes in miniature, of great help. "Sticks with you that way," he'd tell.

"I wish people would listen," he'd say. "Creator knows I've Tried!"

Ho.

Grandfather's Present to...Grandfather!

Grandfather is older, ("Someday I'll again get young") and has had a heart attack and strokes. Still, this hasn't stopped his love of the outdoors. Winter camping OR summer. "Hon, I'm a bit weaker anymore but I NEED to get out. Do some time between me and our Creator alone. CAMP. Sort of difficult to pack in nowadays. Just too much. So, I've been looking for an easier way to go about it. I have my toboggan for winter. Now it's time to find a 'hauler' for summer. Searched my thoughts, the internet and sport shops...nothing seems to fit the bill. But I THINK I've FINALLY FOUND IT. I'm going to buy a three Wheeled BABY JOGGER!"

This he did.

"It folds up, is light weight, the foot rest holds my Wiggy's bag and tent...the seat, my filled pack. It has a hood to help keeps things dry. It's Super Light Weight, and rolls like a dream. I can push OR pull it AND it has a HAND BREAK! To top it off, it was On SALE!"

To test, he did just that. Filling his pack...and all gear. Tying it on securely. Then down (and UP) the steep trail 'road' on their property. Over rocks, around and over bush, then across fallen trees. Sage land to woods, it worked as he'd hoped. This with SNOW on the ground!

Grandmother was not worried, as he was doing this all 'at home.' She'd worry later, when he was off on the real thing.

Beaming, he came back an hour or so later. "IT WORKS! Works GREAT! Now I can hardly wait until mid-spring. LOVE YOU HONEY!"

"Can't keep him down," she tells friends.

Ho.

The Rip

Grandfather and a friend were almost to Hopi land. Heading there to do 'work.' It was quite early in the morning…Sun not long up. A BEAUTIFUL clear morning.

There, high up, a multi-jet engine aircraft was slicing Its way through the sky…leaving Its contrails behind. AND something ELSE!

"Look at that plane," he told his companion.

As it flew forward, it was as if the contrails were a 'Two way zipper'…OPENING BEHIND and CLOSING from even further back. REVEALING…The VOID!

There was NOTHING in the 'opened' part. NOT EVEN COLOR!

"WHAT is <u>THAT</u>!" His friend loudly said. Almost SHOUTED!

"Brother, it is The NOTHING! What we are watching few men have ever seen.

ABSOLUTELY <u>NOTHING</u>!

THIS is what WE exist in. Our sky, our plants, our stars, us:

All.

ALL IMAGINATION.

<u>THOUGHT</u>!

What you and I are witnessing is pure PURITY! The VOID that IS GODCREATOR.

We are honored to witness this.

Why 'He' has chosen to do so is something only 'HE' can explain. This is nothing man is capable of…not even Alien men. Only one has. Only one CAN. The one who dreams ALL. YOU ARE SEEING The 'face' of GOD!

Nothing to see. NOT a THING to See! THAT son, is <u>HIM</u>."

Ho.

The Future Transportation...Today!

Grandfather was grinning 'ear to ear.' He held a copy of an email sent to him from a friend in Australia. "Look at THIS!" He'd say to visitors.

The picture was of two, towed by three draft horses, that were pulling their CAMP TRAILER! They had built it on a frame with rubber 'wagon wheels' and a 'Steering Platform' in front. Their 'Deck' was 'Houseboat' fashion. A Solar Panel atop the camper's roof.

"Isn't this WONDERFUL! THIS IS WHAT IT WILL BE LIKE IN THE FUTURE! WONDERFUL!

HO!

I have seen a small family, traveling through; using STRAY DOGS to pull a three wheeled homemade Dog Cart. Dogs and family HAPPY…and FREE!

No gas or mechanical concerns. Simply GUTS and willingness to travel slowly. They were from California and traveling to Spokane, Washington. All their needs on the cart. Castoff bikes to ride as they tired of walking. WONDERFUL FREEDOM! And an *'I don't give a dang WHAT people think'* attitude. DOING THEIR 'Thing'…using NATURE as their 'way.' Tent as 'home.' Their son was of about four years old, and had already learned to ride the little child's bike. The wife pregnant with their 'soon to be' second child. Her health from all the exercise was in EXCELLENT shape. Quite a family. Kid, Dogs, ALL: GRINNING IN THEIR FREEDOM!

I have seen 'The Goat Man.' He too travels as the others…a small Sheep Herder's wagon, his home. Goats his 'motor.'

HO!

In their sixties, there was another couple. These two had put an old VW camper van on pontoons. Using the motor to run a Stern Wheel Paddle. Had forward and reverse home, with all they needed. All on this pontoon boat. They could dock their craft, undo the belt…and drive to town if needed! 'RIVER HIPPIES!' Traveled the Mississippi river. ALMOST free. Gas kept them from full freedom…but hey, their odd boat cost FAR LESS than a commercial one and made more sense!

I have been to the Far East. Seen Sampan 'homes'…poled and rowed. YOU are the Power Plant.

THIS IS THE WAVE OF THE FUTURE! People will IMPROVISE! People will LEARN you don't need a fancy, high priced HOUSE to have a HOME.

LOVE is the 'home.' Always has been. People have forgotten that. They end up enslaved to expensive house payments, taxes, upkeep, utilities. They've quit LIVING. Trading it for Slavery. NO FREEDOM!

These 'nomads Vagabonds' are GOOD People. Not bums. Not thieves. Just folks who HAVE FOUND THEIR FREEDOM by using their BRAINS…and changing their attitudes on what a 'Home' is. ALL OF THESE PEOPLE Were FILLED with LOVE! They have FOUND THEIR FREEDOM. Free to be DIFFERENT! In this, they have FOUND The CREATOR. THEIR Joy connected to 'HIS' Joy. Ho.

The same holds true with 'trekkers.' Back Packers. Wanderers of the highways and byways of our planet... Canoeists too do this. Some, permanently.

I tell you true, these are the VANGUARDS of our future. The 'Different Ones.' HO.

Yes, DARE to be DIFFERENT. It will be FORCED on you. Why wait? THAT 'FORCE' is PAINFUL. Do it WILLINGLY. KNOWINGLY!

TAKE THE DARE and know FREEDOM! HO."

Vinegar

“Grandpa, YOU SMELL LIKE VINEGAR!” his granddaughter said…nose ‘curling.’

“Should. Got it in my hair, poured some on my neck, shirt and pants cuffs. Didn’t have a forewarning reason to drink any...I’m heading out to heavy tick country. If I’d had known in advance, I’d have drank a full cup for the last three days. Sweat it through the pours then. Vinegar keeps Ticks, Skeeters, Horse Flies, and other bothersome insects away. That or the smudging in the Sacred Herbs.”

“It keeps the bugs away? Even TICKS!”

“Well, the flying bugs won’t land. The crawlers, if they get on you, head DOWN and OFF. Rather smell like vinegar then a MEAL!”

“I’m not sure I’d put that stuff on ME!”

“Honey, you have acne.”

(She looked embarrassed.)

“If you WASHED with vinegar, all would be gone in two to three days. Great for underarm body odor too. Not SOAP. Just straight vinegar.”

(She shuddered).

Best thing in the world for Sun Burns too! Just sop it on. BURNS LIKE CRAZY! Do it again when the ‘sting’ stops. STILL ‘burns.’ Do it one more time…till you feel NO stinging. And you wake up in the morning with absolutely no hurt OR peeling skin. All you have is a BEAUTIFUL DEEP TAN.

You see granddaughter, Vinegar helps and heals in many ways...Even good for animals, when mixed in their feed…or in a delusion, bathing them with it.

Lynnsay, if you only knew what our Great Maker has done for us, it would amaze you. ‘He’ has set up all, just for us. To enjoy, to use for health, to learn from. Honey, life is more than boys and music and ‘self’ fun. All of that is just part of life, but ONLY a PART.

Someday I hope you’ll learn this, and the JOY you’ll experience IN that knowing.

I love you sweetheart. Well, I’m off. See you later honey.”

D.B. Cooper

Grandfather lived under the flight path of the famous mystery of D.B. Cooper…the parachutist who chutes out of a large passenger plane, carrying several thousands of dollars. He has yet to be found.

"MAYBE," said grandfather. For grandfather may know something others don't.

"I lived in Rose Valley. This is part of Longview, Washington...I know the area well. So too many living there. One morning I received a call from an older friend. A small time farmer. He had not heard of that night's event…that a Plane Hijacking had taken place. He called to tell of 'an odd thing' he had come across that morning.
He was out scouting the hillside, opposite his house, for firewood. There was fresh snow on the ground. Hiking up was an Electric Power 'Pole' cut; suddenly he came upon 'the Oddity'…FRESH FOOT PRINTS…but as he told me: from NOWHERE, brother! They just were THERE! No one WALKED IN but someone walked OUT! IN STREET SHOES!"

Hum, D.B. Cooper?

A few years ago grandfather saw a Book on Cooper in the library in Ellensburg, Washington. He checked it out and read.

It was by a woman claiming 'D.B.' was her 'now deceased' boyfriend. He took her to the site area he claimed he came down from.

Grandfather RECOGNIZED ALL THE HOMES/FARMS and OUTBUILDINGS he took her past.

Whoever this person was, he KNEW the area FOR SURE!

He told her he had buried the parachute shallowly, alongside a log as he walked away from his landing IN AN ELECTRIC POWERLINE CUT.

Too bad the old farmer hadn't followed those footprints.

Ho.

Grandfather and Nature

Both grandfather and grandmother enjoyed the 'YOU DO IT' type shows on TV. This doesn't always 'go well' with Sky and others (family/visitors).
"Don't like it, go to the bed room TV," a standard saying with the two.

One show, on gardening (grandmother's favorite to watch) was talking on killing weeds.
Both of them know there are a number of 'weeds' filled with Health Help. One the other hand, the County doesn't see them in this light. "SPRAY or FINE!"

Both cringe on spraying the chemicals used. "Both Costly AND Not Good for our Mother Earth," grandfather would say.

They were constantly looking for a safe NATURAL 'way.' THIS PROGRAM GAVE ONE!

"Boil Water and put on weed(s). Kills them AND their roots."

THAT DID IT! Grandfather headed to the kitchen. Shortly after, carefully carrying a large pan of steaming water…out the door he headed.

Around their porch, there were many culprits. Tilting the pan, each received a good, long, 'shot.'
"Sorry Folks, gotta be. You've plenty of kin out on the Counties Road Ways. They want US to put out money but won't do themselves. Fine us…but ignore their own wrong doing. At least this is WATER…not POISON. All around you can benefit as you 'go on.' At least, we'll see…"

The '*teller*' told TRUE! The weeds passed on, the Earth was not harmed, and the greenery around the now deceased weeds became greener.

"When one realizes they are part of the whole. Caretakers to man, beast, and nature alike, they will need to walk gently upon the Earth. CARING, for ALL. Even to the killing of weeds. I am Thankful for finding this safe way. Except for the poor weeds, it is now a 'Win Win' situation. I THANK THE CREATOR!"

HO.

Grandfather Goes "Ultra-Light" Camping – In Style

He was teaching his two grandsons it wasn't necessary to know 'old ways,' nor 'modern ways' to enjoy a few nights out camping.

"The 'whites' have some really nice things one can buy to camp. Much money can be spent on their ways. At the same time, our ancient ones camped constantly, without the white ways. Those who were nomadic kept things very simple. Needed to. All was back-carried or dog drug. When horses were brought back by the whites, then they started taking more. The horses carrying/pulling. Without their knowledge, you kids need to learn to travel light and painlessly. Both mean: Faster and Farther hikes for you. Come with me, I'll show you how I've mixed the two *ways*."

Taking them into the bedroom, he pulled out a small bundle. Opening it, they saw a Hunter's 'Vest.' This was opened to reveal Its many pockets. Not all were filled. Grandfather started taking things out: a Box knife…a Flint AND small magnifying glass…A Pocket Saw…three Long needles…Fishing line/sinkers/hooks (all in a Zip Lock bag)…a small roll of Parachute cord…a spool of brass wire…some Oversized Band-Aids, Medicine Ointment…and about 16 inches of small diameter aquarium air hose (rolled up).

The back pocket held three lightweight 'emergency blankets.'

Separate was a water container.

"This is all you need to 'cross' the two ways. More can be added if you'd like. This though, is simple. Salt and Pepper shaker I put in before leaving. In the old days licking your arm gave salt…wood ash the pepper, though with knowledge, pepper plant weed seeds, if available. I take free Condiment Packets picked up at Convenience stores as well. Seasonings and jams. Doesn't cost a cent.

You can use a small stick as fork and drink from a large folded leaf as cup, or hand. The small Aquarium hose I use to sip up water and to gently blow on my newly started fire. I don't need to get a face full of smoke/sparks and can easily bend over to sip from a low water spot.

With the vest, I've less than $35.00 here. The vest is the backpack. Your back doesn't hurt with this. No straps to cut into your shoulders. You are able to walk freely.

This is my 'Cross Ways' kit.

I don't need ANY of it…but I'm getting old…handier for me.

I take a Loin Cloth along as well, and spare socks. Saves my clothing. No one 'out there' to offend, anyway."

"What about BUGS?"

"Smoke and Mud takes care of most of those. If I take along my Sacred Plants…the smudging from those, handle all nicely. Aho? I've taught you all of this before. Have you forgotten already?"

(They had.)

"Better pay attention, boys, I won't be with you forever. Aho?"

"Yes grandfather, Aho."

The Toe

Grandfather, both an Inner as well as a 'regular' Heyókȟa', has a…well, rather an Unusual sense of humor. He's noted for it. Especially in his family.

Grandfather had to have his Big Toe amputated. Before the operation, he told the doctor to save it. "It is our way to bury our 'parts.' This was done. He went home with it and put it in the freezer *for spring*."

He was sitting at home when his granddaughter came to use the computer. His VERY bloody swaddling Band-Aid stretched out before him.

Lynnsay wasn't noted for a strong stomach. She looked away.

He gave her a few minutes to get evolved with her emails, then quietly said, "Lynnsay, want to see my stump?"

"NO GRANDPA! I do NOT want to see your stump!" Then returned to her emails.

He waited. Then said, "Lynnsay, want to see my TOE?"

She had stopped to hear what he wanted. "NO! NO! NO! I have already TOLD you I didn't want to see your TOE!"

"Well Lynnsay, I had asked if you wanted to see the Operation, not the toe. This time I've asked about the toe."

She wouldn't look at him. Because she was a bit angry.

He smiled…and waited.

"Lynnsay, are you going to the funeral?"

THIS took her by surprise! Spinning towards him, "FUNERAL!?? WHO DIED?"

"No one. I've gotta bury my toe."

"OH GRANDPA! STOP IT! CUT it OUT!" In her queasiness, anger, and frustration, she was now SHOUTING!

Now for the finality! All he had to do was wait. She was now 'set up' for what laid ahead.

In time, she was done.

"Grandpa, could you drive me home?"

THE TRAP WAS SET! ☺

"Yeah hon, hop in the truck, I'll be out in a minute."

She left. He got up, hopped to the bathroom, and grabbed a washcloth…then to the kitchen. Here he wrapped up a small Fish Food container in the washcloth. Then hobbled to the truck.

Getting in, he faked fumbling around to get the key in the ignition. Container AND keys in the same hand. "Here, hold this." He dropped the wrapped container in her jeaned lap. Getting the key in, he put the truck in reverse, then drive. The trip to be short, simply across the street and up a rough dirt roadway. He left the container in her lap.

Then began the 'banging around' in there.

"What's this, grandpa?"

"My toe," he said. "I thought your brother would like to see it."

SHE GREW 'STRAIGHT'…EYES WIDE! "GET IT OFF! GET IT… *OFF*!" She began SCREAMING!

"Oh for HEAVEN'S SAKE…Here!" he said, as he reached for the container.

HE GRABBED THE CLOTH, Not the CONTAINER! UNROLLING THE CONTAINER INTO HER LAP!

"AHHHHHH! Get it OFFFFFFF!" As the now CLOSER 'toe' continued bouncing in her lap!

His foot went to the brake pedal, he was ROARING IN LAUGHTER! And CRYING from it all! Unable to see, he HAD to stop! His granddaughter beside him…Screaming her head off, unwilling to open her legs, unwilling to touch it with her hands! She was having an absolute FREAK OUT!

Finally, he removed it and told her the truth. She slammed the door as she left. Didn't even Thank him for the ride…☺

More Anger

June has arrived. The time grandfather will no longer do "personal" help. More and more are angry over this. He's gotten a slew of angry ones. Most have been helped time after time. Almost all of those giving nothing in return. Again, one of the reasons grandfather is slowing down.

His most recent angry email held this:

I THOUGHT GOD GAVE FREELY! YOU ARE HIS WORKER. You are WRONG in charging!"

His reply:

Yes, "He" DOES Give FREELY. I've told in my Website you don't NEED to buy from me...that you can GET it all FOR FREE. Simply by reading your Bible.

Want it FREE? GO to HIM! Otherwise, get from me. Your choice. Your option.

I have spent Many Hours with you. On phone calls and with emails. Not ONCE have I received a cent from you.

Now we are done. I have shared. I have helped. You have told me this yourself more than once. Now go. Use what I told. I have GIVEN enough. You have no reason to complain. GROW UP AND GROW! We are done. I wish you all the best. You CAN do it. You CAN Grow in "Him." Now, WILL YOU?

Yet Another

"There is no hope."
"Nothing can be done."
"Teach me more."

Grandfather replied, "I HAVE been teaching! YOU HAVE REJECTED IT.

I tell it CAN be changed.

I tell THERE IS hope.

I tell and TELL. Yet you return with THIS?

You refuse the teacher. You refuse the text Book.

You pay NO ATTENTION. Yet expect to remain in college?

LEAVE! You are discharged. You have continuously failed every test.

There are others needing your chair. Others that WILL pay attention.

YOU ARE ROBBING THEM OF THEIR CHANCE!

Now go. Go, and TEACH YOUR SELF!"

Grandfather is not "Owned"

People seem to think a few bucks gives permanent access to years Of GRANDFATHER'S knowledge and training. It hurts him that this seems to be the case. Most give nothing. Yet expect him to be on immediate call. This is wrong. His life is filled with years of hard earned training. Nearly a lifetime of it. Starting at age ten. This is the case with ALL "Medicine" People.

As many, he feels used and certainly abused.

It is his wife's daily labor that supports their needs. This TOO is true of many in the "Medicine Way." The "unsung heroes." People owe THEM respect. These mates go through "hell" for the help and needs of others who do not SEE…or, frankly, CARE! They think only of THEIR own "needs."

Is it no wonder so many in "Medicine" have ceased?

Is it no wonder many "Medicine" People are no longer with a Life mate?

"Worn down" by the "GIVE me's."

How many out there fall under this category?

In GRANDFATHER'S case: Tens of THOUSANDS!

Then there are some who give…asking not a thing in return. HELPING SUPPORT the ungrateful. The arrogant. The "Thank You-ers." The TARES IN THE WHEAT.

Helping these tares to have water and light…to grow. Those who are killing off the TRUE Wheat. Robbing the energy in their uselessness. People who CARE for others.

Grandfather is often "gruff." He has every right to be. After all, he works the field. His time and labor supporting ALL within it. To work so long, to work so HARD, to raise so much JUNK, is a sad and frustrating thing. Yet he labors on.

The weeds are pulled daily…yet the field is ENORMOUS! WAY beyond the skilled laborer's manpower. Few are field workers. Many tire over time and simply quit.

THE GREAT GARDENER SEES. "He" KNOWS!!!

"My people are over extended. My field taken over by the Sin Weeds. THEY IGNORE ME. However, I warn: I, the GREAT MAKER see the few doing so much. Much now is about useless. I have few volunteers. TOO few. I MUST HELP THE WORKERS! They DESERVE it. Thus, I will send My POWER onto the vast field. I WILL FRY THE TARES! I will lose wheat in this…but they will still go into my Storage Place. They will not be wasted. THOSE I will pick up and SAVE. The rest will be but ash…buried overtime, by the ash that the GREAT BURNING

will bring. I will call the four Spirits to blow the winds without ceasing. Season after Season. Earth Ash and BONE Ash will mix…and the bones will help fertilize the new Field that will begin after this GREAT SEARING. Thus, even the BONES will become of use…FINALLY! I will not let what I have given, be of uselessness. I WILL USE THE BONES! Though dead, they will help give LIFE.
Meanwhile, the TRUE Wheat…scorched and all will be a pleasure to me…a NEW TASTE. Like Smoked peanuts. PLEASING TO MY PALATE! No, they have every right to be with me. IN me! THEY ARE GOOD!

I will bring on terrifying events over the Great field. I will shake the Earth. 'Tilling' it. Ripping it open. EXPOSING the BENEATH to the ABOVE. Bringing up Fresh and NEW Soil. For this soil here is now polluted and needs time to rejuvenate. I will send the Winds. I will send the Fire…by Wars and Grandfather Sun and other ways. THE FIELD WILL BURN! It will PURIFY! FIRE is My GREAT PURIFIER!

Already diseases have entered the field. These have multiplied, as Locusts gone amok. I WILL LET THIS BE! After all, they weaken and kill only the weeds that allow their entry. WEEDS that do NOT Rise to ME. Who do NOT Seek My Healing way. Who grow on in their wanted sickness? Wilted and NOT KNOWING. DEAD on their STALKS! Green? THEY KNOW NOT green…not the GREEN that I provide!
They look around and see others about them, in the same WAY. 'SEE?' I AM 'NORMAL.' There's nothing wrong with ME!

So many Sick, it is NORMAL to them!

Then they see TRUE Wheat. 'DIFFERENT.'

'QUICK, Spread our roots towards THAT one. SOMETHING IS WRONG WITH IT! It needs NO Reason to upset our NORMALCY! KILL IT! It is a WEED!'

That is what the tares think. That is what the tares are aiming at. TOTAL WEED FIELD!

Not in MY GARDEN! I will come and FOIL These Foolish Weeds. THEY WILL DIE!

No amount of screaming and crying will save them. No *'I ACCEPT YOUR SON'* will save them. They 'Accept' only to be spared from the great fire. WORDS…not TRUTH!

I KNOW their HEARTS!

EACH Plant! I KNOW Them!

Yes, there will be 'Great Gnashing of Teeth' indeed...NONE CAN FOOL ME!

The 'Great' weeds and the 'lowly' weeds. I see no Difference. THEY WILL NOT CONTAMINATE MY STORAGE HOUSE!
NONE!
So, I have begun. I will raise infections. I will raise insects. I will raise a GREAT 'Stirring!' One day it will snow. The next the rains will come. The sun will bless an area ONLY TO HIDE BEHIND THE CLOUDS when all the weeds say "AHHH! It is FINALLY a GOOD TIME. Our Season again 'Normal!'

OH, NO IT'S NOT! For I have come onto my field AND CONFUSE IT!

Your Great and Small 'Forecasters,' will be ashamed A LAUGHING STALK! UNABLE to forecast accurately…FOR THEY DO NOT SEE ME…The Great SPIRIT…who stands on the Earth giving My instructions to my Spirit Beings. They are unable to SEE the four called the '4 Horsemen'…EACH WITH A PLOW AND SWORD! NOW riding within the FIELD! Slicing, Tearing, CREATING CONFUSION. An 'UNSEEN ARMY,' of only FOUR!!!

Four, so GREAT, not ALL THE ARMIES in ALL My Creation, can defeat them. COME AT MY COMMAND! Come HIGHLY Incased with PERSONAL BODY ARMOR! MY Armor. PURITY! RIGHTEOUSNESS!

No, man weeds have spent their days in SELF-joys SELF-fears. THEY SEE ONLY SELF! They no longer HAVE the eyes to see THE SPIRIT(S) I AM and who ARE IN THE FIELD. OBEYING!

I, the GREAT GARDNER, am HERE AMONGST YOU! I have come to help the Field Workers you make Life so miserable for. I HAVE COME TO SAVE THEM AND THE EARTH!

Now many things will come across the WHOLE FIELD!

Each a WARNING!

RAISE YOU LEAFS AND PAY HOMAGE TO ME!

If not…SEE, with your Own Eyes…The TERROR OF TERRORS: THE RED SKY!

THE sign that NOTHING YOU DO WILL SAVE YOU NOW! EVER!

Hear Me."

Something To Think About

Grandfather is a 'watcher.' What he has seen over his life, he 'files.' In time this kept knowledge comes out in statements of truth.

"I have watched mankind a long time. What I've seen and learned, I apply to myself. As any Inner Heyókȟa': We see, we learn, we apply.

As all, we see anger, we see happiness. All this from the Holograms we are around. UNLIKE all, we APPLY the *DON'TS* to ourselves. We see each as a lesson. I do not want to disappoint our Maker. It takes time to stop doing the *Don'ts*, but by constantly remembering the WRONG we have witnessed…eventually, we overcome. We cease doing wrong things. At least to a great amount.

Anger is a DON'T.

LOVE is a DO.

PRIDE is a DON'T.

OTHERS ahead of you a DO.

WHINING is a DON'T.

PRAISING 'Him' in ALL things is a DO.

Do you understand?

Know this: It is NOT the GATHERING that counts.

It is the CASTING OUT, SPREADING that do.

Cast HATE, Cast ANGER, Cast NEGATIVITY

And that is what grows in your 'field'...Your 'Garden.'

BAD BEGETS BAD!

'Toss' out (spread) LOVE and COMPASSION…and the Garden SMILES.

So TOO does our FATHER-Creator."

Nature Speaks Knowledge

Grandfather has spoken of this a number of times in the past. Telling tells of experience he's had with various animals. Be it Snakes, Horses, Deer, Coyote, Elk, Cat, Dog, Cattle…all are quite easy to converse WITH…not just TO.
Many have seen him do this…and the results. SEEABLE results to what he says he is saying/hearing.

"As told, ALL has awareness. Not just animals. ALL!
I find Rocks very interesting. Trees that are full of chat. Water as well. Insects, Sand, Clouds, Mountains, Flowers, Bushes, etcetera…ALL able to converse.

Nature senses your MOOD.
Nature senses your Illnesses.
Nature senses, and PRAYS!
Prays and TALKS to the Creator.
Nature WANTS to help. WANTS you to know Peace and Contentment.

Have you not noticed a dog cringe at your anger? THAT DOG KNOWS YOU ARE MAD! Even without a Word spoken to it, it knows your MOOD, and reacts.

When one walks…'STOMPS'…off into the Wilderness, All therein, know your MOOD.

If you go to Cut and Destroy, THEY SENSE THAT.

If you go to hunt/kill, THEY SENSE THAT.

Ever notice the abundance of deer just prior to deer hunting season? Deer all around.
Then…THEY DISAPPEAR! You're lucky to see ONE. Let alone get a shot.

THEY SENSE YOUR KILL MOOD!

Then there are times you NEED their life. You NEED the food they can provide. It is THEN, one steps firmly in your path. A VOLUNTEER!

Have you ever wondered WHY our Big Brother 'went to the Wilderness, OFTEN?'

NATURE is a BALM TO THE SOUL! A PEACE Giver. NATURE HELPS HEAL the Inner Being. Gives it REST. A 'time out.' It does not quarrel with you. It does not nag. It gives REST TIME. Selah, pause and think on this. FOLLOW your teacher, The Christ, who learned, and GAVE! HE IS YOUR EXAMPLE!"

Ho.

The Visitor

He came, the visitor was 'Down.'
"May was a hard month," he told.

Grandfather looked at him long. This one has always been a *down* one.

"No, son, May was a LEARNING MONTH. Look at it like That.

Until you get the reason for 'hard,' EVERY MONTH will be hard!

I have never seen you come with a good report. Nor have I seen you come SHOWING YOU ARE LEARNING!

How often must you come, complaining, to be given the answer…then return again with the same problem: *hard*?

What do they call a forty-eight year old man in the third grade?

GIFTED!

You should be Graduating, Shoot! You aren't even IN the third GRADE!

When are you going to Pay ATTENTION!?

Life is a School, son. Designed to give you GROWTH and MATURITY. Designed to give you YOUR SPECIFIC JOB.

Until you learn that, until you THANK YOUR TEACHER for all 'His' PATIENCE, all 'His' LOVE and COMPASSION…for NOT KICKING YOU OUT OF CLASS because 'He' CARES ABOUT YOU…then, the school will remain…'Hard.'

Why HASN'T 'He' dispelled you? BECAUSE HE KNOWS YOUR POTENTIAL!

I TELL YOU TRUE: 'HE' CARES!

I tell you even MORE a truth: <u>HE'S</u> NOT GOING TO GIVE UP ON YOU! Even if it 'Kills' you!

May wasn't hard. YOU JUST DIDN'T READ THE BLACKBOARD! You sat around PAYING NO ATTENTION! 'Lollygagging,' looking out the window. 'HE' WANTS YOU IN THAT 'OUTSIDE' YOU LOLLYGAG LOOKING AT and LONGING FOR!

However, you must LEARN before you can SAFELY walk the life 'out there.'

What is 2 + 2?

LEARN IT! KNOW what '2 + 2' IS, Or you'll be 'Short Changed' out there...LIFE is a LESSON. One you can use, to HELP you live SAFELY.

Without Paying ATTENTION to the Teachers' constant teachings, YOU WILL BE AS A BLIND MAN WITHOUT A STICK! Wandering about ON THE FREEWAY!

You are BLIND but THINK you SEE!

A CHILD thinks him/her Knows EVERYTHING! Have you noticed that? Have you noticed how THAT gets them into constant trouble? DO THEY LISTEN? Or do they HURT?! KIDS DIE with that attitude!

You, who CLAIM to 'TRUST THE TEACHER,' show NO trust whatsoever. You see ONLY that you are NOT GETTING what YOU Want!

'TRUST?' POOEY!!!

Now, GROW UP and LEARN!

Take each day AS A LESSON!

And GRADUATE! Don't STAGNATE!

The next time I see you, it will be, I HOPE, with a GOOD Report 'card'…Even a D+!

Or don't come back at all. NOT until you do!

I wish you well. Till then, God Bless and goodbye…"

Idle Entertainment

Sky was bored. When in this way he would 'ride' grandfather to entertain him. Grandfather had no time. He was Busy! Still, Sky wouldn't cease. Finally, grandfather said, "Son, get me some Elmer's Glue, some of grandma's thread and bring them here."
He did.

"Now, GO CATCH SOME FLIES!"

"WHAT?"

"Do as I say. There's plenty at the kitchen window. I want BIG flies and I want them ALIVE AND UNINJURED."

After a few minutes, Sky returned with one. "Now what?"

"Get him turned over. Hold his wings and hold onto him. Don't let it go. I'll show you."

Doing so, grandfather placed a tiny dab of glue on the fly's abdomen. He then pulled off about a foot of string. Breaking off that length. He then ran one end into the fresh glue. "Blow on it till it dries." he ordered.

After about a minute, the string was permanently attached.

"OK, let it go." The fly lifted, thread trailing.

"There you go, Sky…you now have a LIVING KITE!"

"Now, leave me be and go FLY IT!"

Sky was ENTHRALLED. The poor fly (soon to pass on of old age), was hours of fun. Landing on the ceiling, it was easy to get the thread and 'undo,' with thread, seeable.

"Sky, LET IT REST. Give him a BREAK!"

Soon other fly's were likewise 'harnessed.' Bits of various colored strings floating throughout the house.

Later, grandfather sniped the threads close to their bodies Outside. Releasing them all unharmed where they belonged.

Sky spent DAYS of this. Taught his friends as well. Grandfather finally had his peace!

Ants...Nature's Guides To Water

Grandfather was 'witching.' Dowsing. In this case, for a viable water source. The great woods opening held many sources. All rather small. "Trickles," he said. He continued walking about, looking for a better flow. Finally, one was found. He was looking for ground water. The property owner having only a shovel to dig and too inexperienced to dig a large and deeper well. Not many have this experience. They hold their dangers.

"All I want is to collect enough to hand water my little garden," he had said.

"Here," grandfather called. "This is the spot a number of the tiny sources meet before continuing on. It's shallow enough. At about five feet. Should fit your needs. If you'd care to, go get your shovel, we'll see what's just down a bit below."

Digging began. The soil dry. "Don't worry about it, keep digging."

At about two feet grandfather said, "Stop. Look. What do you see?"

The man leaned down. "Nothing but dirt here. Dry dirt."

"Oh? Look again."

"Just dirt and ants."

"Yes. Quite a few ants scrambling about. ANTS BUILD THEIR DENS ABOVE A WATER SOURCE. Allowing the water to WICK UP. They *point* to WATER!

Being so small, they can't 'afford' to dig so deep the water floods. It must WICK.

As any, they too must have moisture to survive.

Their presence shows you there IS a water source below. So, THERE is your proof. The ANTS! HO!

The ants that build large 'domes'...these do not need dowsing to find the water source. All it takes is SIGHT. Often you can SEE 'domes' in a line. If you find but one, do a 'circle walk' from that one. Widening your circle more and more. The chances are great you will find others in this manner. Ants are territorial. Their homes distanced from each other. As a bear or a wolf, these little ones have THEIR 'range.' THEIR hunting grounds.

Find the 'line of sight'...one Dome to the next, to the next. Dig on that line and you will find your water. Aho?

These will be rather shallow wells. They will also be year round water givers. Aho?

You will not know the depth nor the 'run,' but you can rely on THESE mound builders THAT THE WATER IS THERE…and PERMANENTLY there. Aho?

When doing a shallow well, I'd suggest two or three Food Grade 55 gallon barrel steel, OR better yet, PLASTIC ones. One atop the other. This forms a decent 'casing.' Wide enough to dip from if need be…or pump from. A screen should be placed on top. This to stop bugs and drowning of field mice, etc. Remember, still water attracts mosquitoes. KEEP IT COVERED. Or build birdhouses around it. Bats and Swallows are EXCELLENT 'getters.' Aho?

I personally prefer the harder 'getting' by non-powered pumps. A Wind Mill is still viable. So too, Solar. Town Bought ELECTRICITY is NOT Reliable! Ask yourself if they are viable. Using BOTH… 'Town and Natural' is good…IF you HAVE 'Town Power,' apply it AND Natural. Hand Lugging is a constant…as long as one has the health and ability. We will have a hand pump. A Modern Stainless Steel one for ours. This in the near future. Pump to a container or direct to our buckets. I bought a WATER CARRYING SHOULDER YOKE to make carrying easier.
Hopefully our well will be ABOVE our home. GRAVITY FED to the house. That is the simplest. Don't forget to BURY or INSULATE any pipes or hose used for this BELOW the freeze depth of your area. Better to Sweat NOW then to have the line freeze later and have to DIG! Aho?

As you are now learning: NATURE IS SOMETHING TO OBSERVE AND LEARN FROM. 'Wild' is MORE than food. Learn that!

Our Creator has given far more than most realize.

Well, my work is done here, Yours is just Beginning! Take your time. Don't over exert yourself. I'm off."

A Rehash To Those Really Willing To Listen

These stories (except the jokes) are based on FACTS. EACH built on the knowledge and experiences of grandfather.

Now, to those WANTING to prepare, REALLY, read on:

READ THE BIBLE…DAILY.

LEARN TO USE THE CONCORDANCE…and USE it!

PRAY ON YOUR KNEES…DAILY.

BELIEVE ALL You READ (BIBLE)…DAILY.

TEST THE SPIRITS OF <u>ALL</u> THINGS three TIMES…INCLUDING THE BIBLE.

WHEN IN DOUBT (BIBLE) CHECK IT WITH THE CONCORDANCE.

REJECT ANY "FALSENESS" MAN HAS INSERTED.

FOLLOW THE "BIG BROTHER"/CHRIST; HE CAME AS AN EXAMPLE.

DON'T FEAR ASKING HIM IN AND TO HELP YOU, REGARDLESS OF YOUR RELIGION.

TRUST HE DOES <u>NOT</u> LIE AND <u>IS</u> HELPING.

DO NOT EXPECT "INSTANT" CHANGE…(It CAN be but TRUST IT IS "IN THE WORKS.")

PREPARE.

LEARN "ANCIENT" WAYS. STUDY THESE (LIBRARY/INTERNET/ETC).

PRACTICE.

GET A PUSH (FOOT) SCOOTER.

EXPECT AND PREPARE FOR NO ELECTRICITY.

EXPECT AND PREPARE FOR NO GASOLINE.

PREPARE FOR LOSING YOUR ABODE.

GET HONEY.

GET GOOD SLEEPING BAGS (WIGGY'S SLEEPING BAGS ARE THE VERY BEST).

GET a GOOD TENT (THREE SEASON AT LEAST) WITH LOW WIND FACTOR.

GET LAND AWAY FROM ALL COASTS AND LARGE BODIES OF WATER.

LAND HIGH UP.

CONSIDER HAVING NO BABIES. ADOPT.

EXPECT NO GOVERNMENT SUBSIDIES.

EXPECT AND PREPARE FOR WAR ON OUR OWN LAND.

EXPECT AND PREPARE FOR FUTURE FAMINE.

LEARN FIRST AID/EMT TRAINING, AND IF POSSIBLE MID-WIFERY.

LEARN TO IMPROVISE.

LEARN, LEARN, LEARN, TO TRUST GOD/CREATOR.

LEARN TO "FEAR NOT."

BUY NO MORE PETS.

BUY WISELY DO NOT "SKIMP" ON THINGS BOUGHT (IF YOU CAN).

EXPECT TO WALK AWAY FROM ALMOST ALL YOU POSSESS.

DO NOT RELY ON YOUR GOVERNMENT(S).

DO NOT TRUST THOSE IN AUTHORITY…GOVERNMENT, LAWYERS, NEWS MEDIA, RELIGIOUS LEADERS, etc.

LEARN THERE IS ONLY ONE WHO IS TRUSTWORTHY: OUR CREATOR.

LEARN YOU CAN "CONNECT" WITH THIS GREAT ONE: CREATOR.

LEARN "HE" <u>KNOWS</u> IF YOU ARE TRUE, OR FALSE AND RESPONDS ACCORDINGLY.

AGAIN AND AGAIN AND AGAIN, FEAR NOT! TRUST!

KNOW THE ABOVE IS FOR ALL, REGARDLESS OF RACE, CULTURE, OR RELIGION.

LEARN there is but ONE CREATOR…with MANY NAMES.

You, reader, will need to <u>KNOW</u> "HIS" NAME. It is: LOVE.

In this, there will BE no "differences," Color, Culture, "Ways," melt at that Ones "LOVE" feet.

IF IT DOESN'T (within you), YOU STILL THEN HAVE MUCH YET TO LEARN.

STRIVE TOWARDS THAT GOAL!

You will also need to:

Learn to *LEARN TO <u>U N L E A R N</u>* to *Learn*!

Years of training in the "Cant's" of life HAVE GOT TO BE REVAMPED.

You have been trained to FEAR, and live in it. Many don't believe this, yet it is the FULL TRUTH!

To you, the reader, all that is told here is meant to help. It is totally YOUR decision to reject or accept. I have long ago learned it is not my RIGHT, not my JOB, and not within my ABILITY, to even TRY to "beat you into submission." YOU reader, have your OWN path. Your OWN will. It is not a "requirement" you take my advice, learning's or teachings.

IT IS <u>YOUR</u> LIFE. Do as YOU please!

I but share and give things to think on. Aho?

"Grandfather, Is Your Life Always' Smooth' and 'Good'?"

"In the *whole of it, it* is ALWAYS 'GOOD.'

'SMOOTH' is another matter. No, it is not 'smooth.' The trail of ANY Pathway is always 'uphill.' Like any little trodden Mountain trail.

In the 'walk of life,' you are Always Climbing. You are headed for the next 'higher peak.' This means you climb one peak, then head down. This 'down' is an easier part of the path. But LOOK BACK! The start of the Life Climb starts in a serene meadow, before you stand the first Climb. Overtime each peak before you is higher than the one you just mastered…thus you are ALWAYS CLIMBING! In time, that wonderful meadow is but a distant memory. The 'Babyhood' of your life walk.

MANY stop their climb. They are defeated by Its harshness. So there they camp. They die in that camp. Never reaching their 'God Hoped For' goal.

Some climb higher than others. The path is filled with bones. Few reach the Last Peak and can look down to 'The Great Hunting Ground.'

There, stretched before them is Eternal Beauty. A Great Plain filled with nothing but good. Eternal PEACE! Eternal 'EASY LIVING.' PURE LOVE!

This vast Plain holds a light above its center. The SON sun. RIGHT ABOVE ITS CENTER.

ALL mankind are sent on this One Path. Sent, but with NO ORDERS to CLIMB! ALL climb a Little though. Then either 'camp' or strive to See that LAST VIEW.
Then the walk down begins. When completed, they…EVERY HUMAN…enters at LEAST the EDGE of this wonderful Plain. Yes, ALL.

Then there ARE those who WALK ON, TO CAMP BELOW THE LIGHTED 'STAR'…the SON sun.

Nonetheless, life is not 'Smooth.'

BUT IT IS 'GOOD,' if you LOOK at it as that. If you comprehend, THERE IS A REASON FOR ALL!

The boulders and loose stones you travel are ALL MEANT TO GIVE ONE STRENGTH. The very PEAKS are ALL MEANT TO GIVE YOU STRENGTH!

When you realize this, IT HELPS YOU 'PRAISE GOD CREATOR IN <u>ALL</u> THINGS!

Many are defeated by the rough, exhausting path. They lay and do not get up.

I understand, it is NOT a 'Smooth' path.

In my life, there HAVE been times I've 'camped.' But I 'SAW' and after awhile, would break camp and begin the climb again.

Will I get to the Last Peak? I do not know. I DO know though I WANT TO TRY!

I still have Determination. My breath has not yet stopped. WILL I be successful??
I too may only reach the 'edge' of that great plain. Perhaps even farther INTO it. I do not know. I just know I WANT. Aho?

My life has disappointments…yet those I've found are but another stone in the path. I CONTINUE to PRAISE and PASS THROUGH the stone. 'Big Brother' is CONSTANTLY WITH ME because I AM CONSTANTLY WITH HIM!

In The GOOD BOOK, it tells: '*DAD' NEVER GIVES MORE THEN YOU CAN BEAR*.
That means a lot to me. THAT STONE <u>CAN</u> BE OVERCOME!
Trust Him. Trust His JUDGMENT. KNOW He LOVES YOU.
HE WANTS YOU <u>STRONG</u>!
FORGE ON! Don't GIVE UP! HE 'BELIEVES IN YOU!'

Trust Him…and PRAISE.

AIM FOR THE CENTER OF THAT PLAIN! Aho?"

Grandfather Mourns

"Tonight I am on bended knees, my Father…to cry.

Please Sir, let my voice be heard. Allow me, O' Father, to face you. Not your back. Please Sir, show me the things I have done to prevent this. I await Sir."

And grandfather kneeled silently.

Thoughts and deeds came. Things that were unpleasing to The Great One. The filth and 'dirt' of the day.

One by one, The Big Brother washed each away. Each washing given Thanks to.

In time, no more came. He was clean.

Now he could envision the Great One turn and look down at him…waiting.

"Papa…your Spirit has fallen on me heavily today. I FEEL SAD. SO sad! I have seen your hurt. All the children within your house, who are paying no attention. Each going about their own thing. Giving little to know heed, to your voice. Your…OUR…house is a mess, sir. My many brothers and sisters lost in their will, their lusts, and their 'gods.' So many living only for the moment. I see this, 'papa'…and I cry.

That's all I can do Sir, cry.

That's all that's left Sir. My tears. I'm sorry. Amen."

And his tears fell down.

The “Be Moaners”

He was telling all about the many times people have come complaining about one thing or another. How he had help them through. Only to have them return, again and again and again on OTHER ‘woes.’

“People fail to LOOK BACK. They never turn around and see the mountains behind them. They only see the one before them and cry. Someday they NEED to look BACK!
Has ‘He’ not seen them through THOSE ‘Insurmountable’ times? THOSE Mountains? YES ‘HE’ HAS, else they would not exist and gotten so far on the ‘path.’

They need to LOOK BACK and SEE! They MUST STOP COMING TO ME! They must GO to ‘HIM!’

I am but an Adviser. A Counselor. I POINT!

‘HE’ ANSWERS! ‘HE’ gets them through. Not ME!

I Pray YOU LOOK BACK! I Pray YOU look UP. I Pray YOU LEARN, from PAST ‘MOUNTAIN CLIMBING’ that ‘HE’ HAS GOTTEN YOU THIS FAR!

LOOK BACK…and STOP CRYING! Stop ‘BeMOANING.’ Look Up, as I’ve pointed you to do EVERY TIME…and TRUST! ‘HE’ will ‘get you through’ once again. Has, so far…"

Ho.

Recession

"You tell, in your Great Vision, you were shown a giant economical collapse in our Country. Can you elaborate on that, grandfather?"

"Well, this is now January 2008. Listen to the panic Wall Street is in. Look at the Housing Market. Check out the BBC News…check out the WORLD. WE ARE STANDING IN THE DOOR FRAME from what I observe. One foot IN, One foot out. ONE MORE STEP IN and you are FULLY IN IT!
I think the major Governments will do some things to advert it, yet, IF SO, it will just be a Temporary 'fix.' IF, mind you!

I was shown three financial 'classes.' Blue Collar, White Collar and the extremely well off. ALL went down!
This was represented by Transportation. The RICH in Private Jets. White collar in Cessna, Blue in Gyrocopters. After the collapse the White were in Gyrocopters, The Blue on bikes and scooters, the Rich though, REGAINED THEIR 'Transportation Jets'…though they NEVER regained their HEIGHT. ALL were deeply changed. DEEPLY!

Looking for a Scapegoat, the CHRISTIANS were blamed. BIG TROUBLE for THEM and their Families! Name Calling and Beatings of their children in school. 'Madness,' in a way.

I have run into a few Christians who are in the 'market.'

'*We will be THE Controlling Force (Wall Street),'* they have told me. Asked me if I 'wanted in.' NO WAY! They claim, '*This is GODS WILL so HIS FOLLOWERS can STABILIZE things.*' First off, I don't think they have the financial means of doing so…secondly, I do NOT think this IS OF OUR CREATOR. I personally think its good intent is UNGodly HAUGHTINESS.

No, I want nothing to do with it. I've seen what Money can do AND what POWER can do! NO THANK YOU!

No, I do not think this is of God at all…

Still, Recession? DEPRESSION would best describe it. The Euro, Chinese interference, other things, will bring us down.
A reason for this: MAKE THE USA WEAK…then ATTACK, Physically.
Ditto on all our War 'helps'…WEAKEN the USA! Spread them THIN…
'THEN we'll HAVE THEM!'

I think they're right, if that's the case.

I've warned many years now. Been called all KINDS of things…but I haven't wavered an iota!

I've told 'PREPARE.' Both for THIS event and events still to come. Right or Wrong, I will continue. If wrong, I too will face our Maker. Then will 'pay the Price.'

I've told, *'Do NOT Believe a WORD I SAY...but CHECK IT'* (and come to your own conclusions). I still say that.

Am I spreading FEAR? Or WISDOM? YOU decide!

I am sharing only what I've been shown…AND CHECKED ON.

Look at our Country today...YOU DECIDE!"

HO!

SMART?

A number were sitting with grandfather. Just chatting of general things. Grandfather adding insight to subjects that were arising. Finally, one said, "Grandfather, HOW did you get so SMART?"

Grandfather looked down, sighed, looked up, and said,

"All this time we've been together and you STILL don't get it?

I am NO SMARTER than ANY…

I am NO DUMBER than ANY…

I suppose, if tested for my 'IQ'…I'd be on the lower side of 'normal.'

I don't know how to spell well. My math is rudimentary. I can't tell sizes below one-fourth or three-fourths on a ruler. Can't look at a socket wrench and tell what size it is by sight alone. Can't tune up an older car…many things, just sorta 'dumb.'

BUT I have ONE THING going for me that I've learned, that most don't: HOW TO CONNECT WITH THE GREAT LIBRARIAN. THE one that knows ALL!
'Dad', the 'Great Creator.'

I've made FRIENDS WITH HIM!

I've learned 'He' is REAL, as I've often told.

Smart? NO! 'HE' is SMART.

I'm just smart enough to CONNECT!

Mankind FORGETS 'Him' and RELIES on their OWN 'Brain power.' Scientists, Doctors…all these 'High Thinkers.'

Oh, they find out some things. Many OTHER Things they THINK they 'KNOW.' IF that were true, WHY DO WE HAVE STARVING? WHY DO WE HAVE POLLUTION? WHY DO WE HAVE WAR?

No, they just 'know' enough to get in trouble.

Man is like a mere child. A child who has found a match and think they 'KNOW' Fire!

In learning how to activate it, by striking it into activity, they say: *'SEE, I KNOW FIRE!'* YET, THEY STILL ARE NOT MATURE ENOUGH TO WATCH OUT FOR SPARKS ! TO WATCH OUT AND STRIKE IN A SAFE AREA! So, in learning, they often end up DESTROYING.

There are times they destroy to the point nothing can be done. TOTAL LOSS!

All because they consider themselves so "SMART."

It is THESE who are on the "dumb" side.

But, no dumber OR smarter than ANY of us!

If YOU are interested in REALLY GETTING ALL THE INFORMATION YOU DESIRE or NEED…GO, LEARN TO CONNECT TO THE GREAT LIBRARIAN!

ANY can do so.

I Have. The Other 12 have. Others have. We're not alone.

'HE' is the 'SMART' ONE…WE are just 'Smart' enough to REALIZE THAT and CONNECT TO 'HIM.'

Now, THAT'S the SMARTEST THING I CAN (and ever WILL be) able to TELL YOU!

Aho?"

Stones etc., Have Powers

Grandfather was teaching a class. Two, in this were 'into' *Rock Healing*. Here is what he told: "Remember, God is in ALL things. This includes ALL stones and minerals. You know the power of a few. Many, but still yet a few.

As plants give energies, so too do various rocks, etc. Yet ALL plants and ALL stones have energies.

Each of Each 'does' things. Things for certain needs of a patient…certain needs of Mankind in general. Not just for illnesses, but for LIFE. Our continued existence. Aho?

Indeed, we ARE 'all one relation.' Working together to allow each to live. Aho?

Being God is IN…being we are ALL withIN…being The Creator is a Living Spirit…being we are ALL His Thoughts, we are all One thing: ENERGY.

This energy has no separation. It is of ONE source and all of the SAME Matter.

With this understanding of ENERGY, you can expand your knowledge of each single stone you are using. In this, you can then be more proficient in their uses. This includes plants, as well.

In this case, we are using stones as the example, yet all five Senses, and things pertaining to them, are on the same 'theme.' Aho?

ALL is ENERGY only 'Placed' within your thought of what you consider 'reality.' Thus, you can physically SEE a stone. This is given for your help…AND growth!
The 'Growth?' TO EVENTUALLY SEE BEYOND PHYSICAL SIGHT! Few will ever do so. *'A Stone is A Stone.'* They see nothing beyond that.

In fact, a Stone is an ENERGY FORM. 'Matter.' PURE DREAMING THOUGHT! PURE One Kind ENERGY.

You have heard of Cholesterol. Little fat cells. Often connected to heart attacks, due to Build Up. These are SOFT 'Stones.' Collecting and damming the blood flow.

ALL Matter is like Cholesterol. A COLLECTION of Energy MATTER. To 'FORM.'
Thus you SEE Trees/Clouds/Rocks/Grasses/Each Other. ALL.

In Stones, some are GIVERS, some are RECEIVERS. 'Collectors.'

Used with the knowledge, which one does to which one, you can use these to your advantage. Remember ALL is MATTER Only. To GIVE, or to TAKE.
Diamonds, for instance, are TAKERS–used properly. THEY ABSORB 'Bad' Energies.

Head injuries within the brain can benefit from diamonds…and a 'dust'…centralized at the 'Baby's Soft Part' of the skull. Or too, sprinkled on the top of the head. A 'Main Diamond' in center of these. Will acts as ABSORBERS. Collecting SHOCK WAVE Energy to themselves from the damaged brain within the skull…then, as Cholesterol, sending that 'bad' to the main 'stone.' They act as 'Bumpers' to all the disrupted energies within the brain. Absorbing the SHOCK(s).
Removal of the main stone on a daily basis and replaced by a fresh main one, is like removing an absorbent gauze pad. The SHOCK (unseen). 'Puss and Blood' is taken away and new 'Medicine' Is applied.

There are ways to cleanse the 'old pad' but that is for another time. The Old Tibetan Monks know best on this. Their way of cleansing crystals are the same for diamonds.

By the way, Chrystal are second in this type of healing work. Aho?

Not as Fast and takes longer, but easier to get. Aho?

Some stones of color Heal. Blues and 'jeweled' greens and others emit Goodness, Serenity, etc.

ALL things WORK for ALL. Done properly, one can use individually to specific needs and purposes.

Yes, stones Heal."

Aho.

Sheesh!

The things people come up with! It Floors US! For instance:

“Grandfather, can you get a curse off me that I’ve had for 40 years now?”

“Possibly. Tell me, what brought this on? Do you know?”

“Yes. It’s something I said.”

“What?”

“I answered ‘YES’ to the question: *Do you take this woman to be your lawfully wedded wife?*”

(GOTCHA!)
☺

What's It Like To Be…You?

"That's an odd question. Why do you ask?"

"Just curious, grandfather."

Grandfather slowly shook his head, side to side, and then let out a quiet, airy 'laugh.'

"Well, you asked. Gives me something to consider on."

"Hum…I suppose it's, gee…how do I tell such a thing?"

A minute passed. Then yet another, as he sat, thinking.

"Guess it's sorta hard. Took me a long to come to where I am. Years, really.

I had to come to like me first, DESPITE me.

Then to LOVE myself. That sounds 'heady,' but it too, had to be.

I had to see me through 'HIS' eyes.

The Great One has done a lot of loving to put ME 'out!'

Took him about forever, I guess. Poor bugger.

I'm not one FORCED into doing anything! Pretty hard headed. Kinda like a brat kid.
'He' had that to deal with. Did too…and still does.

But eventually, I slowly began to learn 'His' Love. All He's done for me, despite me. A lot of patience and Sacrifice was put out on this hardheaded one.

Somehow, I got to seeing myself. What I was. What I had done at the moment. Seemed I was only feeling 'good' when I DID well SPIRITUALLY. The rest of the time was self-centered *'I Want'* indulgences. Really didn't make me happy. Not when I thought about it.

Therefore, I began to see me in a 'new light.' An Ingrate creation of The Creator.

Still, 'He' MADE me. I thought, *This Great One DOESN'T MAKE 'MISTAKES.'*

So, *I guess I'm not that bad*. (BAD as I was!) This is what I began thinking.

Somehow, that helped calm me down. That and trying to understand WHY 'He' made me.

Like I said, I wasn't the nicest guy in the world.

Thinking on how doing GOOD MADE me FEEL good, within…well, I liked that good feeling. Was a lot better than my dark 'fog.'

So, IN 'Him' and BECAUSE of "HIM"…I began LIKING ME! It wasn't long after that, that I slipped into 'HIS' Love. Suddenly I began actually Loving ME! 'HE' DID THIS!

Since then, I have LIKED and LOVED as 'HE' Liked and Loved.

In this, we two became Very Close. I enjoyed this so MUCH that I did NOT want it to go from 'His' LOVE Presence. Due to 'HIM,' we bonded as 'one.' I became 'His' son, 'He' became my FATHER.

With 'His' First Born ('Big Brother' to me) IN me. Dwelling here (he pointed to his heart) I was and am able to please. The Great One time after time. Our bond is VERY Close.

'What's it like to be ME?'

Well, in 'HIM' I am quite satisfied.

'He' gives me duties to do, 'He' teaches me it IS 'Him' doing so, THROUGH Me.

I'd rather obey 'Him' AND STAY IN LOVE with ALL ('HIS' LOVE) then live as the 'world.' I suppose this will one day be my 'undoing' At least to MAN around me. SO WHAT! I AM AT PEACE WITHIN MYSELF. I AM AT PEACE WITH MY GREAT FATHER. I AM AT PEACE with ALL THREE that Makes 'The One.' I may die cruelly. May die in great pain. But that will PASS! And I will be home, PERMANENTLY, with My GREAT DAD/MOM/BROTHER…and very close to this/these '3-in-1' that makes up the ONE.

In this, I live…REALLY <u>LIVE</u>! I would have it no other way.

'What's it like to be ME?'

It is a 'pain'…and a PLEASURE.

The Pain is that so few know this relationship. Many who Claim to, really don't. It hurts me…for I FEEL 'His' PAIN, Deep within ME! Aho?"

Silent Hunting

"Time to go, boys," grandfather told his two grandsons. He handed each a long hollow tube and a handful of homemade darts. Blowguns and ammo. Each dart had been scratched at the tip…and showed brown. Homemade arsenic. POISON.

"Put these (darts) in the rabbit pelt and wrap them well. DON'T SCRATCH YOURSELF WITH THEM!"

Off they went…the 'hunters.'

At the end of the day, they arrived home with one Quail and many stories.

"Tomorrow, another quiet weapon…Bolo."

Each had their own. Handmade. They used fishing weights as the three string weights.

No luck that day. A couple of missed rabbits to talk about.

They were out again the following weekend. THROWING STICKS this time. Weight more on one end, then another. Spin when tossed at a target. Nine ducks and one rabbit came home with them on this trip.

These were just a few of the quiet weapons…game getters…that grandfather was helping them make and use.
Each had learned to make an Atlatl (Spear thrower) and spear arrows for them. Also, Yo Yo throw stone...Traps and Snares. They were learning. Then took a small bird 'getter,' GLUE. Made from Holly Sap.

"Smear this on branches you see birds land on. Birds are of habit. One limb/one spot on that limb is one bird's territory. This glues them to the spot. Literally! Easy pickings."

Yes, he thought survival ways. All quiet…all 'on hand' materials.

"Now, just because you KNOW, doesn't give you the RIGHT to take a life for 'sport.' USE THIS KNOWLEDGE WISELY! We have killed. We have plenty of store bought food in the freezer. You Don't NEED to do this EXCEPT FOR PRACTICE. ONLY USE THIS IF TRULY NEEDED from here on in. Aho?"

On The Spot Fishing

Grandfather and the boys were 'tripping.' A nice clear creek was approached. Good size fish swimming about. TROUT!

"Gee I wish we'd brought our poles," the eldest said.

Grandfather reached down and pulled a number of tall weed leafs. He placed two in his mouth and began twisting each in the same direction, crisscrossing the two as twisted. Towards the end, he twisted two more to the first ends.
He did this until he had about four feet of FISHING LINE!
Next, he snapped off a tiny stick and using a rock, 'pointed' both ends. Tying this to one end of the 'line.' A small stone tied above this makeshift HOOK, as a SINKER. The boys searched about for bait. A grasshopper was put on the Hook and the Line tossed in. After the frightened fish returned, it wasn't long before a greedy fish struck. Grasshopper into its belly...HOOKED. In time, they had enough for a decent lunch.

All from Nature and...KNOWLEDGE.

Dreams

"Life is a dream. Every moment of it. Day or night. Day AND night. Mankind dreams their events…their trials and tribulations…their Own 'good' and 'bad.' All self induced. This is again, the *'Ye are as gODS'* that Scriptures speaks of. I have told ALL about you is a dream. YOURS!

For instance, my youngest grandson…a PROJECTED DREAM OF MY OWN…is a real 'bear' to get up in the mornings. Particularly on school days. It is a 'fight'…it's a Major WAR! Huff and Puff. Slamming doors, yelling. *'I HATE SCHOOL!'* That kind of thing.

Quite frustrating.

Well he, MY DREAM, He is a PROJECTION OF MY INNER SELF being made Manifested. SKY (my grandson) is The REAL INNER ME!

In truth, I DON'T LIKE 'SCHOOL' EITHER! It's often a HASSLE. One I don't care to contend with. SKY IS MYSELF. SHOWING me…ME! Rebellious and that I am often dissatisfied.

I CAN (and DO) learn from this. I KNOW 'he' is ME…deep inside. That this sweet kid, the Berserk KIDBEAR, is The Creator SHOWING ME what I TRULY 'Hold' inside. SHOWING me something about me that needs to be 'worked on.' SKY is a GIFT!

A Gift shared TO me by my Nagual Angel, who can ONLY communicate via Dreams and Visions…and Illnesses. Just obeying Its orders. Just doing its JOB!

INNER Peace, I've found, brings OUTER Peace.

When I have INNER Peace, SO SKY REFLECTS IT and is a real sweetheart.

If I slip, or AM slipping, he (and other 'mirrors') REFLECTS 'anger'/'nastiness'/etc.

IF I'M WISE, I 'catch' that and begin working on getting 'at peace.'
When I'm successful…THE MIRROR(S) CHANGE!
I tell you TRUE: IT WORKS!

You are now at least, aware. 'TRY' ME. TEST THIS…and LEARN from YOUR DREAM(s). FOR LIFE IS ALL A DREAM!"

Ho.

Useless Counseling

She had called before. Her husband missing. Grandfather did a Spirit Travel and located him.

"He's OK. Out 'gallivanting' (womanizing). He'll be back in a few days."

Grandfather doesn't like bad news…or giving it. Still, she had come, seeking.

The husband returned, as told.

About five weeks later the HUSBAND called, "Wife missing."

Ditto on Spirit Travel.

"She's OK. Doing what YOU did. She'll return soon."

Did.

Then HER Again! SAME PROBLEM but this time with a 'twist.'

"Grandfather, I've found another man. What will this lead to? Can you tell me?"

"Yes…to making the Great One (Creator) both Dissatisfied with you, and sad. You were not brought into this life to act as you are. You AND your husband were/are meant for BETTER things. You two are one. Yet both of you are boozing and cheating self. STOP DRINKING and STOP 'GALAVANTING'… You."

CLICK! She had hung up.

"People want to 'do their own thing.' Truth HURTS! They call, asking, and get news they prefer not to hear. THEY SEEK 'GOOD NEWS.'

'Approval' to do UnGodliness.

They KNOW they are doing wrong…yet WANT to CONTINUE in the world's way.

You either do as this world of darkness grins at…or make 'HIM' grin in JOY.

TRY 'HIM.' You'll find YOU GRIN IN JOY, TOO!

Born INTO 'Sin' (Disobedience to God) does not mean YOU <u>NEED</u> TO!

Do you want REAL HAPPINESS in life? FOLLOW BIG BROTHER!"

This is what grandfather was going to tell her.

Ho.

Mixing Of Cultural Ways

Grandfather was out peeling Tipi poles. The sound of the Weed Eater breaking the piece of the morning's silence.

WEED EATER?

Yes.

To PEEL BARK?

Yes.

"My wife accidently hit a pole lying in the grass she was weed eating. It was old and dry. THE BARK FLEW OFF LIKE MAD! She told me of this.

I just incorporated this White Man's tool to my Indian Use. I used to hand peel. Took quite awhile doing a number of poles. Her news was good news to ME! Now, I no longer hand peel. I just let the bark dry on the poles and whack it off with this weed eater!
Sure makes an easier and far faster job of it!

I also now use this 'way' to do hides. I starch them out and go to it with the 'eater.' Fat and left on meat, FLIES! Another hard job speeded up by the White Man's technology. When the hide dries, I go over it again, this time helping to break down Its hardness. Sure helps!

I'm no 'dummy'...I've learned to use many 'ways' of the whites. At the same time, I'm aware of OUR 'old ways.'

Someday, the things of the White man will be too costly...IF you can get them! So, use them to my advantage while I've got them and keep the 'old ways' handy. I won't 'hurt' like the whites...just back to being slower in doing again, is all.

'One Up,' on them.

I LIKE the OLD WAYS of the Whites too. Nonelectrical 'ways.' The ways of their early days here. Most of us have no knowledge of the 'HOW'S' of those days.

Ever see some of *those day's* FURNITURE? WOW! And ALL made without a SPECK of electricity! They were smart in those days. Smart too, today, but TOO SMART for what lays ahead.

I don’t mind many of their modern things. USE THEM! But don’t put my ‘life’ in their Usefulness FOR THE DAYS AHEAD!

We are building our new home using a combination of THEIRS and OURS.

OUR type HOME, but using much of THEIR things to do so. Aho?”

Can People Really Levitate?

To this question grandfather just shook his head.

"Yes, all are quite capable of this. All CAN do so MUCH more then they think. I've told again and again: YOU CAN do '*The Things Of our Big Brother.*' But, AGAIN, you WON'T if you DON'T THINK SO! It and all the other things He exampled…AND OTHERS…are simply CONVINCING YOUR MIND you ARE DOING SO!

You've spent your LIFE in *The Cant's*. TOLD it and BELIEVED it! THAT MUST BE OVERCOME. As I've said, many times, you need to UNLEARN…TO learn.

Reprogram your thoughts and beliefs…and the WORLD of 'MIRACLES' are AT YOUR VERY BECKONING!

I will say this no more. Accept it or reject it. It's up to you.

Any who test this and do NOT DO SO, they are showing only that they are NOT totally in the MINDSET of BELIEVING FULLY.
They SAY they do…yet the *'proof is in the pudding'*…IF they AREN'T SUCCESSFUL…they ARE NOT IN TOTAL REPROGRAMMING!

The DEPTH of the mind is VERY deep. YOU MUST CONVINCE THE "DEEP DEEP." THEN you will levitate. THEN you will be open 'to the Cosmos'…the WORLD of CANS! Not JUST 'Can,' but beyond that…to the 'AM' (cementing the fact).

Aho?"

Innovating

Grandfather and grandmother had a large chest freezer…AND a want for a Hot Tub!

The freezer was old. Set aside to be pitched out.

Not having the money to pay the extras needed to take to the dump (cost more with the compressor)…AND no money for a hot tub, well, that got grandfather to thinking.

He was off to the freezer. Dragged it with his truck to the spot they wanted the hot tub. One he was sure it was in the day's sun, he began. He cut off the electrical cord, leveled the freezer, put steps of blocks to go up into the freezer, drilled a water exit and plugged it, made a small slatted 'box' at one end inside…made a low seat of cedar wood, got out his cheapo electric fishing motor and battery, placed the motor on the slotted box (prop towards the 'open' section of the freezer), filled the freezer with water…placed a black plastic sheeting over the open top…and waited. During the evening, he went out and closed the lid. Opening the next day.

At about two in the afternoon he felt the water."Warm Enough," he declared. Striped and went in. Turning on the motor, he felt its prop's current stirring the water around him.

He sat back and relaxed. Smile on face.

"HEY HONEY, COME ON OUT! It WORKS!" he called.

This was left behind when they moved.

"We'll replace it when we build on the Safe Land. I'll 'Log Cabin' around the next one. Make it look good. Might use a big Stock Water Tank then, though. Might even go to the old way of heating water by using hot stones."

INNOVATE! Don't just SALIVATE over WANTING. *It's* there for you…CHEAPER!…IF YOU THINK a BIT DIFFERENTLY! Aho?"

Grandfather Introduces The Boys To A New Way To Fish

His grandsons arrived, Face Mask, Snorkel, and Fins in hand. Swim suits on. As ordered.

Grandfather had a blown up car inner tube, three old fishing poles and reels…and a coffee can with bait lashed to the tube, also a long fish stringer. Hopping into the pickup, they were off.

Once at the lake, all donned their gear and headed into the water. This was a friend's private lake. No boats allowed that had motors. Otherwise, grandfather would have had a flag to attach to the tube too.

In they went, all baited up.

They swam the shoreline slowly. Finally spotting some good size bass.

He instructed the boys to glide over their nests and dangle a wormed hook before the fish of their choice. "DON'T SPLASH!"

WHAM! Bass are very protective of their eggs.

Time after time, they brought in the biggest ones and put them on the stringer. When tired, they'd rest, an arm over the tube.

"Don't clean a spot out. That will deplete the area…AND the new births. Take only what you KNOW you need."

Each had a laminated fishing license around their neck.

Occasionally grandfather would see a shadow deeper below him. "Might be a sunken tree. Dive down and look. These are good hiding spots. Remember to slowly release your air as you come back to the surface."

The day was quite successful. A family gathering was to be the next day. They got what they needed and all three enjoyed the summer swim.

HO!

Mystery Sights

Over the years grandfather has received requests (?) on sites of mystery. "This is here."/"This is there."/"What IS it?"/etc.

MOST requiring his 'immediate' attention/'telling.'

NONE offering support or pay to go and 'check this out,'

(NOT THAT HE WOULD!)

Almost for 100% SELF-Curiosity.

To these, he just shakes his head.

"So MANY of our Scared Places are now in the 'whites' hands.

Not ONE should be! NONE!

We were given these places to protect! But HUNDREDS have been stolen or destroyed. Highways plowed through them. Airports built on them. Homes, Farms…AND MILITARY have them now. THE WHITES HAVE NO RESPECT! They TAKE. They DIG. They CHIP. They Put in Museums…They DESTROY. They HIDE, and then they want us to tell MORE!

Hell! I KNOW THINGS I WOULDN'T EVEN TELL MY OWN MOTHER!

Our peoples' Scared Grave Sites are dug up for 'artifacts'…and so too, even our very BONES!

TAKE! TAKE! TAKE!
WE want WE want
GIVE US MORE!

Many things stolen or cheated out of. SOLD on eBay…Sold at 'Trade Shows.' Sold to 'Private Collectors'…you name it!

Why should I go and let them have MORE!

I've told enough. I have shared knowledge. This to wake them up to the truth *'there is more out there,'* than they can imagine. TRYING to make them Learn! To get them back to THE SOURCE of ALL Information. THE CREATOR!

No, I have told enough.

They are like a WILD FIRE GONE AMOK! Consuming ALL they can reach and BEGGING FOR MORE! 'Feed me–FEED ME–Sit it at my FEET, so I can EAT!

Yes, there are 'sights'…'*out there.*' Strange MYSTERIES.

SACRED…at least to Us.
They don't KNOW 'Sacred.' THEY KNOW ONLY 'MINE!'

WE were given these places to PROTECT…AND to GIVE THE KNOWLEDGE OUT WHEN THE TIME IS RIGHT!

THAT'S WHY we KNOW. For ALL! The WORLD! At a <u>GIVEN</u> TIME!

Not at MAN'S time, but 'HIS!'

The whites have taken SO MUCH of things THAT WOULD HELP ALL, WithOUT knowing what they have DONE…it is a wonder, WHAT IS LEFT, will now be of ANY USE!

They have KILLED OFF MOST OF THE KNOWLEDGE KEEPERS! Those who KNEW. They have RULED as VENGEFUL 'GODS!' LAUGHING at their 'Authority'…MADMEN! DICTATORS!

And they want us to Give MORE?

Today, THE TIME OF GIVING is REALLY PROTECTED, by us!

THIS is what the Whiteman has done! MADE US <u>NOT</u> WANT 'to give.'

Even the few elders who DO give, are banned by the others. Called 'Uncle Toms.' 'TRAITORS!' By doing what MUST be done!

Today, thanks to the 'Ruler THIEF'S,' ALL will 'pay.' EVEN OUR OWN 'BLOOD!'

Today there ARE HARDLY a KNOWLEDGE KEEPER LEFT! What we have, is people who ONLY KNOW *'This/That'* site IS SACRED! That's ALL they know!

THEY HAVE ALMOST NO 'KEY KEEPERS!' The few left are OSTRACIZED!

Those who ostracize ARE AS 'STUPID' AS THE WHITES!!

The 'Whites' did this to THEM/US!

Now…we die.

"Grandfather, what is the strangest thing you've seen?"

At this question, grandfather laughed.

"Yes, that is true question. Few experience the things I and other Medicine People do. Guess we ARE different.

I have seen some things that have raised every hair on my body, as they were so…unexpected.

But your question is about the STRANGEST. Hands down, it is this:

I was driving down by the Testing Range in the southwest. Tall fencing for miles: 'STAY OUT' signs. The whole government 'bit.' It was the middle of the day. A Beautiful day. A fair amount of traffic but not overly loaded. I was in the right side lane.
An old 'beater' VW 'Bug' began to pass on my left. Dust and dirt all over it.
The driver was a man. Somewhere in the age of high 30's to low 40's. HE HAD NO SOUL!

I mean SOUL-LESS!!!

His eyes were straight ahead, unblinking. No sideways looking. His hands held the steering wheel tightly at 10 o'clock and 2 o'clock. THERE WAS NO 'LIFE' IN HIM! Like a true DEAD MAN DRIVING!

I have NEVER Seen this before (or since), but I HAVE HEARD of it!

I tell you, IT WAS SPOOKY!

Was I afraid? No. Was I Feared? No. But I WAS SHOCKED!

This was no Zombie. Zombies still have their souls. Walk oddly. But not Soulless.

HE HAD NO SOUL!"

"Grandfather, what is the 'weirdest' thing you've had happen?"

"Gosh, you people ask the Darnest questions!"

(Laughter)

"Well, I've had so MANY 'weird' experiences that are hard to say…Hum, do you mean BESIDES getting MARRIED?"

(More Laughter.)

"Hum, well TOO MANY to nail just one, so I'll give you my LATEST. This occurred just last night and ran into early this morning.

Close to nine last night, our granddaughter called from West Virginia. For some reason static started up seconds after her first word. Drowning out what few words I could hear before the line disconnected. I waited about thirty minutes to see if she'd call back. Did, I THINK! ALL static this time…and again the line disconnected.

I then called HER. On her cell phone. Could only leave a message. Tried again a bit later. This time leaving a message to return my call using Our Cell Phone number.
Less than five minutes later, she responded. Or so I Thought. ALL STATIC! So emailed her I'd call in the morning and went to bed.

As I've told, I get up early. SHE called ME before I could call HER."

"Grandpa, I DIDN'T CALL YOU LAST NIGHT!"

"But Lynnsay, it was YOU, YOUR VOICE and JUST THE OPENING WORD you ALWAYS Start Out With!"

"No Gramps, I called NO One yesterday, No one at ALL. It WASN'T ME!"

"Gramps, I think this house is haunted…They have a dog that barks for HOURS while it sits in front of a Chair in the room here! NO ONE IS IN IT!"

"Well, I believe her, fully. I've heard of 'Phantom Calls'…just as I've heard of 'Soulless Humans.' Seems a spirit had been having some fun last night.
So…THERE'S a 'WEIRD ONE' for you!"

The Year 2008

This is being written the 14th of June, 2006. Written to inform you that it appears all Medicine People (that I know), are ALL "LAYING OFF" for a FULL YEAR! This seems to be the case with me, as well.

JUNE SEEMS TO BE "THE CHANGING" MONTH!

MANY CHANGES ARE AHEAD. Changes WE are preparing for. That those "less in touch with Creator" are NOT!

It's as if the Great Creator has given a Silent Phone Call: "TAKE A BREAK! BE WITH YOUR FAMILY. YOU HAVE LABORED TO NEAR DESTRUCTIONS. I AM PROUD OF YOU! TAKE a NEEDED Break…NOW!"

Almost like an ORDER!

It appears only a MINIMAL "work" will be done in this time. Like even HE is sitting back and watching only.
What lies ahead?
Most of us KNOW. Some to a greater extent than others, but we are ALL…AWARE!

I tell you true: THESE "QUIET TIMES" FORETELL A NEW BEGINNING. A NEW LESSON.

So NEW we have NEVER EXPERIENCED ITS LIKE!

A MONTH "off" is hard enough…but a YEAR?! UNHEARD OF!
Will it mean a great changing of Heart?
Will it mean a great changing of EARTH?
Will it mean a Godly REVIVAL? Or a great God REBELLION?

I know not. My friends know not.
We know only…Rest, my children. Rest. FOR THE FUTURE LAYS AHEAD!

Friends, You/I/WE/ALL, MAKE THAT FUTURE! What will it be???? YOU decide.

Ho.

PS: As we know these events have transpired by the time you are reading this…just like many events are in the process of being so or have already done so.

More On The Just Done

Friend(s), I want you to know HOW THE CREATOR "WORKS."

We (of Medicine Ways), as told, seem to be given a "Leave Of Absence."

The Creator God is very much as a General in any army. In this case…even ABOVE a "five star" General.

We, the Medicine People "soldiers" have been on "the front lines" for an unbelievably long time. In "His" role as Supreme Leader, has pulled us back for "Rest and Relaxation." Time to lick our wounds, sleep, hug our loved ones, go to a show, fish, etc.

A time for SELVES AND FAMILY.

We still stay in touch with the "High Command." This on a daily basis. Occasionally given a "job" to do during this. These are minimal.

As a Front Line soldier, I (and we), find "He" gives short term "Leave." THIS IS A GIANT ONE!

ALL "Leaves" mean A NEW LEARNING will take place. "Weapons" of "advanced" "Technology." Given and taught the use of. Then, BACK TO THE FRONT LINES, WE GO!

WE WILL NOW BE GETTING "SUPER WEAPONS" it appears. FAR more advanced than ANY of us have ever used. "SECRET WEAPONS" will come forth. Like NOTHING any one of us had ever Dreamed was available!

A full year off bespeaks a MAJOR BATTLE PLAN IS IN THE WORKS!

That means WE WILL SLOWLY BE PUT BACK ON THE "LINE."

As any who have "time off," we will get rather "fat." Thus, "back to boot camp" to prepare ourselves to get back into the "Frame of Mind" to "DO." In SPIRIT/PHYSICAL/MENTAL.

This will take time, but NOT A LOT OF TIME! So suspect a three month "build up." "Revamping." THEN TO THE NEW WORK/"WEAPONS" we go.

Therefore, at about JUNE of NEXT YEAR, we will start, once again.

To WHAT? WE do NOT know.
Let's hope it is an "occupying forces" of WORLD PEACE "caretakers."

Understanding Today Better

Understand, reader(s), When Scriptures says "There was WAR in the Heavens," it is a statement of FACT.

Armies against armies. ANGEL ARMIES!

This was needed to MAKE Lucifer and his FLEE.

To BRING ALL Soul Bearers to The FREEDOM OF CHOICE.

Otherwise, Lucifer and "his" would have stayed in the Heavenly realm. NOT SPREADING OUT! Therefore, our Creator MADE them leave!

Once they were chased off, in eons of time, Lucifer had his followers spread to EVERY PLANT that SOUL BEARERS possessed. Eventually spreading SELF WILL across ALL!

Our Earth Mother, is THE ONLY PLANET LEFT that still "knows" GOD.

ALL OTHERS HAVE LONG AGO FORGOTTEN!

Now, as we enter this New Era of The GREAT CHANGE, War AGAIN looms. Once again, there will be "War in the Heavens." WE know this time as "Armageddon."

Though I've told WE CAN PUT THIS OFF, it STILL will be! Has TO!

This will bring ALL Soul Bearers BACK TO KNOWING THERE IS A GOD! Only One. Ho.

So, as you read (I hope) the Good Book, see the Plan. See the REASON.

So too, see that The Great CREATOR has EVERYTHING IN CONTROL. ALL!

We here, (our military/Governments/Leaders/etc.) "RUN" <u>EXACTLY</u> AS OUR MAKER'S HEAVENLY DOMAIN!

The DICTATOR Governments HERE are Lucifer's. His conning as Our "Good" here, AS "GOD."

WE ARE A MIRROR OF THE REALM OF "SPIRIT!"

With that, in mind, you will get a BETTER GRASP OF WHAT'S GOING ON! Put on THE FULL ARMOR OF GOD, Reader(s), and FEAR NOTHING AT ALL!
We that do, are the HIGH Warriors in this war. STAND IN HIM! HO!

Grandfather Talks To Christians

Several Christians were in a group talk with grandfather. Some 'against' him, some 'for' him.

"Brothers and sisters, I don't care what you think of me. I really don't. What I care about is what you think of YOURSELVES!

I will be 65 tomorrow. Some here have seen more years than I, most not.

What I am saying is I've been around for quite awhile.

Now understand, as an Inner Heyókȟa', we are trained to observe.

Observing is more than sight. It is observing what is said AND DONE, as well.

One observation I've found is: I HAVE YET TO MEET A CHRISTIAN who is Not AFRAID OF LUCIFER!

Ask yourself this, WAS JESUS?

Did HE run when He was on the Mountain Fasting? Did HE tremble?

NO! He STOOD UP TO him! Not in 'self' but with THE WORD OF GOD.

Using that NON-SELF Way…He went 'toe-to-toe' with him. NEVER WAVERING.

HE didn't flee. LUCIFER was the one who LEFT!

Yet I have yet to find a 'Follower' who does as He, their Example.

I have met many fellow Christians in my years. I have observed. I have Heard, I have Seen, I have TESTED. ALL fear the Dark One!

'What should I DO, grandfather?'

'I have trouble Connecting, grandfather?'

'I CAN'T WIN, grandfather?'

'He is so STRONG, grandfather!'

'Where should I/We GO, grandfather?'

This and many other things, told to me.

ALL showing FEAR!

In addition, THESE call themselves 'CHRISTIAN?'

That word, CHRISTIAN, means CHRIST FOLLOWER.

REMEMBER HIS 40 DAY WILDERNESS FAST!

Lucifer is an ANGEL! WE have FULL AUTHORITY over ALL ANGELS. Lucifer is an ANGEL! Lucifer is an ANGEL! Lucifer is an ANGEL! GOT THAT?!!

WHY do you FEAR this one? ALL he can do is TEMPT!

In his tempting, he temps YOU to BELIEVE HE IS SO STRONG that YOU CAN'T 'WIN.' He LIES, to TEMP You TO BELIEVE!

And BOY! DO YOU!!

I have observed.

IF 'Christian' means FOLLOWER OF CHRIST…YOU ARE NOT A CHRISTIAN. You are a poor excuse to what 'Christian' means.

IF you WANT to be a REAL Follower, RELY ON THE CREATOR'S WORD.
'His' WORD!

STAND UP TO THE LIAR! Make HIM LEAVE!

Note: Lucifer never stopped trying to defeat the Christ. Time and time again, he tried to destroy our Big Brother, the Lord.

Yet, TIME AFTER TIME, HE HAD TO LEAVE!

CHRIST USED THE KNOWLEDGE OF THE WRITTEN WORD TO DEFEAT HIM!

Used what HE 'BELIEVED'…TRUTH! GOD'S TRUTH!

Now YOU must decide: WHO DO YOU BELIEVE?!

WHAT do YOU REALLY Believe!

Do YOU RUN? DEFLATE! DEFECT!?

Are YOU a TRUE ‘FOLLOWER’…or a Wild Wilted Follower?

I do NOT CARE what you think of ME! I care what you think of YOURSELF!”

Praise God In All Things! Do You know How Hard That Is?

This from an irate one. One who has ‘troubles’ after ‘troubles.’ Constantly coming to grandfather. Wanting HIM to ‘push the magic button.’

“Listen, I have told you MANY times how to get out of your messes. YES! PRAISE HIM IN EACH!

‘HARD?’

Can you THINK? Can you SPEAK? Use one or the other UNTIL YOU FEEL JOY and RELEASE!

What’s so dang ‘Hard’ in THAT!???

You are UNWILLING to OBEY ‘His’ METHOD…well, ENOUGH! You are on your own. I’m done with you. Bother me no longer. WE ARE DONE.

Either DO or live in your constant problems! I’ve done ALL THAT’S NEEDED!

I wish you well. Good Luck.”

Grandfather Advises High School Students

Once again, grandfather had been asked to speak in a local high school class.

The subject: Career Decisions.

The students were attentive to his tellings.

"If you are looking for a career that pays well, never goes out of style, and is in constant need, then there's only ONE field to go in: MEDICAL.
Both you guys as well as you girls will need no worries about finding a job, ANYWHERE.

You don't need to be a Doctor or Urologist or X-Ray technician or ANY of those 'higher callings.' All you need is a NURSING DEGREE! The higher, the better.

As things now stand, there will be few machines to use, X-Ray included. These 'specialized' jobs will generally go 'down the tube.' Your learning is about useless to zero. When electricity is down, so too are these specialized fields.

NOT SO WITH A NURSE! They can help even using a CANDLE! Day and Night they will always be needed, and on hand. A NURSE HAS JOB SECURITY!

I've seen many college students graduate on various other career fields. ALL 'sweating it out.' Either ending up in dead end jobs or going entirely into very different jobs. VERY FEW OBTAIN A HIGH POSITION in their chosen fields.

I have YET to see one who has gone into the Nursing Field who is NOT still in it!

Consider this.

Consider too, you, as a nurse, will be SO NEEDED in the future, THE GOVERNMENT WILL PROTECT YOU! Yes, PROTECT!

Physically PROTECT.

So, my young friends, consider what I tell here.

For those of you who WILL consider, the 'road' starts now. GET First Aid TRAINING. If you think this is interesting, then go for Emergency Medical Technician training. Need more? There is a class on ADVANCED E.M.T.
ALL these will be useful to you, even IF you decide NOT to go into the Medical Field.
I wish you well. Ho."

The Fours

Again, another class talk.

"Sir, I'm thinking of going into the army. Do you have any suggestions on what would be best to get into?"

"Son, there are four S's that you should consider. That is, if you aren't interested in Corpsman (Battle Field 'doctor'). THAT is what I'd prefer you go into. Not killing, but SAVING. Beyond that, check into these 4 things:

SOUND
STEALTH
SPEED
SPIRIT

Sound is the FUTURE of war. LASER SOUND. With this there is no, or nearly no, Noise. Nor a Tracer bullet to trace to you, the shooter.
Sound can be as a Laser...PIN POINT accuracy! Or used in 'Shot Gun' spread. It can last but a finger pull on a trigger long, or the trigger held and a weaker/WIDER field of fire can be.
Sound can kill or stun. It can stop a body or tank…OR plane. It can also STRIP A MOUNTAIN! Turning it into a heap of shattered stone.

Sound is a TERRIBLE WEAPON! OR a GREAT HELP Healer, to mankind.

Our Armed Forces are experimenting on Its use. All for DEATH, I'm afraid.

Next is STEALTH. You are already aware of the Stealth Aircraft and Its ability. I need not go further on this. Aho?

Then comes SPEED. LOW FUEL/HIGH SPEED. Eventually 'Mini Tanks and Mini Submarines' will be made. Lightly protected. Able to stop a 50, to maybe a 60 millimeter bullet. The SPEED will be Its survival way.
These will be 1,2 and 3 manned. The COCKROACH SHAPED Mini-Tanks will have the capability to 'Skip-Fly' short distances. Jumping over mind fields, etc.

As of yet these are not yet here in THIS Dimension…but ARE in OTHERS.

SPIRIT: the ULTIMATE 'weapon.' With ONE PERSON IN PROPER MINDSET, THAT PERSON CAN 'FREEZE' A WHOLE ARMY! Then the 'good guys' can go about these 'frozen ones,' disarm them, handcuff them, and lead them into captivity. A 'NO KILL' WAY!

This too is yet to be learned HERE, Aho? Good Luck in your choice. Ho."

Grandfather Is In His Element

It was his 65th birthday. He was heading up to the Safe Land they had. He and a young friend. The young man to do a Vision Quest as grandfather prepared to build.

"I've all the essentials. Even a small generator if needed. My dome frame is within the pickups bed…shovel, pick and some needed tools. All ready to start. I FEEL GOOD!

65 and starting over. Again! A WONDERFUL Age to do so! No Stagnation. No couch potato. Just me, The Creator, Knowledge, and still young enough to do things. WONDERFUL!"

(This to his passenger.)

"So MANY hit 'retirement age'…and do little till they die. Most young OR old, wouldn't venture out anew. Don't know for sure why. Some in fear I guess. Changes don't come easily. I've got a year to get things ready. Root cellar…Water…Abode…All. Then up we go. The three of us. Some 37 miles from town. No 'permanent' electricity. Live 'with the chickens'…and bear and cougar and other free roamers.

It won't be easy. Especially on my wife. She's become complacent with all the modern ways. We've lived this way before though. When we were younger. That helps at least. She knows what to expect. Sky on the other hand…has not a clue. To him, now, it's all an adventure. All 'play.' Will fast wear off, when he has no TV or video games to waste away his time. Gonna take time. For ALL of us! Still, 'ahead of the game,' starting over. Many won't do this, though they DO 'feel' a 'calling.' They will be in for a shock when the 'crap hits the fan.' Too bad, they don't listen to their 'heart.' Their INNER BEING. That's GOD telling, *'OK,THEIR will.'*

I'll be mixing White and Native American here. Use the white's things while we have it…Indian to save money. Thus, I've a generator…until gas or parts make that unusable. Eskimo Lamps with reflectors behind each, for light. My water carrying Shoulder Yoke to haul water if needed. This from the distant river. Going to have a hand pumped well…Creator Willing. The yoke as 'back up.'

Our refrigerator will be on the line of the homes of gophers. Won't FREEZE things, but WILL keep them crisp and cool. Smoking and maybe jerking our meats will be…or buy and eat the same day. Sky's going to learn quite a bit in the next few months! When done, he'll be able to make it on his own, if need be.
Yeah, quite a few changes lay ahead. 'BACK to the FUTURE.' Sure glad I've taken my own advice…Creator's WISDOM…and studied/tested/learned.

I've know this was coming since I was ten. Started Then. Haven't stopped. Now to put it all to good use. Aho?"

Again Grandfather Advises

Grandfather receives many informative letters and emails. Reports of what is happening in various areas on Earth Mother. News not heard on American News Media. From Earth Quakes to Tornadoes to Social Problems and Government Intrusions on freedom. (More and more of 'Big Brother'... ONE World Government...(i.e., The Anti Christ one, that the world is entering).

MANY are 'out' claiming to be 'Informed' by 'Guides,' mostly. Here is his reply to those telling of 'This one' or 'That one':

"Many are 'telling.' In this telling they ALL contain TRUTHS.

JUST ENOUGH TRUTHS TO DECEIVE THE PERSON WHO IS FOLLOWING THESE 'TELLERS.'

You must learn to Check! Check! CHECK!

Do this against Scriptures. ALL FULL TRUTH IS THERE.

Understand Scriptures needs The CONCORDANCE to find 'The Thread of TRUTH' that The Good Book contains. It has been 'messed with' by man over the centuries.

(This is why we have so many Religions and so many Denominations.)

Mankind's error is in not checking. Check, CHECKING that what is taught by the teachings of their Spiritual leaders.

Thus, both those leaders AND THEIR FOLLOWERS will pay dearly at the 'Time of Judgment.'

You tell me of yet one more 'teller.' I have CHECKED, Checked, and Double Checked his website. Here are my findings: I SEE TRUTH there, but my time does not permit the time needed to read all there in. Thus, YOU must check three TIMES on EACH 'Telling.'

It is UP to YOU to KNOW THE SCRIPTURES (with Concordance work) WELL ENOUGH TO KNOW IF ALL TOLD IS TRUE.

IF you DON'T, then you, as many, stand a VERY GOOD...hear me;
A VERY GOOD chance, OF FOLLOWING A 'TELLER' that uses just enough truth TO get A FOOLISH Person TO BELIEVE ALL the teller is saying.

MANY will be deceived.
Many ARE being deceived.

We are in 'The Time of the DECEIVER.' The LIAR!

ONLY WISDOM, Only BIBLE WITH CONCORDANCE USE, can help YOU remain in The TRUE TRUTH! Only by THAT will any be Safe.

Today you must be EXTREMELY CAREFUL! For we are in the OUTLAYING 'MINEFIELD' of the Deceiver's 'Base Camp.'

MANY WILL DIE in this Spiritual Mine Field.

ONLY THOSE WHO WISELY CHECK, CHECK, CHECK, USING THE CONCORDANCE WITH THE 'GOOD BOOK' stand a chance of walking safely through this minefield.

This minefield leads to Destruction of your SOUL: Yet, with WISDOM and PURITY of the 'Thread of Golden Truth' that the Good Book contains, CAN YOU SAFELY THREAD THROUGH THE MINEFIELD.

Now I leave it up to you. I have instructed. You have heard the 'Teacher.' NOW it is up to YOU to Thread safely, or go out and be wounded, or Die.

YOU HAVE BEEN TAUGHT!

'Boot Camp' is over. Go now, with Wisdom, The Good Book, The Concordance, and CHECKING THREE TIMES ON ALL.

We ARE In WAR! Not 'Gonna be.' ARE!

Go get on your Warfare garb. The ARMOR OF GOD, and GET OUT THERE AND FIGHT!

Hear me; this war is TOTAL!

You can FIGHT or stand by as a civilian. TOTAL WAR means CIVILIANS DIE IN MASSES! PLEADING for 'deliverance' as all Hell breaks loose around them.

Now CHOOSE: GODS ARMY, LUCIFER'S, or CIVILIAN.

The choice is yours. YOU HAVE THE TEACHING. HO."

Parallel Time Spot

"You've talked about Parallel Time, grandfather. Even said, the Earth's inner gratings are opening such spots. Is there a particular place one can go to see?"

"You are sitting in one now," he said.

"WHAT! I don't understand, I don't see it!"

"It opens on Its own, brother. As Mother allows within her gratings. Generally, you are very unaware it IS the Parallel Time trip you are in. Unless an event takes place that's, hum…*offbeat,* you'd never know it.

This land we own has a center emitting spot. In the gully by the tipis. Most occurrences take place there. Generally, it covers only a few hundred yards, all in a circle around the center. I've seen this reach out, twice now, to about a full mile radius. At least I've seen it twice, that I KNOW of. It's traced to here, this trailer home of ours, once that I KNOW of. Again, it takes a 'different thing' that occurs, that makes one aware it is open and you're inside it. It's not like turning on and off a light switch…though that IS possible to do."

"How?"

"I don't tell how, so don't expect to learn from me. Still, doable.

There have been some strange things that have occurred here, during these openings. Others have witnessed them. Some have driven by and see 'me' at the tipis, entertaining others. SWEAR BY IT. They weren't seeing THIS me, but the 'me' within that Parallel Time. I've seen others I knew, SWEAR BY IT, that weren't them of THIS Parallel Time, too. Yes, some strange things…

These openings can, and do, open ANYWHERE and at ANY Time. The Times seem to be random, it appears. At least in general. This land HERE, though random too, has the most SHOWN though, that I've seen so far.

Now let's go onto other subjects. Aho?"

"One more question, PLEASE?"

"Hum."

"I've heard ghost stories of Gettysburg battles and things. There are LOTS of GHOSTS, aren't there?"

“Yes, there are…BUT: WHAT is GHOST and WHAT IS PARALLEL TIME SHIFTING! BOTH takes place! Are they seeing GHOSTS? Or ARE THEY IN A PAST PARALLEL TIME!”

“HOW CAN THAT BE…PAST?”

“There IS no time. That’s how It happens. You slip into a LIVING PAST.

There are some who ‘go in’ and SEE…AND ARE SEEN! Startling both parties.

Remember, we are dealing with the NATURAL, as WELL as the SPIRITUAL. Things few understand, or even know about.

Now, enough…”

Grandfather's Opinion Of War

When asked what he thought of warfare, grandfather replied:

"We are constantly 'at war.' This though within the World Of Spirit. Few realize this. At least not its fullness. It is Constant. Awake and asleep.

There are energies unseen, even by me, but there. For and against each individual. I am fortunate in that at least I am AWARE of it…and thus able to help fight these off.

'Tricky' things, these 'unseen.' Still, once aware they CAN be overcome. Ho.

These negative Spirits surround each 24/7. They are 'The Unseen.' Literally WITHIN THE VERY AIR we breathe and walk about in. They send NEGATIVITY as well as TEMPTATIONS.

To overcome you SAY (mentally or aloud) OUT with NEGATIVE, IN with POSITIVE while doing a number of breaths…say OUT as you breathe out. IN as you breathe in…in and out. The air holds Both 'God' and 'UnGod.' You can thus dispel the negatives and have only the positives within you.

This is a very difficult thing, as the negatives go OUT OK, BUT STICK VERY CLOSE BY. Ready at a moment's notice to again enter and 'do.' VIGILANCE must be CONSTANT!

If you catch yourself in UnGodly 'ways,' that means they (negative) are back. They are a real 'pain in the rear.'

Needed though, to give you WILL. Aho?

Now, the War(s) YOU are probably referring to, is the Physical Wars of mankind.

To me, absolutely ASININE!

Mankind in general have strayed so Far off The Creator's Course, they have become self-orientated. That means: *ME! ME! ME!* and *US! US! US!*

No REAL Agape LOVE.

They have forgotten what they were born with.

My 'way' is harsh. Though I pray for ALL, I see no real change of the masses.

My thoughts thus are this: STAY IN YOUR OWN LAND/CULTURE (there in). ALL!

Visiting by legal means, is quite alright.

STAY AND FIGHT EACH OTHER…of your OWN!

Leave the others out of it. Your personal 'problems.'

Do NOT enter into another's conflict. Let THEM Settle IT! EACH!

Eventually each culture WILL settle down. MANY will die. Innocents.

But what is death? Aho?

Then perhaps peace will reign. Should anyway.

Not enough left to fight each other.

SENSE will enter…finally.

No one should be the 'guardian' of another. The 'World's Peace Force.' This puts those as the 'judge.' The *ME/US* 'Masters!'

Let the CREATOR be MASTER!

LET EACH COUNTRY RULE THEIR OWN!

STAY OUT!

It only creates more dissention, Worldwide.

Brother against Brother. Race against race. Cultural ways against cultural ways. HATE!

UNITED NATIONS? CONTROLLERS!

GOVERNMENTS? CONTROLLERS!

RELIGIONS' LEADERS? CONTROLLERS!

STAY HOME AND FIND YOUR OWN BALANCE!

That is my opinion, anyway on as YOU see *war*."

Alternative Ways

Once again, grandfather was asked his thoughts on Alternative Ways, Electricity, etc.

"Gee, where have YOU been? I've told on this many times. I THINK IT'S GREAT. Wind, Solar and Water energy versus 'Store Bought.'

I see a problem though: NOT PRIMITIVE ENOUGH!

Sellers making good money off many who can barely afford these things. Prices still generally so high most can't touch these things. Many going into deep debt to 'save.'

WE ARE SUPPOSED TO BE GETTING OUT OF DEBT, not IN! That's what 'His' Word says.

Is it possible? Yes, but certainly not without its problems!

People are STILL thinking 'Electricity.' MODERN MANS' BIGGEST 'BUG-A-BOO!'

As things are still running…all the money spent will be ABSOLUTELY USELESS!

Debts incurred, 'out the window.'

BATTERIES will need REPLACING in time. NOWHERE TO BUY THEM!

Parts break. NOWHERE TO GET REPLACEMENTS!

Gas to run Generators: GONE!

I tell you true, this MODERN *'Alterative Energy ways'* are GOOD, for NOW…but useless soon!

Stop and think: IF my GREAT VISION holds true…and so far it IS…then you'd be far better off WITHOUT these MODERN Alternative things.

They are OK IF YOU REALIZE they are ONLY TEMPORARY 'HELPS.'

Go into them with THAT Mind Frame and your OK. But to think YOU 'have it made' when the Bison Poop 'hits the fan'…well, you're sure going to be SURPRISED!

To me, those doing these things, IN THE WRONG 'HOPE'…are as a man hanging by one hand at the end of a long rope! Eventually he will tire and fall into the chasm below him.

GO and 'Do' in the RIGHT Knowledge that even THIS is a TEMPORARY 'FIX'...while PREPARING for the day THOSE Things Will NOT work, and you'll be OK.

I too use the modern way of the 'whites.' HOWEVER, I HAVE BACKUP for when these ways 'go down the tube.'

We have a Cistern to catch rainwater and store...AND a Water Pump of Electricity to pump this water into the house. We ALSO have a SIPHON HOSE to use with BUCKETS to do the same 'getting.' As long as water is there, we can get it to go inside, electric or not.

I have a portable Gasoline Pump to collect from creeks etc., AND A SHOULDER YOKE to CARRY Direct from the water, if need be, Both!

Our new abode has Generator and Batteries for electricity...BUT MANY CANDLES and REFLECTORS when THAT 'stops.' Also, we know how to burn Oils and Fats as light and cooking when the CANDLES GIVE OUT!

We Solar Heat our water for bathing, etc., and in winter, wood heat the water.

Do you see? WE ARE IN 'ALTERNATIVE' that is of the 'Whites' AND in the more NATURE...and a far CHEAPER...'way.'

WE can rise and sleep as the Chickens...AND ARE PREPARED TO DO SO.

We are not stuck with High Priced 'You SAVE' things, that modern man seems to THINK they need.

We TOO are 'on the end of the rope'...yet WE have a PARACHUTE!

Won't hurt US to let go!

THINK BEYOND THE MODERN ALTERATIVE! Use it while you can...and can afford, but DON'T STOP THERE! 'DOUBLE UP!' Have BOTH at hand.

THINK AHEAD! WAY ahead!

Those that do will be the wisest.

Why pay someone else to sell you High Priced items that get you in debt AND WILL FAIL in time? Again, in a SHORT Time from now.

Preparing the way we are puts US ahead of those preparing as a 'white man.' Aho."

Preparing To "Find"

Grandfather received a call from a Canadian Cree. The caller coming as the 'middle man.' This between distant Cree tribes Chief and Counsel.

"Grandfather, I'm asked if you'd be willing to come to this reservation to help them find a missing man. Also to ask your fee."

Grandfather thought, prayed and answered, "Yes, I will come, but need the money to get there and back. If they can provide that, yes.

I will drive. Thus gas and a stipend to eat on. I can sleep in my truck and tent. This will be all that's needed to do so. As for 'pay,' that is between them and the Creator.

I ask that cigarettes be given on arrival. This was the way of Tradition from our past. I don't smoke a pipe except in ceremony…therefore cigarettes work well for me. Tobacco is the proper way to give any in 'Medicine.' ALWAYS! Aho?"

And it was so. Agreed on by all.

"I cannot come GUARANTEEING. I can only do what is allowed. They need to know this."

(That too agreed on.)

Grandfather Began prayers…

"Do a five day FAST," was told and so it will be. HO.

This is how he 'works.' First seeking 'Should I?' Then checking the answer three times. Then obeying.

"As long as it's morally correct and causes no one harm, it is usually alright. USUALLY. Not ALWAYS! So I check three times."

This story has similar that these writings contain. The reason for it is to get the IMPORTANCE of SEEK/ASK/FIND, then OBEY to a 'T'…into the readers mind.

Again, IF one GOES BY 'HIS' WORD…DOES as it instructs: the *HOW TO's* ARE THERE…and SUCCESS is inevitable!

Remember TOO the importance of NEVER TAKING CREDIT!

ALL you are is a WILLING ‘vessel.’

‘HE’ does the ‘Doing.’

‘Duplication’ helps the Reader…YOU…to get the IMPORTANCE of what is being shared.

G(o)OD ‘luck’ to you.

HO!

Nosey People

"I've seen you in different garb. Coats mostly. Why do you have so MANY?"

"WHY on Earth would you be interested in my coats?" he asked.

"Well, grandfather, you dress differently. It interests me. Would you tell ME the meaning of your dress?"

"SHHHEEEESSH …Well alright, I guess.

Hum, I have several. One fully beaded. A Cree Coat. Brain tanned, Smoke cured. This is my 'Fancy Coat.' I wear it for very special things only. Important Counsels, etc. It's a beauty. Smells of wood smoke, and VERY pricy. I couldn't afford such. All HAND done in the Old Way. This was given as 'pay' for a healing.

I have another…full fur, Elk hide. Un-beaded but full fur color and small furs as trimming here and there. It is quite old. It's also rather famous. This too was a gift. Just a GIFT. Nothing was done for it! It is VERY long, VERY heavy…and as said, old. SHEDS! But I LOVE IT!

It's a 'utility' coat. Made for heavy winter snows and campfires. It's so THICK it's HEAVY! 'STIFF.' An excellent coat to keep warm in almost any winter one would be in.

This coat was used in a number of movies. The owner rents 'frontier clothing' to MGM, etc. It was rented for me to wear on my GREAT VISION DVD. On taking it back in, I was wearing it. WISHING IT WAS MINE! The owner saw me enter…knew of me and said, "Grandfather, THAT Coat is <u>YOU</u>!" and there and then GAVE it to me! I WAS SHOCKED! Still am. Praise 'Him!'

HO.

I love to use it on quests and winter outings.

I have my regalia coat as well. Wore it twice to Pow Wows, but I don't dance. I wear this in private 'Pow Wows' between myself and Creator. All alone. 'Him,' my drum, and I there, off in the wilderness. I dance. To 'HIM!'

I'm just too 'White Skinned' to dance in a regular POW Wow. No, I keep mine private. Ho.

This coat is of The Greenland Eskimo type. I went to their design and my wife made it for me.

I've had Full Bloods ask me to wear this to their Pow Wows (dance or not). Have. As I watch the full bloods dance in all their finery, and envy…THEY in turn come to ask and look at mine… *'So UNUSUAL.'* THEY envy MINE!

I wore this when running my Sled Dogs as well. A real 'Show Stopper!' Ho!

I have an ANORAK…a 'Pull Over' type. Added a Goose Down hood to it and had a White Arctic Fox put on the hood's front rim. Had it in red fox, but that got too old, so switched. Prefer the red. Will go back to that when I can find the right fur.

The hood can be snapped on and off, as needed.

This is a good Early Spring/Late Fall coat. A lightweight wind/snow and rain breaker. If in REAL cold, Layering is needed or it's too cold.

Hum, let's see…OH, I have two PONCHOS. Made of Alpaca wool…From Ecuador. One WHITE, for ceremony use, one black, for 'every day use.' I ENJOY THESE! I can wear them at anytime. Any season. Cold? Wrap and 'belt' it. Hot? Take off or let the design run 'free.' If a Poncho has a 'fault,' it's within a car. Gotta lift your rear and pull it up in back or you won't get the seat belt on easily.

I have a number of White Man Jackets. Don't care for them, except a simple Levis Jacket. 'Casual.' Don't have one anymore though.

I'm given coats and jackets…wear them a few times, then give them away to native Americans I know who are in need. Better than the thin cheapest they have. Far warmer. Ho.

Got a Suit Coat and Suit Overcoat. Only worn that suit once so far. Guess some ding-a-ling will bury me in this outfit. Won't be MY choice though. UGH!

Maybe there's one or two I'm missing. So MANY. But that's what I've got…OH! AND AN AUSSY Coat! Great on horses or motorcycles! Don't ride either now though. Would be a good Anti-Mosquito coat up north, except would be too hot. I'll probably give this away too.

Think that's about it, I guess. DON'T ASK ME ABOUT MY MOCCASINS and Footwear! Reason for all of THEM too.

If I had my way, I'd be wearing the Elk Coat and LOIN CLOTH. Use my fur Leggings with this in winter. LOVE THE LOIN BREECH-CLOTH!! Probably get arrested…

Therefore, that's that. Tell me brother, being you're nosing around about MY clothing, tell me: what Kinda Skivvies DO YOU WEAR? And is it true you only have 12? So one per month! Sheeeeshh."

Church

Grandfather was asked about 'Church.' Actually more or less TOLD he was 'wrong' in not 'going to Church.' He replied:

"WHO SAYS? WHAT is CHURCH? In WHO'S EYES? YOURS? Or The CREATOR'S?

It appears YOUR idea of 'Church' DIFFERS from 'Dad's!'

Here is a Being who told a King that EARTH IS HIS FOOTSTOOL…and YOU put 'Him' into a BOX!

ALL NATURE IS 'HIS' CHURCH!

ALL CREATION is 'His' CHURCH!

The STARS, The GALAXIES, and the FAR BEYOND is 'His' CHURCH!

'He' is in ALL! And YOU put 'Him' Into a BOX!

A MAN/LUCIFER, BOX!

The 'Box' of: *WE are RIGHT, YOU are WRONG!*

YOUR 'WAY' BOX!

There are THOUSANDS of these BOXES…ALL fighting against Each OTHER!

'OURS IS THE RIGHT BOX. YOURS are WRONG!'

GOD HAS NO BOX! 'He' has only FREEDOM!

'Church' means, 'BODY OF BELIEVERS.'

'BELIEF' means: *TRUST IN/STICK TO/RELY ON HIM, The BIG BROTHER CHRIST!*

WHO IS CHRIST???!

THE TEACHER! THE EXAMPLE! FREEDOM INCARNATE! PURE and PurITY!

THE ONE WHO TAUGHT AND TEACHES WHAT YOU ARE CAPABLE OF! IF you TRULY FOLLOW!

MANS' (Lucifer's really) 'Church' is NOT Freedom. It's CONTROLLING! CAPTURING! DICTATING!

'Follow ME…MAN/LUCIFER.'

YOU PROVE THIS by your VERY ACTIONS! Or it might be better said, *'By your INACTIONS!'*

'I'M Wrong?'

READ THE WORD OF GOD. READ THE DOINGS OF THE EXAMPLE! THEN tell me *'I Am WRONG!'*

WHERE IS YOUR FRUIT, Oh Tree?

The telling of the FRUITLESS TREE that The Christ talked to, had ALL THE LEAFS, ALL THE BARK, and ALL THE BEAUTY, of ANY tree…yet BORE NO FRUIT!

It was MADE to BEAR FRUIT! It stood STAGNATE.

There are TRILLIONS of Trees. ALL are TREES.

A tree is a tree!

YOU were MEANT to be a FRUIT TREE! WHERE IS YOUR FRUIT!

And YOU want ME to go to YOUR NURSERY?

GOD gives ME the Sun, The Moon, The Seasons. WITHOUT THE BOX YOU ARE IN and insist I must be IN! HAND fed by MAN! WHY? WHY am I 'WRONG' standing out here IN NATURE…GOD FED! TRUSTING THAT 'HE' will water me and nurture me AS I NEED. I STAND TRUSTING! YOU 'stand' SHAKING!

'WILL I GET THE FOOD NEEDED BY MY LEADER?'

'WILL I BE GOOD ENOUGH to be NOTICED?'

'If I JUST GO BY THE RULES of my MAN CARETAKER, I SHOULD be OK.'

YOUR LEADER CONTROLS YOU!

Your Leader's BOSS controls your LEADER!

Together they are CULTIVATING FRUITLESS FRUIT TREES!

So I'm Gnarled. Wind Wiped. Haggard looking. DIFFERENT! And STRONG!

But I GIVE FRUIT! I Stand at the Cross Roads FEEDING THE PASSERBY'S!

YOU sit IN A BOX! Whiffing your fragrance of TREE out the boxes' window!

'COME, Join ME! I'm a TREE!'

'Come, look at my BEAUTY. Look at my PERFECTION! JOIN MY FOREST ! I'm a TREE!'

Well it is true…you ARE a tree…a FRUITLESS Fruit Tree! WORTHLESS OF YOUR CALLING!!!!

No Thanks, I'd rather stand outside in the weather. GROWING BY THE GREAT GARDNER'S CARE AND WISDOM! FACING the ELEMENTS! GROWING STRONG in those Elements. AND BEARING FRUIT!

I don't want to be BOXED. Aho?"

"WELL! YOU WILL Be awful LONELY out there *all alone*," the man said, "and you WILL be ALONE!"

"WHAT? ALONE? That is a CROCK! There are HUNDREDS like me all OVER this Earth."

"Oh? WHERE? The Bible says 'GATHER TOGETHER.' WHERE is YOUR GROUP Gathering?"

"Mine? ROOTED IN THE EARTH. We may be far apart but OUR ROOTS REACH FAR! 'DAD' CONNECTS our Roots. WE PLAY 'FOOTSY' WITH EACH OTHER! WE are NOT 'ALONE.' The BIRDS fly our seeds, one to another. UNITING US. WHERE are YOUR BIRDS? Your BOX excludes them, the NATURAL!
WE CONVERSE with MINDHEART thought. YOU just sit and LISTEN! WE are in NATURE. NATURAL. FREE! You sit in a stagnant environment. WE raise OUR LIMBS to the ALL of Creation. T H E CREATOR! You raise YOURS to the CEILING! But your CAPTURED HEARTS HOPE FOR FREEDOM, 'one day.' Just as a ZOO Animal ALSO pines. Trapped behind BARS!
YOU 'hope.' WE <u>KNOW</u>!

To you I say:

OPEN YOUR WINDOWS!

TAKE OFF THE SCREENS.

LET THE BIRDS IN!

For you to want ME in YOUR box…well,

'GET THEE BEHIND ME, SATAN!'

Ho."

Who Is God? Who Am I?

“Grandfather, I have sat at your teachings, read your tellings. You say we are all Daydreams: HIS. You say, *‘all about us is OUR day dreams’… ‘holograms.’* I STILL don’t fully understand. WHO IS GOD? WHO AM I?”

“OK, get a piece of clear typing paper. All white, all blank.”

(She did.)

“Now look at that paper. ‘Pretend’ THAT is GOD. Now, imagine a dime size circle within that ALL GOD. Got it?”

“Yes.”

“That imagined little circle is you. Do you see You in ‘reality’ there?”

“In reality? No, all I see is a blank piece of paper…*God.*”

“Now you’ve ‘Got It!’ You can’t separate the two. BOTH are GOD in that sense. Except the ‘You’ within the whole is much smaller. Yet, at the same time…JUST AS LARGE!”

“Now, go and think on this. DEEPLY. Perhaps you’ll comprehend what I’m saying and trying to get across to ALL the separate ‘I AM(s),’ to help you understand.

By the way, as the ONLY ‘I Am’…do you ‘see’ another little circle on that whole page?”

“No.”

“That’s because no other exists. ALL that you see in ‘Reality’ is YOUR ‘IMAGINATION MADE HOLOGRAMS.’ Yours and yours alone. In TRUE (Spirit) REALITY…the ONLY thing that ‘is’…is The Great Void of PURE LOVE JOY we call GOD. NOTHING EXISTS BUT ‘HIM’…and what ‘HE’ Hologram DREAMS into existences. YOU! The YOU ‘I AM.’

I hope this helps…”

The Buddhist

Grandfather had received a call from a young man he had helped. The call was concerning a friend of his. One in great physical Pain. He asked if he could give her his phone number. Grandfather agreed.

The next night she did.

She told him of 14 years, being in very bad shoulder and arm pain, as well as legs, etc.

She had gone to a Russian Healer who had told her, "God is trying to open your eyes."

That was ALL. She left, not understanding Its meaning.

"Do YOU know, Grandfather?"

"Yes, she was correct. Now you are about to find out Its meaning.

The Pain is brought on by The Creator to WARN YOU ARE NOT 'RIGHT' IN His SIGHT. These are GIFT Warnings! He is trying to GET YOUR ATTENTION!

In your hurt, you have started your search for relief. It has also started your HUNGER to know WHY you hurt.

You went to a Healer. She gave you TRUTH but you didn't understand it. You told your friend. He, in turn, came to me. Now from him to me.

I AM YOUR 'UPSTAIRS' KNOWLEDGE 'Librarian.' You will now learn you have HAD ALL THE NEEDED KNOWLEDGE (to heal) DEEP WITHIN YOUR MIND all the time. ALL you were born with. LONG FORGOTTEN. The door locked by being born into 'sin' and ACCEPTING THAT over the PURE WAY Knowledge you, and EACH, are born with. You've TRADED Sin OVER GOD'S WAY. Now is the time you are to once again OPEN THAT CLOSED DOOR you have.

I AM THE KEY HOLDER. The CARETAKER of the LIBRARY. Your 'door' is about to be opened. Are you a God Believer?"

"Yes. I am a Buddhist."

"It is alright to be Buddhist. There is no wrong in it, BUT this: You are not meant to WORSHIP your Ancestors, you are meant to HONOR THEM. Your WORSHIP should be to HE who

BROUGHT THEM, to BRING YOU! HE MADE ALL. Just to get YOU! You are SPECIAL IN HIS EYES. As too were they.

To read the Scriptures does not make you a Non-Buddhist, but a BETTER Buddhist."

He then went on explaining the 'I AM' and the works of her Nagual. That SHE was THE ONLY ONE. That ALL about her was but a mere dream. That her Nagual was doing Its job of trying to notify her she was 'off track.' She seemed to understand.

He then told her how to get cleansed. Told her of the 'Knee Prayer'/'Seeking Prayer'/'RETURNING Prayer'.

For it was that, that would bring her healing.

The 'WAY' was accepted, and the conversation HEALING WAY was over.

The next night she called again. She had followed the tellings. Had spent 'knee time' and said, "But I received NOTHING! Then, I went to bed. I had a STRANGE DREAM."

HER Dream: "I was walking in a long line of people who were going forth to talk with God. A man came to my side and began to berate me. Yelling at me. Telling me I was 'NO GOOD', 'WORTHLESS', That I had 'NO REASON' TO BE IN THIS LINE…or RIGHT! I don't know what it means?"

Grandfather laughed. "That 'MAN' was YOU, honey. YOUR THOUGHTS of YOURSELF!
You were receiving an answer to your Knee Prayer!
You evidently have a very low Esteem of yourself…"

"OH! IT'S TRUE! It's TRUE! I don't think well of myself AT ALL!"

"Well, Lil' One, GOD thinks well of you! That's why He MADE YOU. He WANTED YOU! To Him, YOU ARE HIS LITTLE 'PRINCESS'!

YOU are telling HIM 'He' made a mistake. 'Was Nuts' THAT HE IS STUPID AND CRAZY!

I think you owe HIM an APOLOGY!

God NEVER makes mistakes. EVER!

You need to realize this. Then get RIGHT. APOLOGIZE! Then CRAWL UP ON HIS LAP AND HUG HIM! Aho?"

She understood and was quite contrite.

She then told grandfather that The WHOLE DAY was spent WITHOUT PAIN!

He suggested an EARTH HEALING 'fix' that would help.

"Go to the grass. LAY ON IT. On your Back. Stretch out your arms UPWARD and PRAISE HIM. Then THANK MOTHER EARTH for HER Energy Healings.
We are made of Earth. We are part of her. She is part of us. You hurt, she hurts!
Between the two, you will notice a GREAT inner Physical Change. A HEALING."

He told, "Plants do more than being Plants. MANY ARE HEALERS! I know of trees that heal women's 'problems.' A patient simply hugs and Loves the tree and wraps her legs around them (the tree) and is INSTANTLY HEALED by that LOVE HEALER BEING.
I have seen Mother Earth take people lying on her 'hair' (grass) and be healed of chronic Back Pain. EVEN DEPRESSION!

I have seen MANY things that you would consider 'strange.'
'Strange' to YOU, but not to US (of 'Medicine'). You have much to learn. Ho.

Remember, THE CREATOR LOVES YOU! Ho"

Later that night, Grandfather had a dream of this woman. In time, this will be shared with her.

This is that dream:

She was herding many sheep. EACH SHEEP WAS A 'Sin' (a Disobedience to God). She was herding them 'Home' (to God).

THE BARRATER WAS THERE at her side. 'Doing his thing.' She ignored him and defiantly kept the herd going toward the fence (of safety). She ENTERED WITH THEM through the gate. Shutting BUT NOT LOCKING the gate. Grandfather called her back to the fence.

"LOCK IT!" he said. SHE OPENED THE GATE and CAME OUT to LOCK IT!

"NO! NO!" He shouted, "GO INSIDE AND LOCK IT!"

She did, JUST AS THE BARRATER CAME RUNNING UP, screaming his Lies!

It no longer affected her. SHE WAS SAFE INSIDE and HE WAS PERMANENTLY LOCKED OUT!"

Aho?

I Don't Know What A "Demon" Is

This was said to grandfather by one wanting to GROW. The person knew there WAS such…but really had no idea WHAT they were. 'Not REALLY.'

"Hum. Well first off, they are REAL. Each is a LIVING entity. BREATHING…but SOULLESS.
They take on many forms. They are capable of SHAPE SHIFTING. At least the 'main' ones.

Each is created by Lucifer.

When The Creator taught Lucifer, there was ONLY ONE THING 'HE' DID NOT TEACH: How to make SOULS!

Thus, no demon has one.

This NONE Knowledge made/makes Lucifer *ticked*."

"If I can't MAKE THEM, I'll CAPTURE THEM! ROB God of them. AS MANY AS I CAN! He'll PAY for this oversight!"

"There is no room for TWO GODS! For a house divided against itself can NOT stand. Aho?

Anyway…Lucifer has the ability to create Beings. Those he makes we call DEMONS.

Each is 'raised' to serve their master. They are not told of TWO to choose from.
Only that ONE…'Theirs' has a competing ENEMY. One who WANTS to be 'The ONE.' The REAL GOD!

So they 'help him' to fight this 'enemy.' Aho?

Lucifer, their Creator, MUST be 'THE ONE' for *'Didn't he MAKE me?'*

They are good at their jobs. Real WARRIORS!

As in any army, there are STRONG, FEARLESS Warriors and weaker ones.

Yet ALL are quite easily defeated BY A SOUL BEARER WHO KNOWS HIS/HER GODLY RIGHTS and USES THOSE RIGHTS CORRECTLY!

The Creator, in 'His' Written Word, The Bible, says: 'Ye are as gODS.' It also says 'YE HAVE AUTHORITY over ALL ANGELS' and too: 'In HIM (the Christ) ALL THINGS ARE POSSIBLE to those who FOLLOW ME (the EXAMPLE).'

Didn't HE cast out demons?

Not only 'YES' but these tellings tell YOU these beings ARE VERY REAL!

YOU HAVE AUTHORITY OVER ALL ANGELS.

Lucifer is just that…an ANGEL!

Thus YOU, IF YOU REALLY HAVE TRUST IN 'HIS' WORD…can 'flip a demon away' as you'd flip an ash off a cigarette.

ORDER LUCIFER to RELEASE hIS WORKERS OUT/AWAY!

They MUST leave because their 'God' MUST Obey! IF you TRULY 'believe.'

It's as simple as that!

Did CHRIST 'Order?' YES! And He WAS Filled WITH GOD. 'God on Earth.' Just as YOU are 'God on Earth' by ADOPTION and ACCEPTING. FULLY accepting. Aho?

Does this 'Make US God?' NO! I said, 'God IN us.' IN!

Just be aware, FULLY, of what your commitment to LOVING GOD is. Aho?

Demons are real WORKING beings. Simply out doing their jobs. In addition, YOU ARE THEIR BOSS! Simply by being Lucifer's 'BOSS!'

Don't get 'heady' over this though. That's EGO! SELF! A TRAP! Those who DO get into this headiness, HAVE BECOME AN UNGODLY PERSON. Nothing more than a SORCERER.

What are Demons? TRICKSTERS, LIARS, DECEIVERS, CONTROLLERS and, at times, POSSESSORS. Each easily handled by someone in Right Standing. Aho?"

False Reports

Grandfather received a phone call on July 9, 2007. Seems his name had come up the night before on a famous night radio show. A Caller called in to say that he was in touch with GRANDFATHER'S GUIDE!

Folks, GRANDFATHER HAS ABSOLUTELY <u>NO</u> 'GUIDE(S)!'

Not ONE!

This is New Age.

This is DECEPTION!

This is NOT of GOD!

CAN THIS BE MADE ANY CLEARER?!!

"What part of 'NO'/'NONE' don't you understand?" grandfather said.

"Never HAD them, never WANT ONE! My guideline is 'HIS' WORD.

My TEACHER is THE EXAMPLE called JESUS .

ANY into this 'guide' stuff are OUT OF STEP WITH THE CREATOR. I PRAY for them…EVERYDAY. For THIS IS THE TIME OF TRICKERY!
And MANY ARE being TRICKED! MANY!

If you hear of one telling as that caller, PRAY FOR HIM/HER.

If YOU are into this…PRAY to get AWAY FROM IT!"

HO!

"Indiana Jones"

This was a comment made regarding a recent trip to Canada grandfather and his grandson made. "Your life reads like an Indiana Jones story."

Grandfather thought on this, then responded:

"Guess you're right. Sorta does. Sure, an interesting life, I've got to admit. Sad thing is, tens of tens of tens of thousands, could have the same life. At least in a big way. Man is so stuck in their age old beliefs and peers' teachings that they refuse to go beyond these. What a shame. Instead, they are hung up on technology. Not Godnology.

Yes, I and others as me DO lead an 'Indiana Jones' life. Adventures most will never know or see. To be honest with you, most couldn't handle it. Just too 'different.' Therefore, they'll never know the freedom in it…being 'different.'

The Big Brother knew AND showed. Tried to help the world know too and Killed for it.

People are so strange…

I Love my life and my calling. Been different. FULL of adventures!

Without full commitment to wanting to KNOW THE FATHER…they will never experience the Freedom out there for them. Too bad and so Sad. Yes, what a shame."

Ho.

Why Don't You Give More "How To's?"

Grandfather was asked this.

"As it stands, you aren't ready for more. A baby must be weaned from Its mother's teat before it can be given baby food. That, before solids.

I have fed what you are capable of. Stronger foods when you could handle them. You'd choke otherwise.

Many things I've told, you have gagged on. Takes time.

It is YOUR Growth that makes what food you are capable of safely eating. I will wisely Not 'force feed' you. No matter how HARD you cry!

If I gave more, AHEAD OF TIME, you'd surly die. Unable to chew. Unable to swallow because you don't chew. Yes, you'd choke and die.

I have told of things of 'solid food' and you hunger. PREMATURELY. You are barely off the teat and call for steak. This is immaturity. No, you are not ready for the REAL meat of 'doing.'

Take what I've presented. Chew on what little 'solids' I've given, THEN we'll see about meats that are more serious. If you don't, then you're not of my 'blood.'

ONE BITE AT A TIME!

Or find yourself another 'Nanny.' One NOT as caring.

Do you understand?"

"Grandfather, What Is Your Greatest Desire?"

This plus, "Peace on Earth?" was asked. Grandfather didn't hesitate.

"To FULLY Emulate our Big Brother, Christ.

In this, YOU would be AS CLOSE TO THE FATHER and HOLY SPIRIT as HE was.

I LOVE the Creator SO MUCH I want nothing less. This to Honor 'Him,' The Great '3 in 1.'

I do not WANT to be 'Christ,' I simply want to be AS He. Simply allow ALL my WILL to AIM AT PLEASING The Great Creator.

Our Big Brother came to example. I have read AND SEEN His Way. THEY WORK!

We twelve (Inner Heyókȟa') all want the same. We 12 all want to SHOW the World...AND BEYOND, that by FOLLOWING, ALL ARE CAPABLE of a MIRACLES and LOVING LIFE!

'Peace on Earth,' starts with PEACE in YOU!

I want that FULL PEACE in ME! I <u>STRIVE</u> for THAT!

How I WISH all who CLAIM 'Agape Love,' HAD AGAPE LOVE!

How I WISH ALL wanted to PLEASE GODCREATOR at LEAST as much as I!

I WISH ALL 'FOLLOWERS/BELIEVERS' LOVED as much as I do, NOW! REALLY LOVED OUR CREATOR...Enough to BE AS HUNGRY AS I AM!

I have much work to do within me. I am not, nor EVER WILL BE, The BIG BROTHER, But I WANT HIM TO KNOW I WANT HIS WAY. FULL LOVE!

THAT is my desire. I do not DOUBT, With 'HUNGER DETERMINATION,' this IS possible. I GET CLOSER AND CLOSER EVERYDAY!

How I Wish ALL felt 'His' Presence. 'His' BEING. 'His' REALNESS! THAT is my 'Greatest desire.' Others and 'Self' IN FULL TOUCH WITH 'HIM.'

Aho?

HO!"

The Old Cree Graveyard

Grandfather was taken by a Cree to his son's recent burial site. Grandfather knew this young man. As so often the case on reservations, liquor and drugs bring death to many Native Americans. This was the case here.

Standing with the silent father, he began to 'see.' Many where there. Ancestors who had not gone on. Staying in their purgatory. Most of the days when 'Christianity' was still in the introduction days. Old and very young were there, gathered around the new gravesite.

After the father finished his prayers, grandfather told what he was seeing.

"Somewhere between 82 to maybe 85 are here with us. All trapped in the 'new religions' teaching. They believed in their cultures' 'way' of the Happy Hunting Grounds and each told this was 'UnGodly' by the Black Robes (Catholic Priests) and others. As always, these 'Christians' wanted to convert the Natives to the 'Right Way.' THEIR WAY. Here now stand many who were introduced to FEAR. The *'go OUR WAY or GO TO HELL.'* A 'hell' they knew nothing of until these deceivers introduced this to The People. Now they stay here…in fear. Would it be alright with you for me to tell them the Truth of the afterlife and possibly get them free?"

The father quickly agreed, for this old graveyard held 'vibes' that scared all the living.

Grandfather retrieved his drum and rattle from his truck. Then he began to sing, etc. 'to entertain them.'

This was happily received by the gathered ones. They were of THEIR life days. It had been a long time without. Ho.

Once all were again happy, grandfather began telling of their being deceived by the well meaning religious ones that had caused fear in their minds/hearts. Told them there truly WAS a 'Happy Hunting Ground'…AND a Heaven FOR the 'Whites.' Each according to THEIR Beliefs. They listened intently.

AND WERE FREED.

Now this graveyard holds NO 'bad vibes.' THE LIVING GO IN TO REMEMBER…without Stress.

Ho.

"How Can We Improve?"

This is another question asked grandfather.

"I have pondered on this many times over the years. Beyond the need to connect to our Great Maker, I have found mankind's biggest problem lays in the Good Books Words: "They hear but are deaf. See but are blind."

Mankind seems bent on not choosing to REALLY pay attention to each other. Another's viewpoint. They instead press forward with their Own "conclusions." Not really paying attention to the view of others. SELF over COMPATIBILITY.

This leads to quarrels within households, cities, and whole countries. It brings divorces to wars. Ill feelings bring inner conflict. This in turn, brings on illnesses. Illnesses bring on death. Either self willed or in massive wars. Individuals to MILLIONS. All because we "see" and "hear" without seeing and hearing.

I, myself, have been at fault in this. It is this that made me ponder. I still do. But have greatly improved over the years.

I do not like quarrels and bad feelings between myself and others. This goes against the One Law of God: LOVE.

I am uncomfortable when in this "out of attunement with Him." EVERY time.

No, I do not like it. Thus, I go off to ponder. More often than not, a quarrel is caused by my OWN not "hearing/seeing."

To cease my inner tension (irritation), I return to the one(s) I have battled, explain, and APOLOGIZE. I seek their forgiveness. This in turn gives THEM Insight. Thus, ALL are helped to grow stronger in wisdom and Spirit. Aho?

Too often mankind "jumps to conclusions." Giving no thought to what another's Reason "is." I have been accused falsely by others who have not pondered or asked. No, they just attract. Using their "False Eyes" or "Hearing." Nary a thought to the "Why" of what I am doing or saying. Misjudging.

As told often, every nation has their own culture ways. OURS in not THEIRS and THEIRS is not OURS. Why force a "forging way" onto others? Each Culture is just trying to reach The Creator in THEIR "way." SEE that! Calm Down. LOVE…and UNDERSTAND others' views. ACCEPT those views. RESPECT Our Brethren. For they Too try to reach God. Do so and Peace will reign. SHOW, don't FORCE. Aho.

And I Thought I'd Heard It All

Another call to check on animals. Two horses and a dog.

"My dog got sick yesterday…can you tell me why?"

Grandfather agreed. Asking the (not well) young dog, "what happened?"

He received this reply: "I was HOT, and that made me feel really bad."

HEAT STROKE!

Telling this to the owner, she then told grandfather, "I had her with me in the car all day yesterday."

She had 'run in' here and there…windows cracked open. Not enough, and too long per stop.

"I'll know better next time…now for my horses. Both were foaming at the mouth yesterday, and one hasn't been eating well lately."

Grandfather entered their small corral. Both horses knew him. One immediately said, "WHAT do YOU want?" She was NOT in her usual good mood! Quite irritable.

"I've come to see why you aren't well, honey. Can you tell me?"

She thought it over.

"My back teeth hurt AND MY JAW. It hurts to eat."

"Anywhere else?"

"Yes, my whole body aches…mostly though my mouth and back hips. I hurt all over."

She was an old one, this mare of 26 years. Old. Grandfather checked her out. All four hoofs had 'white stress bands' across them, a swollen knee…and heavy pain in the back legs/hips. Less so on the front. Rheumatism!

Due to her aching mouth, she had a hard time chewing. This stopped her from eating well…AND thus to FOAM at the mouth (lack of cool water in vegetation). She was just 'getting old.' Old at an ACCELERATED Pace!

Now, not wanting a Bit or even to have her rider on her back. Just one big HURT. Age does that. Often catches up with you 'suddenly.'

This one, being put out to 'pasture' will perhaps live out three more years. PAINFUL years.

Meanwhile the OTHER horse had been frothing too! Grandfather asked HER if SHE was "OK."

"I'm fine."

Then why were YOU frothing!"

"I felt her pain and sympathized is all. 'Sharing.' I'm fine."

This caused grandfather to laugh aloud. He knew of Men 'feeling' labor pains of their pregnant WIVES…but this is/was the FIRST TIME he'd had it 'be' with an ANIMAL!

He explained all to the owner. "WHAT! Sympathy Pains with a HORSE?! I've never HEARD of such a thing."

"Nor have I, my sister, it just goes to show how HUMAN 'others' can be."

And it is so.

Ho.

Ah, Come On!

Some think grandfathers 'nuts,' especially on the subjects of aliens. There's a lot of disbelief there. The *"WE are the ONLY Ones"* belief stigmatism. Basically put out by preachers, etc.

Grandfather, being truthful, doesn't care. He's had his personal involvements with these Soul 'Star Brothers' and KNOWS.

"Did I ask you to "Believe? No. I just tell it is up to YOU to check and decide for yourself. I just give you things to consider…and CHECK ON.

YOU hold that these either don't exist, or are all DEMONS.

I tell you true, Many DO 'take on' forms that appear as these Aliens. DEMONS, in reality. Then too, many are NOT Demons, but true Aliens. Some LOOK Demonic!

But this is all up to You to check on!

I KNOW. I HAVE checked! But YOU stay in your 'hiding' way of belief. In this case: Unbelief.

It doesn't matter to me one bit. I just…Tell.

For your information, there are many 'breeds' walking our planet. AND 'Deceiving' DEMONS! Far more then you can imagine. There are also a few aliens IN THEIR FORM, in Hidden Places, that are on our planet. ABOVE Ground and UNDER, AND sea.

Still, on a weekly basis, IF not on a DAILY basis, you 'rub shoulders' with such 'breeds.'

Often they are the 'Trouble Makers' and 'Bullies' you meet. 'Controllers' mostly. People (as YOU know them) that have an OBSESSION to be 'Known.'

In truth, this is not always THE way that you can "check"…some humans are Demonically Possessed. Some…well, YOU find out!

Yet to be so 'TURTLE' is a foolish thing. You don't WANT to learn. You are AFRAID to find out your 'little Cocoon' has existence outside your protective cocoon 'shield.'

This doesn't bother me at all. It is YOUR Path.

In time, in DEATH, you WILL find I've spoken true.

Hear me: It is not my 'job' to convince you or 'pound you over your head' and 'beat it in' on the REALITY of these others. Mine is but to try to make you AWARE.

I do just THAT. The rest is up to you. Aho?

I tell you true, there is so MUCH you don't know About LIFE! To you, BREATHING is 'LIFE.' You ignore the 'I AM.' The 'WORKING THE DREAM' you are so capable OF!

To me, this is a sad shame on your part.

You come to me with questions, then reject the answers. Wasting MY time AND YOURS! I'd rather you wouldn't come at all.
There are THOUSANDS JUST LIKE YOU! Stay with THEM…and don't waste my time. You'd be doing us BOTH a favor, believe me!

DO 'Aliens' exist?

YES!

WILL you believe? THAT IS FOR YOU TO FIND OUT!

Are they 'Harmful?' ALMOST ALL ARE, to some extent.

Am I in DANGER? KNOWLEDGE FREES!

Will you 'go to Hell' by 'trying to find out?' No you will NOT, but you WILL often be 'flirting' with REAL DEMONS and THINKING OTHERWISE. THIS can lead to 'Future problems.'

YOU ARE NOT SAFE WITHOUT BEING IN FULL PROTECTION IN THE CREATOR.

KNOW THAT!"

Words

Grandfather was teaching. In this, he came to the subject of 'Words.'

"Scripture tells of mans' 'tongue.' WORDS spoken. As you study on this and contemplate, you will find out the IMPORTANCE of what you SAY…AND how you SAY IT.

Words can bring Joy…or great Pain. Healing…to Death.

Words are the BASIS of today's Mans' 'existence.' They are the 'tiny rudder' that steers our 'ship's outcome.'

Be it our PERSONAL Life or our MASSES Life. Words affect EVERYTHING!

It is WORDS that are as Stones tossed into a still pond.

They cause RIPPLING Effects.

Thus, we must 'measure' our words CAREFULLY.

They are NOT TO BE TOSSED OUT LIGHTLY! 'Haphazardly.' ESPECIALLY WHEN ON AN ANGERED 'WAY' of 'being!'

Saying *I LOVE YOU* will make Plants thrive. Animals adore you. The sun Smiles.

'I LOVE YOU' is the STRONGEST GOOD WORDING.

'LOVE' is the STRONGEST G(O)OD WORD!

It repairs. It heals. It makes life GOOD!

WORDS are the OUTWARD REFLECTION of the INWARD MAN!

Speak in ANGER…it contorts even the most angelic face.

HATE spoken aloud, CAUSES GREAT RIPPLING WITHIN THE POND!

ANGER causes BIG 'rippling.'

LOVE is as a Butterfly's KISS…a DIMPLE that does not disturb. It EMBRACES!

Choose carefully what and HOW you SAY…BEFORE SAYING! Ho."

Some Things To Think About

Grandfather told:

"ALL ACTIONS HAVE REACTIONS.

ALL WORDS ARE AN ACTION.

ALL 'LOOKS' HAVE AN ACTION.

ALL, RESPOND TO ALL'S ACTIONS.

LIVE IN A GODLY WAY
AND YOUR LIGHT LOVE OF LIFE
WILL BRING JOY TO ALL ABOUT YOU.
WHEN IT DOES NOT,
KNOW THE OPPOSER IS ALWAYS AT WORK.
THIS ONE HATES LOVE.
THIS ONE <u>FEARS</u> LOVE.

IN LOVE,
YOU ARE IN FULL PROTECTION
FROM THE OPPOSING ONE.
YOU WILL <u>AUTOMATICALLY</u> WIN…
EVEN IF IT APPEARS OTHERWISE.

<u>ONLY</u> in LOVE

DO YOU <u>WIN</u>!"

HO.

What Are We...Really?

By now, you know grandfather has 'thought' on much. The above title is but one of many questions asked.

The answer may surprise you:

"As told, we are Energy. Pure THOUGHT. A 'Dream' of our Creator. Yet we are even more, in a sense.

We are The ULTIMATE ROBOT.

Self-Replicating. Self-Repairing. Able to do all we think ('dream') of.

Yet we are also MORE: we are made up of SELF WILL AND SOUL.

Man, even those great cloners of the Stars, is unable to give these two things to their many eons of clone making.

This ONLY our MAKER is able to do.

This makes 'Him' GOD.

We are MINIATURES of Him. 'Little g's.'

Unlike Him, we can go no further. It is a MENTAL AND PHYSICAL IMPOSSIBILITY.

No SOULS can we make.

No SELF WILL can we make.

ALL ELSE WE <u>CAN</u>, though.

When Scripture's tell us *'Even the ANGELS Envy us'*...this is a true and 'heavy' statement.

They KNOW what they are...AND their Limits.

We are AS THEY...PLUS!"

"What are we...REALLY?"

"Reread all the above. THAT'S WHAT WE ARE...REALLY. Ho."

"Love" versus LOVE

"Grandfather, when does one know TRUE Love for another?"

"A good question. As you no doubt know, there IS 'TRUE LOVE.' One for another, as Life Mate. Let's start first with the OTHER 'love.' This, in truth, is a misguided FEELING. One brought about from one's HORMONES gone AMOK. A natural 'maturing' of the human body. Females are the most strongly affected by this in general. The 'trick' is TO KNOW IT and DEPRESS it when it arises. Males AND Females alike.

Females WANT to be 'IN LOVE.'
As they mature into early teens, they begin thinking of 'The Nesting Time' ahead.
Males, on the other hand, are like ALL males of nature. 'STAGS.' They want to HERD. To 'OWN.' They will FIGHT for this!
The 'more the merrier' is their goal.
They are RULED by the MATING INSTINCT. Not 'Love'…though the Human Male may CLAIM this is love, but still, it is based on LUST, not LOVE.

This is not ALWAYS the case…but I'd venture it is in a GOOD 95% of the cases.

RARE ARE THE YOUTHS WHO ARE MATURE ENOUGH TO KNOW THE DIFFERENCES!

Those who DO, REPRESS THEIR SEXUAL TENDENCIES for the other.

Oh, they HAVE them, but REPRESS them.

This is RESPECT.

Both to the opposite AND to the Creator.

Do NOT allow the other to OVERRIDE YOU. IF the other persists, KNOW S/He is NOT 'in LOVE,' but is 'in Love LUST.' DROP THEM!

They will NOT make a good LIFE MATE!

You must RESPECT 'The Temple' that YOU ARE. This is showing MATURITY…AND your LOVE for the Creator.

Can you?"

"Grandfather, When Do You Know 'The Honeymoon Is Over?"

Grandfather smiled. "This will best be explained in a, well...a 'Crude' way. Forgive me. But it is best so you'll keep the knowledge. Aho? "

"Aho."

"Well, when the two begins their 'To Be Life Path' as one…each acts out their most in 'Perfect way.' HIDING the REAL 'YOU.'

Both are 'on their toes' to give out only the BEST they have. Trying to impress the other on how 'Wonderful' they are.

Doors will be held open for the girls, seats held to the woman's backside, then pushed forward. That type of 'showing.'

Yes, both show their 'correctness.'

THEN COMES THE MARRIAGE!

You will KNOW with the FIRST LOUD Dinner BURP or the (forgive me, please), FIRST (in your presences) FART!

THAT'S when you'll KNOW 'The Honeymoon IS OVER!'

NOW the 'Shield of Pretense' is DROPPED.

(Laughter.)

We call this 'The POPEYE effect.' The 'I YAM what I YAM…TAKE ME AS I YAM.'

It is the TRUE mate each has chosen.

You MUST accept if you TRULY LOVE the mate you have LOVE for! Aho?"

Toys

Grandfather's guests were distracted by his grandson, Sky who was 'cruising' through the TV channels, looking for something of interest. A particular channel caught his eye. TOYS! A program showing the new technological things kids have an opportunity to own. All of High Technology. The two showing were enthusiastic over each they presented, "Look at THIS" – "Look at THAT," etc. Not selling, just SHOWING.

Little robots that spun and mucked about. A dinosaur robot that dipped, stood, moved head and tail, etc. The guests were as enthralled as Sky, "WOW! AMAZING what they can DO!"

The program over, all got back to general conversation again, but ON THE TOYS this time.

"It IS amazing what man can make," grandfather said.

All agreed.

"But so sad."

This took their interest, "Sad? In what way, grandfather?"

"Well, the parents buy these 'Wonderful' toys for their kid. The child puts in a battery, reaches over and hits a switch, then stands back and watch the toys PLAY WITH THEMSELVES! In time, this becomes boring. The toy useless. Just another thing to toss and break or forget. High money…little rewards and certainly no LEARNING on the child's part.

That Dinosaur, for instance…all battery run. A few little Radio Control buttons to push from afar. THAT TOY CAN BE DUPLICATED BY THE PARENTS AND/OR THE CHILD. WithOUT Batteries! Go to the library and get a Book on PUPPETS! Spend time with your child BUILDING the puppet dinosaur! QUALITY Time! Then, when completed, that child is CONNECTED with that dinosaur. No 'finger pushing'…STRINGS! HE or SHE MAKES IT WORK. The child BECOMES the dinosaur! And chances are, the PARENT tries it too. Improving Its movements and teaching the child. UNITY! Aho?

A robot that SPINS? Gee, big deal! GET a TOP or a YO-YO. The child can LEARN from THOSE. Can get INTERESTED by it. Can build up SELF-PRIDE over their accomplishment. Self ESTEEM that will carry on into their adulthood!

What has happened to the big cardboard BOX? Where are the kids scooting down the sidewalk on an old board with skates as wheels? Homemade STILTS? Made BY THEM, not some Company who only wants Money.

You, the parent wanting to please their children, see and buy…'BRAIN THIEVES'…'BIG BUTT MAKERS'…and you wonder why your child is so overweight. Why NOT? Eat, press a button, sit back and watch a toy play with Its self.

We are losing contact with our kids. Few girls know how to sew! NONE, it seems, can KNIT a SOCK. Chances are, neither can YOU!

What about showing your child, girl OR boy, how to THREAD a NEEDLE and SEW ON A BUTTON?

You guys here, try a SLING SHOT. They're cheap enough to buy, yet More FUN to BUILD! Then teach the responsibility of it. Aho?

How about games like Checkers? Chess? Marbles? All to make them use their MINDS, not their EYES watching a toy play by itself.

Barbie dolls? GREAT but CAN get pricy. I can recall my sister, into her early teens, still cutting out, changing 'clothes'…outfit after outfit…of PAPER DOLLS! She'd have ME draw cloths and dolls for her when she wanted something different. These simple dolls helped HER choose her Life path…and ME along MINE!

Modern man has allowed their children to fend for themselves. They no longer start teaching TOGETHER/ACTIVE things, TOGETHER. Instead, 'buy a toy and let me just have mySELF time.'

We are LOSING OUR CHILDREN!

YOU are LOSING your child…because you have ignored their earliest LEARNING Years.

And then you say, 'I CAN'T HANDLE (HIM/ Her/She/He) won't LISTEN!'

Why should they? When WE ignored them in their early growth?

Yes, those Modern Toys are 'wonderful' alright. In truth, they ARE! And there's nothing wrong with them, USED IN MODERATION! Mixed in with YOU. YOU and your child. Don't ignore them. Share their wonderful modern toys But share TOO the Toys WITHIN THEIR MIND. Share YOUR 'Old Ways,' and TEACH. Be and GET Together. You'll BOTH Love it. You in THEIR 'New World,' them in YOUR 'Old World.'

Aho?

Well, I have told the sadness I spoke of. Perhaps you can understand now. Aho?"

Beating the Heat/Cold

Grandfather was dressed to the 'hilt.' All in his favorite color…black. It was 93 degrees and no shade, yet he seemed so relaxed and comfortable to the Crees he'd come to talk to.

"How can you STAND this heat Old One? You aren't even raising a SWEAT! WE'RE ROASTING!"

"It may sound strange, but Hot Drinks are best for hot. Cold Drinks are best for cold. All of YOU are drinking Ice Water. I drink heated drinks. It's that simple.

I learned this from an aged White Cowboy who'd always have a hot coffee in hand while out in the sun. Tried it. Worked, so been doing it ever since.

Now it's up to YOU to test…ho."

Why Don't You Go To Church?

This has been asked by many, "Why don't YOU go to THE Church that has been around you all your life?"

Grandfather replied, "You attend a BUILDING…I attend the FOOT STOOL! You go one to perhaps twice a week. I go DAILY.

I WALK IN IT!

My days are devoted to serving our Lord…our God. THE MAKER of ALL THINGS!

The grasses, the deserts, the tropical Islands. The ALL, that is to me, HOLY.

You often destroy this 'building.' Giving little to no thinking to what you are doing to a Precious thing that is of HIS making. Your ways are not my ways. I HOLD ALL THINGS as 'Sacred.' Do YOU?

No. I see 'you' daily, spending little time but for 'self.' And you call your ways THE way?

Yes, you worship the same Maker that I and my kind do…yet not as fully as do WE.

You claim you are 'Free,' yet bow to the teachings of a long line of men. Men who have never known the Freedom that being in the TRUE ' Church' brings about. The Freedom of PURITY.

You hold to 'laws.'

'Laws' set down by Soul TRAPPERS.

These 'Godly' UNGODLY leaders you sit enthralled in, you follow.

I choose not to. Many like me choose not to.

Yet WE ATTEND 'CHURCH.'

Not YOURS, but HIS!

What IS 'church?' What does THAT WORD MEAN? 'A BODY OF BELIEVERS!'

What does 'BELIEVERS' mean? GO CHECK THAT in your Concordance!

There are many of us who are of THAT 'Church.' Of MANY Religions. MANY Denominations…AND some who are of none. Yet they are Faithfull and IN LOVE with the Great Maker.

Many who understand and LOVE His GREAT GIFT…His Son.

We don't need your 'way' for this. Our salvation is as certain as yours, yet with a Freedom you and yours don't fully comprehend.

All too often your Kind think WE are the 'unsaved.' OH, how UNTRUE THAT IS! We are DEFINITELY 'Saved.'

HE DIED FOR ALL.

Those of us that don't 'commit' our 'Church going' ways to YOUR 'Church going Ways' are IN Church. We are IN AND ON 'Church,' and our CHURCH is WITHIN US!

We are FREE!

I do not tell you that you MUST be as we are. This is a matter of Choice. You are comfortable with yours. WE are as comfortable with OURS. LET IT BE AS THAT!

Worship the Great One AS YOU FEEL FIT.

WE DO!

ANY who 'FOLLOW'…Atheists included, are IN RIGHT STANDING BEFORE HIM!

Any who LOVE…REGARDLESS of culture, color, or 'way,' are IN RIGHT STANDING BEFORE HIM!

If you are uncomfortable with hearing this, Amen, So Be It. I will remain on my course before Him. The course of a FREE THINKER. Free from the 'rules and regulations' of man. Pure and Simple.
AS WAS THE CHRIST."

Ho.

What's Happening Lately…Anything?

This an "E" sent to grandfather. He replied:

Yes…or so it seems. This is one that only time will tell. So won't know if it's truly of our Creator until then. Tested though. All tests positive. Two Tests on each. The finale will be test three. Aho?

As you know, I'm fairly close to "Dad"…AND "Big Brother." Well, the last three nights have been "odd." I see Big Brother maybe three times a year. THIS TIME: three NIGHTS IN A ROW!

This has NEVER happened before.

I won't go into details too far, but He's taken me to "The Tree Of Life" on all three nights. We go to a Giant Limb and he shows me things from that vantage point.

EARTH ON FIRE! SMOKE ALL AROUND…and an ENORMOUS WIND!

Last night the Wind One was shown. It was SO STRONG it JUST ABOUT SNAPPED THE WHOLE TREE! Right near Its base! Really LEANED! Almost destroying it!

He told me "HANG ON!" (This referring to HIM, the "Tree Of LIFE"). I was shown the smoke first…and there, above the smoke layer, were what looked like MECHANICAL "Shark Fins" cruising about. Then, THE WIND!

At first, I was TERRIFIED. REALLY SCARED! Then recalled the night before "seeing" "CLING TO THE TREE OF LIFE (Him) AND YOU'LL BE ALRIGHT!" i.e., TRUST HIM and IN HIM. Aho? Well, DID. Clung VERY TIGHT to that "Limb!" It was bouncing and waving about, as was the Whole TREE!

Next thing I knew, my GREAT FEAR went away and I sat UP…LAUGHING!!!

Despite sitting upright, I WAS SAFE FROM FALLING and the TURMOIL of that VICIOUS WIND! Suddenly ALL FEAR WAS GONE and I was HAVING A "BALL!"

Was like riding a Crazy RODEO BULL! But SO "STUCK" to it, it COULDN'T DISLODGE ME! Therefore, I sat upright and ENJOYED THE RIDE! "Went with the Flow" of the Beast! It was a WONDERFUL Ride! EXHILARATING! HO!

All seen in the last three nights seems to follow along with my "Great Vision." Now, only Time will tell. FEAR NOT! CLING TO THE "TREE"…TIGHTLY!

Nature Saves Grandfather

He was on a long hike, eighteen and a half miles UP. He wasn't getting any younger and had wanted to do this trip since he was in his thirties. Now he had the time. His wife drove him to the drop off site, wished him safety and a good trip, then left. He was on his own. Lifting his pack, he gave thanks and started his climb. His bad knee and hip, hurting before going, immediately started their aching. It was not going to be an easy go.

Some two miles later, limping along, he heard a, "HO!"
Turning to see who called, he saw a spirit native coming towards him out of the woods. "May I join you?" he asked.

"You are welcome my uncle," grandfather replied.
Side by side they walked chatting between them. Then, "I see you are limping my friend, are you alright?!"

"No," grandfather answered. "I hurt. My knee aches. Has for a number of years now, but I want to do this trip."

"I can fix it," the spirit replied (he was, in his day, a Medicine Man). At that, he touched the back of GRANDFATHER'S leg, at the knee. There was a 'PING' sound. THE PAIN WAS GONE! (This has NEVER RETURNED to this day.) Grandfather gave GREAT Thanks. They traveled together for a mile or so more, then the spirit left for his lodge campsite. He invited grandfather to come and spend the night. Grandfather declined as he wanted to make the Mountain top before dark. They parted. Grandfather rejoicing.

Now his hip began aching far more. Each step filled with pain.

"HO!" He heard again. This from yet ANOTHER Native American Spirit. A young man. As before, "May I join you?"

"Welcome, cousin."

As before, they walked and chatted. The younger man telling he was an apprentice of 'The Medicine Way.'

"Here with a small group hunting for deer and bear." His wife and three children and an elder using three tipis.

Grandfather heard, "hunting for deer and bear" but not a word on elk. He brought that up to this young man.

"Elk? There are no elk here."

At this, they both realized their Time Shift walk. In THIS (GRANDFATHER'S) time, the woods were filled with elk. But in the Spirits' time frame, the elk were still Plains animals, not yet taking Wood's Refuge. Their walk spanned for HUNDREDS and Hundreds OF YEARS! Only the OLYMPIC ELK were WOODS ELK (all other PUSHED to the woods FROM THE PLAINS caused by the Whiteman's expansion).

The young man was amazed at their 'Time Jump' differences! Grandfather getting a 'kick' over this. BOTH MEN WERE ALIVE, BOTH MEN in THEIR OWN TIME…while being TOGETHER in BOTH TIMES. Fascinating.

(Grandfather had experienced this a number of times before. The other though, was just now learning it.)

"I see you are hurting, grandfather," the young one said.

"Yes, my hip."

"I can fix that," and with a touch and another 'PING'…the pain was gone (This occurred in about 1992…it is now 2007 and 'IT' has NEVER RETURNED).

They went on, until they came to an opening at the side of the trail (NOW a dirt logging road). 'THERE,' in a natural clearing, stood three Tipis (made of hide). Three children gleefully playing. The young man's wife, a very pretty woman, scraping a deer hide. An old man by another tipi. The wife looked up, smiled, and waved greetings. The children giving 'DADDY' yells. All was in pure bliss.

Again, grandfather was invited to dine and sleep. Again, he declined. They parted.

(This natural glen, in GRANDFATHER'S TIME, was now planted with trees. They stood about 11 feet tall. THIS WHOLE AREA WAS REPLANTED…after Its second CUTTING! This should tell you the GREAT TIME DIFFERENCES the two walked!)

Yet a THIRD Spirit was met on this trip, but this sharing is getting too long…so will be brought quickly to yet, ANOTHER occurrence that happened:

Grandfather was OUT OF WATER. Having shared with the third Spirit, plus. Now he was in Need. MILES still to go. The day HOT.

He began praying.

At this, an ancient (first cutting) HUGE Tree Stump spoke! "Go Upward. There you will find a field on your right. Go into that field. Walk AND LISTEN. Your water is there!"

Grandfather gave the stump an offering of thanks…and then obeyed.

A few hundred yards further up he came to a field, and did as the stump told.
Seeing only wild flowers and tall grasses. No water in sight. But he LISTENED, as told.
He almost stumbled on it before he heard it. A fast trickling of WATER! Bending down, he parted the grasses and there it was…

Not more then perhaps five inches wide at the widest. Pure, Cold and DELICIOUS!

He drank his fill. Then filled his containers. He sat at Its side giving thanks to all. ALL TENDING TO HIS NEEDS. ALL from the GREAT CREATOR. The One *IN ALL THINGS.* ☺

This ends this telling, though not the ALL of it. That for another time, perhaps?

This told, all TRUE, to show YOU…"GOD IS IN ALL THINGS"

Shared to tell If YOU 'connect'…you CAN SURVIVE! HO.

(REMEMBER THIS TELLING.)

Fear Monger!

This told to grandfather several times.

"Oh? DON'T YOU SEE WHAT I TELL IS TO MAKE YOU SEE YOURSELF…NOW?!

If you, think these things bring FEAR…it's because you ARE fearful. Like it or not.

I SHARE The HOW TO of HOPE! Hope IF these 'bad things' DO take place!

To FOLLOW is MORE than to TRUST! Most will 'Trust'…'THEN'…and TOO LATE!

Most will CLAIM 'trust'…and SOB AS THEY SHAKE…in FEAR!

Want an example? HOLOCAUST!

Start LEARNING while you still have a chance. Learn, PLUS TRUST!

WHY DO YOU THINK HE SHOWS ME THESE THINGS!

To show YOU where YOU STAND!

MANY ask ME…because they think ME 'holy.'

That tells Me that THEY CONSIDER THEMSELVES <u>LESS</u> then 'Me!'

This is Not at ALL true, yet still, they do…and here's Big Brother, 'CONCERNED' about ME!

Where does THAT put YOU???!

Now, look within yourself. DEEPLY, and SEE CORRECTLY these Tellings/Showings!

THEY ARE FOR <u>ALL</u> OF US!

There are NO 'ACCIDENTS!'
There is a REASON FOR ALL!

Before accusing falsely…GO TO 'DAD' with THESE TWO THINGS in mind!

FIND OUT THE REASONS!!!

This then Makes you WISE. Aho?"

Grandfather, Do You Envy Anyone?

"Envy? I Envy the child. I Envy their Innocence. I Envy their BELIEVING. I Envy them and the 'Mentally Impaired,' who are as a child.

Yet, I Envy even more, those we call Ancestors. Those now 'gone' FOR THEY WILL NOT FACE WHAT LAYS YET AHEAD!

All 'gone.' All safe. Yes, I 'Envy.' Ho."

The Boy Scout Meeting

Grandfather walked into the house, having just returned from Sky's first Boy Scout meeting.

"What's the matter, honey?" His wife asked.

"Well, there was a good sized group there. Nine boys plus Sky. I sat with four parents and in a while the two leaders joined us. The boys were planning an upcoming Scout Jamboree and the adults were discussing 'needs.' Looking for the cheapest prices on things they wanted the kids to have. Trouble was, everything they 'wanted' cost money, was very livable and yet FREE from within nature!

This is LEADERSHIP??!

The Theme of the jamboree is SURVIVAL.

Their way is SURVIVE WITH a HARDWARE Store and PHARMACY On Your BACK!

I was AGHAST! I had no IDEA 'Scouting' had slid so FAR, Honey. Not a CLUE!

Talking FLINT and STRIKER 'kits.' SO SMALL, PARTS GET LOST when dropped!

ROPE?

SUUURRREEE…EVERYONE going out is going to lug ROPE Around? Never happen!
They don't know how to MAKE rope 'On the Spot!'

One thing after another!

The only GOOD thing spoken of was on getting LED Head Lamps. THOSE ARE WORTH IT!
But even THESE aren't necessary for night vision.

Here I sat with The BEST OF THE BEST in our Counties Scout Troops and listened to…NO KNOWLEDGE.

Shoot! Sky can run CIRCLES around even their EAGLE SCOUT in Survival. REALLY!

I outta pull him out but these kids need to learn. So too the elders.

Now, to 'DO' and not 'invade' the leaders' possible egos. They are a Loving and DEVOTED bunch. Just so…soooo…well…White."
Ho.

Country's Leader

"Grandfather, who do you want as our Country's next leader?"

This by a young man visiting the elder couple.

"Son, The Creator sets up all governments. Each for a reason. Some are reasons we don't understand, yet all have 'His' reason.

I've told one is to pray for their Government. This daily. Few do.

The Lord's Prayer 'On EARTH as it is in HEAVEN' is very pointed. Our Big Brother wanted only the BEST for this Earth.

Who prays as He today? Are there any? Those who do, is it of Rote?…or Heart?

It takes many to make a change. Only ONE to start it. Our Great Brother started it. It is up to US to 'follow.'

Who I will cast ballot for is my decision. As is yours. Let's keep this within ourselves.

Do not just listen to the Speeches, but PRAY DILIGENTLY…and hear HIM.

Whoever wins, PRAY FOR THAT WINNER and those behind him.

Know this: It matters not which man is king.
It matters only which man is THE 'KING'!"

Earth Change/Messenger Change

Grandfather told, "I've noticed that since the big Indonesian Tsunami event, that this has disrupted the meaning of Natures 'signs.' Signs I could always depend on have totally changed now. I am in the process of finding *'what means what'* all over again.

I don't know if this is so with others, but certainly is for me.

Seems that tiny Earth 'hesitation' threw everything out of 'sink.' It's going to take me time to re-know. Probably get it all figured out and another change will wipe THAT out!

This has to be expected as it is THE Time. Stranger will be taking place. As time goes by. Yes, it is time for this.

Madness will escalate worldwide. We are already seeing this taking place. Oddball shootings at schools and in various places…the Taliban Whackos using 'ignorant' people to go blow up…Many things.

The BAD will be 'good,' the GOOD will be 'bad.' Yes, it is foretold. It is TIME.

Indeed, our world is a mess and going to get FAR MESSIER."

"Why?"

"BECAUSE WE ARE NOT RIGHT IN 'HIS' EYES. Get right, OVER 85% of us, or we continue into the time of Armageddon. Get RIGHT and we change this path. We will then leave it to our future generation(s) to slip and fall…or continue peacefully.

It is all up to US and it ALL starts with EACH Individual.

I am speaking to the *'I AM…YOU ARE NOT.'* What has happened and IS happening, is caused by EACH *'I AM's'* PERSONAL SELF. Your Deep, Deep 'inner' you. I am speaking to your own INNER FEARS that you are projecting in hologram form. EACH *'not standing Right in the Creator's eyes.'*

'HE' KNOWS YOUR HEART! That 'Heart' is your 'Deep Deep.' SO DEEP YOU DON'T REALIZE it is YOU who is causing these turmoil…OR goodly happenings.

He sees you FAR BETTER than YOU SEE YOURSELF.

You can't Con GOD CREATOR.

You CAN con your SELF though. Have. Are…and now face the results.

FEAR = MADNESS

MADNESS = FEAR

RIGHT STANDING = No FEAR, No Madness…and NO MORE EARTH CHANGES.

It = INNER PEACE, INNER JOY

And THAT = HEAVEN ON EARTH…as it was and is MEANT to be.

THAT 'Righteousness' = PURE AGAPE LOVE!

For God Creator is LOVE.

I, this 'I AM," is telling MYSELF….'YOU' MY HOLOGRAM, to CALM DOWN AND TRUST. CALM DOWN and have PEACE.

I am speaking to ME…the YOU 'I AM.'

Now that YOU 'I AM' must do the SAME.

I have found truth. I have told 'self.' MY Inner Peace IS. I walk to reach out to all the *I AM's* we each are.

I'm tired of looking for new 'signs.'

HO!"

Dare To Be Different

Grandfather has often told this.

In this, grandfather has done some 'unusual' things. He *'practices what he preaches'*, just to find out if they'll work. More often, they do…somewhat. Take, for instance, his PAPER CANOE!

Old plywood was used to frame out the eight foot canoe shape. Old 2 by 4's made into sawhorses to hold all. Everything was scrounged except five gallons of shellac.

All was setup in their small living room. Their poor daughter had to get on her knees to get to her bedroom. Crawling under his 'boat.' Poor kid.

Once his frame 'mold' was done, he took an old roll of chicken wire to make the hull. That done, he began brushing shellac on several sheets of old newspapers over the wire.

"Waterproof and LIGHT," he proudly proclaimed.

When dry he lifted the hull off the form and shellacked more paper on the inside.

"Done," he said.

"No, it needs ribs," his wife said.

"Nah, the spreader stick I have in will do it," he replied.

As often the case, the wife was correct. ☺

When the weather was right, grandfather took his latest 'invention' to a local river for a tryout. A long tree branch his paddle.

As he pulled out his 13 pound canoe, an elder gentleman was getting into his neighboring truck. Seeing what grandfather had…he shut his truck door and fell in step beside grandfather. Without a word, the two walked to the small beach.

Grandfather tied a long kite string to the thwart spreader and looked about for a stick to tie the other end to shore. The old man stretched out his hand and held the end. Again, not a word spoken between the two.

Grandfather gingerly got aboard and gently shoved off into the fast wide waters. He began 'paddling.'

"It WORKS!" he shouted in glee! "IT WOR……!"

The word unfinished the second time. For a SHADOW was coming up over his shoulders. He quickly looked around to see what it was. THE STERN! Then the BOW started folding upwards to him. THE CRAFT WAS BENDING…and grandfather at its center!

Like a closing clamshell, he was being engulfed!

Then the old man began pulling him to shore. Just in time.

Grandfather rolled out into the shallows, stood and looked at his creation. Pulling it ashore, he took it and the string in hand and walked back to his truck.

“Needs ribs,” he said. The elderly man said not a word.

As both headed to their vehicles' doors, the old man turned to grandfather and said:

“Son, I'm 82 years old. I thought I've seen it all. Now I KNOW I HAVE!”

Roaring with laughter, he left.

OLD/AGING

"Grandfather, you have told 'aging is curable.' That we can reverse our age. Yet EVERYONE gets old. It's natural! IS IT TRUE!?"

"I don't speak lies, nor idly. I give Truth only. Of course, it's 'natural.' You cannot stop the seasons. Still, you CAN stop your LOOKS. You can be '100 seasons old' but LOOK as if you've lived but 20, or whatever. That age look is your choice. Death is as natural as is Life.

I have observed people all my life. I know what STARTS aging. I know what continues the LOOK of it.
I tell you true: EACH HAVE ACCEPTED THE 'SIN' FULLNESS WAY over the TRUE Way. I have seen 'Old People' leaning on canes. Using Walkers. Walking OLD! Bent, stooped being 'feeble.' I see and am so sad for them, 'Accepters.'

MANY can EASILY reverse that and STILL 'BE Old'…but with a difference! Having the look of youth but with the wisdom of an elder. WALKING TALL! STRIDING, not shuffling. It's all a MINDSET. You get what you BELIEVE! Have you observed these 'feeble ones?' Surely, you have. We all have."

"WHY ARE THEY LIKE THAT?"

"They are THIS WAY TO ATTRACT 'PITY'…to get OTHERS to 'Feel Sorry' for them. They WANT ATTENTION! The, *'Look, I'm OLD. PITY me. RESPECT me,'* syndrome. Or should I say SINdrome?

You see far more females then males out on the street. Helped along by a younger one. A Daughter or son or yet ANOTHER 'Old One.' Men have a tendency of staying In. LETTING CARES COME TO THEM!

In truth, this 'Old' syndrome is a less 'Obtrusive' way of the ALZHEIMER'S CON! Less severe but with the same desired results: *TAKE CARE OF ME FOR I AM TIRED OF TAKING CARE OF YOU!*

So they 'age.' It's a less SEVERE 'way' of Alzheimer's 'ACCEPTABILITY.'

Do you wish to LOOK OLD yet not FEEL OLD? Then STOP STOOPING. STRETCH YOUR MUSCLES. Learn you don't NEED that Cain! STAND UPRIGHT. STRIDE, don't Shuffle. FEEL HEALTHY. FEEL YOUNG! In this way you CAN reverse your course. Be an EXAMPLE of 'PRIDE'…not 'SORROW.' Men have a tendency of bending their knees when standing. Women, with your backs standing Up RIGHT, STAND UP, In a WELL and STRONG WAY! Keep that up and you BECOME IT!"

Sky's First Sweat

Grandfather had his 'just turned 11' grandson with him on travels to Canada and the Crees.

Grandfather had explained the etiquettes required among these good people. Sky was being attentive and doing quite well. Impressing the elders.

Then came his first Sweat Lodge experience.

Knowing this was the Native way of 'church,' he was looking forward to it.

What he DIDN'T realize is the Cree's Sweat IS HOT HOT HOT!

Grandfather gave him a large beach towel to cover with and help hold back the heat.

"Put it over your head, son, if you get too hot. The heat can scorch your ears badly. Lay on the ground if need be. Heat rises. It's hotter when sitting upright. Let us know if you want out. There is no shame in doing so."

At GRANDFATHER'S request, Sky was sat next to the 'door.' This to allow fast egress if required.

All went in. A large group of 12 or so. Sky by one side of the entrance, grandfather at the back with the leader. The door (of heavy cloth) pulled shut and tucked tightly, allowing no light to penetrate. These after a number of heated stones were first placed inside.

Before the water was applied to the glowing stones, a member of the group needed to get something he'd forgotten outside.

All were already sweating from the un-steamed stones' heat. The door was opened to allow the man to retrieve his object.

As the cloth was lifted, there was Sky…NOSE TO DOORWAY, ON the Ground and FULLY COVERED by his towel!!!

Grandfather said, "What are you doing THERE? The Heat hasn't EVEN STARTED YET!"

All burst out laughing!

Sky sheepishly sat upright but kept covered. The heat was nearly unbearable to him!

"For your sake, Sky, I will keep the heat as low as I can, but this is a SERIOUS Sweat, I warn you. Thus, it will STILL be hot…just not as hot as we normally do. Can you take it? Or would you care to leave now?"

"I'll stay," a muffled reply came.

Again, the door was shut and secured. No air penetrating, nor outside light. Only the stones gave light.

The beginning prayers were said. The Prayer Ties (colored cloth that each were in charge of praying into) were put on the willow frame overhead. The Cree's instructing Sky.

Grandfather remained silent.

Then the first water was splashed on the stones. Steam INSTANTLY hissed and covered all.

"Are you alright, Sky?" asked the leader.

A mumbled, "yes" from his covered form.

(This to suppressed quiet laughter from all.)

Sky 'held.' Grandfather was both surprised AND pleased.

In time, the pipe was lit and passed around. Each giving thanks for The Creator's 'hearing' the audible prayers said. The smoke rising. Mixing with the heavy steam.

Prayers 'Lifted' to heaven. Ho.

The pipe was handed to Sky. As was the custom for all within. Sky received, gave thanks, and proceed to 'draw.'

He had NEVER Smoked. But he was 'game!'

Inhaling (not required but no one told)…suddenly he 'Exploded' into Heaving Coughs and Gags!

LAUGHTER! (All, having memories of THEIR first time!)

Sky made the first 'round,' but that's all he could take!

He sat out the last three. To all, he did well.
HO!

Escape

A meeting with a few who have been following GRANDFATHER'S knowledge led to this question:

"Grandfather, you have told of different Plains and Dimensions and Parallel places... Places only speculated as a possibility by today's Scientists. You say you have entered such…Correct?"

"Yes, I and others have done so. Some deliberately, some by accident…and some by a deliberate act of the Creator. Why do you ask?"

"Well, I…we…were just wondering…can one STAY in, say, another Parallel space and escape what may take place?"

"Yes. It's been done."

"Can YOU?"

"Certainly, and I have. For short periods only. This, MY choice."

"Why don't you just GO…and STAY?"

"That would go against my Great One's desire. I am to stay Right where I am.
It would be easy to 'run' yet you don't understand the results. To go to a Parallel Time Place for a length of time, well, this forces the 'You' that is there, to TRADE with you! He or She comes HERE, to THIS Parallel time.

A 'trade' and not one I'm willing to make on another.

No, I will stay, as ordered.

SELF preservation IS of SELF…at least in THIS way.

Running is usually Fear Based.

To cause ANOTHER'S death so YOU can LIVE 'safely,' is not a Godly act. At least to me it isn't.

No. I will stay…and Trust HIS will. Aho?"

Why?

“Why do people spend their money on building an expensive ‘meeting place’ to worship our Great One?

Why do they not meet in homes, as did the original Followers?

Why not meet in a rented large place, or in the wilderness, occasionally, to *be as one*? Sharing what each Smaller Group has learned and what each are doing?

Why don’t people needing Christ’s Love SEE it, with monies NOT spent for a fancy building, but instead, Helping THEM? Monies spent on helping the Elderly, etc…

WHY?

We call ourselves ‘followers’ yet go about doing UN-Christ-like ‘ways.’ Not UN-Godly, just not as He did.

Did HE collect money, stop, and build a building?

WHY do WE than do so?

ARE WE TRULY *FOLLOWING*?

It WILL return. It MUST! The original ‘ways’ WILL BE FORCED UPON US…the TRUE ‘Followers.’

Why not start NOW?

WHY MUST WE BE FORCED?

Why not DO AS HE EXAMPLED and STOP these Man’s Ways of MADNESS?

Why?”

???

Grandfather As A Kid

"What was your childhood like, grandfather? You sure are 'mellow.' Were you BORN this way?"

"All are little sister. All are. Things change as one gets day by day older. I was no exception."

"How far back can you remember?"

"I don't know. Pretty young though. Still a baby. I remember I hadn't learned to roll over yet. That's going back pretty far."

"WOW! Why do you recall THAT?"

"Hum. You ask, so I suppose I should answer. Wasn't the best memory.

My mother had lifted and bathed me. She had me on a towel, drying me off. I can still see it! Her love was as a warm cuddle. You could see it in her EYES!

My father came in. I can still see THAT as well! He was commenting on something. Talking to mom. Suddenly he reached down and 'tweaked' me. My 'private.'

Next thing that happened, was just Automatic…was, well, I PEED. DEAD 'Shot'…RIGHT INTO HIS LEFT EYE! It was a perfect *shot.*"

(Laughter.)

"Wasn't funny for HIM! His face grew into a RAGE. He lifted his hand to hit me…HARD! Mom STOPPED IT!

I think I was able to understand words, though I was as yet unable to speak myself. I heard her yell at him, *'RAY! NO!'* As she grabbed his arm, *'IT WAS YOUR FAULT! NO!'*

Then she lowered her voice and told him, *'He's just a BABY…YOU shouldn't have DONE THAT! Now, GET OUT OF HERE!'*

He left, but sure was mad! Mom was too, but not at me…at Him.

Must have impressed me, cause I STILL REMEMBER!

I think babies know more about than adults know about.
We come INTO this World, KNOWING. Maybe unable to EXPRESS, but Knowing!

That reflex was my Inner KNOWING what my father did WAS NOT RIGHT!
'Nailed him' the only way I could.

Even young, we have our 'defenses.' At least to a degree. He never did it again. Aho?"

The lady looked embarrassed. "Maybe I didn't need to know that…"

"Yes you did. Now you'll remember to be VERY CAREFUL OF WHAT YOU ASK FOR! BE WISE! You'll never forget it, what I've just told. IT WILL HELP YOU.

May I suggest you ask no more questions without thinking of possible outcomes FIRST, from here on in? Aho?"

"Aho."

Reader:

This young woman is now quite a bit older. SHE HAS NOT FORGOTTEN.

You can 'see' it in her hesitant thought, before she 'acts'…ALWAYS!

REMEMBER: There ARE <u>NO</u> Accidents! There is a REASON for ALL!

Aho?

Sky Is Taught Simple Basics

"Grandpa, how come you never get lost?"

Grandfather laughed.

"I DO get lost, Sky. Put me in a city and I have NO Idea where I am. In the wilderness, that's another story though. To know direction I know that the Sun always comes up from the East and goes down towards the West. That's all I need to know my direction.

Son, look around. Where is the sun?"

"Over that way," Sky pointed.

"Yes, and it is still morning. So it's still rising. Now, put it directly behind you. At your back."

(He did so.)

"OK, you know your back is now East. This puts your Left shoulder towards the South.
Your Right shoulder to the North and your front towards the West. By simply knowing where the sun is, you become your own Compass.
If the sun is directly overhead, it is Noon. Wait a few minutes to see where it heads. It heads west. So you then know that way is west, behind you is east. Your left side is South and your right side is North. It's as simple as that.

For BETWEEN the four directions you use simple math. Like cutting a pizza into four part: East to West/South to North. In between 'cut the pizza' BETWEEN these four sections. Now you have East BY South, IN BETWEEN THE TWO. Do the same on the 'pizza' and each 'cut' give you the IN BETWEEN directions. The 'BY' part. Do you understand?"

"Yes."

"OK, do so now. Let me see. Where is South?"

(Sky put his back to the rising sun and pointed south.)

"Good, now where is South East?"

(Sky showed correctly.)

"North East?"

(Again, correct.)

"Very good Sky. You know for sure and have proven so. Your testing is complete. Now onto similar:

At night, it is the MOON that is the Night 'sun.' It too rises and falls in the same manner as does the sun. The two are as a dog, chasing Its own tail. Aho?"

"Aho."

"When you are unable to see EITHER, then you go by OBSERVATION. As you know, here our winds are almost always from that direction (pointing west). It goes EAST from there. So again you can position yourself accordance and know your directions."

"But what if it's dark and there IS no wind, grandfather?"

"Again, ALWAYS BE AWARE of EVERYTHING. Don't just go taking a walk…walk AND OBSERVE at the same time. Here our winds are pretty heavy. LOOK AT THE LEAN OF THE TREES. Look at the BUSHES. WHERE are the MOST Branches and leaves? The LESSER always FACE THE MOST COMMON WIND DIRECTION. The MOST 'Hide' behind the Stalk or Tree MAIN 'Stem.' Thus, you know HERE the direction, West to East.

By being OBSERVANT you can ALWAYS know your needed direction. Aho?"

"AHO!"

"OK, one more thing: to SPEED UP your walk, simply look for an object that stands out in the direction you are going. A tall tree, a Mountaintop. ANYTHING in that given direction. Then walk to it. There, again check and again look at an 'aiming' point to walk towards.

Alright, lesson over…oh walking compass."

"Well, not really. What about cities?"

"Two ways: CARRY a compass is one. But the best in this situation is to ASK SOMEONE!"

Bird In A Cage

In a recent phone conversation, a woman told grandfather she, “Feels like a bird in a cage.” She was searching for truth. Had been looking for over four years.

They had talked quite awhile before her ‘bird’ statement.

“People already KNOW. You, for instance, tell me you are feeling like a bird in a cage, flapping your wings against it, trying to fly free. Many have told me similar.

I tell you true: you have the answer for your own freedom, right there in that statement, but you don't contemplate even on your own words.

We are all given the ability to be free. It depends on your Hunger WI LL.

Yes, even a caged bird can get out. Can fly FREE!

What does a bird do while in there? It EATS. It Poops and it Pees.

POOP and URINE create RUST. Persist and eventually the bottom will fall out of the cage. You will BE FREE at last!

The most powerful food you can eat is the Word of God.

The most powerful drink you can drink is:
THE EVERLASTING ‘Water’ from the ‘Well of LIFE.’

The more you partake of these two things, the faster your freedom will be!

Listen to your own words. THINK on what you say. You have carried your OWN WAY OUT all along. BORN with it! Aho?

HO!”

Warfare Weapons…"Elsewhere"

Grandfather and others were talking of our Technology. WARFARE Technology.

"We here are 'advanced' in ways our public knows little or nothing about. Our Governments' have gotten information from 'others.' Some of our Unknown 'Black' military have and DO WORK with 'others.' I have seen some of this with my own eyes.

(Others of us have as well).

Our SURFACE Governments do NOT KNOW of the BLACK.

Still, even the 'others' do not know OTHER warring areas. Areas of Other DIMENSIONS.

I have seen some of this too.

I have gone into a Parallel Time that was at war. Russia against the U.S.A. We were losing.

We were desperate for anything that could turn the tables.

Enter ME. Not THIS me, but the 'me' OF THAT Parallel Time.

He 'I' was an inventor. Working on his own.

His ideas rather radical. Making SMALL better than BIG.

Each side had Navy Ships/Tanks/etc. Each was being destroyed. That's why that 'me' went small.

He came up with a very little one, two and three men Submarine. A 'station' sub. This to be dropped off by a 'Mother' sub. Several were aboard this 'Mother.'

Each 'Minnie' had barely room to move. So little room, those manning it SIT ON THEIR OWN TOILET! This toilet had a 'solid' backrest that could lean back to sleep. Not a FULL straight 'lean' but at a low angle that the Average person(s) had their legs under at a sitting position. This craft was CRAMPED!

Foods were on the bulkhead (wall) and other things as well. Minor medical needs, etc. I 'followed' the 'me' designer from first thought to inception of building. These craft were too fast to make 'flimsy,' but VERY DEADLY! Crews volunteered.

The building was much as OUR auto factories. An Assembly Line affair.
There were MANY, and in a very short time.

I saw the one and two man/men 'minis' took 'over.' They were also faster to produce.
Three men 'minis' were too large.
Each sub had an UMBILICAL CORD (Air Snorkel)...that floated on the water's surface, LOOKING LIKE BELL KELP. Just another piece of Flotsam and Plankton to a casual observer.

These subs were SHORE HUGGERS, and rarely went deeper then perhaps 35 to 50 feet.

As they were dropped off by the 'mother,' the crew worked toward the shore, nestling in the kelp beds and corral.

There they sat. DEAD STILL. For DAYS at a time! A three week Maximum.
These subs had no 'wheels' (props as we know them). Theirs were several short Flaps along a long rubber set of 'chains.' These would lock as they were pushed backwards, and as they lifted into the subs underbelly, those there would unlock. Thus, only the exposed BOTTOM flaps would be 'stiff'...pushing the sub forward.

They tried reversing if needed. It didn't work. So on each side were similar, but not as wide on each. These were the REVERSE(ing) 'props.' Think Military TANK Threads...and you'll get the palpitation idea.

These 'flaps' were locked by MAGNETS. The bushings the RUBBER 'chains' ran on, were of HARD RUBBER. THIS CRAFT was EXTREMELY QUIET. There was no 'Prop Wash' to hear OR SEE.

As for armament...each had one to two small HIGHLY EXPLOSIVE fast Torpedoes, AND too, small ROCKETS. Each crewmember had highly sensitive (to sound) Ear 'phones' on. These lil' subs PACKED A WALLOP! Thus, with them (and their brave crews) the war WAS being swung around to our favor.

MANY enemy ships were waylaid. It got that 'Shore Hugging' was almost Suicide to them.
At sea, our regular subs and ships took over. Between the two types...well, you get the picture.
Aho?

This other 'Me' also invented a tiny tank. VERY, VERY FAST! Very lightly armored, too. KEVLAR 'sheathed.' They were shaped like a COCKROACH. A real GROUND Hugger.
One to two crew it. Usually only one. The reason for this was to spread out our manpower. More could be put on the front line with one man. WE WERE RUNNING OUT OF SOLDIERS!
These had two 50 caliber Machine guns AND rockets as armament.

These lil' tanks COULD 'LEAP' over small sections of land. MINEFIELD areas. Leaped like a big Locust! Done in a 'Hovercraft' way. Their drawback was exact to Set off mines. A number would be hit, yet their speed so great, and the NUMBER on the 'field' so LARGE...well, the enemy had very little chance and fled before them. With these on 'field,' they too helped 'turn the tide.'

Due to the subs and tiny tanks…our Country's limited building resources were stretched greatly. Each built 'assembly Line' fashion and with little, hard to find (massy) metals.

Did we win? I don't know. Left. Know THIS though: SMALL and LESS was BETTER! Aho?

This has not been the only 'Times' I have seen us at war. Others have seemed to all seen LOSING. Then went FROM High Technology TO…SIMPLE.

One Parallel Time war we were using KITES and small Clear Helium Balloons. Some to drop grenades, some to watch for troop movement. VERY SIMPLE 'Technology' that helped TREMENDOUSLY. The kites TOO of clear ,CHEAP, 'plastic' sheeting. DARN NEAR INVISIBLE!

The Balloons were tithed to the ground by three strands of 'wire.' THEY STAYED ALOFT DAY AND NIGHT! No fire to heat and keep them up was seen. I don't know what was used to keep them flying during the cool of night. They just hung there…with cameras watching at 360 degrees sweep. Night vision and Heat seeking Cameras aboard. Our bases were safe from intruders because of them.
I have seen much. Enough to know, SIMPLE WAS WINNING!

HO."

Godly Believers Are At War!

“I get SO DEPRESSED,” one told grandfather. “So MANY are deceived. So MANY WANT to go ‘do,’ but ALONE. WHAT can I DO? They refuse to LISTEN!”

Grandfather slowly shook his head, then said, “Of COURSE you’re depressed. YOU ARE PLAYING ‘GOD’!”

“No I’m NOT! I seek His want and will, Always!”

“Yes, AND forget the Most IMPORTANT: TRUST! Why if you do, are YOU so darned ‘depressed?’ WHO’S DOING THE WORK? In these cases: YOU. I tell you true, HE can handle THEM. YOU have No NEED to fret. It’s A LIE! You’ve stepped onto a MINE, Satanically PLANTED.

You are DEPRESSED because YOU FORGOT TO TRUST THE CREATOR TO HANDLE HIS CHILDREN As HE Sees FIT! ‘SAVING’ People is NOT YOUR BUSINESS! It’s HIS! Now YOU feel ‘Injured.’ It’s your OWN DARN FAULT!

Look at your Godly Walk in this way: You are a SOLDIER. One in a GIANT MINE FIELD. YOU have a MINE DETECTOR: The WORD OF GOD. Yet you are NOT TURNING IT ON! ALL have a detector. Most DON’T turn it on…and pay the price. Depression is ONE OF THE INJURIES the mine(s) Cause! Just ONE of them.

These ‘mines’ are DESIGNED to STOP or SLOW YOU…and YOU ARE ALLOWING IT! You go from One Mine to Another. You end up slowly LIMPING across the field, or LAY WHERE YOU ARE.

TURN THE DANG DETECTOR ON!

When you can see this; that YOU are the CAUSE of your ‘hurt’…Then GET YOUR REAR UP. APOLOGIZE! This is ‘Calling the Medic’…BIG BROTHER. HE will repair you. HE will make you Whole again. YOU Then FORGE AHEAD, LOVE Attacking SAFELY!
LOVE is GOD. Just SHOW THAT!

See these ‘mines’ as GIFTS. Gifts to MAKE YOU AWARE. WISE! ‘LIFE’ IS CONSTANT WAR! PRAISE Him and GET UP! ‘SEE’ and NEVER Take Off or Tilt ANY of your ‘Armor of God.’ Even TILTING it can EXPOSE YOU TO HARM!

‘See’ it that way and you will NEVER come to ME again, ‘moaning in depression’ or other ‘problems.’ Frankly, after hearing this, AND YOU RETURN ‘MOANING’ again…I WILL TELL YOU ONLY TWO MORE TIMES. After That…DON’T COME BACK! Either LEARN or stay wounded TILL YOU DO. I Am NOT YOUR GOD! Selah.”

"You Sure Enjoy Your 'Job", Don't You?"

Another statement from one.

"Yes, I do. Frustrating as it's been. Yes.
I get to see people CONNECT. Get to see people RETURN. Get to see some 'DO' and not 'need' me. I GET TO SEE PEOPLE KNOW that The Creator is A LIVING BEING! That THEY can WALK WITH HIM, FEARLESSLY! And IN AGAPE LOVE, and 'DO!' A number of various things I have gotten to see, but this the most rewarding. Ho.

I have learned people CAN be 'as He,' WITH HIS HELP.
It's Mind Boggling!

Many want to be a 'Medicine' Man or Woman. NOT CALLED to it, and yet, by connecting, THEY ALMOST ARE!
Very close to it indeed.
Yes, I love my job.
I feel this walk has made me as 'Marco Polo'...seeing WONDROUS THINGS!

People thought him 'a liar' and quite a 'story teller,' yet he was proven JUST THE OPPOSITE. HE explored the 'unknown Earth world.' I EXPLORE the unknown World of SPIRIT.

Yes, I LOVE MY JOB.

HO!"

A Class With Grandfather

Grandfather had been asked to teach at a distant city. Agreeing, he arrived to do the Friday evening, all day Saturday, and a half day Sunday class.

As was the Inner Heyókȟa' way, he had all bring 'The Good Book.' Using this, he had all read the verse(s) pertaining to the lesson(s) next to be taught.

"The thing you are about to be taught derives from this, written in Scriptures. Mostly I will teach the 'How To(s)' of it ONLY. It will be up to you to put these into Fact. I WILL actually have you DO two or three things HERE...the rest will be you, on your OWN. These, I will help you with, will give you confidence that the Good Book tells true. I will teach as the ancients were taught. In this, you will see that The Good Book AND our 'Indian' ways ARE ONE in results. Aho?"

With first (reading the bible basics) of the teachings...after each, they began Using the Indian way. In this, the group (of some 25) they LEARNED (Did), TELEPATHY 'on demand' and LEARNED (Did), TALKING TO NATURE, as well as TIME TRAVEL.

"Alright, that's enough. You've READ it...and now you've DONE it. YOU KNOW THE GOOD BOOK DOES NOT LIE. You've learned that and learned HOW WE 'Indians' do it. At least those of old. These three actual doings should be enough. You've EXPERIENCED THEM. The rest I will just tell the HOW. YOU, learn ON YOUR OWN, to Experience THEM. In this you Test the Word of The Creator AND ME."

He then proceeded telling the 'Indian how on: Self Healing (KU), NAGAL (angel use healing), Healing Others, Age Regression, Death, Baptism, Catching A Vision, Working the DREAM, Shape Shifting, Invisibility and other things...All Biblically based.

Then he taught POWER PRAYER and POWER READING (of the Good Book).
Then the importance of the Concordance . This *'to rid the manmade dust from the Creator's Golden Thread of Truth,'* the Good Book has. (Learning how to Strip Mans' injections into His Word over the centuries).
"THIS leaves ONLY the Truth...His GOLDEN WORD," he said.

They were a good group and soaked up the teachings. What they do about it, remains to be seen.

Grandfather "Coyote"

The Coyote is THE TRICKSTER, in Native American lore. All Heyókȟa's are such Clowns/Tricksters. Grandfather is an Inner Heyókȟa, AND a Heyókȟa.' One can never know what to expect from these two groups. They Love 'surprising.'

This Story is of one 'incident' Grandfather pulled on another; a white friend traveling with him.

They were visiting friends. This at an expensive Bermed Home construction site, way up in the wilderness. The friends had quite a camp area set up. Much like a Safari 'set up.' Huge tent/Picnic table/LP fancy gas cooker/Out House…the 'Works.'

Here is where grandfather, his friend, and the visiting Architect stayed.

GRANDFATHER'S younger friend was a 'Full Bore' Vegetarian.

This way of eating meant his Bowel Movement was 'delayed' for days. When he DID 'go,' you could count on close to an hour wait until he was finished. Aho?

It was summer. A Full Moon out and warm. A beautiful night. All three bedded down within the tent.

Just about asleep, the friend decided it was time to visit the rental/plastic Out House. Disturbing the other two, as he turned on lights and rummaged about for his boots and clothing. His idea of 'quiet' did NOT fit the other two. Finally, he turned off the lights and tripped out the doorway. ZZZIP...ZZZIP went the big zipper. Then, despite the full moon, he dragged his untied boots, tripping on tree roots, grating on the gravel, coughing and mumbling to his destination.

Both inside knew sleep was useless. It would all replay Itself on his return.

After some ten minutes, grandfather knew the younger was out to 'sit'…and knew it would be about an hour before he returned.

"I've got an idea," he told the architect. "It will be at LEAST two hours to do, so you can get SOME sleep in the meantime." At that he rose and dressed (no light needed), quietly he unzipped the door, leaving it so.

Silently he approached the outhouse. Knowing the occupant was 'concentrating' as he tried to get out his 'Rabbit Balls' scat. An endless 'job.'

As he got closer, he walked bent over…BEAR LIKE! He began a slow 'meandering' suffering BEAR walk. *'Just a bear passing through'* type noise. As he was coming close he began 'Sniffing' and low 'Grunting.' He knew he was being heard. The door's inside lock Clicked!

Yup, he 'had him!'

He went to the door, Smell and Sniffing around it. Then reached out and gave it a slight push. Then HARDER. He then grunted loudly and did a finger scrape.

NOT A SOUND FROM INSIDE!

He ambled around the whole structure. "Growl…Growl…Sniff, Sniff, Sniff."

He then turned away, into the moonlight. Letting his shadowy silhouette be seen through the plastic wall of the outhouse. Grunting 'angrily,' he disappeared. Going to a fire log pile. Here he sat behind it and had a good LONG smoke. Giving his friend plenty of time to feel secure enough to get off the seat he was glued to. THEN HE RETURNED!

He could hear his friend sit back down.

Doing as before, this time he added to it all. He 'ambled' over to the very close Picnic table. FOOD HAD BEEN LEFT ON IT. INCLUDING a bag of 'Nice Salty POTATO CHIPS!'

He began 'pawing' at the open cans, grunting and growling.

" PING !" Went one can across the gravel…

"PING…BANG," the others. All this less than ten feet from the outhouse .

Then came THE CHIPS! Rattling and ripping at the bag, grandfather made Smacking Noises. Grunts of satisfaction left his lips. He then took a handful of chips and crunched them. Tossing these and the sack onto the ground. He then AGAIN tried that outhouse door!

Finally, at the moonlit side of the outhouse, using the moonlight as 'back drop,' he spread open his coat and stood erect. Growling loudly, he ambled off. Once again 'disappearing.'

This time TOWARDS THE TENT!

Here he sat and had THREE cigarettes! Then reached down, picked up a stone and tossed it at the outhouse! BANG!! Then went inside the bed.

Close to 20 minutes later, a TERRIFIED young man came TEARING IN! "BEAR! BEAR!" he was SCREAMING!!!

There is more to this, but time doesn't permit.

Suffice to say: HE CAME OUT <u>CLEAN</u>! ☺

"What Is The Most Difficult Healing You've Done?"

"First off, the 'you' you are referring to, have the *'I have done'* connotation. I DO NO HEALING! 'HE' Does! Remember that. Aho?"

"I'm sorry. Yes, Aho!"

"Thank you. As for this question, beyond a doubt, it was on one badly injured in a motorcycle/car accident. There were two on the bike. Both badly injured. The wife far more than the husband. Both, friends of mine.

When he was well enough to call me, he did. This from the hospital they were in.
He told me what had happened. That he was pretty broken up (bones) but was deeply concerned about his wife. Her skull had been severely injured. The doctors had to put her into a coma state to repair the damage. She was 'now out of it' but her memory was 'shot.' Incoherent and confused. Would I come?

Asking for silence, I went to the Creator. Seeking 'His' will. I received: "GO."

The next morning I arrived.

Both were together. In the same room.

I was first told to touch/empower a 'Quick Healing' on the husband's broken bones and pain. Then to his wife.

Her eyes were SPINNING…unfocused. The Doctors had told her husband she would never be able to recover. That she would need to be put into a 'home' and would be 'like a vegetable' until she died. They know nothing of the Power of the Creator.

"GO INTO HER MIND!" I was ordered.

I did so. WHAT a MESS! THOUGHTS/MEMORIES COMPLETELY ASUNDER! There was NO 'reason' within! No beginning…middle…or to the now. SHE HAD NO CONNECTION WITH HER LIFE! ALL were streaking about…as does emboweled INDIVIDUAL 'memories.' I had NEVER seen or experienced this in all my life!

'Now what, Lord?' I prayed.

'CATCH THE MEMORIES. CONNECT THEM.'

I knew nothing of her life. Nothing of her day by day learning, and I had to start from her FIRST MOMENT. The BIRTH Memories…then 'catch' as best I could. Stringing the memories (as best I could) to the very moment we were there together.

Talk about HARD!!! Catching EXPLODED 'SHRAPNEL' streaking about the brain, incased in a 'balloon' called her Cranium. A VERY difficult task! She was in her fifties. That's a lot of MEMORIES!

With my hand holding hers, I stood there seeing and scathing. 'Stringing' the 'wild Beads' and 'catching' as best I could. TRILLIONS OF THOUGHTS!

In time, the 'beads' were restrung. Not perfectly, but on one 'controllable string.'

'ENOUGH,' I was told…and came out.

She looked about her…eyes no longer confused or spinning. She saw her husband and Smiled. SHE REMEMBERED! Then she began to speak. She recognized me, the accident…a lot of things.

My job done, I left.

They were BOTH sent home some two weeks later…much to the Doctor's total surprise. (So I was told.)

I keep in touch…she still has problems memory wise, but the 'string' seems to be like a Magnet thing. Still stray thoughts returning to their rightful place in her Life Thoughts.

GOD IS GOOD!

HO!"

The Judges

Grandfather was with friends. Six. One, the youngest, had just told of a 'buy' he was getting. Almost in unison, the others (BUT grandfather) let out some rather uncalled for 'comments' to this poor fellow.

"THAT'S THE DUMBEST DANGEST THING I've EVER heard you do!"

"THAT'S STUPID!"

"DON'T DO IT!"

Things like that.

Grandfather remained silent…then:

"Let's get GRANDFATHER'S view on your 'wonderful buy.' You respect His judgment."

All but the one agreed.

"Alright, being you all feel my thoughts are of value, I will do so.
I see four men telling off one. I've know all here a number of years now. I am aware of YOUR financial 'problems,' as you have told me.

You, Tom (looking at him) have three cars, two are 'Junkers' to repair, and two trucks. You have shared how 'bad' your 'living' is. Yet you are looking into yet ANOTHER truck! Here you tell me you are sinking for needs of money and yet you go on adding to the problem. All this with only you and your wife to drive all those acquisitions. And here you are yelling the loudest.

EACH of you are in similar straights…and STILL you spend.
Now you jump on a man who asked for NO advice and CERTAINLY NOT FOR JUDGMENT.

He simply TOLD.

'Judge not least YOU BE judged.' I'd advise you think on this.

People are funny. We are all willing to Jump, all willing to Condemn, yet very few look at themselves BEFORE they 'Go Off telling.'

FEW THINK BEFORE THEY LEAP!

I tell you true, most toss their 'slag' on the slag heap. That heap gets bigger and bigger. Taller and taller, and EVERY PIECE is UNSTABLE. You see a Mountain and recognize it as such.

This Mountain I speak of are your Major 'sins.' It is easy to see and thus easy to remember. You go to your knees and beg forgiveness for that 'Mountain DEED'...yet never seem to see the massive Slag Heap that keeps building higher and higher. DAILY Small DEEDS. In time that adds up to a heap HIGHER than the mountain.

You walk away from prayer THANKFUL for the Mountain removal. Giving great praise. Yet RIGHT NEXT TO THAT NOW EMPTY SPOT trembles the Slag Heap! It WILL fall down! YOU CAN COUNT ON IT! Either before 'passing' or after. IT WILL ADD TO YOUR DISCOMFORT! It IS adding to your discomfort. Your aches and pains, illnesses and accidents, your 'Woes,' are ALL PART OF THAT SLAG HEAP'S Trembling. You are getting hit with Its constants 'Rock Slide!'

Here you've all judged. NONE looking at themselves. Not at first...and generally not EVER. His telling is 'HIS MOCCASINS.' HIS! Not ONE of you can tell me YOU'VE walked in HIS moccasins. YOU'D DARN WELL HAVE TO LIVE WITH HIM TO SEE THE 'WHY' OF HIS DECISIONS! WHY do YOU Judge? What RIGHT have YOU to DO SO?!

WHO MADE *YOU* GOD!

(They sit stunned at his words.)

I tell you true: If you want to HELP...then NEVER DO SO IN A CONDEMNING WAY. EVER!
IF one asked for advice...then do so...WISELY.
If they DON'T...THEN KEEP YOUR MOUTH SHUT and just LISTEN.
IF you truly feel, what is being shared is Morally Wrong or Harmful...PRAY FOR THAT PERSON.

My brother, Think. THINK on your own mistakes. Your own moccasin path. Look back.
See...THINK...what 'stupid things' YOU have done.
GET YOUR SLAG PILE DOWN...and THEN you can Advise.
ADVISE, not 'Tell.' Aho?

Now understand, you asked, if you hadn't, I'd still be silent. Aho?"

And Again

Grandfather was with a group of Knowledge Seekers. He had shared many hours over a two day period. Still they didn't seem 'to get it.' They were stumped on the 'I AM' teaching.

"Your question (to one) shows me you do not fully understand. All here seek power. Power to overcome. Power to help others. Power to comprehend life. To comprehend the 'I AM' is to comprehend Life, Illnesses, Accidents and even death itself. Without comprehending the 'I AM' is to NOT comprehend and Do all that you seek.

Without it, you will learn to walk, somewhat…but with a severe 'limp.' You must grasp the 'I AM' FULLY, or be very limited. Any here who CAN grasp, are fortunate. Can YOU?
I don't know. All I can do is teach it. The actual 'doing' lies completely with you.

Again, you must learn that this life is but a mere dream. Nothing more. That YOU are the ONLY ONE IN EXISTENCE. When you learn this, indeed you CAN 'Move a Mountain.' LITERALLY.

You aren't…Not CAN'T…AREN'T…because you are not fully comprehending the 'I Am.'
THIS 'LIFE' IS YOUR DREAM!

You see war, accidents, illnesses, death, aging and 'bad' all about you. YOU HAVE ACCEPTED THIS AS 'REALITY.' Yet what you are seeing…what you are experiencing…is simply YOUR OWN INNER FEARS and TURMOIL (and what not) being PROJECTED before your very eyes. THIS IS INNER FEARS, etc., which are being 'played out' in the Projection of the HOLOGRAMS that YOU 'send.' Just simply HOLOGRAMS. Holograms of YOUR INNER THOUGHTS. Thoughts, if you will, in 3D.
YOU ARE PROJECTING ALL THESE 3D <u>MOVIES</u>. 'Movies' of your OWN 'writing.'

'THOUGHTS are REAL,' the Good Book says, and HERE IS PROOF!

If you are stuck on 'Horror movies'…you PROJECT 'horror movies.'
If your interest is on 'Love Novels'…that's what you begin to see in your 'Life Movie.'
If your interest is on Lust and Sex…so will you live.
If it's on 'Success'…so it is 'seen.'
If on being Godly…that Too becomes your 'reality.'
If it's on 'Poor Me'…then you will live in the misery of that. Never achieving anything but 'rejection,' pain, etc. A 'Hard LIFE.'

YOU ARE THE 'I AM!'
YOU are the DREAMER!
It's YOUR DREAM!
Understand the 'I AM' and then begin WORKING YOUR DREAM.

It’s your RIGHT. A GIFT our Creator has GIVEN YOU.

Understand THAT, and you WILL UNDERSTAND HIS STATEMENT: ‘YE are as gods!’

What more can I say?”

Sorry, I Can't "Buy" That

One who had listened to the 'I AM' teaching, was looking rather 'disturbed.'

"I'm sorry, dude, I can't *buy* this teaching! If I am the only 'I Am'…how the hell does you OR I, explain such things as Aliens! UFOs! They are REAL. I'VE SEEN THEM! And I can't accept I simply MADE THEM UP! How can I 'makeup' something I've NEVER KNOWN OF! I've been *with you* until this. I can believe it's possible to Project life as a Hologram; that all about me is a Hologram. Sent to teach me about things within me. UP TO THIS then, I think you are FULL OF CRAP! Sorry…"

Grandfather heard him out. ALL in the group did and ALL were now perplexed. All, BUT grandfather. HE started to SMILE instead.

"Son, you say you can possibly accept this 'I AM,' till you think on the 'Impossible'…Aliens, etc. It is apparent you are simply listening to me. You are not listening in CONTEMPLATION.

Those aliens you see ARE of YOUR Making, as well. OF CREATOR GOD, AS WELL. TEACHERS of your Inner Self, AS WELL.

They are there to Show You your INNER FEARS OF THE UNKNOWN! Your FEAR of WANTING TO GO DEEPER INTO GOD. Your 'Undiscovered.' YOUR '*BORN WITH*' ABILITIES LONG FORGOTTEN.

'HE' is SHOWING YOU that YOU are FIGHTING AGAINST 'HIM.' FIGHTING agents REMEMBERING. FIGHTING AGAINST <u>GROWTH</u>! And ARE AWARE OF IT!

You sit there, smug that you have me. No, you haven't. You are too set in your 'reality way,' you don't WANT to accept. Yet you've COME. Come to LEARN.

You sir, are in CONFLICT! WANTING to learn, have been TAUGHT, yet UN-WANTING to UNDERSTAND!

ALL ABOUT YOU is OF YOU, FROM YOU, and TEACHERS TO YOU. Even ALIENS!!

Now if you recall, I've told you and all here, *'Do NOT Believe a WORD I SAY…TEST IT!'*

You have not. You sit smug in your Locked 'way.' That's alright with me. It's you're decision and it's your right. It shows me how CLOSED you are to COMPLETE TRUTH FREEDOM!

SELAH!"

"Grandfather, Why Are You So Rough On Christians?"

This asked by one of several he was meeting with.

"Sister, I have been around Christians all my life. I've seen their Caring, their Love, their Heart…and too that there are many who are in The Church, not because they believe, but that they FEAR. Those are there to 'save their rears' so that IF there's a God…they DON'T want to 'go to hell.' Simply being on 'the safe side.'

They are told:
'Ask Christ in and You Are SAVED.'
'Go to Church or go to hell.'
'Read the Bible and join us and you will be Safe.'
'WE are the Only RIGHT ONES.'

Everyone WANTS to be safe. Everyone WANTS to 'go to Heaven'…IF there IS an afterlife. Who can blame them?
It's not just Christians that feel their way is the 'Only way.' ALL CULTURES have their 'Way.'
Wars are fought over, *'WE are right, YOU are wrong.'*
All simply trying to 'help' everyone else.

My own race, Native American, have been and still are, deeply affected by these types. Often 'brow beaten' into a Way that, in reality, is as Right as those of the 'brow beaters.'
God, Allah, etc., is LOVE. Love includes TOLERANCE. Love includes UNDERSTANDING. Love includes ONENESS.

Here is a Master…a master of Total LOVE, who wants to not lose a One of 'His' Creation…who FORGIVES AND LOVES…and Forgives. But WE DON'T! Christians' claim 'to follow.' If that were true, THEY'D NOT CONDEMN. They'd simply LOVE.

Like a lit candle in the night, moths come to that light. WHY FRY THEM?!
Are we to be 'Bug Zappers,' or a SAFE LIGHT?
LOVE DOES NO HARM!

IF one were TRULY into LOVE, they'd be MANIFESTING IT…not just TALKING about it!
LOVE CONNECTS THE Love Creator to You.
LOVE heals. Love GIVES. Love is SHARED. Shared by MANIFESTATION.
Big Brother MANIFESTED. He was MORE than talk. He WALKED it!
SHOWED it. And GAVE it.
He forced none…THEY CAME at their own volition.
He *said*, 'I HAVE FOUND THE WAY OF LOVE. I HAVE FOUND MY FATHER. I HAVE FOUND GOD IS LOVE.'

He *said*, 'FOLLOW WHAT I DID TO Find, and JOIN ME IN MY JOY! I HAVE LEARNED. I'VE DONE THE *GROUND BREAKING*...FOLLOW ME!'

The Good Book shows what He did TO FIND. He EXAMPLED. It's all in WRITING.
Yet the Christian World just...Sits. WHERE IS THE MANIFESTATIONS?! WHERE IS THEIR CONNECTION PROOF? Where?

Yes, I am hard on these who make claims...and DENY the WORKS of those 'claims.'

These are the same ones I 'walk with.' I call myself a 'Christian.' A FOLLOWER of Christ's way...the way of LOVE.
I have found Him, 'Big Brother,' KNEW THE TRUTH. I've FOLLOWED to TEST, and HE WAS RIGHT! AGAPE LOVE CREATES 'MIRACLES!' MANIFESTATIONS.

Yes, I AM hard on my fellow 'believers.' THEY LIE ABOUT THEIR BELIEFS!

I have been amongst them a long time. I KNOW they LOVE. I KNOW they MEAN WELL. I KNOW they CARE. And I Know they themselves, are lacking. Talk is cheap. Even a babbling person can TALK. IT IS TIME TO FULLY CONNECT and MANIFEST!

I want them to realize this. I have tried, for YEARS, to tell them, *'There's more to Christianity then Talk.'* It has done no good. 'SWEET TALK' has FAILED! We have NO MORE TIME FOR FENCE STRADDLING!

We are on the verge of Change. A change brought on by The CHRISTIANS and OTHERS, (who CLAIM: They 'Love'), LACK OF MANIFESTING (Agape Love). Now the WORLD will pay the price. ALL will pay.

I have 'sweet talked' and Manifested quite awhile now. Walking the walk. Talking the talk. FOLLOWING THE LORD Christ 'Big Brother.'

All it seemed to do was to get people to COME TO ME to be their 'miracle worker.'
MANY of these 'Believers'/'Christians.' It Appalls me.

They read the same Book I do...yet have NOT TRULY CONNECTED. So, I 'get hard.' I KNOW WHAT THEY 'HAVE' and WANT THEM TO HAVE THE SAME.
I LOVE them...and it's time they grow up. As a matter of FACT, it is ALMOST PAST TIME! ALL 'GOD LOVERS'...no matter their 'way' and God Name, Need to CONNECT. TOTALLY! For the SAKE OF THE MASSES!

Am I 'tough' on Christians? Yes, I am, yet if you know me well, you'll see I'm tough on ANY who claim 'THEY LOVE GOD.'

Hate is NOT God. “WE ARE RIGHT…YOU MUST BE LIKE US ‘OR ELSE’ are NOT of God. ANY, of ANY Religion that slips into these categories, is NOT of God (no matter what name you call this one).

PEACE is. LOVE is. BROTHERHOOD is. TREATING EVERYONE WELL is. SHOWING is.

If, perchance, you are ‘offended’ that I say LIVE LOVE/SHOW LOVE…perhaps that means you may feel some Guilt. I’m not accusing you…I’m asking YOU to ‘accuse’ yourself. Check WITHIN you. ARE you falling short? DO you need help? DO YOU WANT TO?!Well, help is there for you. JUST ASK!

Remember, you came to ME; I did Not come to YOU.
Remember too, I tell, ‘DO NOT BELIEVE ME…CHECK!’

This life is for everyone…though not everyone WANTS it.
Then too, many want…but FREELY. Without the HUNGER to LEARN!

We are no longer BABIES. We are EXPECTED to learn to use a fork. EXPECTED to dish into the food AND DO SOME SELF FEEDING.

This requires a bit of SELF EFFORT on your part.

IF you are hungry enough, YOU WILL LEARN TO EAT. With OUT being Bottle Fed all your life! Yes, I AM ‘Rough’ On ALL. BECAUSE I LOVE YOU!
Recently, I partook in making a DVD. My second such. In the first, I was serious. Filled with sorrow. In the second, though much covered the first, I was almost always in Laughter.
This has offended some. I was ‘Flippant’ and ‘Sarcastic.’ WHY the DIFFERENCE?

BOTH were done in The Spirit. The Holy Spirit.
I was not acting. I was SEEING.
In the second, SEEING how ALL I’VE TOLD OVER THE YEARS was being treated in a *‘Won’t be in MY time, so why worry’* way.

Oh, FOOLISH GENERATION!

I saw this.

The sadness was Overwhelming within me. It was either LAUGH over the futility of it all…my Time and Sacrifice and Faithfulness to my Creators commands…OR GO ‘MAD!’
I CHOSE LAUGHTER! I was not, AM not, being ‘Flippant’…THE ‘see-ers’ that SAY that are! NOTHING WILL CHANGE THEM! Not until it’s TOO LATE! And THESE are ‘Christians’??

UGH.”

"I don't Believe In Witchcraft...It Doesn't Exist... Nor The Devil"

"That's an interesting statement," grandfather replied. "Yet you say you believe in God. Odd."

"Why Odd?"

"Well, God says they both exist. There are Scriptures pertaining to both. Actually, several. This tells me you have no respect for God, OR what 'He' had written in the Good Book. From the angel Lucifer to the King who went to a witch to seek advice from a dead person...not to mention Christ on His forty day fast.

Seems to me you are one who writes your Own 'Bible.' *Pick and Choose*, then fill in, as YOU like."

(Anger showed in the eyes of the listener.)

"True. You don't like truths. It shows. Your talking to one that is not willing to sit by and let you get away with things. You've come seeking Me. 'To Learn,' you say. Well, you're learning and don't like it.

If you don't believe in witches, etc., it's too bad you haven't traveled with me. You'd BELIEVE THEN!

I've traveled to a home where a possessed one would go into a far-off look, stand up, and float across the room. Under demonic control.

I've seen witchcraft being worked on many. Seen it tried to work on me, too.

I've even seen LUCIFER himself, face to face. Saw him run too, at the name of Christ our Big Brother.

I've had Pastors seek my help in ridding homes of demons...and people.

These things I HAVE SEEN! Yet you 'Don't Believe.'

Odd. One is blinding you at this very moment. Giving you the lie temptation, these things 'don't exist.' You've accepted. This has led you away from the LIVING WORD OF GOD. You are Duped and don't even know it.

You don't want to hear Truth. Leave now and consider what I have said. I wish you well.

Grandfather Tells Of "The Good Time"

When asked if he has ever seen a "Good Time" for the human race, grandfather told this:

"I have been taken into our future. From tomorrow to MANY hundreds, even THOUSANDS of years from now. I have seen things of ungodly horror to what you refer to 'Good Times.' YES! Definitely, 'Good Times' will be. A time of our population's rebuilding…and well past, to when we return to 'as now'…AND WORSE.

As told, mankind will be in shock for a number of years after the 'flip' and our *Mother's* three part roll. As told, it will take some 30 to 40 years to un-shake that shock and start again to get *back to LIFE*. LIVING. It is during that RE-GROWTH Time I see as the BEST of the 'Good Times.'

I saw small villages, people grouping together as one, who lived in African type huts. I've told of this. Here Living started in a big and wonderful way. There was PEACE On ALL The Earth! Forests were returning. Man fought no more with each other. Animals, Birds, Fish and even Insects…as well as the human race, once again 'laid back' and lived 'as one,' in Harmony. The Plant Life reemerged. ALL allowing ALL to live 'as one.'
It was WONDERFUL TO BEHOLD!
PEACE! Blessed PEACE! Oh what a thing to SEE! WISDOM Everywhere!

Mankind had learned their lesson. HO!

An interesting…no, a FASCINATING thing I was shown was a 'Cloth' these future people came up with, somehow. Like GOSSAMER. SUPER Light Weight. Pastel colors. FLOWING. All but a certain group wore this. The other group wore a rough 'Sack Cloth'…very course and as the style worn during Christ's walk. 'Tonics,' etc. These were 'HOLY Men and Women. Their 'badge.'

I have tried to duplicate the 'Flowing Cloth.' I was and am unable to. I have told of this cloth before as well. As told, it was FLOWING. In this 'mass Size,' it could be wrapped three times. 'Layering' according to the weather. Three wrappings for the coldest of weather. Much like a bird's fluffing of their feathers for insulation. How I wish I could duplicate this Now!

The people had learned things that their ancestors knew thousands of years ago. Things I've shared we can do Now, but don't believe it. Though groups were not extremely adapt at these. At least not the 'common' man. The Holy Ones were another matter. They did these things as easily as breathing. These 'Holy Ones' were the wisest of all men/women. They traveled about as 'Judges' and Godly Advisers. Often they would teleport to an 'in need' area and then WALK to the exact spot. They ALL could levitate…and would, to cross rivers, etc. They PREFERRED to WALK just for the 'Smell The Roses' JOY of it. Ho.

I do not know if what I will now tell is BEFORE/DURING or AFTER this 'time,' but I was shown NUDITY of some. Not 'Indecent,' but 'FREE.' Much like an animal. There was no shame in this. CLOTH LESS and 'FREE.' Yes, much as an animal.
Those in this 'way' were experiencing the ALL of BEING ALIVE! A 'nature tough' only one unashamed of no covering can have.

I am telling you what I SAW. Personally, I prefer a covering. To ME, the Loin Cloth is sufficient. I am not 'into' full nudity. Aho?

But these in this way were as WILD Ones. FREE! But not GONE 'Wild.' Aho?

Yes, this time frame to ME, was the BEST of 'The GOOD TIMES.' Aho?"

Grandfather, Always The Clown!

Heyókȟa's are the Countries…CLOWNS! At the drop of the hat, he changes tense moments into ones of LAUGHTER. This is one of his recent ones:

He had to get an EKG at his white Doctor's orders. He took his 11 year old grandson (Sky) with him. They both entered the room. Grandpa took off his shirt and laid it on the table. He had done this before and knew the 'routine.' Sky though had never seen it. As the electrical tabs were being placed on his chest and arms, Sky watched closely…somewhat concerned. Each tab had an 'electric' wire attached.

"What are they going to DO with you Grandpa?"

Seizing the moment, grandfather replied, "They are going to electrocute me, Sky."

"WHAT!"

The nurse looked up and said, "It won't hurt, son."

"Is that right grandpa?"

"Oh, maybe a LITTLE…" (Winking at the nurse). All set, she had Sky stand by the 'reading machine' to show what was going on. Sky was full of interest.

"Ready?" She said. His back was to grandfather. The seeing was turned on. Sky looked, then to grandfather to see HIS reaction.

There was grandfather…TWITCHING and 'VIBRATING' on the table…mouth open saying, "ZZZZZT…ZZZZZZT!"

Sky's eyes POPPED! Then realized grandfather had pulled yet ANOTHER 'Gag'…he began to ROAR in LAUGHTER…then too, Grandfather!

"Hold STILL, HOLD STILL!" the nurse was nearly SHOUTING (she had not seen what was going on behind her back). This made them BOTH Laugh even HARDER! Suddenly Sky 'Back Fired.' TWO ENORMOUS 'Toots' in a row! "I'm Sorry! (between laughter), I didn't mean IT…they just SLIPPED OUT!"

(SO TOO DID THE NURSE! She didn't come back in for a good fourteen minutes!)

They were still giggling at all this as they drove home. Suddenly Sky quieted, looked at grandfather, and said "Grandpa? What will YOU be, when YOU grow up!"

Nature Even Provides Music!

The whole family was at the Pacific Coast beach in Oregon, a rare time. All there, three grandkids, daughter, and even GRANDFATHER'S wife.

Strolling along the beach, gentle breezes and warm sunshine. Just enjoying.

At the surf line, Bell Kelp laid here and there. Grandfather had the children fetch one for all. Grandfather took out his penknife and began cutting the Bell ends into a 'horn,' then slowly sliced the long pointed ends of each. Until he got to the hollow each has. Here he began cutting small sections off until the right diameter to fit lips. He reamed that inner hole's edge. Lifting the 'Horn,' he preceded to blow. A Deep 'Fog Horn' tone came out. Blowing harder, he was able to create three different tones…much to the family's delight!

Each blew theirs. Seven on nature's horn, they walked along, toning. This drew the attention of other strollers. Two came to him seeking how. These two were from San Francisco and in the San Francisco Philadelphia Harmonic, as HORN PLAYERS! Grandfather had then picked different sizes/lengths of kelp.

"The smaller, the Higher the tone pitch," he told. In no time at all, they too joined the group. Shortly, they started thinking. Borrowing GRANDFATHER'S knife, they cut 'finger holes'…as on a flute. IT WORKED! Talk about SOUND! These guys knew how to PLAY! Not just Sound, but NOTES OF MUSIC!

"How did you learn that, grandpa?"

"Oh, learned it from an old Maine Lobsterman, long ago."

"COOL!"

Grandfather knew many surprising things. Always alert to 'different.'

Using this same knowledge, he once had his brother pull alongside a 'rip' tide. The boat was small, the fog thick. Big ships passing all around. His brother was a bit uncomfortable.

"Wish I had my bottle Air Horn," he said. Did, when grandfather was done! (Sounded like a LARGE SHIP!) His brother, "The Apple?" was flabbergasted!

"Nature gives things far beyond food and beauty, brother. Even the STARS CAN SING," grandfather told Him.

Ho.

"Actions and Reactions"

Earth is as a still pond. ONE'S ACTIONS can destroy its stillness…or allow it to remain.

See your actions in that light. To spoil its beauty see yourself as a small pebble. You can either drop it into its stillness and create Long Lasting ripples, or refuse to toss.

Yes, even a Small pebble dropped creates ripples…yet there are those who decide a BOLDER would 'do better.' ALL affects ALL.

HOLD YOUR TONGUE! HOLD and FORGIVE your ANGERS AND FRUSTRATIONS!

Live in PEACE.

This gives YOU inner Peace. THIS GIVES ALL Peace!!

FORGIVE. LOVE. CARE! THINK!

Our WORLD reacts to *YOURS*."

Ho,

Grandfather

Do You Mean...

"Grandfather…that can be Far Reaching. Even on to the Actions and Reactions of SICKNESS! Do you mean we do and CAN 'react' to what we are being TOLD? That if a Doctor says, *'You are dying of cancer, etc.,'* you REACT to that, and DIE of accepting what you are TOLD!?!

"YES! Yes, Yes, YES! You have FINALLY *GOT IT!*

Hear me: If you are told ANYTHING and accept WHAT YOU ARE TOLD By MAN, YOU ARE FAILING TO BELIEVE WHAT OUR MAKER SAYS!

HE says we are MEANT to live to an AVERAGE AGE of 130 Years…Scriptures are FILLED with tellings of HUNDREDS of 'Year old' People. There's a telling of an 'Old' lady that was SO BEAUTIFUL that a KING LUSTED FOR HER. A gal IN HER eighties! It also tells of 'SIN'… DISOBEDIENCE OF MAN…GOING 'DOWN HILL' Due to ACCEPTING MAN over GOD. MAN'S 'Word' Over 'HIS' WORD. THIS is a SIN!

Listen to me: there is a TV Commercial on the air now of a lady who had cancer and was told she had two months to live. Her sister called another Doctor. A 'Cancer center.' They gave 'many Tests' and told her 'NO EXPIRATION DATE.' She NOW HAS NO CANCER!
I do not know what treatments they gave. The FACT IS, NONE WAS NEEDED! Those WORDS ALONE DID THE HEALING! Anything else was just Medicine Man PSYCHOSOMATIC 'Doing'… SHOW! She did NOT want to die. So she ACCEPTED THIS CENTER'S TELLING. THAT is THE VERY MOMENT HER HEALING BEGAN!

We of the 'Medicine Way' get patients who do NOT want 'bad things to be.' So WE PUT ON A 'SHOW!' They BELIEVE IN THAT 'SHOW' and WIN! WE WORK WITH THE MIND. THAT in turn MAKES THE BODY REACT! We give POSITIVE…Positive. NOT NEGATIVE… Positive!

HOPE, not HOPELESSNESS! And they react to THAT and are 'healed.'

Have you ever noticed The LOOKS on people's faces when they hear 'bad news?' How CRESTFALLEN they LOOK? *'I HAVE CANCER/Diabetes/etc…'* and INSTANTLY the *'Oh NO'* (I'm 'DEAD') LOOK, given by the Told One. THIS IS 'VERIFYING' the TELLERS FEARS! SPEEDING UP THEIR DEMISE! The LOOK Alone SPREADS FEAR! The TONE the Teller uses SPREADS FEAR! The telling from the FIRST Told, to OTHERS, CONCRETE THAT FEAR! Friends and family hear, *'Have you HEARD, So and So HAS CANCER/etc.'* THE FEAR SPREADS and IS INFECTIOUS! FEAR acts as a DEATH VIRUS! And the person DIES!

THAT 'sick' person HAS BELIEVED MAN over GOD! FEAR over 'FEAR NOT!'

Do they 'Praise God IN all Things?' Or do they 'Praise' because they are told To, BUT DON'T REALLY MEAN IT?!

You PRAISE until YOU MEAN IT! REALLY mean IT!

Hear me: FEAR IS FROM LUCIFER! This angel is REAL, Yet ALL HE CAN DO is TEMPT! He has BILLIONS of People TO HELP HIM CEMENT HIS LIES! Doctors INCLUDED!

BILLIONS who Do NOT Believe the GREAT CREATOR…'GOD,' OR 'HIS' WRITTEN DOWN WORD! NO! They are CARRYING ON THEIR ANCESTORS' Long Ago ACCEPTANCE of 'SIN.'

'The Sins' of the Fathers' CARRY ON to THE 'SONS.'

It is YOU, the INDIVIDUAL, WHO CAN BREAK THE CHAIN REACTION!

YOU!

If you need help in so doing, GO TO OUR BIG BROTHER! ASK!

He could have come DOWN FROM THAT CROSS, but had a MORE IMPORTANT thing to PROVE. That LIFE CONTINUES! That there IS 'LIFE AFTER DEATH!' He HAD to die TO PROVE THAT TO YOU and ALL! AND TO HIMSELF!

HOW can YOU succeed? 'FOLLOW ME' He TOLD!

It's as simple as that. LOOK AT HIS WAYS OF EXAMPLING. FOLLOW THOSE WAYS! SEEK HIS HELP, for He's BEEN THROUGH IT…and 'PASSED!' Need help? ASK HIM FOR IT! He's there For You! He is STILL VERY MUCH ALIVE!
NOT as a 'spirit' but a BREATHING (as us) BEING, LIVING IN ANOTHER 'LAND'…HEAVEN!

THAT LAND EXISTS! It is as FIRM AS OURS! It is just on a different 'Plain.' HE LIVES/WALKS/TALKS and KNOWS THERE…JUST as He learned HERE!

HE is, in this KNOWLEDGE WAY, the 'FIRST BORN.' The ONE who LEARNED FIRST! Yes, WHAT YOU ACCEPT HERE, causes REACTIONS ALL AROUND YOU. Even to EARLY DEATH!

HEAL Others by BREAKING THE CHAIN of LIES your ANCESTORS' accepted. Change to HEALTH. Change from FEARS too: *'UP YOURS Lucifer! I REFUSE YOUR LIES! I ACCEPT MY MAKER'S WORD over your LIES. GO TO HELL!'*

The *'Get Thee behind me, Satan'* the Christ told: He KNEW it was THE DECEIVER that was using Peter's Tongue…and TALKED DIRECTLY TO THAT DECEIVER. That LIAR. THE ONE TRYING TO RIP OUT HIS BELIEF KNOWING. He was NOT talking to PETER!

It is YOU who must change. YOU who spreads 'good' or 'evil.' WARS to 'PEACE ON EARTH!'

'Our Father, who art in heaven, LET IT BE HERE AS IT IS THERE!' (Paraphrased.)

Now, BREAK THE CHAIN! LIVE a LONG and GOOD LIFE! SPREAD <u>GOOD</u> 'tidings'…NOT LIES, but TRUTH! CHANGE YOURSELF AND YOU CHANGE ALL!

Now, SELAH…Go, and THINK ON THESE THINGS.

Ho."

Sky Fails A Test…And Wins!

Grandfather's grandson, Sky, hopped into grandfather's truck after school. He had a soft grin on his face.
"Grandpa," he said, "We had a test today and the teacher gave me an 'F.' She told me I was wrong on something and I told her I wasn't. She said I was *crazy*."

Grandfather said not a word, waiting for his grandson to complete the telling.

"It was on 'Inanimate things.' Trees, plants, and things. Things she said that live but don't think and talk and stuff. I went down the list on those that do and those that don't. We were to check those that do. ALL do grandpa, so I marked them all as DO!"

Grandfather was grinning, just as Sky, now!

"So she gave me an F. She is wrong, grandpa."

"YES Son, she is wrong. But she doesn't know it. Your teacher is a good woman. She has never LEARNED, Sky. She's as almost ALL the people on our Mother. Almost all have forgotten. Almost all just go by what THEY are taught. This is what she has been taught…and therefore teaches as 'right.' Like all, she never tries, Sky. She is also a Christian…or so she tells. Yet she doesn't Check what the Good Book Says. She just goes on what is taught by others who call themselves 'Christians.' She's a Follower of MAN, Sky, NOT of our GOD Creator.

Forgive her, son. She's just another ignorant one. She means well. Remember that.

SHE may have given you an 'F,' but you've got an A+ in MY BOOK…AND IN GODS!"

Sky's eyes were full of Merriment…JOY!

"I wish she'd come and learn from YOU, Grandpa. THEN She'd know!" and began to laugh.

They BOTH laughed, ALL THE WAY HOME!

Ho.

The Gifting Basket

Grandfather was explaining to several of a way of 'giving your *sins*,' to the Father.

"This is a way some within our Nations do it. It is meaningful, beautiful, and very effective. It is called '*The GIFT(ing) BASKET*.'

In this you Image a Beautiful Basket. Imagining or seeing it into existence. Remember: Thoughts are REAL…thus, what you have imagined by imagery or by 'seeing', is indeed real.

Take your time. Make it in any shape you want. Of any materials you want. It is a basket of Love.

For you who know not how to 'build a basket,' do a box. Wood or cardboard, it matters not.

Once you have this 'completed', go to your knees before Him. Go into Power Prayer, as I have explained. At each 'sin' reminder/showing, take that disobedience, seek forgiveness, be cleansed and then place that sin into your imagined container. Do this with each, till you are cleansed fully.

Now WRAP the container with the most BEAUTIFUL Wrapping you can imagine. Wrap it and decorate it if you please. All this is done in your thoughts. Again, Thoughts are REAL. Aho?

When all is complete, physically lift the container to our Creator…telling 'Him':

'Father, I have a present for you.'

See or Sense 'Him' reaching down and taking it from you. See it being taken up, until it is gone.

What you have done is GIFTING, ALL THE GARBAGE you have accumulated…All the SINS you had, TO GOD! As a GIFT! A PRESENT! That basket is filled with Stinking ROT and Ungodliness. Pure FILTH!

Our Father takes this GLADLY from you, 'His' Child. It is GONE. And you have SEEN it leave. SEEN it Taken. It has become very REAL to you now. 'HE' TOOK IT AND NOW PERMANENTLY OWNS IT! HO."

Sins Of The Fathers

In yet another group teaching, one asked about the Scriptures comment on the *'Sins of the father's going on to the child.'*

"A good asking, my brother. It will take time to answer, so bear with me.
First off, The GOOD BOOK is, beyond doubt, the most misunderstood Book on Earth. Even the many great Bible Scholars fall far short of what it tells. Good as they are.
This doesn't mean to reject their knowledge. It means to learn it and GO DEEPER. You would be remiss not reading their findings.

'*God is IN ALL things.*' Remember this.
As I've shared, we are of 'His' thoughts. 'His' DAYDREAM.
If 'He' didn't daydream you, you would not be. It is that way with everything. Space and all in it, to the tiniest of things. Even that that's smaller than an atom.
ALL are 'His' thoughts.
Thoughts a100% ENERGY.
Thus, we…All Creation…are of one source and all are of the same identical energy.
'One RELATION.'

When the Creator made the first human pair, man and woman, our *today's* race started there.

Each Soul Bearer is of three: Body/Mind/Spirit. I have told you what the three are already.

Of the three, the MIND SOUL is the 'y' of the existence of the other two.

The soul holds ALL that each has done. Thoughts/Reactions/Actions and Deeds.

The first two humans were totally innocent beings when first created. No sin was in them.
Sin entered when they disobeyed their Makers orders and did the opposite.

THAT SIN…that DISOBEDIENCE TO GOD...was thus automatically imbedded into their soul. There Permanently.

THAT was thus WITHIN THEIR BODIES.

When they mated and conceived their firstborn and their next, etc., that Disobedience Memory was in each of the parents. The mother's EGG, the father's SPERM.

Just as I've told a Replanted Body Organ, from one who died to one who lives, carries the deads Soul into that one, the soul of the Living…thus do the Souls of the mating human pair Insert THEIR Soul Memories Into a newborn.

Thus the CHILD carries the SINS of Its parents. It comes automatically!

Think on this. The first to be made many, many years ago. Their offspring mated too. These held the SINs of the first two. They TOO sinned. And on and on. Right up to YOU today…and me. ALL THESE SINS of ALL OUR ANCESTORS AUTOMATICALLY DWELL WITHIN US. Like a disease, we carry this mass collection.

Each new child is born PURE and SINLESS. BUT, we are born INTO sin. Surrounded BY it and born WITHIN it…or IT within us, as the case actually is.

It is true, we need not ACCEPT disobeying. That's each new ones right…AND ability.

ONE refused sin ways. Our Big Brother. Ho.

ALL OTHERS…ALL our ancestors chose to accept sin though. Thus, it carries on to you and me.

THE SINS OF THE FATHERS/MOTHERS ARE IN OUR GENES!

We cannot escape this. It's automatic.

Again, WILL allows us to accept or Reject.

Only the ONE chose to continue his life NOT disobeying. One of, what? Trillions?

Born as we, innocent, He chose to REMAIN as born. Innocent. Ho.

He had HIS Will…just as we do OURS.

IN CHOOSING TO REMAIN INNOCENT, He BROKE AWAY from His Parent's Soul Sins they carried. Starting a NEW 'Blood Line.'

Yet He never married and allowed that bloodline breakaway to help His offspring.

There was NO NEED TOO! Man is BORN to DECIDE to go GOOD or BAD ALREADY. Aho?

Again, it is SELF WILL that is mankind's worse enemy.

The gift of The Creator.

It is what makes US different from ANGELS.

Know this, as Lucifer came into the Garden Of Innocents, he is in OUR 'garden of innocents'…the Innocents we are first born from. Aho?

Now you know why man is born with '*The Sins of the Fathers/Mothers.*'

Can we ESCAPE it?

We can, if we chose as Christ did, but we don't. Thus, we are TRAPPED.

Trapped? *NOT* REALLY! For our Creator made a WAY OUT! 'His' Son, the FIRST BORN of the UN-TRAPPED.

Now, if we WANT to be UN-TRAPPED, we need only go to 'Him' and HIM. Asking for forgiveness AND HELP. We INVITE the BIG BROTHER IN!

It's as simple as that. YET THIS HAS A CONDITION.

You MUST MEAN IT!

Many who ask, ask ONLY to 'save their rears' Just in CASE there IS a 'Heaven and Hell.'

It is these who will be surprised on 'The Day Of Judgment.'

'But I ASKED HIM IN! I CALLED Him LORD!'

Scripture tells this: Not ALL who says *'LORD, LORD'* will ENTER THE KINGDOM OF HEAVEN!

Again, the HEAVEN and the HELL you are taught of in Church, etc., are only PURGATORIES. TEMPORARY!

It is those who are SERIOUS about changing, and 'work' at it, which will enter.

You can NOT 'WORK' your way to Heaven, but you CAN 'work' at REALLY WANTING TO PLEASE YOUR NEW FATHER!

Note: I said NEW father.

For when you decide, you REALLY want to Change, and ASK CHRIST IN TO HELP…YOU ARE THEN 'Born Again.' Only THIS time, ADOPTED INTO THE FAMILY of the FATHER, the SON, The HOLY SPIRIT, i.e., The FAMILY OF GOD!

You have CUT ALL TIES to ALL your ANCESTORS…AND your Earth Parents.

BORN again…INNOCENT. ANOTHER CHANCE! This time, DO it RIGHT!"

"But grandfather, I HAVE done that! HAVE 'asked Him in,' and STILL I sin!"

"Yes, old habits are not easy to break. Yet with our Big Brother's HELP…AND His BLOOD SACRIFICE…AND YOUR DETERMINATION TO BE A CHANGED 'New One,' In TIME, THE OLD WAYS LEAVE. At times, SOME are gone from you INSTANTLY…yet others stay on. ALL WILL GO IF YOU ARE DETERMINED. ALL WILL GO IF YOU TRUST 'Big Brother' IS HELPING.

Hold to that TRUST…and ALL WILL BE NO MORE!

You are NO LONGER TIED to the EARTH BOUND Ancestors 'carryover' of the SINS within the bloodline SOUL MEMORIES you have been carrying.

You are now born into a NEW Blood Line…an <u>ALL</u> GOD Blood Line. You have DIED to SIN and BORN AGAIN NEW!

Too many give this nary a thought, unfortunately.
They WANT Un-entrapment…they SAY…but CLING to the WORLD THEY CLAIM THEY WANT AWAY FROM!

You can NOT serve TWO masters!

'Dad' says, *'CHOOSE! MAKE UP YOUR MIND! I WON'T ALLOW 'Sharing.' It's either him (Lucifer/sin) or ME! I HAVE SACRIFICED MY SON, the ONLY who CHOSE to STAY IN Born with INNOCENTS for YOU! My <u>ONLY</u> SON! I will NOT let YOU 'PLAY GAMES' WITH THIS SACRIFICE! CHOOSE!'*

Yes, we fail. We sin. Yet, IN TRUST, we WIN! It's all a matter of INTENT…TRUST…and WANTING to look UP! So, QUIT looking DOWN! Look UP! THIS is what gets you UN-TRAPPED.

He came for ALL. NO EXCEPTIONS! Color, Looks, Beliefs, Cultures, deeds…they all mean NOTHING to HIM. NOTHING!

The ONLY THING 'HE' WANTS is HONEST WANT!

No 'piddling around' wants; REAL INTENT to change.
Without it, you will be the one 'surprised.' One of MANY, who say, *'But I called Him LORD!'*

HE KNOWS YOUR HEART.
Let's hope YOU do. Ho."

A Question Grandfather

"Yes?"

"Well, it's an old one, but I'd like to hear your input on it. If a tree falls in the forest, and no humans are there, is it heard?"

"Child, perhaps a HUMAN won't, but ALL ELSE will. Fellow trees, to all plant life will know. Each is 'human' in THEIR way. Each feels each pains, hurts, joys, etc. Every tree is related, as are we humans. Each has Eyes, Hearing and full Awareness. I know this is very hard for you to comprehend. It's too 'foreign' to you. 'Crazy'…yet I speak true.

Yes, its falling is heard."

Ho.

"Why Are Parallel Times Now Occurring?"

"It has always happened. As a 'fluke.' It is happening MORE now though. Why? OUR EARTH IS SHIFTING. This starts deep inside. Plates are grating against plates. This creates a static electricity effect. Just as one occasionally sees 'balls of lightning' appearing above a rubbing plate, an Earthquake warning. Perhaps not an IMMEDIATE thing to be, but an area to Watch. Now the inner and deeper plates are rubbing…creating 'riffs'…Rips on our surface CHANGING THINGS.

The openings created are things like Parallel Time shifts, and other happenings. Dimensional Shifts are included as well. All this is natural. This has happened each time our Earth has changed Its axis. The trick is to be aware of this and not go 'mad' during it.

I say MAD. As in CRAZY.

We are all made from our Mother Earth. Same components started us out. We are thus IN TUNE with her. What affects her, affects us. By being AWARE, you will save yourself from this madness. You, as an Aware One, will FLOW with it. Many won't. They will 'snap.'

BE AS A GREEN REED. BEND! Be NOT as a STIFF reed, Dry and standing proud…the 'I AM REED' proud. This STIFFNESS will BREAK THE REED!

Be PLIABLE, LEARN and BEND!"

Grandfather Cooks Dinner

Grandfather was invited to lunch by several Mexican migrant workers. The food 'Blew Him Away.' Chicken legs and wings in Salsa Sauce. It melted in his near toothless mouth! He never got the recipe! Spent several years trying to duplicate it, to no avail and was heartsick over it.

Still, he prevailed.

Grandfather was/is not one that gives up easily…he goes by *'Seek and you will find, Knock and it will be given unto you.'* He knew things often don't come fast and easily…So he kept on...For YEARS!

Then one morning a thought came to him. One he had never tried. 'BOIL.'

With this also came a 'seeing.' That night he bought the legs, wings and a large bottle of salsa. The next day he filled a large pan with all, adding some water. Then he brought this to a boil…stirring as it heated. With this done, he placed and covered the meats into it. He then turned the heat down to the number 3 'simmer' and put a lid on it. He left for town shortly after.

Some four and a half hours later he was back. Opening the still simmering food, he forked out some meat. THAT was IT! THE EXACT TASTE HE'D BEEN SERVED so long ago.

Dinner was done! STEAMED to PERFECTION. The salsa permeating the meat.

Later his wife and grandson came home to 'Perfection.'
The meat falling off the bones…tortilla chips on the side to dip. At the first bite, each was in love!

"No WONDER you liked it so much, honey!"

Sky now cooks this when his friends come over. There is NEVER ANY LEFT!

Ho.

"Grandfather, Can Love Be Created?"

At this, grandfather's eyes lit, a soft smile came across his lips.

"Oh yes, little lass, it can. Indeed it can, or at least helped along," he spoke softly.

"I'm surprised most, no, I take that back…ALL, haven't found that answer. It can be created through MUSIC. As the main 'starter.' Let me explain.

Recall I have told that: *'you are what you eat?'* To *'Use the five senses?'* That we ARE *'all related?'* That we all, *'come from the same mind-womb of the one called Love?'* And too, we are *'of the same elements of our Mother, the Earth?'*

What do all these things have in common? Think about it."

She did, but the look on her face showed she could not find the binding one.

"Child, each I've mentioned correlate with the one answer. What I have given you is on the same 'way' of the Scriptures 7th code. Given much thought, you begin to see connecting 'glue.' An 'adhesive.' But, adhered to WHAT?

Love is not just an EMOTION, it is ENERGY. Energy created by our Great Maker. Energy…THOUGHT…then becomes FACT, with…SOUND.

When you sing to a child, a wee one, it SOOTHES. It brings PEACE. Calmness. The child sleeps. Warmly tucked into your arms. No fear. No cares. No worries. Simply Trusting, Loving, Protected BABYHOOD.

CAN Love be created? YES, by MUSIC!

Music is based on the heart beat of all. Our mother Earth has a heartbeat. The Stars have a heartbeat. All life is based on the Heart Beat of…love.

All around us, every land, every people, use the simple tone of but one instrument: The DRUM. Originally, the FEET were the 'drum,' then was added the toeing by Sticks and by Rocks, and too the clapping of hands. Then was added the vocal sounds: Hums, Yips, Yells. All very primitive, but all on the same theme: THE HEART BEAT.

As is the Heart, so too is the MIND.

'You are what you eat.' YOU ARE WHAT YOU HEAR Too! What you LISTEN TO is FOOD FOR THE BRAIN! LISTEN: WARRIORS receive WAR BEATS to work themselves into

FRENZY. In that Sound Way, Soldiers are lead to war, BRAVELY, by Drummers, Fife players, Bagpipes. THEY GO TO THEIR DEATHS IN ONE MIND! All, controlled by SOUND.

Today's kids thrive on Hard Rock…Music on HATE/Destroy/Kill/Rebel...And they do. Reacting in mass or singularly. THEY 'EAT' of a Grating 'OFF TONE.' An IRRITATING Tone NOT OF LOVE.

How can we, 'man,' Create LOVE? EAT LOVE SOUND!

All mankind, of even those of the STARS, have ONE THING IN COMMON: MUSIC!

IF we can COMBINE OUR MUSIC of GOOD FEELINGS, we can CREATE GOODNESS TO ALL ABOUT US. LOVE!

As told, MUSIC is the 'Main Starter.' START THERE. THEN, use ALL five SENSES in a Godly, Correct manner. Within these five Senses, PROPERLY USED, Love COMES IN. Thus, yes Love…CAN be CREATED.

Ho."

"Grandfather, Do We Need To Fast To Get A Vision?"

"NO! Visions can come at ANY time, in wakening state to early sleeping state...WITHOUT fasting. If the Creator wants to show you something, HE WILL DO SO!

Your job is to SEE and then to CHECK on what you've been shown.

I fast many times. From extremely long to only one meal. In the wilderness to just going about my day. It is a WRITTEN COMMAND TO FAST.

I have had many visions, yet few are during a fasting time. I do not share ALL my seeing and those I do are shared with very few. The vision I call my 'Great Vision' I was TOLD to share with ALL.

No, it does not require fasting to be shown. Ho."

"Would it be permitted to ask another question?"

"Certainly Ask."

"Well, you fasted 69 days. The 'vision' given, isn't that more a BODY STARVED HALLUCINATION?"

"Son, I suppose ALL visions ARE 'Hallucinations.' At least of a sort. On my 69 day fast, I took Vitamins and Minerals daily. I kept my health up. I was not fasting for a vision…I was just FASTING. I had no idea how long I would do so. I went by what felt right. It turned out to be that long, was my MIND 'Starved?' It may have STARTED to be. I QUIT THE MOMENT I BEGAN THINKING 'WRONG.' This LONG AFTER the vision was given.

I started when I felt Right to start…and quit when it was THE TIME to quit. When I began NOT THINKING CORRECTLY…in this instance, when I had DELAYED Reactions in decisions, I QUIT! I literally drove STRAIGHT TO a Drive In restaurant and bought a hamburger. To be less than eight minutes after realizing.

Are they 'hallucinations?' Tell me this, ARE THEY…when they COME TRUE!"

"I Have A Hard Time Forgiving"

"Most do. To forgive is a wonderful thing. An EXPERIENCE. It truly makes you FEEL GOOD inside. Yet many SAY they 'Forgive' yet keep coming back to the REMEMBRANCE of the occasion they have 'forgiven.'

I've found that Forgiving and FORGETTING are two different things, yet they work together. You see, I've found: FORGIVING is REMEMBERING that you…FORGAVE!"

Winter Camp

It was late when grandfather and Sky set up camp. Swirling snow and very close to zero Degrees. Shoveling off a flat spot, they laid down insulated silver 'cloth.' This to keep the cold from rising through the tents floor. Frozen ground made staking difficult but grandfather had come prepared. The hatchet did the job.

They were using their favorite tent. A three man/three seasons Clip Flashlight. Their Wiggy's sleeping bags were the best made. Sky to sleep in the 60 Antarctic and grandfather in the Zero degree Wiggy's HUNTER. Both were extra long and wide. Each preferring to snuggle in. The three man tent, with all gear, was wonderful for two.

"Two Man tent is too small for two," grandfather had said. "Great for ONE though." In Bags and In Tents, he didn't mind the extra weight. Preferred it for comfort. Sky too. They used the 'Indian sled' grandfather had made and were using Ojibwa Snowshoes.

"I wouldn't have any BUT Ojibwas," grandfather said. "They part thick willows, you don't need to 'spread eagle' walk. I've tried many styles. To me, these are THE 'Shoes' to own!" He had bought pairs for each grandchild, his wife, and himself. The campsite was right in a large open field. No wind or snow protection at all. This to teach Sky 'Extreme camping.'

"With insulation under the tent, never beyond the tents floor, Sky…always a bit Less. Otherwise, water will collect on it and seep into the floor…" and with snow piled about two feet high on the sides and back…'home' was ready.

"The snow tightens the cloth AND keeps wind seepage from coming in from below," grandfather said. They had the Rain Cover over the tent so the snow was against that.

Sky, in unzipping the opening, went too fast. Catching the zipper onto the overlapping cloth. Not knowing better, he kept yanking. Really, 'locking' the zipper…and the flap wide open still. "STOP!" grandfather shouted. Sky froze!

"I Didn't KNOW," he was close to tears.

"It's OK son. You are here to learn. Next time when you feel the zipper 'lock', stop IMMEDIATELY or it gets worse. ALWAYS PULL A ZIPPER VERY SLOWLY. Many zippers have been broken due to going too fast. You'll learn. That's what this is all about. Aho?"

"Yes grandfather." It took awhile but eventually all was right again. Sky headed out for firewood.

"All set?"
"Yes."…and the campout began.

Breaking Camp

Due to the heavy rains and snows…and where grandfather set up the campsite, ALL Wood gathered was SOPPED! Grandfather had expected this but said nothing to Sky. The poor kid surged the area HARD looking for firewood. He LOVED a campfire.

Try as they could, no wood took to flame.

"We will COLD CAMP, Sky. There will be times you will not DARE have a fire. This is good. You will learn you can still enjoy nights out, fireless."

Sky didn't look too pleased but was willing.

"No use standing here in this cold, let's get into our bags and swap lies!"

The night went well. Sky like a turtle with head in shell. Deep within his oversized bag…snoring away. Grandfather awoke to do his morning prayers. He used this awake time to tap the tent's accumulated snow off Its top and sides. Insulating the tent from the weather even more. He worked WITH nature, not against it. Twice that night he did this, and each time cut out an air hole at the head and base. Not allowing a dangerous situation within. The tent was low and small. Not a Dome style but one designed to let winds slip easily over. A 'ground hugger'…yet towards the versatile, easy 'setup' room needed.

Finally, Sky awoke. As expected, 'bored.'

"I can't get back to sleep, grandpa."

"Want to go in and have breakfast?"

"Yes."

This they did.

Later, they went back to bring things home.

They turned the two bags inside out to allow perspiration to evaporate. Shaking the bags to rid of any debris first…then draped over the shower's rod. Later they redid the 'turning' and stuffed each into their sacks. They then hung the two sleeping mats/dried and put those in yet another sack. The tent was last. It too turned inside out and shaken before drying after, as above and put into ITS sack.

"Take Good Care of your gear son. Always! Do all possible to not roll and pack anything that's wet. They will mildew and rot…AND make a COLD sleep in winter. Aho?"

"AHO!"

The snowshoes were slow dried by standing upright in the tub…checked for cuts, etc., then stored in a dark place. The sled toweled off and stored as well. All was back to normal.

"Can we do this again, grandpa…SOON?"

"You bet, son, Very soon! WITH Fire."

A Broken Heart

The teen came to grandfather. The *'love of his life'* (AGAIN) had broken off with him. He bemoaned this fact to grandfather.

"I wonder, Why?" he said.

Grandfather looked at him and answered, "Son, it's your mustache."

"My MUSTACHE!"

"Yes. She told me your kisses were weak enough, without having to sift it through one of THOSE things!"

☺

Grandfather Battles The County

It seemed the local 'Government' has only one thing in mind: RULES.
These to bring in more money to their coffers. 'Coffers' that just seems to give raises for their 'people' and to hire MORE of their 'people.' Permits for everything. Rules to obey or be heavily fined.

"Now I'm not against rules. Quite often they have good reason. Not ALL though. Least not to me. I had nine dogs. My own sled dogs. All males and all 'fixed.' Big Malamutes. A pretty quiet bunch in general. One day an 'official' letter arrived. I was running a KENNEL! And this 'UNLICENSED.' I called them and asked, *'What constitutes a Kennel?'* The reply, *'Boarding other dogs and breeding.'*

When I told them they were all MINE, all MALES, and all FIXED…they gave in. I was 'legal.'

This went on and on. One 'illegal' thing after another. Each time I beat them. But I'm fed up with these dingbats. Moving to a more 'lenient' county.

All States have rules. It's a matter of knowing them and TWISTING THEM to your advantage that will get you by.

HAS to be done, for your pocket Book and your sanity. Not BREAKING their rules, but learning them to YOUR advantage. It CAN be done!

I was told I needed a SEPTIC TANK to live on my land in my TIPI! A few thousand dollars for a Tipi POT? Ridiculous! I spent $75.00 for an Out House Permit. So much for their money grabbing Building Permits!

I was living in a camp trailer on our land. 'AGAINST THE LAW!' BIG daily fine to live beyond six months at a time in one (we are 'Recreational land'). I told them, 'OK…I moved into this on January 6th. I still have over a month.' So, some weeks later, another *'YOU ARE BREAKING THE LAW. YOU ARE ONLY ALLOWED TO LIVE IN THAT TRAILER FOR six MONTHS AT A TIME, YEARLY!'*

Called them, *'I moved in on January 6th, it is now December the 26th of a NEW YEAR! So, I HAVE six MONTHS TO GO in this NEW YEAR!'* Beat them at their own game.

Here they tax your home on the number of CLOSETS! Build with NONE or ONE (vacuum cleaner/etc.). Others tax by the number of bedrooms. Build with ONE BIG bedroom that uses Fabric Folding curtains!

Other areas you are tax FREE if on STILTS or one SKIDS or HAVE NO PERMANENT ROOF. USE THEIR RULES TO FIGHT AGAINST THEM!

Is a DOME a ROOF or a WALL??? Worth looking into. Are you in a low rain or snow area? A Heavy Vinyl ROOF can replace a wood TAXABLE one. See?

I am building a small 'cabin' Dome on our new land. *'What's THAT? A Root Cellar?'*

I'll build another as a Smoke House. (Hey, we have food we store and I DO Smoke!) *'Lie?'* Maybe. I prefer BENDING to accommodate my life style without THEIR money making 'Rules.' Will I get away with it? Don't know. Probably for a while. Enough time to get the money needed to fit their 'rules.'

The way things are going, rules won't matter. Only survival will. 'They' will be worrying about their OWN rears and not mine. Our economy and future war will have ALL scrabbling. *'Where to LIVE? How to EAT? How to GET THERE'*...not the 'job' will be their concerns...and this pretty soon, at that.

Knowing their rules AND THUS HOW TO BEND THEM to YOUR advantage is WISE.

There was one who lived by this. Breaking 'THEIR' Rules constantly: Jesus! HO.

'I have come to SET MEN FREE.'

Ho."

Thanksgiving

"Grandfather, soon Thanksgiving Day is about to come. Why on EARTH would you Indians celebrate it! What do THEY/YOU have to be *'THANKFUL'* For?"

Grandfather looked the asker directly into his eyes, then said:

"It is true we of the true overseers of this land have been sorely mistreated. This from the Pilgrims first day upon our shores. It is told on that day our ancestors hid as these strange two legged sat down their *canoes'* sails and waded to the land. Now here they began to explore. In this they came upon the Peoples' winter Food storage, entered…and raided the foods. I do not doubt these tellings.

It is also true we, the People, saved their lives a bit later when they were hungered. The first' Thanksgiving' day. In truth, we gave of our compassion. Doing as The Great Spirit would want any to do.

Yes, we were out bred and out fought. Eventually losing our great Eden to the newcomers. BUT WE NEVER FULLY LOST OUR TOUCH WITH THE WORLD OF SPIRIT.
The WORLD of ONE SUPREME BEING! Even till today.

For THAT, I am THANKFUL.

Now our trials are reversing. Folks as yourself, come to us seeking truth. Seeing that your churches are as dry bones, that your way has brought little more than destruction. You young people search and the Great One says, *'LOOK! I STILL HAVE A FEW WHO CARRY THE LIGHT. GO TO THEM!'*

At first, we were leery, 'You have taken so much of what has always been ours. Now you come to take what little we still have, our *touch*?'

Many still think this way and refuse to release what little they still have of that. We are fast losing the touch. WE HOARD. This to our race's shame.

We were Given, TO GIVE!

The Great Spirit knew you would be in need once again. This time, not to sustain the body, but to SUSTAIN YOUR SOUL.

Some of us recognize this, and give. Some refuse. Some condemn those of us that do this *'We are ALL One Relation'* walk. We who recognize, The Great Spirits Love is not for us alone. Despite that, we few *'givers'* carry on, as all should. OF THAT, I AM THANKFUL!

For you, who truly SEEK, I am Thankful for THAT AS WELL!

No, I do not 'thank' for the overthrow of our lands…nor the lewdness your people have brought. But I AM Thankful THAT WE CAN HELP HEAL YOU!

Yes, for that, I give 'THANKS.'

Perhaps we will be instrumental in returning all to the realization there is more to Life than the so called 'civilized' ones know.

You are LOST. You hear the 'voice in the wilderness': MAKE STRAIGHT THE WAYS OF THE 'LORD'…AGAPE LOVE!

That I was born wearing one shoe of the Whites and one moccasin of the People…that The Great One has allowed me to 'bridge' between our ways and your ways AND THAT THERE ARE OTHERS DOING THE SAME…for THAT I am TRULY THANKFUL!

That EVERY 'NATIVE' OF OUR LAND is a LIGHT, just by BEING! Whether they know it or not…I AM THANKFUL! For WE ARE YOUR REMINDER OF WHAT YOU LEFT.

Now the Black Line and Red line are REVERSING! OF THAT, I AM THANKFUL!

As Black Elk came to tell of the coming of the Whiteman, My name was given to tell that NOW, the REDMAN…our SACRED ONENESS…Is coming. Nigh, It Is HERE!

To ALL of the 'Red Skin,' just for BEING, I AM VERY VERY THANKFUL!

I just wish THEY were, as well. THEY JUST DON'T REALIZE THEIR IMPORTANCE OF BEING BORN IN THAT SKIN.

WE are the CONSCIOUS OF ALL THE EARTH! The PHYSICAL Conscious!

In that I am able to tell you this: I AM THANKFUL!

Ho."

"Grandfather, Do You Have Any Regrets?"

"Other then, so few listening? Yes, I have regret. I have been in the 'White World' almost too long. This to help the world know they have the ability to change, and change our everyday situations. As you know. What you don't know has its price.

I've had to ignore my 'red side' to do this. The side, I love dearly. For the sake of All, I've had to often overlook the few…My 'People.' The Native American. This, I regret.

I have not done a Bear Dance in some five years. I have had only one Sweat in more than that. I've had no time to go on a Quest, in nearly seven years. Haven't had 'Quiet Time' in nearly five years. All my time has been to get to the Earth's masses, leaving the Red few, in second place.

This is a side I love much, and Miss Much.

I need to return.

The simplicity of it is beautiful. Also AWESOME. In this 'way' is Simplicity, Inner Peace (at least to me) and of Purity. It's a way of innocence.

I have given my time and energies to a massive household. It is time to go to my room. 'Home.' Back to the Moccasins, I have as well.

I so MUCH, want to go 'home.' Just me and 'dad,' hand-in-hand, in this garden of Inner Peace that still a few of the old 'Medicine Way people' have. I miss that.

Because of my White skin, I have not been considered 'Indian' by my native brethren. Because of my White skin, my white brethren have not taken me seriously, as 'Indian.'

It took me YEARS to get comfortable WITH mySELF. Walking in two worlds is HARD.

I've gotten used to it though.

I do not dance at Pow Wows, I dance in private, to the Creator. Never alone. 'He' dances with me.

Yet I have had no TIME to dance, in many years. Too busy trying to help the world.
I need to get back to my roots: American 'The People' INDIAN. For it is THAT blood that runs beneath my white skin.

I have fought ‘the Good Fight’…Now it is time to go to where I am most comfortable…my ‘home.’

I will NEVER be accepted by my red brethren, or my white ones. Oh, a few, yes, but just a few. I’m used to it now. I am no longer a lonely man in a world that seems to ‘categorize.’ It still saddens me, I must admit, but that’s the way it is. Yes, I’ve gotten used to it.

I came from God, I will return to God…in the forests, alone…and eventually to the Great Land.

I am not alone. I am lonely only when I THINK: *‘I am alone.’*

Yes, I regret. I regret I have had to be away SO LONG!

Ho.”

The Drum

"Grandpa, I wish I had my drum." This as Sky and grandfather set high atop grandfather's 'praying hill,' overlooking the Kittitas Valley.

They had come to 'just be with The Creator'…smelling the spring's newness, watching the stars and generally enjoying all that 'He' had given.

"Forgot it, huh?"

"Yeah. It would sure be nice to have Its sound, now."

Grandfather reached to the back seat of the truck and brought forth an empty two liter plastic pop bottle. Taking off the cap, he handed it to his grandson.

"Hold it at its base. Cup it there at Its base with your hand. Use the other to lightly beat Its side with your fingers, Sky. You have there a very soft toned drum. It's very soothing."

Sky did as directed. It added to the pleasure of that of the '*All Around.*'

Too Bad There's No Cure For Hair Loss

This brought laughter to all. All but GRANDFATHER, that is! HE looked SHOCKED!

"GOOD GRIEF! THERE IS!! I'd forgotten ALL ABOUT IT! What an IDIOT!

Here I am balding away AND I KNOW A CURE! DANG!"

"What IS IT?"

"Whoa…I'm here to teach you to Connect and learn things on your OWN. Not to just 'give you a FISH!'

I will give you hints. If you're REALLY interested, then YOU take these hints AND FIND OUT FOR YOURSELF."

Two balding men and a thinning woman looked disappointed.

"Sorry about that…but you've got to learn sometime. This is one of those learning's. OK, Most…not ALL…but MOST Hair Loss is caused by lack of blood circulation to the scalp. Nature provides certain stimulants that bring that look back. There are both an ANIMAL and a PLANT stimulator. Actually a number of both. FIND ONE AND YOU ARE ON YOUR WAY!"

"Which One?"

"Go ask the plant. Go ask the four-legged. I've taught you 'God is in all things'…that nature has AWARENESS and that you CAN converse. DO as I've told and ASK THEM."

"That's not fair…"

"It's not 'fair' to take up my time either! It's not 'fair' to GIVE and see you return and return, time after time either. So, if you TRULY WANT, Truly HUNGER, then you already know how to get your answer(s).

Don't look DISAPPOINTED in ME! GET OFF YOUR 'DUFF' AND GET BUSY!

HO!"

You Don't Believe Miracles Exist?

"On the contrary. They most certainly DO. What I've learned are most of what mankind calls 'miracles' are Natural cures…once you learn how to do so.

I will tell you of one I call a true miracle. One that happened to me just recently.

As many know, I'm an utter 'DUH' when it comes to computers. WAY beyond STUPID! For the life of me, I can't grasp the computer 'geek' talk. NO Book explains in 'Farmereez.' Well, this has stalled me, even to writing lessons, OR Books.
I have to hire one to get them in correct readable and presentable.

After hiring to get these done right, most of any profits are eaten up by that alone.

A Book I've worked on for well over a year, was about to be scraped (This one folks!)…To get it ready for printing was WAY over our heads. Upwards of $60,000.00.

An IMPOSSIBLE situation.

But then came my MIRACLE!

In prayer over this quandary, I was deep in contemplation. SUDDENLY *'DO IT YOURSELF'* popped into my mind.

'Nah, impossible.'

Then MORE came:

'You have FRIENDS willing to teach you, in YOUR WAY, how to DO. SEEK THEM.'

You have a Computer, you CAN learn to USE IT with these helpers.

You have only your OWN FEARS to overcome.

GOD is NOT a God of FEARS!

I began to think, 'Gee, Maybe…'

At THAT THOUGHT, my eyes were led to the left. There, FLOATING EFFORTLESSLY, was the GRANDEST Native American Eagle I HAVE EVER SEEN!

This is RARE in our winter months. I've only seen an eagle here in winter, once before.

IMMEDIATELY I WAS AT PEACE!

I sent out a 'HELP!' request. It was answered IN MINUTES!

I HAD MY VOLUNTEER!

Within less than an hour, I learned things I've never been able to do on a computer before. Not just ONE thing, but THREE!

Three in UNDER AN HOUR! And here I've spent over SEVEN YEARS of being UNABLE TO DO! And this ON MY VERY OWN, WITHOUT HELP!

It's like a DAM has burst. A MIRACLE! A REAL one, to ME!

ONLY 'DAD' can do THAT!

Yes, I certainly DO 'believe in miracles!'

HO!"

Reader, what you will now read is what I write like:
"I was 1 day going 2 C-ATL, and saw 3 that needed help… "
Translation: "I was one day going to Seattle, and saw three that needed help."

Do you ever see any who might want to go somewhere? Maybe to Spain or Africa to maybe China? I SPELL MY WAY, I hit WRONG KEYS, I MISSPELL BADLY, and THIS BOOK WAS IN THAT 'WAY'…LOTS to REPAIR! See?

THAT YOU ARE READING THIS BOOK, IS A MIRACLE!

HO!

“Grandfather, What Is Your Take On The World Today?”

“Well, to be blunt, not good. I'm watching my Great Vision get into it deeper and deeper. Look at our situation today: We are in the throes of a World financial collapse. The U.S.A. is going to be hurting, Big Time, at any day, as I see it.

To recoup, war repairs that, but there's ALWAYS a Loser. We in the U.S.A. have gotten ourselves so involved with alliances WE are in danger. If we don't back our allies, then THEY are in danger. If we pull out of the ‘Arabia’ wars…some, who have allowed us to use their Country as a staging area, well, once WE go, THEY are exposed. REVENGE against them will more than likely take place. As an Ally, we are obligated to go help. This is not easy. THEY are in the ‘area,’ WE are far away. WE will have to ship Everything THERE, to 'help.’ We are already well beyond our financial means. This means chances are, WE go WELL beyond our means…or simply don't go to help.

Breaking our ‘contract’ of Alliances(s). THIS WILL NOT BE FORGOTTEN! Suddenly we ARE *‘The Great Satan’* To ALL Muslims. If we DO go, here in our own Country, to the masses, we (Government) are ‘Satan’ too! As I see it, we have been backed into a corner that CAN have no escape.

Go ‘There’ to die, or stay HERE to die…or CHANGE OUR WAYS back to Love and let 'HIM' protect us…and ALL. THAT (to me) is our ONLY WAY OUT.

So far, this ‘out’ is being ignored. This has been exampled many times. The last: HOLOCAUST!

The Jews claimed, ‘Godliness,’ that claim was with mouth only (in most), not Heart.

WE are JUST LIKE THAT here.

Tongue, not true HEART.

It wasn't until the Jews stood before the death chambers, that they became SERIOUS!

Too Late.

WE are going to be LIKE THAT, too!

Hope? Yes…in being COMPASSIONATE to others’ *ways* and KNOW we are ALL RELATED. PEACE towards each other. LOVE towards each other. CARING about ALL.

IF the VAST MAJORITY can enter these 'ways', then things will calm down. Yet, the way things ARE going, well, man will turn to man. The ‘peace giver’…THE TRUE ANTI-Christ. Lucifer HIMSELF!

This is where we are heading for RIGHT NOW.

When that occurs, The Death Camps’ HOLOCAUST will not be in a One Country…it will be in THE WHOLE WORLD.

I'm telling you because you've asked.

Whose fault is it? Not our President. Not our Congress or Senate, but YOU. You ALONE! MILLIONS of ‘You.’ People who do Not obey these words: ‘PRAY FOR YOUR GOVERNMENT(s)’. This on a DAILY basis.

No, you MAY pray, but DAILY. Most pray for CHANGE of LEADERS…because they HATE the Leaders now in power. Yet our Creator says, 'He' GIVES US OUR GOVERNMENT LEADERS.

If 'HE' Gave, WHY DO YOU HATE? WHY DO YOU COMPLAIN?

'He' doesn’t say to do THAT. Yet most do. In this, you are telling 'HIM' that 'He' IS UNTRUSTWORTHY…perhaps MEAN…maybe even STUPID. You, as a parent: How long would YOU put up with this from your OWN children?

Well, our Maker has 'His' limits too…and YOU ARE GOING TO FIND THAT OUT UNLESS YOU APOLOGIZE and TURN AWAY from ‘doing’ your OWN ‘Thing.’

You may think I'm being a bit ‘crazy’ here. That's alright. So far I HAVE BEEN BACKED that what I've shared, is TRUE. I do not doubt, AT ALL, that what I've told WILL BE VINDICATED.

Look about you now. Look back on my years of warnings. ARE YOU SO BLIND YOU CAN NOT SEE it IS HAPPENING?

Well, I see no great change, therefore I do not see much hope. ‘What is my *take* on the world today…Doom.”

“Well, we've still time. The sky hasn't turned red yet.”

“You’re right, but it’s looking pretty darn PINK, to Me!”

HO.

"Grandfather, You Are A Miracle Worker"

"I know because I am a nurse at the hospital in Blain. The one you brought a woman from the brink of certain death to full recovery."

"On the contrary my sister. HE cures. Not me. Yet there's more. Do you recall I told you I AM YOU?"

"Yes."

"Well sister, I MEANT JUST THAT! You see, YOU are 'The Miracle Worker.' We ALL are! I have shared the Holograms. I have shared that I am your 'Up Stairs' knowledge. That I am YOUR OUTREACH in your seeking Truth. I have shared the word 'CAN'T' and 'CAN' are both POSITIVE words. That you GET WHAT YOU SAY. That you GET WHAT YOU EXPECT.

Billions have read The Good Book. BILLIONS! Some can quote it, verbatim even. I TELL YOU TRUE…of those BILLONS, perhaps ONLY TWELVE SOULS UNDERSTAND IT! Twelve, sent today, FOR today. To awaken any who seeks TRUE truth TO that TRUE TRUTH.

Big Brother was, and is, the ONLY who holds the Full Knowledge of Mans' abilities. He tried to teach this. Both in words and by deeds.
The 'perhaps twelve' I speak of, includes myself. Though we are VERY weak at this ourselves. This I readily admit.

Some call me, as you…some even say I am a prophet. In the New Testament, you can read what a prophet does. In that, I suppose I am, yet I leave that for others to say. I lay no claim to it. Even as Christ said, *'YOU say this…I let others say.'*

I can honestly take no credit for good done. I only follow. He is in me. Dwells within my being. As I've told, *'If you see any good in me, it is He doing that good. If you see any bad coming from me, it is ME.'* You see only 'good.' ASK THOSE CLOSEST TO ME. They are with me daily. THEY Know! No, there is no 'good' in me. In SELF. Only when I am aligned with Him am I seen as 'good.' Ho.

Call me as I am: YOU…in/of your own 'upstairs' knowledge.

As I deal with many 'I AM's,' I see each as an outreach of my own Deep, Deep Inner SELF. My OWN Thoughts PROJECTED. I have a close family member about to be jailed. This for some time. VERY close to me. I seem to be 'callous' to those that know.
'Uncaring'/'Unloving'/'Indifferent.' This is not at all true…at least in the knowledge I Fully KNOW. That person is an OUTREACH of MY OWN Deep. Jail time is ME, trying to ALIGN

that ungodly Deep, Deep to PURITY. Allowing this so I can have INNER PEACE. To the observer I am NOT being a good person by not 'backing.' No, I am CLEANSING my INNER THOUGHTS. Hopefully, this will do this alignment and there will once again be Inner Peace within myself...my 'FAMILY' that has projected in this way. I '*Practice what I Preach*,' I KNOW of what 'life' is all about.

To try to get people to understand, I am a 'cast out.' I do not 'align' to their common thought-ways. I am the 'BORN WITH' Knowledge that they don't want to face and that they have walked away from. A 'Thorn in their side.' The REMINDER. The INNER SELF that is PHYSICALLY 'Shaking them up.' People are basically quite comfortable in their pathways...and don't WANT to be reminded of what they have accepted over what they CAME WITH. Thus, I am 'enemy' to many. I AM AN ENEMY TO ONLY My SELF, really. My Deep, Deep WANTS to sin. Therefore, my fights are many. I am Born INTO sin. It is Appealing as all get out. Self pleasures. I HAVE COME TO HATE IT! My HEART belongs to GOD. My COMMITMENT is a REAL COMMITMENT.

Over the years, this has gotten much stronger in me. Daily...DAILY...I align more and more with LOVE. The TRUE GOD! It's a nice way to go, but it is a HARD way to go. You are constantly battling sin. The Holograms are constantly SHOWING you your Deep, Deep. It never ceases. ONLY YOUR FULL COMMITMENT gives you a good chance of becoming, *'One, with the Creator.'*

Yes, the 'work' of WANTING TO WALK WITH HIM is HARD! Yet, I have found it SO SATISFYING, It's Worth EVERY MOMENT of it, to me.

You have sat with me for several hours now. You have HEARD much, but until you DECIDE to CHECK yourself, what I have told...it's mere Words. NO KNOWLEDGE is REAL KNOWLEDGE until you <u>KNOW</u>! Not 'know'...not 'Know'...not kNOwING ABOUT...but <u>KNOW</u>!

You will walk away with much to THINK on. Go BEYOND 'Thinking'...go into VERY DEEP thinking – CONTEMPLATING! Then TEST IT! The Creator will see that, and PROVE to you all I've told is TRUE FACT!

Do NOT 'test' Him via SELFISH matters. The 'PROVE IT'...*Let me win the Lottery*. Instead, let Him PROVE it by HIS WAY! He WILL do so in a way you cannot deny is PROOF. Aho?

Yes, go with an open mind...a 'crack' in the 'Door' of the 'Up Stairs' knowledge. I have done all I can do to open the 'door.' From now on you are on your own. As you learn, Practice and DO.

Warning though: NEVER TAKE CREDIT! EVER!

No, I am not a 'miracle' worker. It's just YOU showing YOURSELF 'things' you have hidden deep within yourself.

'*YE ARE as gODS!*'

HO."

Food For Thought

Long List...sorry but may be of interest to all here.

Regarding the FOOD SHORTAGES – WE (USA), are NOW GETTING INTO.

I'm starting to get 'panic' mail. People who have CLAIMED to 'believe' what I've foretold in 'Listening.' LISTENING MY FOOT! Now finding UN-STOCKED SHELVES at the Supermarkets! HAVEN'T PREPARED! Have NOT paid attention and NOW 'Panicking.'

"What can me/We DO, Grandfather?"

Want to say DIE...but can't.

HEAR ME, WHILE YOU STILL CAN (if YOU CAN)...stock up on FLOUR (PUT in five Gallon Plastic/LIDDED Pails). KEEP FROM RODENTS and 'Fresh.'

Go to FEED STORE and BUY a BIG BAG of HORSE SALT! Yes, you are READING RIGHT! Not a BLOCK but like a ROCK SALT. This has EVERY Vitamin and Minerals PEOPLE BUY at Pharmacies. GRIND IT AND USE AS YOUR REGULAR SALT. YOU WILL SAVE HUNDREDS OF DOLLARS! A BIG BAG costs UNDER thirty dollars and will LAST for YEARS! Giving you your NEEDED Vitamins/Minerals...GRIND into Table Salt form.

HONEY! In five gallon batch if you can. PRICY but WASN'T seven years ago when I went public and told. LOOK FOR THIS as our bees ARE DYING and prices will go SKY HIGH!

POPCORN...the type you NEED to put in PAN to Pop.

Store CEREAL!

SAVE BONES and boil as MEAT STOCK! (YOU will start eating A LOT of STEWS AND SOUPS SOON!)

DON'T WASTE Potato SKINS: WASH and cut out Skin 'eyes' before PEELING! SAVE THOSE SKINS, and oven cook OR deep fat fry...POTATO CHIPS!

Do you like ASPARAGUS? SAVE THE HARD ENDS YOU SNAP OFF! Makes VERY GOOD Soup!

BUY at LEAST ONE GOOD (in Color) 'EDIBLE PLANTS' Book! You will WANT to eat! And you WALK BY/ON FOOD EVERY DAY!

Won't hurt to look into Edible INSECTS as well! GET ON THE INTERNET AND COPY OFF information...INCLUDING How to COOK them. I know this turns stomachs...maybe you won't eat them but IF YOU MIX WITH OTHER MEATS AND FEED THEM TO YOUR FAMILY (without telling) THEY WILL...NEVER KNOW! THEY stay healthy, you save money or the Insects Live and you STARVE TO DEATH! Your 'choice.'

CONNECT TO our 'DAD' in THIS TIME. Shut up and LISTEN! IF you do HE WILL SHOW YOU PICTURES and TELL of food sources and Water sources.

GET Soup and Meat STOCK (cans).

Milk drinker? GET DRIED MILK. IF mixed and LEFT IN REFRIGERATOR the 'fakeness' GOES AWAY. Won't be 'Fatty' but FAR BETTER than JUST MADE.

Hear me: WE WASTE TOO MUCH! THINK before you toss out! Even leftovers should be frozen and then added together as a STEW.

THINK, Folks...THINK!

These are just a TINY BIT and BASICS. Advice ONLY. I do NOT WANT <u>YOU</u> 'Crying' to me BECAUSE YOU HAVEN'T PAID ATTENTION! If you don't listen NOW...TOUGH!
I've done all I can for you…good luck...DON'T WASTE! Aho?

Grandfather

Learn To Enjoy Life

"Hon, both of you need not be 'outta touch' when in Corporate American Lifestyle. The 'trick' is to treat your job/days as FUN! Like a 'Romp on the Playground.' Let NOTHING 'bother' you. Be nearly CHILDLIKE. ENJOY YOUR LIFE. Your JOB, Your TRIALS, etc., AS AN ADVENTURE! PLAY in it! Almost JOKE with it!

LIFE can be FULL of 'LIFE'…or a DREDGE. It's how you 'attack it' that makes it enjoyable or...well 'hard.'

Mankind sees 'Hardships.' 'Misery.' Thus, life becomes difficult. YOU end up always seeking something to make you happy...AND HAVE IT RIGHT WHERE YOU ARE! You're just not SEEING IT as a CHILD SEES IT. Aho?"

A Letter To You The Reader

Brother/Sister,

At the beginning of this Book, I told 'there are a number of repeats.' Know that these are each based on individual interactions. Repeated so that you may, hopefully, understand Its/Their importance.

This Book has been both fun and difficult to write. It shows the joy I, "Grandfather" have had in Following the Inner Heyókȟa' "way" we call "Purity." It also shows the sadness of these results.

As I sit here typing, I have just returned from my early morning prayers. This was on contemplating what I have experienced throughout my life. The training I received and Its results. I have been greatly honored to be called into the service of an Inner Heyókȟa' Medicine Man. Greatly honored to learn what I/we have…and saddened over the seeing of the state of mankind.

To live in the Knowing (of a person's life) is to live in a "fog" of disbelief. DISBELIEF that others have not "seen." Why have we 12 been the only ones that have? It perplexes me.

I ask that you think on your life…your EXPERIENCES…as the GROWTH RINGS of a mighty tree. These rings are Its Life story. Tightly together, they show STRENGTH…Wide Apart shows DISTRESS.YOU ARE LIKE THIS at the end of your lifespan. "Rings" to be READ, by our Creator.

WHY are some rings SO FAR APART? WHAT brought on this GROWTH distress?

WHY are some so CLOSE TOGETHER? WHAT brought on this SPIRITUAL STRENGTH?

When you "Stand before Him," you will be shown these rings…AND shown the REASON you show these. They are your SOUL'S "DIARY." Your FULL LIFE. All in the "WRITING OF THE RINGS."

Over my years, I have met thousands of people. Many in various Religions and/or Ways of Thought. I have seen the good and the ugly. EACH a hologram OF MY INNER SELF. These are ME! MY fears. MY "ugly and dark" side…and MY Godly side. ALL "living Projections" on MY inner self.

When I tell that each is the ONLY "I AM," I MEAN IT!
When I tell YOU CAN LIVE IN A PERSONAL PARADISE, I MEAN IT!
When I tell THIS is ALL A DREAM, I MEAN IT!

When I tell "WORK THE DREAM," I MEAN IT!
When I tell "You CAN CHANGE THE DREAM (your LIFE)," I MEAN IT!
When I tell "BIG BROTHER" (Jesus to you) IS (and WAS) THE CREATOR'S WALKING EXAMPLE , I MEAN IT!
When I tell HE IS WILLING TO HELP YOU DO THIS "MIRACLE" WALK , I MEAN IT!
And When I tell BELIEVE NOT A WORD I SAY…CHECK, CHECK, CHECK for YOURSELF…I MEAN IT!

We are ALL meant to live a Coexistence in HARMONY. THIS is what I HAVE FOUND TO BE TRUE.

"God"/"Allah"/ "She"/"He"/"The Void," or Whatever you may think of/as our Creator (if and when you do)…it all boils down to only One: THE CREATOR is LOVE.

WHY do I live in THIS dream? Friend, LIFE, no matter IF you change it to "all good," is still LIFE. My "Diary." NO MATTER "WHERE" YOU LIVE IT, you are ALIVE TO Live (it).

I have found Life's Secret…LIFE is ME! The "I AM, YOU are NOT." That YOU are MY OWN Fears/Desires and WILL.

Just as yours are.

I pray YOU…the ONLY "I AM," can understand and see this too. IT WILL BENEFIT YOU TO LEARN THIS. (At least I Hope so.)

Many desire to learn only the SELF-way. The way of "sorcery" and eventual eternal…well, do I dare say it?

Doom.

THAT EXISTS, so…

PLEASE: BEWARE!
PLEASE: Be AWARE!

Choose wisely. BETTER YOUR DREAM for the benefit of ALL (for ALL beyond YOU, are an INNER YOU being PROJECTED, so that YOU can SEE your "Inner You"). By IN bettering, THIS "CALMS" YOUR Inner "SPIRIT"…your LIFE!
You become STABLE in your spirit. ALIVE in the Warm Seas of the gentle waves of your Life. AS FREE AS THE GENTLE BREEZES of…PARADISE.

This Book was designed for YOU, the ONLY "I AM" and for ME, the ONLY "I AM."

Aho?

May all the “spanking,” tellings, lessons and the occasional humor within this Book, end up being a Blessing to you.

I PRAY IT DOES!

May the Creator BLESS YOU (as “He” has me).

Ho.

If you like what you have read here you can visit my blog http://redelkspeaks.com, and look for my next books to be published (children’s book) “Let There Be Eggs” and my “How To” teachings from over the years all in one booklet. You can find more information regarding building homes cheaply on hub pages by Ghost, “How To Build A Survival Cabin On A Shoestring Budget.”

Now, for the:

Ending!
(The "I AM," the "Holy Grail")

You are now familiar with "The Way of PURITY."

"Who" I am.

"Why" I am.

"WHAT" I am all about.

I AM the Results of Following His teaching.

You have experienced my Personality. "Me."

I have hidden little. My ups. My downs. Failures and triumphs are within here.

As you can see, I am no one special. I have, and DO, make mistakes.

I am mere…Man.

Yes, I (this one) have learned "more than normal." This learning I have shared with you, my Brother/Sister.

I leave you with this:

Know the "I AM." Catch Its Full importance. Do all possible to comprehend it. IT IS THE ELIXIR OF LIFE!

With Its FULL GRASPING, your Dream CAN BE CHANGED.

Love/Youth/Health …Whether of your liking…Long life/Financial security, etc., are all THERE. ALL in the FULL GRASPING of what our Great Teacher came TO teach.

IT IS THE TRUE "HOLY GRAIL" and has been IN you, all this time. Ho.

Red Elk,

("Grandfather")

www.ingramcontent.com/pod-product-compliance
Lightning Source LLC
Chambersburg PA
CBHW060308240426
43661CB00059B/2695
9780615445991